Dear Pacific Boondocs

Pacific once again showed us what great hospitality is. Thank you very much for the great event & hope you enjoy this book.

Best regards
Pritash
& Bikash

Mike

CW01642789

Praise for

The Fortune at the Bottom of the Pyramid

"C.K. Prahalad argues that companies must revolutionize how they do business in developing countries if both sides of that economic equation are to prosper. Drawing on a wealth of case studies, his compelling new book offers an intriguing blueprint for how to fight poverty with profitability."

Bill Gates
Chairman and Chief Software Architect,
Microsoft

"The Fortune at the Bottom of the Pyramid *belongs at the top of the reading list for business people, academics, and experts pursuing the elusive goal of sustainable growth in the developing world. C.K. Prahalad writes with uncommon insight about consumer needs in poor societies and opportunities for the private sector to serve important public purposes while enhancing its own bottom line. If you are looking for fresh thinking about emerging markets, your search is ended. This is the book for you."*

Madeleine K. Albright
Former U.S. Secretary of State

"Prahalad challenges readers to re-evaluate their preconceived notions about the commercial opportunities in serving the relatively poor nations of the world. The Fortune at the Bottom of the Pyramid *highlights the way to commercial success and societal improvement–but only if the developed world reconceives the way it delivers products and services to the developing world."*

Christopher Rodrigues
CEO, Visa International

"An important and insightful work showing persuasively how the private sector can be put at the center of development, not just as a rhetorical flourish but as a real engine of jobs and services for the poor."

Mark Malloch Brown
Administrator
United Nations Development Programme

"Most people recognize that poverty is a major problem in the world, yet they throw up their hands and say, 'What to do?' Not so C.K. Prahalad. The Fortune at the Bottom of the Pyramid *gives us hope and strategies for eradicating poverty through profits that benefit all. Pass this book on to those who need to read it."*

Ken Blanchard
coauthor of *The One Minute Manager®* and
The Secret: What Great Leaders Know–And Do

The Fortune at the Bottom of the Pyramid: Eradicating Poverty Through Profits

Revised and Updated 5th Anniversary Edition

C.K. Prahalad

Many of the designations used by manufacturers and sellers to distinguish their products are claimed as trademarks. Where those designations appear in this book and the publisher was aware of a trademark claim, the designations have been printed in initial capital or all capitals.

The author and publisher have taken care in the preparation of this book, but make no expressed or implied warranty of any kind and assume no responsibility for errors or omissions. No liability is assumed for incidental or consequential damages in connection with or arising out of the use of the information or programs contained herein.

Original Edition entitled *Fortune At The Bottom Of The Pyramid, Revised And Updated 5th Anniversary Edition, The: Eradicating Poverty Through Profits, First Edition,* by Prahalad, C.K., published by Pearson Education, Inc, publishing as Wharton School Publishing, Copyright © 2010

Indian edition published by Dorling Kindersley India Pvt. Ltd. Copyright © 2010

All rights reserved. This book is sold subject to the condition that it shall not, by way of trade or otherwise, be lent, resold, hired out, or otherwise circulated without the publisher's prior written consent in any form of binding or cover other than that in which it is published and without a similar condition including this condition being imposed on the subsequent purchaser and without limiting the rights under copyright reserved above, no part of this publication may be reproduced, stored in or introduced into a retrieval system, or transmitted in any form or by any means (electronic, mechanical, photocopying, recording or otherwise), without the prior written permission of both the copyright owner and the above-mentioned publisher of this book.

ISBN 978-81-317-3080-5

10 9 8 7 6 5 4 3

This edition is manufactured in India and is authorized for sale only in India, Bangladesh, Bhutan, Pakistan, Nepal, Sri Lanka and the Maldives. Circulation of this edition outside of these territories is UNAUTHORIZED.

Published by Dorling Kindersley (India) Pvt. Ltd., licensees of Pearson Education in South Asia.

Head Office: 7th Floor, Knowledge Boulevard, A-8(A) Sector-62, Noida (U.P) 201309, India.
Registered Office: 11 Community Centre, Panchsheel Park, New Delhi 110 017, India.

Printed in India by Saurabh Printers Pvt .Ltd.

Contents

BONUS MATERIAL

Videos relating to the case studies and bonus case studies are located on the book CD. You can also download them at the following Web site:

www.whartonsp.com/Prahalad

Ebook readers can view extended case studies at the end of the ebook, following the index.

Preface

This book is a result of a long and lonely journey for me. It started during the Christmas vacation of 1995. During that period of celebration and good cheer, one issue kept nagging me: What are we doing about the poorest people around the world? Why is it that with all our technology, managerial know-how, and investment capacity, we cannot make even a minor contribution to the problem of pervasive global poverty and disenfranchisement? Why can't we create inclusive capitalism? Needless to say, these are not new questions. However, as one who is familiar with both the developed and the developing world, the contrasts kept gnawing at me. It became clear that finding a solution to the problems of those at the bottom of the economic pyramid around the world should be an integral part of my next intellectual journey. It was also clear that we have to start with a new approach, a "clean sheet of paper." We have to learn from the successes and failures of the past; the promises made and not fulfilled. Doing more of the same, by refining the solutions of the past—developmental aid, subsidies, governmental support, localized nongovernmental organization (NGO)–based solutions, exclusive reliance on deregulation and privatization of public assets—is important and has a role to play, but has not redressed the problem of poverty.

Although NGOs worked tirelessly to promote local solutions and local entrepreneurship, the idea of large-scale entrepreneurship as a possible solution to poverty had not taken root. It appeared that many a politician, bureaucrat, and manager in large domestic and global firms agreed on one thing: The poor are wards of the state. This implicit agreement was bothersome. The large-scale private sector was only marginally involved in dealing with the problems of 80 percent of humanity. The natural question, therefore, was this: What if we mobilized the resources, scale, and scope of large firms to co-create solutions to the problems at the bottom of the pyramid (BOP), those 4 billion people who live on less than $2 a day? **Why can't we mobilize the investment capacity of large firms with the knowledge and commitment of NGOs and the communities that need help? Why can't we co-create unique solutions?** That was the beginning of my journey to understand and motivate large firms to imagine and act on their role in creating a more just and humane society by collaborating effectively with other institutions.

It was obvious that managers can sustain their enthusiasm and commitment to activities only if they are grounded in good business practices. The four to five billion people at the BOP can help redefine what "good business practice" is. This was not about philanthropy and notions of corporate social responsibility. These initiatives can take the process of engagement between the poor and the large firm only so far. Great contributions can result from these initiatives, but these activities are unlikely to be fully integrated with the core activities of the firm. For sustaining energy, resources, and innovation, the BOP must become a key element of the central mission for large private-sector firms. The poor must become active, informed, and involved consumers. Poverty reduction can result from co-creating a market around the needs of the poor.

We have to discard many of the "for and against" views of the world. For example, "are you for globalization or against it?" is not a good question. Globalization, like all other major social movements, brings some good and some bad. Similarly, global versus local is not a useful debate. The tensions are real. Very early in my career, I learned that even within the multinational corporation (MNC), that is not a settled debate.

Similarly, the debate between small (for example, microfinance) and large (for example, multinational firms) is not a useful debate either. Large business can bring efficiency. NGOs can bring creativity to solve the problems that face us all. Certainly, I wanted to avoid the paternalism toward the poor that I saw in NGOs, government agencies, and MNCs.

This book is concerned about what works. This is not a debate about who is right. I am even less concerned about what might go wrong. Plenty can and has. I am focused on the potential for learning from the few experiments that are going right. These can show us the way forward. I do not want the poor of the world to become a constituency. I want poverty to be a problem that should be solved. This book is about all of the players—NGOs, large domestic firms, MNCs, government agencies, and most importantly, the poor themselves—coming together to solve complex problems that we face as we enter the 21st century. The problem of poverty must force us to innovate, not claim "rights to impose our solutions."

The starting point for this transition had to be twofold. First, we should consider the implications of the language we use. "Poverty alleviation" and "the poor" are terms that are loaded with meaning and historical baggage. The focus on entrepreneurial activities as an antidote to the current malaise must focus on an active, underserved consumer community and a potential for global growth in trade and prosperity as the four to five billion poor become part of a system of inclusive capitalism. We should commence talking about underserved consumers and markets. **The process must start with respect for Bottom of the Pyramid consumers as individuals. The process of co-creation assumes that consumers are equally important joint problem solvers.** Consumers and consumer communities will demand and get choice. This process of creating an involved and activist consumer is already emerging. The BOP provides an opportunity to turbocharge this process of change in the traditional relationship between the firm and the consumer. Second, we must recognize that the conversion of the BOP into an active market is essentially a developmental activity. It is not about serving an existing market more efficiently. **New and creative approaches are needed to convert poverty into an opportunity for all concerned. That is the challenge.**

When the basic approach was clear, the opportunities became obvious. The new viewpoint showed a different landscape and a focus on early and quiet attempts by some firms to explore this terrain. Unilever and its Indian subsidiary, Hindustan Lever Limited, was one such early experimenter. Around 1997, I found a kindred spirit in colleague Professor Stu Hart at the University of Michigan Business School (UMBS), who was approaching similar problems from a sustainable development perspective. We produced a working paper called "The Strategies for the Bottom of the Pyramid." Needless to say, not a single journal would accept the article for publication. It was too radical. Reviewers thought that it did not follow the work of developmental economists. Nobody noticed that we were offering an alternative to the traditional wisdom of how to alleviate global poverty. Thanks to the Web, various revisions of the working paper circulated freely. Surprisingly, a number of managers read it, accepted its premise, and started to initiate action based on it. Managers at Hewlett-Packard, DuPont, Monsanto, and other corporations started a venture fund and dedicated senior managers' time and energy to examine this opportunity. Meanwhile, the Digital Dividend conference organized by Dr. Allen Hammond and the World Resources Institute in Seattle in 1999 provided a forum to examine these ideas in depth. I have not looked back. Since 1997, I have used every possible platform—academic, managerial, and governmental—to push the idea of the BOP as a market and a source of innovations. During the last five years, slowly at first but now more rapidly, a large number of NGOs, academics, and managers have started to discuss the need for an alternate approach to poverty alleviation and the potential role of the private sector and entrepreneurship as one of the critical elements.

The publication of the two articles, "The Fortune at the Bottom of the Pyramid," in *Strategy+Business* (January 2002) with Stu Hart, and "Serve the World's Poor, Profitably" in the *Harvard Business Review* (September 2002) with Allen Hammond, facilitated the process of widespread discussion within corporations. Today, the discussion is not about "whether" but how fast and where. We have come a long way.

In the fall of 2002, several MBA students at the UMBS came to me and said that they would like to work with me on BOP issues and that they were intrigued by the ideas they had seen in print and my message in numerous lectures on campus and outside. I was not easily convinced. I imposed extraordinary demands on them to convince me that they really cared. They convinced me overwhelmingly. They were ready to travel, explore opportunities, and endure the painful task of assembling convincing evidence. That was the start of the now widely accepted XMAP projects (a variant of International Multidisciplinary Action Projects [IMAP], which UMBS has long supported with faculty mentoring). The X in XMAP stood for experimental. The enthusiasm of the students, especially Cynthia Casas and Praveen Suthrum, provided the glue and helped see the project through administrative difficulties. I am grateful to all the MBA students whose dedication made this book possible.

This book is in five parts. In Part I, a new introduction outlines the progress in the BOP agenda since the publication of the book in 2004. It is an update five years later that confirms the growth and sustainability of the idea. In Part II, which was part of the original 2004 edition (left unchanged), we develop a framework for the active engagement of the private sector at the BOP. It provides the basis for a profitable win–win engagement. The focus is on the nature of changes that all players—the large firm, NGOs, governmental agencies, and the poor themselves—must accept to make this process work. Part III contains letters from CEOs of major corporations supporting the approach, while Part IV describes cases, in a wide variety of businesses, where the BOP become an active market and brought benefits, far beyond just products, to consumers. The cases represent a wide variety of industries—from retail, health, and financial services to agribusiness and government. They are located in Peru, Brazil, Nicaragua, Mexico, and India. They represent a wide variety of institutions working together—subsidiaries of MNCs, large domestic firms, startups, and NGOs. They are all motivated by the same concern: They want to change the face of poverty by bringing to bear a combination of high-technology, private enterprise, market-based solutions, and involvement of multiple organizations. They are solving real problems. The newest of these case studies, that of Jaipur Rugs, opens a new perspective on building global supply chains that benefits the BOP producers. Part V contains the videos that accompany the case studies (available on the CD and www.whartonsp.com/Prahalad).

The BOP consumers get products and services at an affordable price, but more important, they get recognition, respect, and fair treatment. Building self-esteem and entrepreneurial drive at the BOP is probably the most enduring contribution that the private sector can make. Finally, decision makers do not often hear the voices of the poor. We tend to make assumptions about how they feel.

On the CD and Whartonsp.com are video stories that attempt to tell the story primarily from their perspective. Each of the research teams—MBA students—went with video cameras and recorded their conversations with the BOP consumers and with the company managers. We collected more than 100 hours of video as part of the research. We presented the story from the point of view of the BOP consumers, the so-called poor. They are the primary storytellers. They tell us in their language—from Portuguese to Hindi—their view of what the involvement of the private sector and the resultant transition have meant for them. The three parts—the rationale for and the approach to private-sector involvement, the in-depth case studies, and the voices of the BOP consumers—are all an integral part of the book. They are intended to focus not only on the intellectual but also on the emotional arguments for encouraging private-sector engagement.

No research of this nature can be done without the active support of firms and managers. They gave us open access, their time, and their insights. Their enthusiasm was infectious. None of us who were a part of the research need any more convincing. We do know that the entrepreneurship and inventiveness of dedicated managers can bring a sea of change rapidly. That is true across the world. We could not have documented the richness of the transformation taking place at the BOP through the efforts of dedicated management teams without an unstinting effort by the students. The biographies of the students who were involved in developing the case studies are given at the end of this book.

Research of this nature, on the cutting edge, cannot take place in an academic institution without the active support of the dean. Dean Robert J. Dolan bet on the initiative. Associate Dean Michael D. Gordon remained a constant source of encouragement to me and to the students in all stages of the project, from obtaining enough video cameras to providing substantive inputs to the research. His deep belief and commitment to the research agenda were critical to the project. Several of my colleagues provided support. I owe special thanks to Associate Dean Gene Anderson, Associate Dean Izak Duenyas, and colleagues Andy Lawlor and Jan Svejnar, former director of the William Davidson Institute.

It was fortuitous that Kofi Annan, then Secretary General of the United Nations, constituted a special commission on Private Sector and Development under the auspices of the United Nations Development Program and its administrator Mark Malloch Brown. As a member of the Commission, I had a chance to share my ideas with the members of the Commission and staff and found a useful platform for dialogue. Nissim Ezekiel, Yann Risz, Sahb Sobhani, Jan Krutzinna, and Naheed Nenshi showed great willingness to debate and challenge many of the ideas presented in this book. I have benefited from their dialogue. It is my hope that the body of work represented in this book influenced the thinking of the Commission as well.

No project of this size can be done without the active support of a wide variety of people. Cynthia Shaw (UMBS) and Fred Wessells provided editorial assistance in reducing the mountain of data we had collected on each case study into a manageable document. Russ Hall provided additional editorial support and helped in considerably improving the case studies and the text. Many of my colleagues, including Prof. M. S. Krishnan, Prof. Venkat Ramaswamy, Prof. Michael Gordon, and Ron Bendersky (Executive Education, UMBS) helped with detailed suggestions for improving the text. Hrishi Bhattacharyya (Unilever), Allen Hammond (World Resources Institute), and Jeb Brugmann and Craig Cohon (Globalegacy) provided useful insights. The Wharton Business Publishing team has been exceptional in its support and belief in the message. Jerry Wind (Wharton) accepted the idea of this book with great enthusiasm, and Steve Kobrin at Wharton continues the school's support and encouragement. Throughout all the editions, the publishing teams, led by Tim Moore, were remarkable in their support. Their commitment to this book has been a source of strength. Patti Guerrieri was always willing to help and produced yet another revision of the manuscript with patience and quiet competence. Kimberly Ward (UMBS) oversaw the entire project, and Brian Greminger worked magic with the videos. Both of them, by their dedication to the students and to the overall project, were a source of inspiration. Finally, the students stayed with the project for more than a year, always managing to do more and accommodating what must have appeared to be random demands on their time.

The biggest supporters of this project were my family. Our children, Murali Krishna and Deepa, and the latter's husband, Ashwin, kept me going when I was willing to give up the idea of writing a book-length manuscript. As always, my wife, Gayatri, was my source of strength. She deeply believed in the cause and accompanied me to a wide variety of on-site visits, be it Jaipur Foot or the Shakti Amma. She willingly created the space and time for me to work on this project.

It is my hope that this book provides the impetus for a more active engagement of the private sector in building the marketing ecosystems for transforming the BOP.

C.K. Prahalad
San Diego

Guide to Readers

The book is organized in five parts. The purpose of this guide is to outline the scope and the rationale behind each part. This should make it easy for readers to navigate through the book.

Part 1: Private Sector and Poverty: Progress During 2004-2009

This part contains the new introduction to the book. It provides a brief outline of the progress made since the book was launched in the later part of 2004. The focus is on what we have learned from the efforts of both global and local firms' initiatives on the emerging "rules of engagement" with the BOP.

Part 2: The Original Text of the Book

We have consciously kept the original text as is. There was no attempt to update the chapters. The goal was to preserve the integrity of the text and do the updating—our learning over the last five years—in the introduction.

Part 3: CEO Reactions to the Concept and the Book

We asked ten CEOs to reflect on the concept of the role of the private sector and BOP markets, as well describe the impact this book has had on their efforts, if any. These CEOs represent a wide variety of organizations. These firms represent a wide variety of industries, geographical origins, sizes, and heritages. The letters from the CEOs reflect their voices. These ten views included in this part also contain the views of a Dean of a business school and a prominent NGO.

Part 4: Cases Studies and CEO Comments

In this part, we have included one new case. Jaipur Rugs demonstrates how a global supply chain can be built with the poor of India as the providers of the sophisticated capability to weave world-class hand-knotted rugs using imported wool from Australia and exporting finished carpets to the United States.

We have left the other cases as they were in the original book but added an update section.

The updates were written by the CEOs of the companies. Each CEO took stock of the progress they have made since the time the case was written. We are pleased to say that all the initiatives have grown and made great progress. Each one has written their own version of the changes, and you will see a wide variety of lengths, focus, pride, and accomplishment in each one of these updates.

Part 5: Video Clips

Each case has a video attached to it. The role of the video is to give a sense of people, locales, the impact of the private sector initiatives on their lives, and their views of what has changed for them. This is the perspective from the BOP.

The videos are available on the book's CD and online at www.whartonsp.com/Prahalad.

Focus: Multiple Perspectives

As can be seen from the organization of the book, the goal was to provide multiple perspectives. We start from the author's review, to CEOs who have started new initiatives during the last five years, to progress made by those whose pioneering work gave the impetus to the book in 2004. Most importantly, it retains the voices of the BOP consumers, producers, investors, and innovators in the videos.

About the Author

C.K. Prahalad

"...he may well be the most influential thinker on business strategy today."

BusinessWeek

Internationally recognized as a specialist on corporate strategy and value-added of top management in multinational corporations, C.K. Prahalad has consulted with many of the world's foremost companies. In addition to being the Paul and Ruth McCracken Distinguished University Professor of Strategy at the University of Michigan, he serves on the board of directors of NCR Corp., Hindustan Lever Ltd., and the World Resources Institute.

A prolific author as well, his book, *Competing for the Future* (co-authored with Gary Hamel), was a national bestseller and was the Best Selling Business Book of the Year in 1994. He also co-authored *Multinational Mission: Balancing Local Demands and Global Vision* (in 1987 with Yves Doz) and *The Future of Competition: Co-Creating Unique Value with Customers* (in 2004 with Venkat Ramaswamy).

He has been named among the top ten management thinkers of the world in every major survey for more than ten years.

PART I

Private Sector and Poverty: Progress During 2004-2009

New Introduction: Private Sector and Poverty: Progress During 2004-2009

Five years is not a long time to evaluate the diffusion of an idea; much less its impact on the ground. It has been less than five years since the book *The Fortune at the Bottom of the Pyramid: Eradicating Poverty Through Profits* was published. The first article on the subject appeared in 2002.[1] At the time, the proposition that the private sector had a critical role to play in alleviating global poverty was generally met with skepticism. The idea that they could have the greatest impact through creating profitable businesses serving the 5 billion people who represented the "invisible, unserved market" was even more radical. I am profoundly grateful for the people in government, nongovernmental organizations, and large corporations who were willing to listen and experiment. The poor, of course, have long been hungry for change. Their enthusiasm and insights have been a huge inspiration to me.

We are a long way from solving the problem of global poverty. But I find reason to be optimistic that the conditions for creating significant and sustainable change are emerging rapidly. First, the idea that the private sector can and should be involved in creating market-based solutions for the world's poorest consumers is gaining credibility. The market success of some multinationals that have taken up the challenge has created momentum. Respected business leaders such as Bill Gates championing the cause of *creative capitalism* has also contributed to a shift in perception.

Second, actively engaging with consumers in Bottom of the Pyramid markets has resonated with consumers in developed markets as well. The attitudes of the general public have begun to shift away from direct aid to an exchange of ideas and capital. For as little as $25, anyone can evaluate business plans and extend micro loans to Bottom of the Pyramid entrepreneurs through Kiva.org. A few clicks on Novica.com grants access to a network of traditional crafts and artisans, and purchases are accompanied with a note from the artist. Cell phones are a part of the lives of the rich and poor alike. Today, citizens are engaging with each other in ways that would have been difficult to imagine even a few years ago. As a result, awareness of the conditions and nuances of the Bottom of the Pyramid is increasing. This has translated for the push for companies to help in uplifting the Bottom of the Pyramid from civil society, governments, and nongovernmental organizations.

Support—or pressure—for companies to be involved in the Bottom of the Pyramid will not create sustainable growth. The original inspiration for this book—eradicating poverty through profits—seems more tangible today than it did five years ago. There is evidence today that the innovations in the Bottom of the Pyramid can and have produced profitable business, and consumers in these markets have shown that they are as savvy and demanding as those anywhere else. Through my work with the United Nations Development Commission and large multinationals, the most encouraging lesson in this journey has not been in just the validation of the business model originally put forth. Far more significant is the emergence of the Bottom of the Pyramid as a platform for global innovation in some cases; a development which has important implications.

In this introduction to the 2009 edition of this book, I briefly assess the impact of the idea and include the perspectives of executives who have led major initiatives in Bottom of the Pyramid markets. I also address some of the emerging questions regarding Bottom of the Pyramid markets. There are five major themes I talk about explicitly:

1. How has the role of the private sector evolved in poverty alleviation?
2. What have large firms, including multinationals, learned as they actively pursue nontraditional opportunities in the Bottom of the Pyramid markets?
3. What are the key lessons for developing these market opportunities?
4. Are these markets forcing a "new social compact" for business?
5. What are the emerging "rules of engagement" that should inform our approach to Bottom of the Pyramid markets?

The Role of the Private Sector

Until recently, little attention was paid to the role of the private sector in poverty alleviation. The Millennium development goals were originally developed without recognition of the role that the private sector could play. It was later that the social compact with the private sector was formulated by the then Secretary General of the United Nations, Mr. Kofi Annan. The pioneering work on this topic was done by a Blue Ribbon Commission organized by the United Nations Development Program on private sector and poverty. The report was issued in 2004.[2] I had the privilege of serving on that commission. The United Nations Development Program is now fully engaged with the idea of the private sector's contribution to poverty alleviation.[3] Similarly, organizations such as the World Economic Forum have focused private sector groups in developing solutions to poverty—be it the Social Entrepreneurship Forum or the group of firms collaborating to fight global hunger. The acceptance of the role of the private sector in poverty alleviation by civil society is somewhat mixed. Some are willing to accept a role for the private sector and some, as should be, are more skeptical. However, increasingly, large private sector firms and civil society organizations are learning to work together in a collaborative fashion. There is growing recognition that marrying the local knowledge of the nongovernmental organization with global reach of the multinational firm can create unique and sustainable solutions. Needless to say, the private sector cannot solve all problems but can bring technical and financial resources, the disciplines of organization, accountability, and entrepreneurial drive to bear on the problems.[4]

Who and What Is the Bottom of the Pyramid? What Have We Learned?

There is a lot of discussion on what the Bottom of the Pyramid market is and who constitutes that market. The original definition of the Bottom of the Pyramid was based on a simple premise. The concept was originally introduced *to draw attention to the 4-5 billion poor who are unserved or underserved by the large organized private sector, including multinational firms.* This group, until recently ignored by the private sector, could be a source of much needed vitality and growth. The assumptions influencing the focus on the Bottom of the Pyramid were also explicit: "*Four billion poor can be the engine of the next round of global trade and prosperity. Serving the Bottom of the Pyramid consumers will demand innovations in technology, products and services, and business models. More important, it will require large firms to work collaboratively with civil society organizations and local governments. Market development at the Bottom of the Pyramid will also create millions of new entrepreneurs at the grass root level—from women working as distributors and entrepreneurs to village level micro enterprises* (page 2 in the original book).

Needless to say, four billion people cannot be a monolith. They represent extreme variety—in their levels of literacy, rural-urban mix, geographical mix, income levels, cultural and religious differences, and every other conceivable basis for segmentation. This extreme variety does lead to multiple perspectives on the Bottom of the Pyramid. The Bottom of the Pyramid is like a kaleidoscope. No single view illuminates the total opportunity. Every twist helps focus on a specific facet of the opportunity or problem. This variety supports major disagreements among scholars and practitioners on what constitutes the Bottom of the Pyramid. Moreover, the term Bottom of the Pyramid evokes different images. Not surprisingly, readers tend to attribute their own definition to the idea. I called it the Bottom of the Pyramid because that was the reality as I saw it. The goal was to ensure that the rich—the top of the pyramid—could be sensitized to those who are less fortunate. Some did not like the idea of the bottom of the pyramid; they called it the Base of the Pyramid—a bottom-up view.[5] Segmenting the 4 billion was not far off. Some talked about the Next Billion.[6] Some focused on the Next 4 Billion.[7] Some focused on the Bottom Billion.[8] Some tried to get back to the old ways of categorizing the market as A to E; categories C, D, and E constituting the BOP. There is also significant debate on who are at the Bottom of the Pyramid—people living on less than $2/day? Less than $1/day? What about people earning more than $2/day but still in poverty without adequate access to world class (not the same as luxury) goods and services? The extensive study by World Resources Institute/International Finance Corporation has given granularity to the composition of the next 4 billion by country and by income level. It has also shown that Bottom of the Pyramid consumers account for $5 trillion in Purchasing Power Parity terms.

The Bottom of the Pyramid debate has led to new perspectives on the opportunity. There is a focus on the Middle of the Pyramid, or the aspiring middle class. A recent study by the *Economist* concluded that half the world can be classified as the emerging middle class; defined as a population living on $2–13 at 2005 Purchasing Power Parity prices. They have discretionary income and spend on education, health, energy, transportation, and personal care. This market by some estimates includes 2.6 billion people in 2005 and is rising fast. Asia alone is expected to have approximately 60 percent of the global middle class.[9] Many firms now classify the Bottom of the Pyramid market as "emerging consumer markets" or just emerging markets. Obviously this is a more emotionally neutral term. More important, this view of Bottom of the Pyramid markets—the emerging consumers—shows the respect and the commitment of managers in large firms who have spent time and resources to understand this opportunity. This is a significant change from the position even five years ago.

We can draw multiple lessons from the heated debates about what constitutes the Bottom of the Pyramid during the last five years:

1. There is a clear recognition that four billion micro consumers and micro producers *constitute a significant market and represent an engine of innovation, vitality, and growth.* This is a *new category for all*—be it managers, governments, or civil society organizations. We need to understand it. It is clear, however, that this emerging market will force a fundamental rethinking of our approach to business.
2. The 4 billion people who constitute the Bottom of the Pyramid are not a monolith. For those who want to engage in this opportunity, there is *no single universal definition of the Bottom of the Pyramid that can be useful.* The definition must fit the focus for productive engagement. For example, micro-finance organizations in India might have a different definition of the poor from ones in Kenya or Brazil or the USA.

3. We can choose to serve any segment of the 4 billion. No institution—a firm or nongovernmental organization—needs to serve all of the Bottom of the Pyramid. They can pick and choose. Serving the "next billion" is as legitimate as serving "the bottom billion."
4. There is a segment of the 4 billion who are so destitute, so deprived, and so consumed by war and disease that they need other forms of help. Government subsidies, multilateral aid, and philanthropy are all legitimate tools to deal with this segment. Even here, *our goal should be to build capacity for people to escape poverty and deprivation through self-sustaining market-based systems.*
5. Active engagement at the Bottom of the Pyramid markets requires a new and an innovative approach to business. *Retrofitting business models from the developed markets will not work.*[10]

I believe that the debate of what the Bottom of the Pyramid is will continue. But the world of business is moving beyond definition. The concept of the emerging consumer allows each firm to decide which segment of the Bottom of the Pyramid it wants to serve. Some firms, such as Unilever that have a long history of working in developing markets, now focus on "Straddling the Pyramid"—participating across the entire spectrum of opportunities often with the same category of products. It is fair to say that the idea of the Bottom of the Pyramid as an opportunity has taken root. Does this mean that it represents a viable business?

Bottom of the Pyramid as a Business Opportunity

While the cases in this book were intended to illustrate that there are viable business opportunities at the Bottom of the Pyramid, there was a lot of skepticism. Over the years, there is accumulating evidence that this segment represents a viable business. Consider for example, the growth of the cell phone. By 2011, more than 4 billion cell phones will be in use. Most of this growth is in the Bottom of the Pyramid markets. From sub-Saharan Africa, China, Southeast Asia, India, and Latin America and Eastern Europe, there is not a single country where the poor have not taken to the cell phone. India alone added approximately 11 million new subscribers in January 2009. Many successful firms have emerged out of this opportunity. Many are new firms, and many are new businesses in older firms. Mobile Telephone Networks from South Africa, CelTel in Sub Saharan Africa, a dozen competitors in India led by Bharati Airtel, and Globe in the Philippines are some examples. The market capitalization of the three of the top five (two are not listed) leading players in wireless in India is approximately $57 billion as of June 2008. In January 2009, in a depressed market, it was $38 billion.

The cell phone revolution has demonstrated beyond doubt that there is a market for world-class goods and services if they can be made available at affordable prices. For example, a "cell phone minute" costs less than $ 0.01 in India, probably the lowest rate per minute anywhere. The industry had to create its own ecosystem of mini entrepreneurs who sold prepaid cards and also charged the cell phones. The Bottom of the Pyramid business is quite critical for both the infrastructure players, such as LM Ericsson, and device makers, such as Nokia and Motorola.

The spread of the cell phone has made this the device of choice for not only communications but also some computing, entertainment, and the delivery of a wide variety of services such as medical care (as described in the Voxiva case in this book and reconfirmed in the update). Financial service organizations are also rapidly developing systems to use the cell phone for financial transactions (see the ICICI case update). Remittances are routinely handled through the cell phone. The cell phone, we can say, has shown that the Bottom of the Pyramid is not just a market but also a source of innovations in business models and applications. It has transformed the lives of the poor. We can "do well and do good" simultaneously. Most important, the rate of diffusion among the Bottom of the Pyramid around the world has shown how willing and capable the poor are to accept and benefit from advanced technology. The cell phone has broken several long-held beliefs: *There is no market at the Bottom of the Pyramid; they won't pay, they will not accept or do not need advanced technologies; the Bottom of the Pyramid cannot be a source of innovation; and multinationals do not need them.* Maybe some multinational firms can ignore this market. Not if you are Nokia, Motorola, Nestle, Unilever, or Microsoft. However, being a multinational or a large domestic firm does not guarantee success; *the capacity to adapt and innovate at the Bottom of the Pyramid does.*

A large number of firms have benefited from a focus on the Bottom of the Pyramid markets. They span multiple geographies and industries. For example, the success of the following local firms is common knowledge. The goal here is not to give an exhaustive list but an indicative list.

Brazil	Casas Bahia (retail)
	Habibs (fast food)
	Bradesco (banking)
Mexico	Elecktra (retail, banking)
	Bambi (food)
	Patrimony Oy (housing)
Philippines	Globe (telecom, water)
Bangladesh	Grammen (micro finance, telecom, food)
India	Amul (dairy)
	Aravind Eye Hospital, Jaipur Foot, Narayana Hrudayalaya (health care)
	ITC e-Choupal (agriculture)
	SKS Finance (micro finance)
	Airtel (telecom)
South Africa	Pick and Pay (retail)
	Mobile Telephone Networks (telecom)
Chile	Savory, by Nestlé (ice cream)
	Brestler, by Unilever (ice cream)

More importantly, we see a large number of multinational firms either start new initiatives in Bottom of the Pyramid markets or reinforce their existing presence in the Bottom of the Pyramid. Some notable new entrants are such well-known firms as Microsoft (software), DSM (food supplements), Royal Philips (health care), Thomson Reuters (information), GlaxoSmithKline (pharmaceuticals), Intel (computing), Vodafone (telecom), ING (microfinance), and Monsanto (agriculture). Again this is an indicative list. Many of the CEOs were gracious enough to share their experiences and what they learned with us. Their letters are included in this volume.

The large private sector is learning rapidly that there is a significant market at the Bottom of the Pyramid. In some industries the size and attractiveness of the Bottom of the Pyramid markets are well established. Retailing, fast-moving consumer goods, micro finance, telecom, and agri-business, belong to this category. Computing, health and wellness-oriented food, health care, education, pharmaceuticals, and energy are emerging as major opportunities. Affordable and modern housing, water, and transportation are still elusive at the Bottom of the Pyramid. Firms are also learning that this market cannot be approached with the mindset of their traditional markets. There is a need for experimentation and innovation. We certainly will witness more efforts in this direction. We need to ask: Why can't we create markets in every sector that we have created in telecom through wireless? Why not apply the same level of innovation, eco system development, and focus on affordability as we did in cell phones? This question is asked more and more in corporate boardrooms.

Key Lessons from Experiments

Even at this early stage of experimentation at the Bottom of the Pyramid, multinational firms are learning valuable lessons. Although the market is large and potentially lucrative, this potential cannot be realized unless managers are willing to experiment and innovate. They have to selectively "forget" traditional developed market approaches to business. The dominant lessons follow:

1. *The innovation sandbox (embrace constraints)*: The primary task of the private sector is often converting the Bottom of the Pyramid consumers from unorganized, inefficient local monopolies (for example, local moneylenders, local medics) to an organized and efficient private sector. In some cases, it is to ensure that Bottom of the Pyramid consumers are aware of the new products and services (for example, micro insurance). *Awareness, Access, Affordability, and Availability* are the key ingredients to market development at the Bottom of the Pyramid. It is useful to start with an *innovation sandbox,* a set of critical constraints that must become non-negotiables in the developmental process. The innovation sandbox must be specific to the firm, its target segment, and the business. However, some broad guidelines apply. In most cases, we can include
   (a) *Scalability*. Unless the solution can be scaled, it is little use in changing people's lives. Moreover, most Bottom of the Pyramid businesses tend to be low margin, high volume, high return on capital businesses. The businesses are volume-sensitive and scale is critical.

(b) A *new price-performance envelope* or a new value proposition is critical. Affordability dictates that we must start with a *Price-Profit = Cost* and not *Cost + Profit = Price* perspective.

(c) *Modern technologies*. Increasingly it is becoming obvious that dramatic cost reductions are not possible without a judicious use of modern science in the development of products, services, and information technology in delivery of those services.

(d) *International standards* of quality, safety, ecological sustainability, and aesthetics.

We can conceive of these constraints as the boundaries of an innovation sandbox, and all innovations must take place within it. These boundary conditions, when set, must not be relaxed.[11]

All elements of the business—capital intensity, work flow, volume, manufacturing and logistics, design of products, its maintenance, pricing, use of people, skill development, and building an ecosystem of specialized suppliers—must be challenged and examined without relaxing the self-imposed constraints. A typical innovation sandbox might look like Figure Intro.1.

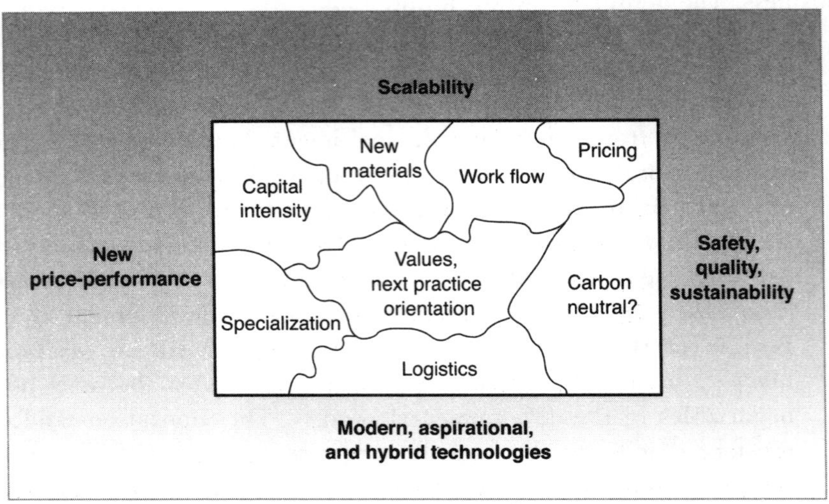

Figure Intro.1 The innovation sandbox.

Within the sandbox, there can be multiple innovations—be it centered on capital intensity or workflow. This approach—constrained innovation—is a critical ingredient to create fresh thinking in the organization. None of the boundary conditions can be met with traditional ways of doing business.

2. *Build an ecosystem:* Because the Bottom of the Pyramid markets have remained underserved by the organized private sector, they have remained local and fragmented. To build a scalable model, managers must invest time and energy to build an appropriate ecosystem. For example, it is impossible to enlarge the market for cell phones without building a large network of micro entrepreneurs who will sell prepaid cards. There are more than one million such entrepreneurs—some established neighborhood and village grocery stores that added this to their portfolio and some new entrepreneurs in India today. Similarly, to get access to rural markets, Unilever built a large network of shakti ammas—rural entrepreneurs who educate and distribute their products. Micro finance firms built and use self-help groups. ITC created village level operators of kiosks. Often, these ecosystems include micro entrepreneurs, micro producers, small- and medium-size enterprises, and nongovernmental organizations. Market development at the Bottom of the Pyramid needs a new ecosystem. The ecosystem inevitably consists of large and small firms. A typical ecosystem as is obvious from the multiple cases in this book and elsewhere will consist of (a) large firms, (b) small- and medium-size enterprises, (c) micro entrepreneurs (as in shakti ammas or farmers), (d) civil society organizations, and often (e) the public sector. All have to collaborate to build a viable business. As a group, they constitute the ecosystem, and each contribute differently to the overall task of accessing and serving the Bottom of the Pyramid consumer. During the last five years, many such ecosystems have evolved. It is easier today to attach oneself to an existing system if it is appropriate. It is appropriate to say that in the Bottom of the Pyramid

   Ecosystems > Investment Capacity

   No amount of investment is a substitute for the skills and knowledge that an ecosystem can provide. The message is "don't go it alone."
3. *Co-create solutions:* Managers who are used to developed markets are often surprised by the sophistication and demands of the Bottom of the Pyramid markets. It is not just about making cheap versions of the products sold in developed markets. Bottom of the Pyramid markets demand that managers acquire "local knowledge and local trust" before they develop markets—be it micro consumers or micro producers. It is unrealistic to expect farmers to sell their meager

crops to ITC and abandon their local trader unless they develop trust in ITC. Similarly, don't expect people to abandon their moneylender before they know that the micro-finance arm of the bank is reliable and will stay with them. Neither should we expect them to change their habits before they are confident that the new animal feed is both efficacious and will be available when needed.

There are three different pressures that must be understood. The role of the private sector is to bring world-class products and global standards of quality and safety to these markets. At the same time, the solutions must be locally responsive. *Global-local tension* is real. Secondly, to provide high quality at low cost, firms must focus on capital intensity of the business and the overheads. Traditional ways of doing business will not do. A *lean business and organization* is required. This represents a major tension in multinational firms as this challenges their existing business models. Finally, firms have to *rapidly learn* about the local consumers, their needs, and their aspirations at low cost.

Large private sector firms are finding that they need to collaborate with others to accomplish these goals. Gaining local knowledge, accessing specialized skills, reducing capital intensity and overheads, gaining trust, and becoming locally relevant requires that they start co-creating solutions. No firm has all the skills and the capability to do this. It is desirable that managers learn to co-opt both consumers and civil society and other institutions to build a co-creation platform. British Petroleum is developing a biomass stove for the rural poor with input from consumers, nongovern-mental organizations, and the Indian Institute of Science. The nongovernmental organizations help identify and build a network of jyoti Ammas—local village level entrepreneurs who sold the stoves. They also help build a network of biomass pelletizers.[12] In the Bottom of the Pyramid collaborative capacity and integrative capacity (the capacity to integrate the contributions of multiple players into a coherent whole) is more valuable than investment capacity. It is fair to say

Collaborative Capacity > Investment Capacity

Co-creation reduces investment needs as more share in the investment. It reduces risk as the key players jointly develop the solution. For example, in the case of British Petroleum, the BP team, the Indian Institute of Science, nongovernmental organizations, and the village level consumers, jointly developed the stove. Managers must learn that the Bottom of the Pyramid markets require a new level of collaboration between civil society and the private sector. It also requires a new respect for consumers as co-creators of solutions and not just passive recipients of a product or service.

4. *A new concept of scale:* Scale can be achieved in many ways. The Bottom of the Pyramid forces us to think differently. Consider the question: "I want to build a dairy that is world scale with a capacity to process 6 to 7 million kilograms of milk per day. How do I plan for it?" This question often gets people calculating how many cattle and how big a cattle farm one should have. Amul in India, the largest processor of raw milk in the world, originates the milk in 10,000 plus villages covering more than 2.2 million farmers. Each one might have only one or two heads of cattle. But by building village level collection centers that aggregate raw milk from a large pool of farmers, and processing it centrally, Amul built *virtual scale.* By paying the farmers for quality (for example, volume and fat content) and by sophisticated logistics from collection centers to world-class processing units, Amul totally avoided the problems of managing large herds centrally. Decentralized origination, centralized processing, and marketing seem to be the key.

   This model is becoming fairly popular. Nestle just replicated the Amul model in the Northern Indian province of Punjab. They collect and process 1.5 million kgs of milk a day from farmers. ITC collects soybean and wheat from more than 2.5 million farmers in a similar fashion with ITC e-Choupal. Jaipur Rugs uses more than 40,000 contract workers spread all over northern India to weave rugs using traditional and new patterns. The Aravind Eye Care Facility uses village level camps to identify those who need surgery. Last year they examined 2.2 million outpatients and treated 285,000 who needed surgery. It is safe to say that the capacity to organize highly distributed and independent suppliers (for example, farmers) and contractors (for example, weavers) or potential consumers (for example, patients) and build a reliable logistics systems is more critical than investment capacity. ITC, Jaipur Rugs, and Amul are nodal firms. They provide the intellectual infrastructure, standards of performance, customer interface, and the technology backbone. It is safe to say that in the Bottom of the Pyramid

   Building a Nodal Organization > Investment Capacity

The Bottom of the Pyramid allows a new approach to scale and organization. Further, most of these organizations are very lean. Most of the systems are self-regulating and do not need much supervision.

5. *Use technology*: It is normal to assume that Bottom of the Pyramid markets are not high-tech markets. Those managers who grew up with the concepts such as "product life cycle view of international business" (meaning that all new technology solutions are developed in the West, and they move to poor and developing countries over time) will find Bottom of the Pyramid markets providing a big surprise. You will find Aravind or Narayana Hrudayalaya using the latest medical technology. For example, Narayana Hrudayalaya prefers digital to analog products even if they are expensive. An analog X-ray machine might be inexpensive, but the film is not. Capital expenditure is lower but variable costs are higher. A large throughput system (scale) makes this an unattractive proposition. Further, digital X-ray allows pictures to be uploaded for examination by experts at remote locations. Similarly, Airtel uses the most advanced technology. It converted its fixed costs into variable costs by outsourcing infrastructure investments to LM Ericsson and IBM. Airtel pays a fee for each consumer added; a variable cost.

   The use of information technology to manage the logistics and manufacturing infrastructure is widespread. ITC depends on its network of PCs to engage and connect with the farmers. The ITC network is the heart of its operation. Jaipur Rugs is starting to invest in an IT system that tracks each weaver and each order along its highly distributed system. Remittances and rudimentary banking functions are moving to the cell phone. There is a tense negotiation between telecom operators and the financial services firms in Africa and India.

   The lessons are clear. Advanced technology is critical for ensuring the quality of product or service delivered. More important, advanced technologies wisely deployed reduce the overall costs (for example, cost per patient, cost per minute of cell phone usage, cost per transaction), if the investments can be leveraged with high levels of usage. Capital expenditure in the absolute (for example, $1 million dollars) is different from asking what if we had 5,000 patients per week rather than 50? Secondly, advanced technologies lead to innovative and new applications, such as cell phone-based banking.

Finally, IT solutions provide real-time information on inventories in the system, receivables, and the changing patterns of consumption. Well-developed IT systems provide real-time alerts to managers.

6. *Sustainability will emerge as a source of innovations at the Bottom of the Pyramid*: The planet is under stress—be it access to water, deforestation, pollution, or green house gas emissions. This is a familiar story. What if we added an additional 3 to 4 billion people as micro producers and consumers to the current 2 billion? Sustainability will become a major impediment. Nobody can deny that the poor have a right to a better standard of living—be it access to safe water, better food and sanitation, and better education. The pressure to serve an additional 3 to 4 billion and at the same time protect the environment will focus attention on sustainability as never before. New innovations, large and small, will be needed. For example, given interruptions in power and water supply, an Indian firm, Godrej, has introduced a washing machine that remembers when the power was cut off in the washing cycle. When power resumes, it starts where it left off rather than from the beginning. This saves both water and power. Packaging is getting its due attention. Biodegradable and new forms of packaging are becoming an imperative. So are new sources of renewable energy. We should expect to see the Bottom of the Pyramid as a major source of ecologically sustainable innovations in the near future.
7. *The challenge is market development*: The biggest challenge to managers who are trained to "serve existing markets efficiently" is to change their mindsets when they approach BOP markets. The cell phone or microcredit are good examples. Airtel had to develop the market. The tele-density in India in 2002 was so low that it was pathetic. They and others had to build an urban and now a rural market for connectivity and value-added services. In every instance of success, managers had to "forget" traditional ways of approaching the business and develop a new and innovative approach. For example, Airtel had to give up on average revenue per customer or user (ARPU) as a measure of attractiveness and focus on the contribution per minute of cell phone time. This is true for Airtel as much as for ICICI, Aravind, or Voxiva. The goal is to build new markets, organize the "unorganized markets," build new ecosystems, and create new business models. The challenge is about innovating the management processes within the firm that allows managers in the

field to defy received wisdom and build a model that works. It is beyond "recontextualizing" the existing business models. It is about management innovation and market development.

8. *Bottom of the Pyramid markets are evolving rapidly*: It is important that we recognize that the Bottom of the Pyramid markets are evolving rapidly. Just measuring the Bottom of the Pyramid segments by income (as is done normally) hides the interesting transitions that are taking place in the market. It is better to use life style measures (LSMs) of the Bottom of the Pyramid consumers. What life style do they aspire to? What life style do they invest in? How do we explain a resident of a slum without clean drinking water and sewage, focusing on kitchen appliances, cell phones, and color televisions? How do we explain a poor mother investing in her son's education through private tuition even when she goes hungry? Or a farmer investing in his cattle before improving his house? Two forces are at work here. First, individuals are making choices to their life style that do not necessarily follow our perceptions of what someone at a particular income level should do. Better informed and better focused on the aspirations for themselves and their families, their decision-making criteria are changing rapidly. We see it in their approach to health care, education, and connectivity. Secondly, the economic pyramid, as predicted in the original version of this book, is slowly morphing into a diamond; not all around the world but certainly in major markets such as China, India, South Africa, Turkey, Brazil, and Indonesia. This will have a profound impact on the opportunities for growth.

We could add to the lessons learned. However, it is important to note that this is a rapidly changing and evolving opportunity. As micro consumers, micro producers, and micro entrepreneurs and innovators, the poor are rapidly becoming sophisticated and demanding. Managers need to develop the capacity to anticipate and continuously adapt.

Business and the New Social Compact

Business leaders who have engaged themselves actively with the Bottom of the Pyramid have started to reexamine the role of business in society. Many CEOs have come to look at business with a new lens—the Bottom of the Pyramid lens. Mr. Patrick Cescau, the retired CEO of

Unilever, is one of them. His views reflect the growing appreciation of the role of the private sector in protecting the planet and at the same time serving the poor.

"For one, there is a growing recognition that the social and environmental challenges facing us in the twenty-first century are so complex and so multi-dimensional that they cannot be solved by governments alone. Industry has to be part of the solution. But perhaps the biggest catalyst for change has been the increasing awareness within business itself that many of the big social and environmental challenges of our age, once seen as obstacles to progress, have become opportunities for innovation and business development. We have come to a point now where the agenda of sustainability and corporate responsibility is not only central to business strategy but has become a critical driver of business growth."

Recently, Bill Gates surprised his colleagues by suggesting that we need to reexamine the role of capitalism. His solution was to move to "creative capitalism."[13] He defined it as

> There are two great forces of human nature: self-interest, and caring for others. Capitalism harnesses self-interest in a helpful and sustainable way, but only on behalf of those who can pay. Government aid and philanthropy channel our caring for those who can't pay. But to provide rapid improvement for the poor we need a system that draws in innovators and businesses in a far better way than we do today.
>
> Such a system would have a twin mission: making profits and also improving lives of those who don't fully benefit from today's market forces. For sustainability we need to use profit incentives wherever we can. At the same time, profits are not always possible when business tries to serve the very poor. In such cases there needs to be another incentive, and that incentive is recognition. Recognition enhances a company's reputation and appeals to customers; above all, it attracts good people to an organization. As such, recognition triggers a market-based reward for good behavior. In markets where profits are not possible, recognition is a proxy; where profits are possible, recognition is an added incentive.
>
> The challenge here is to design a system where market incentives, including profits and recognition, drive those principles to do more for the poor.
>
> I like to call this idea creative capitalism, an approach where governments, businesses, and nonprofits work together to stretch the reach of market forces so that more people can make a profit, or gain recognition, doing work that eases the world's inequities.

Then there are those who promote the idea of Social Capital. This movement is led by Prof. Mohummed Yunnus of Grameen Bank fame. There is a lot of ferment and discussion in understanding the role of markets and the role of capitalism. There are skeptics. Many wonder whether market-based solutions are the answer. The real issue we must focus on is not whether markets can solve all problems. They might not. The real issue is this: "How do we bring to bear *the entrepreneurial and innovative energy of private enterprise to solve the critical problems facing humanity?*" In many cases, as we have already seen, private enterprise must work collaboratively with civil society, governments, and aid agencies and philanthropy to create innovative solutions. For these solutions to be sustainable, creating a surplus (profit) is critical.

These debates are healthy. I do not believe that we should look for an easy or quick solution to these complex questions. We must cultivate the ability to experiment and refine our thinking. Although the final outcome of this debate is not clear, it is obvious that private sector involvement in Bottom of the Pyramid markets has spawned a new debate. It has challenged our assumptions about the role of business in society. Businesses recognize that they must regain their social legitimacy. This will be determined by how businesses approach poverty and sustainability. Our focus on the role of capitalism and the Bottom of the Pyramid might be hiding a bigger and intellectually more demanding question and a bigger opportunity.

Democratizing Commerce: The Challenge for the 21st Century

I believe that the real challenge for the 21st century is democratization of commerce. Often, the debate about private sector involvement in the Bottom of the Pyramid centers on questions such as "Is globalization good or bad for the poor?" If we phrase the question this way, almost by definition, there will be people taking either side. However, if we accept globalization is like gravity and that there is no point in denying gravity; but great benefit to defying it and build a plane, then we can ask the question differently: "How do we make the benefits of globalization accessible to all?" This formulation of the question allows us to be more creative and entrepreneurial. Therefore, I would like to define "democratizing commerce" as *bringing the benefits of globalization to all micro consumers, micro producers, micro innovators, micro investors, and micro entrepreneurs*.

As shown next, we start with the assumption that everybody must have the right to the benefits of globalization. This implies that as individuals we have multiple roles—as consumers, producers, investors, innovators, and entrepreneurs. At a minimum, all must be treated with dignity and self-esteem—as micro consumers. They must be able to exercise choice and must have access to world-class goods and services. World class does not mean luxury. A cell phone that the poor get is world class; it might not have a fancy case, a fine camera, or a great color display. But in its core functionality, it is no different. Treating people as consumers is not the same as creating a wasteful consumer culture. The CEO of the Acumen Fund, Jacqueline Novogratz, had this to say:

> We agree with Dr. Prahalad that choice is where dignity starts, and that the world will change only when we view truly low-income individuals as full participants in their local economies and communities, as producers and consumers, rather than as passive recipients of charity.

We have to start with respect for individuals irrespective of their current condition. Deciding "what is good for them" is against the very spirit of co-creation. Yes, we can educate them on the risks and benefits of choices. But they must exercise their choice. Those of us who have had the pleasure to see firsthand the extraordinary intelligence of the "uneducated" and how they "make do with what they have" are convinced that capability building for personal choice is a critical component of democratization of commerce.

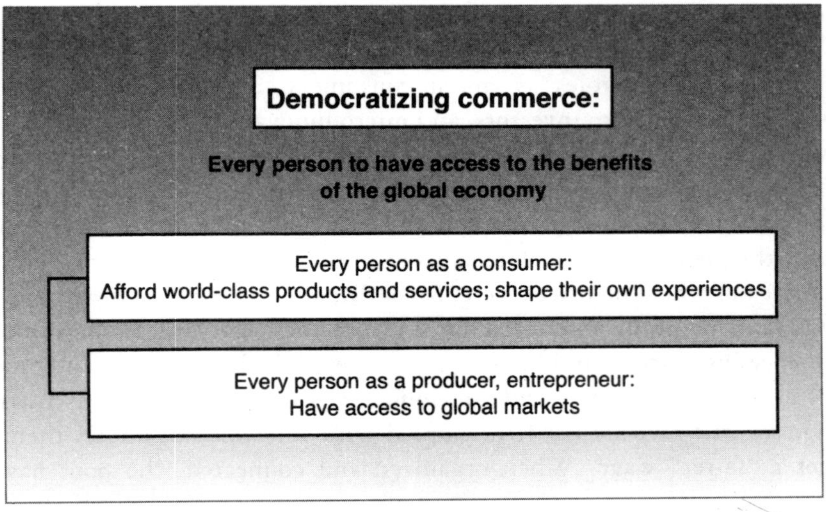

Figure Intro.2 Democratizing commerce.

Although we treat all with respect as "consumers," we must also ensure that all can participate in the global economy as micro producers, micro entrepreneurs, and micro investors. Increasingly, this is becoming a reality. The case of Amul, ITC e-Choupal, Jaipur Rugs, and Nestlé are examples of connecting rural, subsistent farmers to regional, national, and global markets. There are now a large number of examples of organizing the poor to ensure that they have the benefits of information—as in the case of farmers using cell phones to check weather and price information before they sell to farming cooperatives or working with large firms such as ITC or Nestlé. At the same time, individuals must have access to become entrepreneurs. The story of village level entrepreneurs—Shakti Ammas (Unilever), Jyoti Ammas (BP), Grammenn Bank, and self-help groups all over the world, demonstrate that given a chance, the poor are willing to be entrepreneurial and invest in their own success. There are those entrepreneurial women who start a "salon" in their neighborhood, to those who settle for a more traditional opportunity of raising cattle or chickens. The key is that they learn to be self-reliant, confident, and capable of understanding investment and returns, credit, and profit. Finally, we have to provide opportunities for them to save and become micro investors. Access to savings accounts and modern finance is key to fulfill this role. Many of them are also innovators. Today, there are opportunities for them to be organized and their innovations recognized. Prof. Anil Gupta has built an incredible database of micro innovators from villages, and this role is getting recognized.

Democratization of commerce is based on everyone having the right to exercise their roles as micro consumers, micro producers, micro entrepreneurs, micro investors, and micro innovators. *Access to information* removes the first impediment to building this brave, new world. Information asymmetry has always been at the heart of poverty. It was information asymmetry that allowed local moneylenders to have sway over the poor farmers; or buyers have advantage over fishermen who had no idea of what the prices were. Secondly, *access to credit and micro finance products* (including micro insurance) from the organized sector—micro-finance institutions and banks—allows people to build equity and escape usurious moneylenders and continuous struggle with poverty. *Access to regional and national markets*, coupled with information, allows them to get a "fairer" wage. When organized and connected, the poor have a fighting chance to get a fair wage for their work. Finally, they, as micro innovators, can find a market for their innovations if they are organized.

I do recognize that what we are seeing are a "ray of hope" and weak signals that suggest that we can democratize commerce. We have to actively engage the private sector in a collaborative relationship with civil society, governments, and philanthropists. However, the organizing idea that illuminates this new social compact must be

- Respect for the rights of the individual
- The use of transparent transactions or a focus on market-based solutions
- Scalability to solutions
- Reducing the rural-urban, rich-poor divide through information technology and organization
- Focus on entrepreneurship and innovation
- Focus on ecologically sustainable solutions

Five years after the initial publication of this book, I am more excited and energized about the possibilities of the Bottom of the Pyramid than ever before. The capacity for change and creative thinking I have seen from everyone who has embraced the challenge—from nongovernmental organizations, multinationals, and the poor themselves—has been inspirational. A change this ambitious cannot happen overnight. There have been setbacks, missteps, and disappointments. But that is true with all fundamental change. I am hopeful that the debate about the Bottom of the Pyramid has shifted away from convincing people that there is a market to debating how best to serve it. I am confident that the simple fact that so many more people are searching for answers will lead to better and more complete solutions.

It used to be that the rich felt a sense of entitlement. I hope that as a result of more companies engaging with the poor, they too begin to feel a sense of entitlement—to dignity, choice, and mobility. I believe that this change will help not only people across the world, but society and the environment as well, because it will require change and innovation on a massive scale. It is too early to pronounce Bottom of the Pyramid markets an unqualified successes. I think, however, there are enough signals to illustrate that the "invisible hand" of entrepreneurs reaching out to the invisible markets of the world has the capacity to help create the solutions that people—and the planet—so desperately need.

Endnotes

1. C.K. Prahalad and Stuart Hart: *The Fortune at the Bottom of the Pyramid, strategy+business*, First Quarter, 2002.
2. United Nations Development Program: Blue-Ribbon Commission's Human Development Report, 2004.
3. United Nations Development Program: Creating Value for All: Strategies for Doing Business with the Poor, July 2008.
4. Jeb Brugmann and C.K. Prahalad: *Co-Creating Business's New Social Compact, The Harvard Business Review*, 2007.
5. Stuart Hart coined the term Base of the Pyramid to describe the same 4 billion poor. This is more intellectually appealing. In current debates, both terms—Bottom of the Pyramid and Base of the Pyramid—are used interchangeably. BOP stands for both formulations.
6. Niti Bhan and Dave Tait, "Design for the Next Billion Customers," *Core 77: Design Magazine & Resource*, April 4, 2009.
7. The Next 4 Billion: A study done by World Resources Institute and IFC.
8. Paul Collier, *The Bottom Billion: Why the Poorest Countries are Failing and What Can Be Done About It*, Oxford University Press, 2007.
9. Burgeoning Bourgeoise, A Special Report on the New Middle Classes in Emerging Markets, *The Economist*, February 14, 2009.
10. C.K. Prahalad and Kenneth Lieberthal: *The End of Corporate Imperialism, The Harvard Business Review*, Harvard Business School Press, November, 2008.
11. C.K. Prahalad: *The Innovation Sandbox, strategy+business*, 2006.
12. Jeb Brugmann and C.K. Prahalad: *Co-Creating Business's New Social Compact, The Harvard Business Review*, 2007.
13. Bill Gates: Address to the World Economic Forum, 2008.

PART II

The Original Text of the Book

The objective of this section is to *build a framework* for poverty alleviation. We start with a simple proposition. **If we stop thinking of the poor as victims or as a burden and start recognizing them as resilient and creative entrepreneurs and value-conscious consumers, a whole new world of opportunity can open up.** Four billion poor can be the engine of the next round of global trade and prosperity. They can be a source of innovations. Serving the BOP consumers will demand innovations in technology, products and services, and business models. More important, it requires large firms to work collaboratively with civil society organizations and local governments. Market development at the BOP can also create millions of new entrepreneurs at the grass roots level—from women working as distributors and entrepreneurs to village-level micro enterprises. These micro enterprises will be an integral part of the market-based ecosystem. It requires organizational and governance innovations as well.

The vision that is presented in the following pages is the co-creation of a solution to the problem of poverty. The opportunities at the BOP cannot be unlocked if large and small firms, governments, civil society organizations, development agencies, and the poor themselves do not work together with a shared agenda. Entrepreneurship on a massive scale is the key. This approach can challenge the prejudices about the "role and value added" of each group and its role in the economic development at the BOP.

In these chapters, you find the opportunities for co-creation among the various players. More important, the poor themselves are willing to experiment, learn, and change. While we focus on the role of the private sector, the importance of collaboration across the various groups becomes obvious. The interconnectedness of the approach to economic development and social transformation as visualized below becomes obvious.

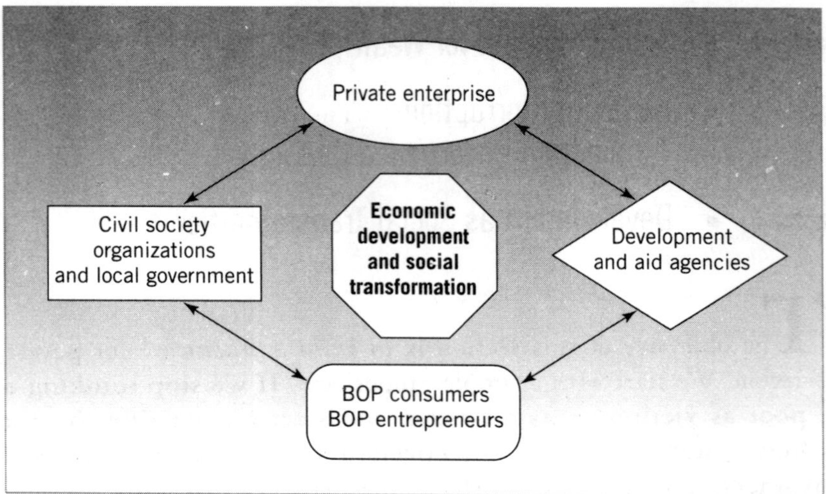

Part II outlines how that can be accomplished by isolating principles from successful, large-scale experiments involving the entire private sector ecosystem. Most of the examples of successful experimentation are taken from the case studies included later in the book. The bottom line is simple: It is possible to "do well by doing good."

I

The Market at the Bottom of the Pyramid

Turn on your television and you will see calls for money to help the world's 4 billion poor—people who live on far less than $2 a day. In fact, the cry is so constant and the need so chronic that the tendency for many people is to tune out these images and the message. Even those who do hear and heed the cry are limited in what they can accomplish. For more than 50 years, the World Bank, donor nations, various aid agencies, national governments, and, lately, civil society organizations have all fought the good fight, but have not eradicated poverty. The adoption of the Millennium Development Goals (MDG) by the United Nations only underscores that reality; as we enter the 21st century, poverty—and the disenfranchisement that accompanies it—remains one of the world's most daunting problems.

The purpose of this bock is to change that familiar image on TV. It is to illustrate that the typical pictures of poverty mask the fact that the very poor represent resilient entrepreneurs and value-conscious consumers. **What is needed is a better approach to help the poor, an approach that involves partnering with them to innovate and achieve sustainable win–win scenarios where the poor are actively**

engaged and, at the same time, the companies providing products and services to them are profitable. This collaboration between the poor, civil society organizations, governments, and large firms can create the largest and fastest-growing markets in the world. Large-scale and wide-spread entrepreneurship is at the heart of the solution to poverty. Such an approach exists and has, in several instances, gone well past the idea stage as private enterprises, both large and small, have begun to successfully build markets at the *bottom of the pyramid (BOP)* as a way of eradicating poverty.

The economic pyramid of the world is shown in Figure 1.1. As we can see, more than 4 billion constitute the BOP. These are the people who are the subject matter of this book.

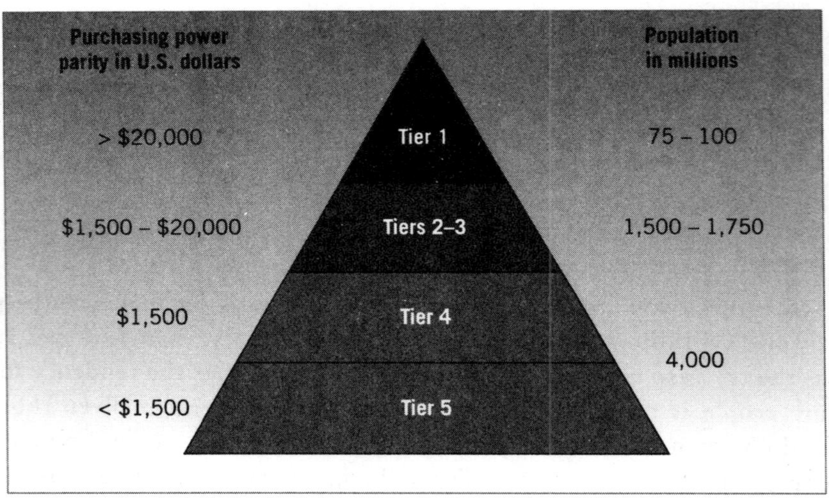

Figure 1.1 The economic pyramid. *Source:* C.K. Prahalad and Stuart Hart, 2002. The Fortune at the Bottom of the Pyramid, *strategy+business*, Issue 26, 2002. Reprinted with permission from *strategy+business*, the award-winning management quarterly published by Booz Allen Hamilton. www.strategy-business.com.

THE BOTTOM OF THE PYRAMID (BOP)

The distribution of wealth and the capacity to generate incomes in the world can be captured in the form of an economic pyramid. At the top of the pyramid are the wealthy, with numerous opportunities for generating high levels of income. More than 4 billion people live at the BOP on less than $2 per day. They are the subject matter of this book.

As you turn these pages, you will discover companies fighting disease with educational campaigns and innovative products. There are organizations helping the handicapped walk and helping subsistence farmers check commodity prices and connect with the rest of the world. There are banks adapting to the financial needs of the poor, power companies reaching out to meet energy needs, and construction companies doing what they can to house the poor in affordable ways that allow for pride. There are chains of stores tailored to understand the needs of the poor and to make products available to them.

The strength of these innovative approaches, as you will come to appreciate, is that they tend to create opportunities for the poor by offering them choices and encouraging self-esteem. Entrepreneurial solutions such as these place a minimal financial burden on the developing countries in which they occur.

To begin to understand how all of this is remotely possible, we need to start with some basic assumptions:

- First, while cases certainly can be found of large firms and multinational corporations (MNCs) that may have undermined the efforts of the poor to build their livelihoods, the greatest harm they might have done to the poor is to ignore them altogether. The poor cannot participate in the benefits of globalization without an active engagement and without access to products and services that represent global quality standards. They need to be exposed to the range and variety of opportunities that inclusive globalization can provide. The poor represent a "latent market" for goods and services. Active engagement of private enterprises at the BOP is a critical element in creating inclusive capitalism, as private-sector competition for this market fosters attention to the poor as consumers. It creates choices for them. They do not have to depend only on what is available in their villages. If large firms approach this market with the BOP consumers' interests at heart, it can also lead to significant growth and profits for them. These characteristics of a market economy, new to the BOP, can facilitate dramatic change at the BOP. Free and transparent private-sector competition, unlike local village and shanty-town monopolies controlled by local slum lords, can transform the "poor" into consumers (as we illustrate with examples). Poverty alleviation can become a business development task shared among the large private sector firms and local BOP entrepreneurs.

- Second, the BOP, as a market, provides a new growth opportunity for the private sector and a forum for innovations. Old and tired solutions cannot create markets at the BOP.
- Third, BOP markets must become an integral part of the work of the private sector. They must become part of the firms' core businesses; they cannot merely be relegated to the realm of corporate social responsibility (CSR) initiatives. Successfully creating BOP markets involves change in the functioning of MNCs as much as it changes the functioning of developing countries. BOP markets must become integral to the success of the firm to command senior management attention and sustained resource allocation.

There is significant untapped opportunity for value creation (for BOP consumers, shareholders, and employees) that is latent in the BOP market. These markets have remained "invisible" for too long.

It is natural for you to ask this: If all of this is so obvious, why has this not yet occurred?

The Power of Dominant Logic

All of us are prisoners of our own socialization. The lenses through which we perceive the world are colored by our own ideology, experiences, and established management practices. Each one of the groups that is focusing on poverty alleviation—the World Bank, rich countries providing aid, charitable organizations, national governments, and the private sector—is conditioned by its own dominant logic. Let us, for example, examine the dominant logic of each group as it approaches the task of eradicating poverty.

Consider, for instance, the politicians and bureaucrats in India, one of the largest countries with a significant portion of the world's poor. India is home to more than 400 million people who qualify as being very poor. The policies of the government for the first 45 years since independence from Great Britain in 1947 were based on a set of basic assumptions. Independent India started with a deep suspicion of the private sector. The country's interaction with the East India Company and colonialism played a major part in creating this mindset. The experience with the indigenous private sector was not very positive, either. The private sector was deemed exploitative of the poor. This suspicion was coupled with an enormous confidence in the government machinery to do what is "right and moral." For example, the government of India initiated a series of large industrial projects in the public sector (owned by the Indian government) in a wide variety of industries, from steel to food distribution and global trading in essential commodities. India's general suspicion of the private sector led to controls over its size and expansion. Some sectors of economic activity were reserved for small-scale industries. In textiles, for example, the "hand loom sector" dominated by small firms was given preference. There was no credible voice in public policy for nurturing market-based ecosystems that included the large and the small in a symbiotic relationship. The thinking was cleanly divided among the public sector (mostly large firms with significant capital outlay as in steel), the private sector with large firms strictly controlled by the government through a system of licenses, and a small-scale sector. The focus of public policy was on distributive justice over wealth creation. Because of the disparities in wealth and the preponderance of the poor, the government thought its first priority must be policies that "equalized" wealth distribution. Taxation, limits on salaries of top managers, and other such measures were instituted to ensure distributive justice. The discussion further polarized around the somewhat contrived concepts of rural poor and urban rich. The assumption was that the rural population was primarily poor and the urban population was relatively rich. However, the data increasingly does not support this distinction. There are as many rural rich as there are urban poor. Poverty knows no such boundaries. In the developing world, more than one-third of the urban population lives in shanty towns and slums. These traditional views reflect the philosophy behind actions taken by bureaucrats and politicians. During the last decade, a slow but discernable transition has been taking place from the traditional to a more market-based outlook.

This much-needed and desirable transition is in its infancy. The dominant logic, built over 45 years, is difficult to give up for individuals, political parties, and sections of the bureaucracy. This is the reason why politicians and bureaucrats appear to be vacillating in their positions. Most thinking people know where they have to go, but letting go of their beliefs and abandoning their "zones of comfort" and familiarity are not easy. We also believe that it is equally difficult for a whole generation of BOP consumers to give up their dependence on governmental subsidies.

We have explicitly focused on ideology and policy and not on the quality of implementation of projects focused on the poor, be it building roads and dams or providing basic education and health care. The distinct role of corruption, which seems so endemic to developing countries in general, deserves separate treatment (see Chapter 5, "Reducing Corruption: Transaction Governance Capacity").

Private-sector businesses, especially MNCs (and large local firms that emulate their MNC competitors), also suffer from a deeply etched dominant logic of their own, which restricts their ability to see a vibrant market opportunity at the BOP. For example, it is common in MNCs to have the assumptions outlined in Table 1.1. These assumptions dictate decision and resource allocation processes for developing countries and BOP markets in particular.

Table 1.1 The Dominant Logic of MNCs as It Relates to BOP

Assumption	Implication
The poor are not our target customers; they cannot afford our products or services.	Our cost structure is a given; with our cost structure, we cannot serve the BOP markets.
The poor do not have use for products sold in developed countries.	We are committed to a form over functionality. The poor might need sanitation, but can't afford detergents in formats we offer. Therefore, there is no market in the BOP.
Only developed countries appreciate and pay for technological innovations.	The BOP does not need advanced technology solutions; they will not pay for them. Therefore, the BOP cannot be a source of innovations.
The BOP market is not critical for long-term growth and vitality of MNCs.	BOP markets are at best an attractive distraction.
Intellectual excitement is in developed markets; it is very hard to recruit managers for BOP markets.	We cannot assign our best people to work on market development in BOP markets.

Adapted from C.K. Prahalad and Stuart Hart, *The Fortune at the Bottom of the Pyramid*, *strategy+business*, Issue 26, 2002. Reprinted with permission from *strategy+business*, the award-winning management quarterly published by Booz Allen Hamilton. www.strategy-business.com.

These and other implicit assumptions surface in every discussion of BOP markets with managers in MNCs and those in large domestic firms in developing countries that fashion their management practices after those at successful MNCs. These biases are hard to eradicate in large firms. Although the dominant logic and its implications are clear, it is our goal in this book to challenge and provide counterpoints. For example, BOP markets enable firms to challenge their perspectives on cost. We will show that a 10 to 200 times advantage (compared to the cost structures that are oriented to the top of the pyramid markets) is possible if firms innovate from the BOP up and do not follow the traditional practice of serving the BOP markets by making minor changes to the products created for the top of the pyramid.

Most charitable organizations also believe that the private sector is greedy and uncaring and that corporations cannot be trusted with the problems of poverty alleviation. From this perspective, profit motive and poverty alleviation do not mix easily or well. Aid agencies have come full circle in their own thinking. **From aid focused on large infrastructure projects and public spending on education and health, they are also moving toward a belief that private-sector involvement is a crucial ingredient to poverty alleviation.**

Historically, governments, aid agencies, nongovernmental organizations (NGOs), large firms, and the organized (formal and legal as opposed to extralegal) business sector all seem to have reached an implicit agreement: Market-based solutions cannot lead to poverty reduction and economic development. As shown in Figure 1.2, the dominant logic of each group restricts its ability to see the market opportunities at the BOP. The dominant logic of each group is different, but the conclusions are similar. During the last decade, each group has been searching for ways out of this self-imposed intellectual trap. To eradicate poverty, we have to break this implicit compact through a BOP-oriented involvement of the private sector.

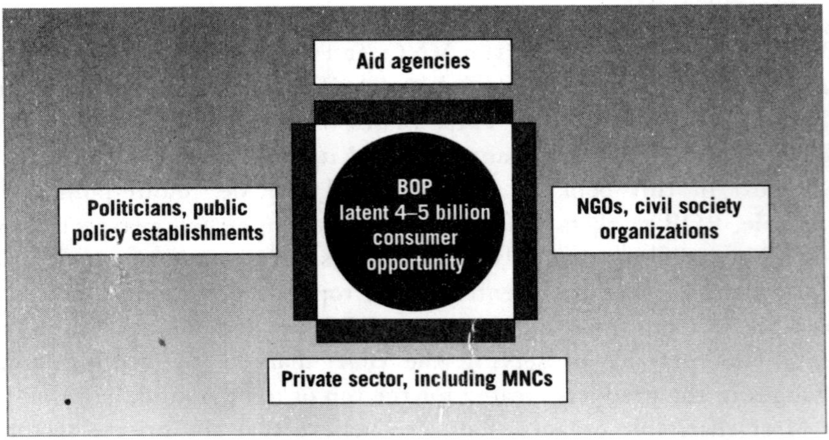

Figure 1.2 The influence of dominant logic.

We have to change our long-held beliefs about the BOP—our genetic code, if you will. The barrier that each group has to cross is different, but difficult nonetheless. However, after we cross the intellectual barrier, the opportunities become obvious. The BOP market also represents a major engine of growth and global trade, as we illustrate in our subsequent stories of MNCs and private firms from around the world.

The Nature of the BOP Market

The nature of the BOP market has characteristics that are distinct. We outline some of the critical dimensions that define this market. These characteristics must be incorporated into our thinking as we approach the BOP.

There Is Money at the BOP

The dominant assumption is that the poor have no purchasing power and, therefore, do not represent a viable market.

Let us start with the aggregate purchasing power in developing countries where most of the BOP market exists. Developing countries offer tremendous growth opportunities. Within these markets, the BOP represents a major opportunity. Take China as an example. With a population of 1.2 billion and an average per capita gross domestic product (GDP) of U.S. $1,000, China currently represents a $1.2 trillion economy. However, the U.S. dollar equivalent is not a good measure of the demand for goods and services produced and consumed in China. If we convert the GDP-based figure into its dollar purchasing power parity (PPP), China is already a $5.0 trillion economy, making it the second largest economy behind the United States in PPP terms. Similarly, the Indian economy is worth about $3.0 trillion in PPP terms. If we take nine countries—China, India, Brazil, Mexico, Russia, Indonesia, Turkey, South Africa, and Thailand—collectively they are home to about 3 billion people, representing 70 percent of the developing world population. In PPP terms, this group's GDP is $12.5 trillion, which represents 90 percent of the developing world. It is larger than the GDP of Japan, Germany, France, the United Kingdom, and Italy combined. This is not a market to be ignored.

Now, consider the BOP within the broad developing country opportunity. The dominant assumption is that the poor do not have money to spend and, therefore, are not a viable market. Certainly, the buying power for those earning less than U.S. $2 per day cannot be compared with the purchasing power of individuals in the developed nations. However, by virtue of their numbers, the poor represent a significant latent purchasing power that must be unlocked. For example, all too often, the poor tend to reside in high-cost ecosystems even within developing countries. In the shanty town of Dharavi, outside Mumbai, India, the poor pay a premium for everything from rice to credit. Compare the cost of everyday items of consumption between Dharavi and Warden Road (now redesignated B. Desai Road), a higher-income neighborhood in Mumbai. The poverty penalty in Dharavi can be as high as 5 to 25 times what the rich pay for the same services (see Table 1.2). Research indicates that this poverty penalty is universal, although the magnitude differs by country. The poverty penalty is the result of local monopolies, inadequate access, poor distribution, and strong traditional intermediaries. Large-scale private-sector businesses can "unlock this poverty penalty." For example, the poor in Dharavi pay 600 to 1,000 percent interest for credit from local moneylenders. A bank with access to this market can do well for itself by offering credit at 25 percent. Although 25 percent interest might look excessive to a casual observer, from the point of view of the BOP consumer, access to a bank decreases the cost of credit from 600 percent to 25 percent. The BOP consumer is focused on the difference between the local moneylender rates and the rates that a commercial bank would charge. The bank can make a reasonable profit after adjusting for risk (10 percent over its traditional, top-of-the-pyramid customers). We argue later that the BOP consumers do not represent higher risk.

Table 1.2 The Poor and High-Cost Economic Ecosystems

Item	Dharavi	Warden Road	Poverty Premium
Credit (annual interest)	600–1,000%	12–18%	53.0
Municipal grade water (per cubic meter)	$1.12	$0.03	37.0
Phone call (per minute)	$0.04–0.05	$0.025	1.8
Diarrhea medication	$20.00	$2.00	10.0
Rice (per kg)	$0.28	$0.24	1.2

Source: Reprinted with permission from *Harvard Business Review.* "The Poor and High Cost Economics Ecosystems." From "Serving the World's Poor Profitably" by C.K. Prahalad and Allen Hammond, September 2002. Copyright © 2002 by the Harvard Business School Publishing Corporation, all rights reserved.

These cost disparities between BOP consumers and the rich in the same economy can be explained only by the fact that the poverty penalty at the BOP is a result of inefficiencies in access to distribution and the role of the local intermediaries. These problems can easily be cured if the organized private sector decides to serve the BOP. The organized sector brings with it the scale, scope of operations, and management know-how that can lead to efficiencies for itself and its potential consumers.

The poor also spend their earnings in ways that reflect a different set of priorities. For example, they might not spend disposable income on sanitation, clean running water, and better homes but will spend it on items traditionally considered luxuries. Without legal title to land, these residents are unlikely to invest in improving their living quarters, much less the public facilities surrounding their homes. For example, in Dharavi, 85 percent of the households own a television set, 75 percent own a pressure cooker and blender, 56 percent own a gas stove, and 21 percent have telephones. In Bangladesh, women entrepreneurs with cell phones, which they rent out by the minute to other villagers, do a brisk business. It is estimated that the poor in Bangladesh spend as much as 7 percent of their income on connectivity.

Access to BOP Markets

The dominant assumption is that distribution access to the BOP markets is difficult and, therefore, represents a major impediment for the participation of large firms and MNCs.

Urban areas have become a magnet for the poor. By 2015, there will be more than 225 cities in Africa, 903 in Asia, and 225 in Latin America. More than 368 cities in the developing world will have more than 1 million people in each. There will be at least 23 cities with more than 10 million residents. Collectively, these cities will account for about 1.5 to 2.0 billion people. More than 35 to 40 percent of these urban concentrations will be composed of BOP consumers. The density of these settlements—about 15,000 people per hectare—will allow for intense distribution opportunities.

The rural poor represent a different problem. Access to distribution in rural markets continues to be problematic. Most of the rural markets are also inaccessible to audio and television signals and are often designated as "media dark." Therefore, the rural poor are not only denied access to products and services, but also to knowledge about what is available and how to use it. The spread of wireless connectivity among the poor might help reduce this problem. The ability to download movie and audio clips on wireless devices might allow firms to access traditionally "media dark" areas and provide consumers in these locations with newfound access to information about products and services. However, this is still an evolving phenomenon restricted to a few countries.

The BOP does not lend itself to a single distribution solution. Urban concentrations represent a problem distinct from that of the distribution access to dispersed rural communities. Worldwide, the cost of reach per consumer can vary significantly across countries. A wide variety of experiments are underway in these markets to find efficient methods of distributing goods and services. One such experiment, Project Shakti at Hindustan Lever Ltd. (HLL) in India, is a case in point. HLL created a direct distribution network in hard-to-reach locales (markets without distribution coverage through traditional distributors and dealers). HLL selected entrepreneurial women from these villages and trained them to become distributors, providing education, advice, and access to products to their villages. These village women entrepreneurs, called Shakti Amma ("empowered mother"), have unique knowledge about what the village needs and which products are in demand. They earn between Rs.

3,000 and 7,000 per month (U.S. $60–$150) and, therefore, create a new capacity to consume for themselves and their families. More important, these entrepreneurial women are increasingly becoming the educators and access points for the rural BOP consumers in their communities. This approach is not new. Avon is one of the largest cosmetics operations in Brazil and has used a similar approach by leveraging more than 800,000 "Avon ladies" as distributors to reach even the most remote regions of Amazonia.[1]

The BOP Markets Are Brand-Conscious

The dominant assumption is that the poor are not brand-conscious. On the contrary, the poor are very brand-conscious. They are also extremely value-conscious by necessity.

The experience of Casas Bahia in Brazil and Elektra in Mexico—two of the largest retailers of consumer durables, such as televisions, washing machines, radios, and other appliances—suggests that the BOP markets are very brand-conscious. Brand consciousness among the poor is universal. In a way, brand consciousness should not be a surprise. An aspiration to a new and different quality of life is the dream of everyone, including those at the BOP. Therefore, aspirational brands are critical for BOP consumers. However, BOP consumers are value buyers. They expect great quality at prices they can afford. The challenge to large firms is to make aspirational products affordable to BOP consumers. These consumers represent a new challenge for managers with increased pressure on costs of development, manufacturing, and distribution. As a result, BOP markets will force a new level of efficiency in the MNCs, as we demonstrate in Chapter 2, "Products and Services for the BOP."

The BOP Market Is Connected

Contrary to the popular view, BOP consumers are getting connected and networked. They are rapidly exploiting the benefits of information networks.

The spread of wireless devices among the poor is proof of a market at the BOP. For example, by the end of 2003, China had an installed base of 250 million cell phones. India had an installed base of approximately 30 million. The Indian market is growing at about 1.5 million handsets per month and reached 100 million handsets by 2005. Brazil already had 35 to 40 million. Both the current market size and the growth rates suggest that the BOP market is a critical factor in worldwide wireless growth. Telecommunications providers have made it easier for BOP consumers to purchase handsets and service through prepaid cards. The proliferation of wireless devices among the poor is universal, from Grameen Phone in Bangladesh to Telefonica in Brazil. Further, the availability of PCs in kiosks at a low price per hour and the opportunity to videoconference using PCs are adding to the intensity of connectivity among those at the BOP. The net result is an unprecedented ability of BOP consumers to communicate with each other in several countries. The technology of wireless and PC connectivity allows the BOP population to actively engage in a dialogue with each other, with the firms from which they want to purchase goods and services, and with the politicians who represent them.

Connectivity also allows the BOP consumers to establish new patterns of communication away from their villages. With cell phones and TV, the BOP consumer has unprecedented access to information and opportunities to engage in a dialogue with the larger community. As a result, word of mouth among BOP consumers is becoming a potent force for assessing product quality, prices, and options available to them. The spread of good bargains and bad news can be rapid. For example, in India, it appears that some consumers found worms in chocolates sold by Cadbury, a large and very successful MNC. Ten years ago, this would have been a nonevent, but with access to multiple and fiercely competitive TV channels, wireless, and Internet, the news spread so rapidly across India that not just managers within Cadbury but all managers involved in the "fast-moving consumer goods" industry were surprised and worried.[2]

BOP Consumers Accept Advanced Technology Readily

Contrary to popular belief, the BOP consumers accept advanced technology readily.

The spread of wireless devices, PC kiosks, and personal digital assistants (PDAs) at the BOP has surprised many a manager and researcher. For example, ITC, an Indian conglomerate, decided to connect Indian farmers with PCs in their villages. The ITC e-Choupal (literally, "village meeting place") allowed the farmers to check prices not only in the local auction houses (called *mandis*), but also prices of soybean futures at the Chicago Board of Trade. The e-Choupal network allowed the farmers access to information that allowed them to make decisions about how much to sell and when, thus improving their margins. Similarly, women entrepreneurs in southern India, given a PC kiosk in their villages, have learned to videoconference among themselves, across villages on all kinds of issues, from the cost of loans from various banks to the lives of their grandchildren in the United States.[3] Chat rooms are full of activity that none of us could have imagined. Most interestingly, in Kerala, India, fishermen in traditional fishing boats, after a day of productive work, sell their catch to the highest bidders, using their cell phones to contact multiple possible landing sites along the Kerala coast. The simple boats, called catamarans, have not changed, but the entire process of pricing the catch and knowing how to sell based on reliable information has totally changed lives at the BOP.[4] The BOP consumers are more willing to adopt new technologies because they have nothing to forget. Moving to wireless from nothing is easier than moving to wireless from a strong tradition of efficient and ubiquitous landlines.

The Market Development Imperative

The task of converting the poor into consumers is one of market development. Market development involves both the consumer and the private-sector firm. We consider the risks and benefits to the private-sector firm later. Here, we reflect on the incentives for the BOP consumer, who is so far isolated from the benefits of access to regional and global markets, to participate. What are the benefits to the BOP consumer? Our examples are drawn primarily from the stories that appear in the book.

Create the Capacity to Consume

To convert the BOP into a consumer market, we have to create the capacity to consume. Cash-poor and with a low level of income, the BOP consumer has to be accessed differently.

The traditional approach to creating the capacity to consume among the poor has been to provide the product or service free of charge. This has the feel of philanthropy. As mentioned previously, charity might feel good, but it rarely solves the problem in a scalable and sustainable fashion.

A rapidly evolving approach to encouraging consumption and choice at the BOP is to make unit packages that are small and, therefore, affordable. The logic is obvious. The rich use cash to inventory convenience. They can afford, for example, to buy a large bottle of shampoo to avoid multiple trips to the store. The poor have unpredictable income streams. Many subsist on daily wages and have to use cash conservatively. They tend to make purchases only when they have cash and buy only what they need for that day. Single-serve packaging—be it shampoo, ketchup, tea and coffee, or aspirin—is well suited to this population. A single-serve revolution is sweeping through the BOP markets. For example, in India, single-serve sachets have become the norm for a wide variety of products, as shown in Table 1.3.

Table 1.3 Creating the Capacity to Consume: Single-Serve Revolution

Single-Serve Value at Retail		
Rs.	**$**	**Typical Products**
0.50	0.01	Shampoo, confectionary, matches, tea
1.00	0.02	Shampoo, salt, biscuits, ketchup, fruit drink concentrate
2.00	0.04	Detergent, soap, mouth fresheners, biscuits, jams, spreads, coffee, spices
5.00	0.10	Biscuits, toothpaste, color cosmetics, fragrance, bread, cooking oil, skin cream

Note: Shampoo and biscuits are shown under different price ranges because these items are available in multiple single-serve and low unit pack quantities.

The number of products sold in the single-serve format is rapidly increasing. The format is so popular that even firms producing high-end merchandise have to adopt it to remain viable long-term players in the growing markets. For example, in the shampoo business, the situation in the Indian market is shown in Figure 1.3.

Measured in tons, the size of the Indian shampoo market is as large as the U.S. market. Large MNCs, such as Unilever and Procter & Gamble (P&G), are major participants in this market, as are large local firms. Because the poor are just as brand-conscious as the rich, it is possible to buy Pantene, a high-end shampoo from P&G, in a single-serve sachet in India. The entrepreneurial private sector has created a large market at the BOP; the penetration of shampoo in India is about 90 percent.

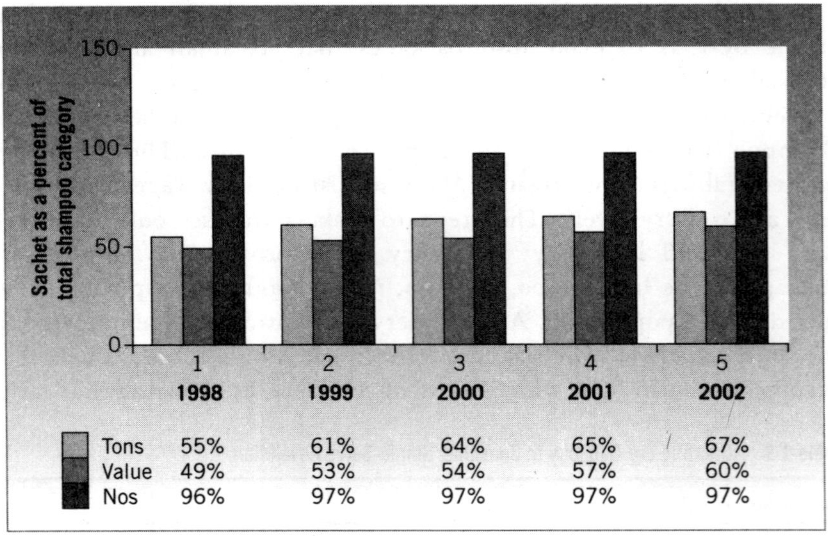

Figure 1.3 Single-serve sachet as a percentage of total shampoo market in India.

A similar approach to creating capacity to consume is through innovative purchase schemes. More BOP consumers in Brazil can buy appliances through Casas Bahia because the firm provides credit even for consumers with low and unpredictable income streams. Through a sophisticated credit rating system coupled with counseling, Casas Bahia provides access to high-quality appliances to consumers who could not otherwise afford them. At the same time, the firm ensures that its consumers are not overstretched. The default rate is low at 8.5 percent, compared to more than 15 percent for competitor firms. Casas Bahia has also created a new pool of repeat customers. CEMEX, one of the world's largest cement companies in Mexico, follows a similar approach in its "do-it-yourself" business focused on the BOP market. The idea is to help the consumers learn to save and invest. By creating a pool of three women who save as a group and discipline and pressure each other to stay with the scheme, CEMEX facilitates the process of consumption by bundling savings and access to credit with the ability to add a bathroom or a kitchen to their homes.

Creating the capacity to consume is based on three simple principles best described as the "Three As":

1. *Affordability.* Whether it is a single-serve package or novel purchasing schemes, the key is affordability without sacrificing quality or efficacy.
2. *Access.* Distribution patterns for products and services must take into account where the poor live and their work patterns. Most BOP consumers must work the full day before they can have enough cash to purchase the necessities for that day. Stores that close at 5:00 PM have no relevance to them, as their shopping begins after 7:00 PM. Further, BOP consumers cannot travel great distances. Stores must be easy to reach, often within a short walk. This calls for *geographical intensity of distribution.*
3. *Availability.* Often, the decision to buy for BOP consumers is based on the cash they have on hand at a given point in time. They cannot defer buying decisions. Availability (and therefore, *distribution efficiency*) is a critical factor in serving the BOP consumer.

Of course, the ideal is to create the capacity to earn more so that the BOP consumers can afford to consume more. The ITC e-Choupal story illustrates how farmers with access to the Internet and thereby access to the prices of commodities around the world can increase their incomes by 5 to 10 percent. These farmers can decide when and how much to sell based on their understanding of the likely price movements for their products. Modern technology not only allows them to realize better prices, but also to improve their logistics. The aggregation of food grains allows for efficiencies for both the farmer and the buyer.

By focusing on the BOP consumers' capacity to consume, private-sector businesses can create a new market. The critical requirement is the ability to invent ways that take into account the variability in the cash flows of BOP consumers that makes it difficult for them to access the traditional market for goods and services oriented toward the top of the pyramid.

The Need for New Goods and Services

The involvement of the private sector at the BOP can provide opportunities for the development of new products and services.

Amul, a dairy cooperative in India, has introduced good-quality ice cream at less than $0.05 per serving, affordable by all at the BOP. This product is not only a source of enjoyment; the milk in it is also a source of nutrition for the poor. Now, Amul is planning to introduce a natural laxative-laced ice cream called "isabgol-enriched." It is too early to tell whether the product can be a success. However, the experimentation is what the game is about. Similarly, the popularization of pizza by the same company allows the poor to obtain an adequate quantity of protein.[5] PRODEM FFP, a Bolivian financial services company, has introduced smart automated teller machines (ATMs) that recognize fingerprints, use color-coded touch screens, and speak in three local languages. This technological innovation allows even illiterate BOP consumers to access, on a 24-hour basis, high-quality financial services.[6] CEMEX, as we saw earlier, provides access to good quality housing. Through Tecnosol, the BOP consumers in rural Nicaragua have access to clean energy from renewable sources—solar and wind power. Previously, these consumers did not have access to grid-based electricity and were dependent on more expensive sources, such as kerosene and batteries. Now they have energy that is affordable enough to run their households. Casas Bahia not only sells appliances, but has also introduced a line of good-quality furniture oriented toward the BOP markets. Furniture has become one of the fastest growing businesses for the company and a source of pride and satisfaction to its consumers.

Dignity and Choice

When the poor are converted into consumers, they get more than access to products and services. They acquire the dignity of attention and choices from the private sector that were previously reserved for the middle-class and rich.

The farmers we interviewed at an ITC e-Choupal were clear. The traditional auctioning system at the government-mandated markets (mandis) did not offer them any choices. When they went to a mandi, they had to sell their produce at the prices offered on that day. They could not wait for better prices or haul their produce back to their villages. More important, the local merchants who controlled the mandi were not respectful of the farmers. One farmer remarked, "They make rude comments about my produce. They also raise the prices in the auction by $0.02 per ton. It is as if they have already determined the price you will get and they go through the motions of an auction. It used to be very demeaning." Not any longer. Now, the same farmers can access information on the Web across all the mandis and can decide where, when, and at which prices they want to sell. Similarly, women in self-help groups (SHGs) working with ICICI Bank in India also have had their dignity restored. As a group, they decide which borrowers and projects receive loans. This involvement of women in leadership development and in learning about finances and bank operations has given them a new sense of personal worth. The single-serve revolution has created a revolutionary level of choice for consumers at the BOP. For example, the "switching costs" for the consumer are negligible because she can buy a sachet of shampoo or detergent or pickles; if she is not satisfied with her purchase, she can switch brands the next day. Firms must continuously innovate and upgrade their products to keep customers interested in their brands, thereby improving quality and reducing costs.

Trust Is a Prerequisite

Both sides—the large firms and the BOP consumers—have traditionally not trusted each other. The mistrust runs deep. However, private-sector firms approaching the BOP market must focus on building trust between themselves and the consumers.

This is clearly evident when one visits a Casas Bahia store. BOP consumers here venerate the founder, Mr. Klein, for giving them the opportunity to possess appliances that they could not otherwise afford. Although the shanty towns of Sao Paulo or Rio de Janeiro can be dangerous to outsiders, Casas Bahia trucks move freely around without worry. The same is true for Bimbo, the provider of fresh bread and other bakery products to the BOP consumers in Mexico. Bimbo[7] is the largest bakery in Mexico, and its trucks have become symbols of trust between the BOP consumers and the firm. The truck drivers are so trusted that often the small store owners in the slums allow them to open their shops, stock them with bread, and collect cash from the cash boxes without supervision. Both Casas Bahia and Bimbo believe that the truck drivers who deliver their products to the BOP consumers are their ambassadors and neither company will outsource the delivery process. In fact, all managers at Bimbo must work as truck drivers for the company to become better educated about their customers.

MNCs often assume that the default rate among the poor is likely to be higher than that of their rich customers. The opposite is often true. The poor pay on time and default rates are low. In the case of ICICI Bank, out of a customer base of 200,000, the default rate is less than 1 percent. The default rate at Grameen Bank, a microfinance pioneer in

Bangladesh, is less than 1.5 percent among 2,500,000 customers. The lessons are clear. Through persistent effort and the provision of world-class quality, private-sector businesses can create mutual trust and responsibility between their companies and BOP customers. Trust is difficult to build after 50 years of suspicion and prejudice based on little evidence and strong stereotyping.

Benefits to the Private Sector

We have identified the immediate benefits of treating the poor as consumers and the poverty alleviation process that can result as businesses focus on the BOP. It is clear that the consumers (the poor) benefit, but do the private-sector businesses benefit as well? The BOP market potential is huge: 4 to 5 billion underserved people and an economy of more than $13 trillion PPP. The needs of the poor are many. The case for growth opportunity in the BOP markets is easy to make. However, to participate in these markets, the private sector must learn to innovate. Traditional products, services, and management processes will not work. In the next chapter, we discuss a philosophy of innovation focused on BOP markets.

Endnotes

1. Helen Cha, Polly Cline, Lilly Liu, Carrie Meek, and Michelle Villagomez. "Direct Selling and Economic Empowerment in Brazil: The Case of Avon." Edited by Anuradha Dayal-Gulati, Kellogg School of Management, 2003.
2. Syed Firdaus Ashraf. "Worms Found in Chocolate Packet," rediff.com, October 3, 2003.
3. See multiparty videoconferencing, www.n-Logue.com.
4. Saritha Rai. "In Rural India, a Passage to Wirelessness." *The New York Times*, August 4, 2001.
5. Harish Damodaran. "Try Amul's New Ice Cream and—Be Relieved." The Hindu Business Line, September 8, 2002.
6. Roberto Hernandez and Yerina Mugica. "What Works: Prodem FFP's Multilingual Smart ATMs for Micro Finance." World Resources Institute, Digital Dividend Web site, digital dividend.com, August 2003.
7. www.bimbo.com.

2

Products and Services for the BOP

As we saw in the previous chapter, the BOP can be a viable growth market. During the last decade, many MNCs have approached BOP markets with an existing portfolio of products and services. Because these product portfolios have been priced and developed for Western markets, they are often out of reach for potential customers in BOP markets. More important, the feature-function set has often been inappropriate. As a result, the promise of the emerging BOP markets has been largely illusory.[1] At the same time, developmental agencies have also tried to replicate developed country models at the BOP with equally unsatisfactory results. The development assistance community has invested billions in Western mechanical waste water treatment facilities in the developing world. Many if not most of these facilities were no longer operating within a year of their completion because the local "markets" could not afford the electricity to operate them, did not have a steady electricity supply, or lacked an adequate supply of chemicals and spare parts.

MNCs do recognize that only 5 to 10 percent of the population of China or India can represent a new market of 50 to 100 million each. MNCs can more easily tap into the top of the economic pyramid in emerging economies such as China, India, or Brazil, and these markets can be substantial. Although the affluent in these markets might appear to be similar to "traditional" consumers in developed countries, they are not. They tend to be much more value-conscious. Regardless, the goal is to reach the entire population base, including the BOP. How can MNCs capitalize on this emerging BOP opportunity?

A Philosophy for Developing Products and Services for the BOP

The BOP, as a market, challenges the dominant logic of MNC managers (the beliefs and values that managers serving the developed markets have been socialized with). For example, **the basic economics of the BOP market are based on small unit packages, low margin per unit, high volume, and high return on capital employed.** This is different from large unit packs, high margin per unit, high volume, and reasonable return on capital employed. This shift in business economics is the first surprise to most managers. As we observed in Chapter 1, "The Market at the Bottom of the Pyramid," creating the capacity to consume—the single-serve and low unit pack revolution at the BOP—can be the first surprise for product developers trained in the West. "How can anyone make money at $0.01/unit price at retail?" is often the question. Similarly, in the West, product developers often assume that the required infrastructures for the use of products exist or that Western infrastructure can be made economically viable and will function properly in these markets. In a developed market, access to refrigerators, telephones, transportation, credit, and a minimum level of literacy can all be assumed. The choice of technologies is not constrained by the infrastructure. However, in BOP markets, the quality of infrastructure can vary substantially, especially within a country as vast as China, Brazil, or India. What is available in Shanghai or Mumbai is not an indication of the infrastructure in the hinterlands of China or India. For example, the supply of electricity can be quite erratic and blackouts and brownouts are common. **Advanced technology solutions, such as a regional network of PCs, must coexist with poor and indifferent**

electrical and telecom infrastructures. Hybrid solutions that integrate backup power sources with PCs are a must, as are customer interfaces. For example, India boasts more than 15 official languages and 500 dialects, and 30 percent of the total population is illiterate. How then can we develop user-friendly interfaces for products that the poor and the illiterate can understand and utilize? Surprisingly, illiteracy can lead to acceptance of the state-of-the-art solutions. For example, illiterate consumers can "see and hear," not read. Therefore, video-enabled cell phones might be more appropriate for this market.

These challenges are not isolated conditions. Involvement in BOP markets challenges assumptions that managers in MNCs have developed over a long period of time. A new philosophy of product development and innovation that reflects the realities of BOP markets is needed. This philosophy must represent a different perspective from those that we have grown accustomed to in serving Western markets.

Based on my research, I have identified 12 principles that, taken together, constitute the building blocks of a philosophy of innovation for BOP markets. In this chapter, we discuss each of these principles with specific illustrations drawn primarily from the detailed case studies of successful innovations at the BOP included in this book.

Twelve Principles of Innovation for BOP Markets

1. Focus on price performance of products and services. Serving BOP markets is not just about lower prices. It is about creating a new price-performance envelope. Quantum jumps in price performance are required to cater to BOP markets.
2. Innovation requires hybrid solutions. BOP consumer problems cannot be solved with old technologies. Most scalable, price-performance-enhancing solutions need advanced and emerging technologies that are creatively blended with the existing and rapidly evolving infrastructures.
3. As BOP markets are large, solutions that are developed must be scalable and transportable across countries, cultures, and languages. How does one take a solution from the southern part of India to the northern part? From Brazil to India or China? Solutions must be designed for ease of adaptation in similar BOP markets. This is a key consideration for gaining scale.

4. The developed markets are accustomed to resource wastage. For example, if the BOP consumers started using as much packaging per capita as the typical American or Japanese consumer, the world could not sustain that level of resource use. All innovations must focus on conserving resources: eliminate, reduce, and recycle. Reducing resource intensity must be a critical principle in product development, be it for detergents or ice cream.
5. Product development must start from a deep understanding of functionality, not just form. Marginal changes to products developed for rich customers in the United States, Europe, or Japan will not do. The infrastructure BOP consumers have to live and work in demands a rethinking of the functionality anew. Washing clothes in an outdoor moving stream is different from washing clothes in the controlled conditions of a washing machine that adjusts itself to the level of dirt and for batches of colored and white clothes.
6. Process innovations are just as critical in BOP markets as product innovations. In developed markets, the logistics system for accessing potential consumers, selling to them, and servicing products is well developed. A reliable infrastructure exists, and only minor changes might need to be made for specific products. In BOP markets, the presence of a logistics infrastructure cannot be assumed. Often, innovation must focus on building a logistics infrastructure, including manufacturing that is sensitive to the prevailing conditions. Accessing potential consumers and educating them can also be a daunting task to the uninitiated.
7. Deskilling work is critical. Most BOP markets are poor in skills. The design of products and services must take into account the skill levels, poor infrastructure, and difficulty of access for service in remote areas.
8. Education of customers on product usage is key. Innovations in educating a semiliterate group on the use of new products can pose interesting challenges. Further, most of the BOP also live in "media dark" zones, meaning they do not have access to radio or TV. In the absence of traditional approaches to education—traditional advertising—new and creative approaches, such as video mounted on trucks and traveling low-cost theatrical productions whose job it is to demonstrate product usage in villages, must be developed.

9. Products must work in hostile environments. It is not just noise, dust, unsanitary conditions, and abuse that products must endure. Products must also be developed to accommodate the low quality of the infrastructure, such as electricity (for example, wide fluctuations in voltage, blackouts, and brownouts) and water (for example, particulate, bacterial, and viral pollution).
10. Research on interfaces is critical given the nature of the consumer population. The heterogeneity of the consumer base in terms of language, culture, skill level, and prior familiarity with the function or feature is a challenge to the innovation team.
11. Innovations must reach the consumer. Both the highly dispersed rural market and a highly dense urban market at the BOP represent an opportunity to innovate in methods of distribution. Designing methods for accessing the poor at low cost is critical.
12. Paradoxically, the feature and function evolution in BOP markets can be rapid. Product developers must focus on the broad architecture of the system—the platform—so that new features can be easily incorporated. BOP markets allow (and force) us to challenge existing paradigms. For example, challenging the grid-based supply of electricity as the only available source for providing good-quality, inexpensive energy is possible and necessary in the isolated, poor BOP markets.

It might appear that the new philosophy of innovation for the BOP markets requires too many changes to the existing approach to innovation for developed markets. It does require significant adaptation, but all elements of innovation for the BOP described here might not apply to all businesses. Managers need to pick and choose and prioritize. Although effective participation requires changes to the philosophy of innovation, I argue that the pain of change is worth the rewards that will be reaped from the BOP and from traditional markets. Further, when we recognize the issues involved, innovation can be quite an energizing experience. I also plan to illustrate with a large number of examples that a wide variety of organizations—MNCs, local firms, and NGOs—are successfully innovating with vigor in these markets and are making a great difference in the quality of life of low-income customers and low-income communities. This is of particular importance to MNCs. Because innovations for the BOP markets challenge our established ways of thinking, BOP markets can become a source of innovations for the developed markets as well. **Innovation in BOP markets can reverse the flow of concepts, ideas, and methods. Therefore, for an MNC that aims to stay ahead of the curve, experimenting in BOP markets is increasingly critical. It is no longer an option.**

Making It Happen

Let us begin with each of the principles involved in innovation for the BOP, identify the rationale for it, and analyze examples that illustrate what can be done to incorporate it.

1. Price Performance

Addressing the market opportunity at the BOP requires that we start with a radically new understanding of the price-performance relationship compared to that currently employed in developed markets. This is not about lowering prices. It is about altering the price-performance envelope.

Price is an important part of the basis for growth in BOP markets. GSM handsets used to sell for $1,000 in India. Not surprisingly, the market was quite limited. As the average price dropped to $300, sales started to increase. However, when Reliance, a cell phone provider, introduced its "Monsoon Hungama" (literally Monsoon Melee) promotion that offered 100 free minutes for a mobile, multimedia phone with an up-front payment of $10 and monthly payments of $9.25, the company received 1 million applications in 10 days. Of course, price is a factor. Equally important is the performance associated with the price. The applications available through the Monsoon Hungama offer, for a mere $10 down payment, are quite incredible, including news, games, audio clips of movies and favorite songs, video clips, astrology and numerology, city guides, TV guides, stock quotes, and the ability to surf the Internet. The phone itself is fashionable and state of the art, using CDMA technology.[2] Today, India is the fastest growing wireless market in the world. During the last quarter of 2003, India was adding 1.5 million new subscribers per month! Both GSM and CDMA technologies are readily available, as are a host of features and pricing options. The regulatory process is also rapidly evolving. This milieu can be confusing at best. However, most value-conscious consumers do not seem to be concerned. There are so many comparisons of the alternate technologies, features, and payment schemes that are debated in newspapers, on TV and radio, and in magazines, that consumers are well informed. Even those who cannot read tend to consult with others who can. Word of mouth is so powerful that the consumers seem to have found an efficient process—combining analyses offered by journalists, companies, consumer reports, and their friends—for evaluating the price-performance options available to them.

How can we provide a high level of price-performance to a consumer population that exists on less than $2 per day? The changes in price-performance that are called for must be dramatic. Let me illustrate. Consider a cataract operation. It can cost as much as $2,500 to $3,000 in the United States. Even most of the poorest in the United States can get access to this surgery through health insurance (Medicare and Medicaid). In other developed countries such as the United Kingdom, the nationalized health services pay the cost. Now, consider the poor in India or Africa. For these mostly uninsured individuals to even consider cataract surgery, it would need to be priced around $50, a fraction of what it costs in developed markets (about 50 to 75 times less than in the United States), and the quality of surgery cannot be any less. Variation in quality in restoring eyesight is unacceptable. For a successful cataract operation in BOP markets, the quality of surgery must also include postoperative care of semiliterate patients in unsanitary environments. Commitment to quality in BOP markets must be broad-based: identifying patients for surgery, most of whom have had limited medical care in the past, much less visits to the hospital; preparing them for the procedure; performing the operation; and postoperative care. The Aravind Eye Care System, the largest eye care facility in the world, is headquartered in Madurai, India. Doctors at Aravind perform more than 200,000 state-of-the-art cataract surgeries per year. Their price is $50 to $300 per surgery, including the hospital stay and any complications in surgery. However, more than 60 percent of Aravind's patients get their surgeries for free with no out-of-pocket payments by patients, insurance companies, government, and so on. With only 40 percent of paying patients at such seemingly low prices, Aravind is nevertheless very profitable. The cost of the surgery, for all the patients taken together (paying and free) is not more than $25 for a basic cataract operation with intra-ocular lens (IOL).

Similarly, access to financial services for the poor provides a challenge to conventional wisdom. Saving with a bank is a new idea for most people at the BOP. They have hardly any savings to begin with and whatever they have they wear it on them (as jewelry) or keep under their mattresses. Simple steps such as saving $1 per week and starting an account with as little as $20 can provide the impetus to cultivating the savings habit among the poor. **Building the savings habit and giving them access to the basic building blocks of financial services must precede providing them with access to low-cost loans or rain and crop insurance.** How does a large global bank approach this market and provide world-class (if a limited range of) services starting with a $20 deposit? Citicorp started $25 deposit-based banking services, called Suvidha, in Bangalore, India. Suvidha was oriented toward the urban population and was entirely based on an ATM, networked, 24/7 model. In the first year, Citibank enrolled 150,000 customers. This was the first time a global bank approached consumers with a $25 deposit option. Now several Indian banks offer similar service, both branch-based and ATM-based, in both rural and urban areas.

BOP markets, be they in telecom, personal care, health care, or financial services, impose interesting business design criteria. MNCs have to fundamentally rethink the price-performance relationship. Traditional approaches to reducing prices by 5 to 10 percent will not suffice. We should focus on an overall price-performance improvement of 30 to 100 times. This calls for a significant "forgetting curve" in the organization—an ability to discard traditional approaches to price-performance improvements. However, these efforts can be justified only if the markets are large and global and the returns are more than commensurate with the risks. Although the margin per unit might be low, investor interest in BOP markets is based on expectations of a large-volume, low-risk, and high-return-on-capital employed business opportunity. BOP markets represent an opportunity to create economic value in a fundamentally new way.

2. Innovation: Hybrids

The BOP market opportunity cannot be satisfied by watered-down versions of traditional technology solutions from the developed markets. The BOP market can and must be addressed by the most advanced technologies creatively combined with existing (and evolving) infrastructure.

More than 70 million Indian children suffer from iodine deficiency disorder (IDD), which can lead to mental retardation. A total of 200 million are at risk. IDD in many parts of Africa is equally daunting. The primary source of iodine for most Indians is salt. Indians do eat a lot of salt, but only 15 percent of the salt sold in India is iodized. Iodine is added by spraying salt with potassium iodate (KIO3) or potassium iodine (KI) during manufacturing. Salt, to be effective as a carrier of iodine, must retain a minimum of 15 parts per million of iodine. Even iodized salt in India loses its iodine content during the harsh conditions of storage and transportation. Indian cooking habits account for further iodine loss. The challenge in India (and similar markets in Africa) is clear: How do we create iodized salt that will not lose its iodine content during storage, transportation, and cooking but will release iodine only on ingesting cooked food?

In an effort to address the immense iodine loss in Indian salt, HLL, a subsidiary of Unilever, recognized that chemicals can be protected by macro and molecular encapsulation. HLL first attempted macro encapsulation (similar to coating medicine with a covering). Although this process kept the iodine intact, it was difficult to guarantee the exact amount of iodine as the miniscule size of the salt crystals complicated the process. HLL thus decided to try molecular encapsulation. Called K15 (K for potassium, 15 ppm), the technology encapsulates iodate particles between inorganic layers, protecting iodine from harsh external conditions. The inorganic layers are designed to only interact with and dissolve in highly acidic environments (that is, a pH level of 1 to 2, as in the stomach). Here, iodine is released only upon ingesting food, only negligibly before that. The tests to validate this technology under the harsh conditions of Indian spices and cooking methods required that the researchers resort to techniques developed by the Indian Atomic Energy Agency, using radioactive tracers. The tracers did not alter the chemistry of the iodine but could detect it throughout the simulated cooking process. To be marketable, though, the iodized salt so developed must also retain its attractiveness (whiteness, texture) and, needless to say, must be priced comparable to iodized salt using the traditional methods (ineffective as a carrier of iodine) and noniodized salt. The technical breakthrough in applying molecular encapsulation of iodine in salt is now a patented process. Unilever is already leveraging this innovation from HLL to other countries such as Ghana, Ivory Coast, and Kenya, where IDD is a problem.

The concept of hybrids appears in strange places. Consider that the dairy industry in India, Amul, is organized around 10,675 cooperatives from which it collects 6 million liters of milk. Amul collects milk from the farmers in villages by providing village collection centers with more than 3,000 Automatic Milk Collection System Units (AMCUS)—an integrated milk-weighing, checking (for fat content), and payment system based on electronic weighing machines, milk analyzers, and a

PC-based accounting and banking system for members. Amul makes 10 million transactions and payments in the neighborhood of Rs. 170 million. Payments can also be made instantaneously. This integrated electronic system sits in the middle of the traditional Indian village in the milk cooperatives. Many of the farmers feel that, for the first time, they have been treated "right"—the weighing and testing are honest, they are paid without delays, and they can now become part of the national milk network without leaving their villages.[3]

3. Scale of Operations

It is easy to succeed in a limited experiment, but the market needs of 4 to 5 billion people suggest that the experiments must be commercially scalable.

NGOs and other socially concerned groups are by far the lead experimenters in BOP markets. For example, we can demonstrate that a combination of photovoltaic and wind-based energy systems can be built for less than $1,000, consistently deliver the necessary power, and be acceptable as a single-family or village solution. However, how do you scale it to cover 1.5 billion people who live without access to grid-based electricity? What is involved in scaling these successful experiments? Can small local entrepreneurs and NGOs accomplish this transfer of technology across geographies?

Scale of operations is a prerequisite for making an economic case for the BOP. Given a stringent price-performance equation and low margins per unit, the basis for returns on investment is volume. Only a few BOP markets are large—China, India, Brazil, Mexico, and Indonesia. **Most of the markets, such as the African nations, are poor and small. The prerequisite for scalability of innovations from these markets is that they are supported by organizations that have significant geographical ambitions and reach.** MNCs are ideally suited for this effort. Further, size allows MNCs to make the necessary financial commitments behind potentially successful, innovative ideas. How can HLL leverage its learning, know-how, and "know-why" developed in marketing salt in India and take it to Nigeria, Chad, Ivory Coast, and China?

It is clear, therefore, that pursuing the promise of BOP markets challenges the dominant logic of both MNCs and NGOs. MNCs can benefit from learning how to engage with NGOs and local community-based organizations to co-create new products, services, and business.

NGOs can benefit from partnerships with MNCs, through which they can leverage MNC know-how and systems to scale innovations broadly.

4. Sustainable Development: Eco-Friendly

The poor as a market are 5 billion strong. This means that solutions that we develop cannot be based on the same patterns of resource use that we expect to use in developed countries. Solutions must be sustainable and ecologically friendly.

Consider the use of water. In the United States, domestic use of water per capita is around 1,932 cubic meters per person per year. In China, it is 491 cubic meters and in India, 640 cubic meters, respectively. There is not enough water available in most parts of the world to support demand.[4] Even if it is available, the quality of water available varies from indifferent to poor. For example, in Chennai, India, there is an attempt to collect rainwater from rooftops and store it in wells. So far, scarcity has not altered usage patterns. Water usage continues to be a critical component of high standards of living in the Western world. The question that BOP markets pose for us is this: Can we develop products that provide the same level of functionality with no or minimal use of water? For example, can we wash clothes without water? Can we refresh ourselves without a shower? Can we flush toilets without much water, as is done in airplanes? Can we recycle water for multiple uses within an apartment complex (in urban settings) and within a village (in rural settings) in a closed loop system? Can we conserve water in agriculture through innovative cultivation methods?

In the United States, each person generates 4.62 pounds of waste per day. If everyone in China adopted Western standards of waste per capita, there would be more than 5.5 billion pounds of waste per day.[5] There are not enough places to dump this amount of garbage! Packaging can play a crucial role in the sustainable development of markets in the BOP. With 5 billion potential users, per-capita consumption of all resources, including packaging materials, can be crucial. Even recycling systems might not be practical as the rural markets are dispersed and waste collection for recycling might not be economically viable. At the same time, packaged goods are one way of ensuring product safety. The dilemma is real. So far, MNCs and others have not suggested a practical solution to the packaging problem, nor do we have a comprehensive approach to energy and water use. Water might get the attention of MNCs sooner than energy as the availability of quality water, even for human consumption, is becoming difficult in BOP markets and, in some cases, developed markets as well. The growth of bottled water is an indication of this trend.

The goal here is not to be alarmists. The BOP will force us to come to terms with the use of resources in ways that we have not so far. Whether it is in the use of fossil fuels for energy and transportation, water for personal cleanliness, or packaging for safety and aesthetics, ecological sensitivity will become paramount. I believe that more innovative, sustainable solutions will increasingly emerge from serving the BOP markets than from the developed markets.

5. Identifying Functionality: Is the BOP Different from Developed Markets?

Recognizing that the functionality required in products or services in the BOP market might be different from that available in the developed markets is a critical starting point. In fact, developers must start from this perspective and look for anomalies from their prior expectations based on their experiences with developed markets.

Take prosthetics as an example. The artificial limb, as a business and good medical practice, is not new. It has been around for a long time and every war, starting with the American Civil War, has given a boost to its usage. Lost limbs due to accidents, polio, or war are common. India is no exception: There are 5.5 million amputees and about 25,000 to 30,000 are added each year. However, most of the patients needing prosthetics are poor and illiterate. For a poor Indian, regaining the ability to walk does not mean much if he or she cannot squat on the floor, work in the field, walk on uneven ground, and not wear shoes. As Mr. Ram Chandra, talented artist, sculptor, and inventor of the Jaipur Foot, the Indian alternative to traditional prosthetics, said, "Indians do not wear shoes to the temple or in the kitchen." Jaipur Foot's design considerations are based on unique functionality, specific to this market, and are easy to recognize, as shown in Table 2.1. The design requirements can be divided into two parts. Design must take into account the technical and medical requirements for various foot movements, but this is not enough. We can build a prosthetic that can perform all the functions required. However, if it is not within reach of the target customer—here the BOP patient—it does not help. Therefore, we need to superimpose the business requirements, not just appropriate prices, but how the individual is likely to use the prosthetic.

Table 2.1 Jaipur Foot: Design Considerations

Activity	Technical Requirements Functionality 1	Business Requirements Functionality 2
Squatting	Need for dorsiflexion	Work needs, poverty, lack of trained manpower, time for fitting
Sitting cross-legged	Need for transverse rotation	
Walking on uneven ground	Need for inversion and eversion	
Barefoot walking	Need for natural look	

Source: Our synthesis of discussions with Jaipur Foot team.

The design considerations isolated by the design team of the Jaipur Foot were uniquely oriented to BOP problems (for example, in India, Afghanistan, Bangladesh, Pakistan, Cambodia, Congo, and Vietnam) in fitting prosthetics and are not the problems that designers would contend with in the United States. Functionality 1 describes the technical requirements that are unique to BOP consumers in India. Contrary to popular assumptions, this set of design parameters increased the required functionality of prosthetics compared to what is available in the United States or Europe. Functionality 2 describes the additional unique requirements at the BOP level. For example, farmers in the BOP must work in standing water in paddy fields for about eight hours every day. Vendors in the BOP must walk long distances (about 8 to 10 km per day). Therefore, prosthetics for consumers in the BOP must be comfortable, painless, and durable. The poor cannot afford frequent replacements or hospital visits. They travel from all over India with their families to get treatment at Jaipur Foot but cannot afford boarding and lodging, much less stay for an extended time in a new location. The prosthetics must be custom-fitted in a day. From the perspective of Jaipur Foot, the prosthetics must be fitted with less than fully trained physicians, as there is a shortage of doctors and hospital space. The job of fitting a custom-developed artificial leg must be "deskilled." On top of this, prices must be reasonable, as most clients are poor. They cannot afford the typical $7,000 to $8,000 per foot cost of prosthetics. At best they can afford $50.

This might appear to be a daunting and impossible task. How can one develop a prosthetic that is more advanced in functionality, for 1/200 of the cost, can be custom-fitted by semiskilled paramedics in one visit (one day at the clinic), and last for a period of four to five years? By accepting these prerequisites, the Jaipur Foot team, led by master craftsman Ram Chandra and Dr. P.K. Sethi, a trained physician, developed a prosthetic that meets all of the criteria for less than $30. This innovation has helped farmers to farm again and a renowned Indian classical dancer to perform onstage fitted with a prosthetic.

The needs of consumers in BOP markets might not be obvious either to the firms or to the consumers. Certainly, the consumers might not know what can be accomplished with new technology to improve their productivity. Managers need to invest the necessary effort to gain a granular understanding of the dynamic needs of these consumers.

India is a country with more than 1 million retail shops. Most of the shops are tiny (around 300 to 400 square feet) and cater to the immediate neighborhoods in which they operate. Despite space constraints, each might offer well over 4,000 stockkeeping units (SKUs). These stores stock unpackaged (for example, rice, lentils, oils, salt) and packaged products that are both unbranded and branded. Most of the store owners are semiliterate and work long hours. The average sales volume per month is about Rs. 400,000 ($9,000) with thin margins. Can these stores be possible targets for a state-of-the-art point-of-sale (POS) system? TVS Electronics, an Indian firm (and a part of the TVS group of companies), focused on this market as a potential opportunity for a POS system. To start, its engineers spent several weeks in the store observing operations and the store owners' approach to management. More than 1,000 hours of video ethnography and analysis by engineers preceded the design of the POS system. The specification of the system was set as follows:

1. Robust system (must accommodate heat, dust, poor training and skills).
2. Stock management with alerts.
3. Payment modalities (cash, credit card).
4. Identification of slow-moving items.

5. Bill printing in multiple languages (English and 11 Indian languages).
6. Power back-up (built-in uninterruptible power supply).
7. Handheld bar code reader.
8. Internet-enabled.
9. Easy-to-learn and easy-to-use interface.
10. Priced attractively for this market.

As of the end of 2003, TVSE machines were field tested in more than 500 stores. The company already has on order more than 5,000 units in industries as varied as petrol stations, railway stations, and pharmaceutical outlets. The design of the POS and its cost structure allow TVSE to migrate this platform seamlessly to other applications.

6. Process Innovation

A significant opportunity for innovation in BOP markets centers around redefining the process to suit the infrastructure. Process innovation is a critical step in making products and services affordable for the poor. How to deliver is as important as what to deliver.

We referred to the Aravind Eye Care System, a profitable institution where 60 percent of the patients are nonpaying patients and the remaining 40 percent pay about $50 to $300 for cataract surgery. What is the secret? The visionary founder of Aravind Eye Hospital, Dr. Venkataswamy (Dr. V, as he is affectionately called), says he was inspired by the hamburger chain, McDonald's, where a consistent quality of hamburgers and french fries worldwide results from a deeply understood and standardized chemical process. In-depth attention to inputs and process steps guarantees high-quality outputs. Dr. V has developed and standardized the Aravind process, in which the first step is more than 1,500 eye camps where the poor are tested for vision problems and those needing help are admitted. They are then transported to hospitals. This is different from the more popular on-site eye camps in villages and small towns in India. The conditions of sanitation and medical care in such camps cannot be controlled, and they can be in specially designed hospitals developed for this purpose. In the Aravind process, technicians, often young women drawn from the local areas and trained in eye care only, supplement the work of doctors. Patient preparation and postoperative work are done by these technicians. Doctors perform only surgeries. The process flow allows a doctor and two technician teams to perform more than 50 surgeries per day. Because the process is so well developed, technicians and doctors are so carefully trained, inputs are fully controlled, and the system and values are rigidly enforced, Aravind boasts of an outcome rate that is among the best in the world. The IOL, part of the modern cataract operation, is manufactured at Madurai, the central hub of Aravind, and exported to multiple countries, including the United States.

Amul, the largest and best-known dairy in India, is yet another example. Amul, as a system, is one of the largest processors of raw milk in India. Milk collection is totally decentralized, yet Amul has innovated processes by which collection is reliable and efficient. Villagers, with a buffalo or two, bring their collection to the village collection center twice daily. The milk is measured for volume and fat content and the villager is paid every day. The collected milk is transported to processing facilities in refrigerated vans. Amul's centralized, large, and highly efficient world-class processing facilities pasteurize and package the milk for retail consumption. Amul also converts raw milk into primary products—milk powder, butter, and cheese—and secondary products such as pizza, ice cream, and Indian sweets. Amul handles marketing and promotion for a heterogeneous customer base centrally.

The Aravind and Amul stories appear to be quite different, but they have many similarities. At the heart of their extraordinary success lie the process innovations they made, as shown in Figure 2.1. The genius of these innovations is the way these two groups—in such different industries—have maintained the local infrastructure of the villages and brought to them the most advanced facilities in their respective fields. Amul connects the farmer with two buffaloes to the national and global dairy market and gives the farmer an identity. Aravind brings the world's best technology at the lowest global cost to the poorest villager and gives him or her the benefit of eyesight and dignity. Neither starts with the idea of disrupting the lives of the poor. Both aim to improve the quality of the life of the poor profitably. Neither compromises on world-class quality. Both have, through careful consideration of process innovation, achieved the requirements we set forth for successful BOP innovations: price performance, scaling, innovative high-technology hybrids, and sustainable, ecologically friendly development.

	Aravind	Amul
Origination	Use of more than 1,000 eye camps around the "catchment area." Detailed routines for the conduct of eye camps. Selection of patients for treatment.	Collection of milk from individual farm families from over 50,000 villages and 500,000 families. Guarantee quality by inspection at point of origination.
Transport to Central Facilities	Patients transported by bus to Aravind hospitals. Often relatives accompany to comfort patients.	Milk transported to main processing facilities by refrigerated vans.
Processing Facility	Specialized, world-class facilities and highly trained doctors and nurses. Clear, innovative work process for surgery.	Specialized, world-class processing facilities to convert raw milk for retail consumption and for milk by-products — powder, butter, cheese, ice cream.
Post Processing	Post-operative care and counseling. Follow-up. Research center focusing on preventable eye disease around the world.	National and global marketing of Amul brand of products.

Figure 2.1 Process innovations for the BOP.

7. Deskilling of Work

In most BOP markets, there is a shortage of talent. Work must, therefore, be deskilled.

One of the major goals facing the developing world and, by implication, the developed world, is active surveillance of the spread of infectious diseases. The spread of Severe Acute Respiratory Syndrome (SARS) across Southeast Asia and from there to Canada is a case in point. The World Health Organization (WHO) and Centers for Disease Control (CDC) recognize that active monitoring of the origination of these diseases in remote regions of the world is critical. Voxiva, a startup in Peru, created a system to monitor disease patterns. Peru suffered a devastating attack of cholera in 1998 in which more than 11,000 people perished. Peru offers a challenge for the active monitoring of diseases in the remote and mountainous regions where access to the Internet and PCs is scarce. Voxiva created a device-agnostic system. Health workers in remote areas can contact health officials in Lima, Peru, through wireless devices, landlines, or the Internet using a PC. More important, each of the health workers in remote areas was given a card with pictures of the progress of the disease. For example, the symptoms of smallpox over a period of time were captured in photographs. Anyone looking at a patient could relate the actual lesions on the patient to the corresponding picture and make a judgment on how severe the disease was. He or she simply had to telephone the central health authorities in Lima and identify the location and the severity of the case by mentioning the number of the picture on the card. The card, in a sense, was a way of capturing the knowledge of experts and identifying the stages of severity. With this simplified diagnostic process, health workers in the field need not be highly trained, nor do they need access to a complex communications network. They just need a telephone to call the health officials in Lima. Voxiva deskilled the diagnostic and surveillance problem in two ways: by reducing the need for a complex technology backbone for real-time communication and for diagnosis of the problem at the local, unskilled level as well.

CEMEX, a Mexican multinational firm in the cement business, started a project called Patrimonio Hoy (Patrimony Now) to help the poorest people build their own homes. The poor in Mexico add, whenever they can, an additional bathroom, kitchen, or bedroom to their homes; endeavors that are expensive. They often do not know exactly which materials are required. They often cannot afford to buy all the materials needed at the same time. For example, they might buy and store sand in the street, in front of their homes, until they can afford to purchase other materials. A significant amount of the materials would be wasted or lost. In response, CEMEX started a program of savings for the poor. A group of three women could start the savings program, and over 76 weeks they would save enough to buy a bathroom or a kitchen. The women knew before they started the savings program what kind of a room they could add, including its size, appearance, and materials needed to build it, including cement, steel, paints, tools, and so on. All the necessities would come in a package, and CEMEX would hold it in storage until the customers were ready. Further, they provided technical assistance and advice from skilled technicians on how to "do it yourself." Since the launch of this program, CEMEX has helped more than 300,000 families build additions to their homes.

8. Education of Customers

Innovation in BOP markets requires significant investments in educating customers on the appropriate use and the benefits of specific products and services. Given the poor infrastructure for customer access, innovation in the educational process is vital.

More than 40 percent of India is media-dark, so TV- and radio-based messages are inappropriate methods to reach these consumers and educate them on product and service benefits. Not surprisingly, in BOP markets, education is a prerequisite to market development. Consider, for example, the incidence of stomach disorders, especially diarrhea, among children. More than 2 million children die of this malady every year, a totally preventable cause of death. The cure is as simple as washing one's hands with soap before eating. HLL discovered that by this simple process, diarrhea-related fatalities could be reduced by at least 50 percent. Incidentally, HLL could also increase its volume of soap sold. However, the problem was how to educate people on the need for washing hands with soap and to convey the causality between "clean-looking but unsafe hands" and stomach disorders. HLL decided to approach village schools and educate children on the cause of disease and how to prevent it. HLL built simple demonstrations using ultraviolet dirt and bacteria detectors on "clean-looking hands." The point was that washing hands in contaminated running water might give the appearance of cleanliness, but such water harbored invisible germs that cause the damage. They co-opted teachers and NGOs and used their own "evangelists" who went to village schools and spread the messages of cleanliness, washing with (HLL) soap, and disease prevention. The children often became the most educated in the family on hygiene and, therefore, began educating their parents. The children became the activists and the advocates of good and healthy practices at home and HLL reaped new profits.

To access and educate consumers at the BOP, more than a single format and approach is called for. Often, collaboration between the private sector firms, NGOs, the public health authorities (Ministers of Health), and the World Health Organization can be of great value. However, collaboration is not without its attendant problems. Although all these organizations might agree on the broad agenda of improving public health, each has a slightly different approach and mandate (that is, politicians are also very concerned about public image). As HLL learned, collaborating with local authorities and the World Bank can cause innumerable and unforeseen problems. Although this multiparty collaboration is difficult, collaborating with the ministers (and their bureaucracies) who have as their mandate better health can be a positive step. NGOs, which are also focused on improving the lives of the poor and have deep local knowledge, can be a great help, after they can accept a commercial solution (as opposed to a charity-based or government-subsidy-based approach) to the problem.

The methods used for educating consumers can also vary. In media-dark zones, billboards painted on walls have been a staple in most developing countries, as are truck-mounted demonstration crews with catchy jingles that attract crowds in villages. In the case of Aravind Eye Hospital, well-publicized eye camps in villages conducted with the cooperation of local enterprises, NGOs, and schools are a good way to educate people on eye care and access patients who need surgery. Aravind developed a strict procedure for holding these eye camps, which are used for preliminary examination of patients. All surgery is performed in specially designed hospitals.

9. Designing for Hostile Infrastructure

The BOP markets exist in a hostile infrastructure. Design of products and services must take this into account.

Consider the design of PCs for a rural network application in northern India. ITC was building this network for connecting Indian villages in a seamless supply chain. E-Choupal, literally "the village meeting place," was designed to enable the farm community and ITC to collaborate and have a constant dialogue. The PCs placed in the village had to work under conditions unthinkable in the West. For example, the voltage fluctuated between 90 and 350 volts against a rated 220-volt transmission. Sudden surges in the current were quite the norm. Early installations were burned out and rendered useless in a short time. Further, the supply of electricity was uneven, often available for only two or three hours per day. ITC engineers had to add to the installation an uninterruptible power supply system, including surge protectors and a solar panel that would allow at least three to four hours of uninterrupted, quality electricity to operate the system. For communication, they had to depend on the satellite network rather than regular landlines. All this added to the cost. However, without this complete system that can operate in the "hostile" village environment, the entire project would have failed.

Consider the provision of good-quality water for the BOP market. Water treatment must eliminate particulate pollution, microbes, viruses and cysts, and organic and inorganic compounds. In addition, if we can supply improved taste and nutrition, it could be a welcome benefit. Systems have been developed to eliminate the "bad stuff" from water, including simple filters to complex systems. However, "purified" water from these systems can still be parceled out in unhygienic containers and touched by unclean hands. The benefits of water purification can be totally offset by what can best be described as the "last step" problem: the last step from the purifier system to consumption. Part of the system design must include the way water is dispensed and stored immediately before actual consumption.

10. Interfaces

The design of the interface must be carefully thought through. Most of the customers in BOP markets are first-time users of products and services and the learning curve cannot be long or arduous.

In designing the POS system for grocery stores, one of the main considerations was the nature of the interface. For example, each store had its own terminology and there were no set standards. Further, each store, based on its clientele, had a particular portfolio of fast-moving items. The software architecture, therefore, had to be designed so that the system could be customized easily and rapidly for each store.

Interface design can also provide some interesting and unexpected surprises. For example, in the case of rural agricultural kiosks, EID Parry found that its customers prefer an English-language interface to their PCs rather than the local language (Tamil). Wireless customers in India and Bangladesh took to the new technology more rapidly than expected. Indian housewives—rich and poor alike—are avid users of SMS messaging; on average they send 60 messages per day. Farmers in the ITC e-Choupal network, in a short period of time, were sufficiently knowledgeable to navigate the Web to check on soybean prices at the Chicago Board of Trade or the latest cricket score. The BOP can be a source of surprises on how rapidly new technologies are accepted and assimilated.

The PRODEM FFP interface in Bolivia is yet another case of creative interface design. The retailer Elektra in Mexico caters to BOP customers and also introduced fingerprint recognition as a basis for operating the

ATMs in its stores so customers need not remember their nine-digit ID codes. The opportunities for innovation—iconic, color-coded, voice-activated, fingerprint and iris recognition (biometric-based) interfaces—are more likely at the BOP than in developed countries. How we interpret the future of interface design is critical and significant research is necessary.

11. Distribution: Accessing the Customer

Distribution systems that reach the BOP are critical for developing this market. Innovations in distribution are as critical as product and process innovations.

ICICI started as an institutional lender and has grown to become the second largest bank in India. Its move into retail banking started in 1997. As such, it is a newcomer and has had to compete with banks such as the State Bank of India with more than 14,000 branches and a 200-year history in retail banking. To compete, ICICI redefined distribution access; by moving away from the approach of building branches as the primary source of access to retail customers, ICICI was able to innovate. ICICI defined access through multiple channels. Today it is the largest PC-based bank in India with more than 5 million active PC banking customers. ICICI also has the largest and fastest-growing base of ATMs in India. As of August 2003, it had an installed base of 1,750 ATMs. Further, in acquiring The Bank of Madura (which had built a strong base of rural distribution through self-help groups in southern India), it gained access to 10,000 such groups involving more than 200,000 customers. In addition to its own initiatives in building retail access, ICICI also formed partnerships with large rural marketers such as ITC and EID Parry to access farmers through their networks. Over a period of six years, through this unconventional approach to retail customer access—PCs, ATMs, self-help groups, NGOs, microfinance organizations, large rural marketers and their networks, Internet kiosk operators, and some traditional branches of their own—ICICI had a retail base of 9.8.million customer accounts and was growing at a rapid rate.

HLL, a subsidiary of Unilever, is a well-established marketing powerhouse in India. HLL serviced urban markets through dealers and suppliers and boasted the best distribution access in India. However, the company found that it was unable to access remote villages through the traditional system. As a result, HLL started a program whereby village women are involved in distributing their products in villages that were not fully serviced by HLL's existing systems of suppliers and dealers. The program, called Shakti, empowers women to become entrepreneurs. HLL's CEO, M.S. Banga, believes that this additional arm of distribution will eventually provide coverage in the 200- to 300-million-person market at the BOP currently not served by existing systems.

Avon has been extremely successful in using direct sales in Brazil. Avon built a $1.7 billion business based on direct selling. Avon representatives become experts who provide guidance to customers, minisuppliers, distribution channels, and providers of credit.[6] Amway has had similar success in India and has built a direct distribution system covering more than 600,000 Amway representatives and a total revenue base of Rs. 500 crores ($110 million).

12. BOP Markets Essentially Allow Us to Challenge the Conventional Wisdom in Delivery of Products and Services

By its very nature, success in BOP markets will break existing paradigms.

All examples used in this book challenge conventional wisdom. They challenge the current paradigms in innovation and product and service delivery in fundamental ways.

For example, Jaipur Foot and Aravind Eye Hospital challenge the assumptions behind how health care can be delivered. By focusing on one disease and one major process, these great institutions have pioneered a way of gaining scale, speed, extremely high quality, and unbelievably low costs. Their systems are being replicated by others in India and around the world. For example, several hospitals in India are increasingly specializing in cardiac care. The cost of a bypass operation in India is now as low as $4,000, compared to $50,000 in the United States. In fact, Indian groups are now negotiating with The National Health System in the United Kingdom to fly British patients into Delhi and operate on them at lower costs, including travel, than they could in the United Kingdom without compromising quality of care.

BOP markets accept the most advanced technology easily. In the wireless market, CDMA coexists with GSM in India. Customers and operators see 3G as a viable alternative. Access to audio and video clips and news and stock quotes are considered basic services. These services are available at $10 down per handset and $0.02 per minute of long-distance calling. Building a customer base of 1 million new customers in 30 days also appears to be normal.

As the innovation for public health surveillance invented by Voxiva has demonstrated, innovations from the BOP can travel to advanced countries. Voxiva's solution is now being used by the U.S. Food and Drug Administration (FDA), Department of Defense, and the Centers for Disease Control (CDC).

Energy innovator E+Co is demonstrating that it is possible to develop hybrid systems that are local, economic, and sustainable. Although not yet a full-fledged commercial success, this experiment is challenging current thinking about reliance on grid-based electricity.

Enabling people to buy by accessing markets creatively and designing affordable products for them breaks the long-held assumption that BOP markets are not viable. A wide variety of firms—HLL, CEMEX, ITC, Amul, and ICICI—are demonstrating that this can be done profitably.

BOP markets break our traditional ways of thinking and acting. This might be their biggest allure and challenge alike. Unless we are willing to discard our biases, this opportunity will remain invisible and "unattractive."

Conclusion

Getting the right combination of scale, technology, price, sustainability, and usability requires that managers start with a "zero-based" view of innovations for the BOP markets. Managers need a new philosophy of innovation and product and service delivery for the BOP markets. The 12 principles that constitute the minimum set of a philosophy of innovation are critical to understand and apply. Needless to say, they challenge the existing assumptions about product and market development. By forcing managers in large enterprises to rethink and reexamine their assumptions about form and functionality, about channels and distribution costs, BOP markets can serve as catalysts for new bursts of creativity. The biggest advantage is often in challenging the capital intensity and the managerial cost structures that have been assumed in MNCs.

Large firms, especially MNCs, can learn a lot from their active participation in BOP markets. It can help them improve their own internal management processes and bottom line. We examine how MNCs can benefit from their involvement in the BOP in the next chapter.

Endnotes

1. C.K. Prahalad and Kenneth Lieberthal, "The end of corporate imperialism." *Harvard Business Review*, July–August, 1998.
2. Anil Kripalani, "Strategies for Doing Business in India." Lecture delivered at the TiE San Diego chapter, August 26, 2003. akripalani@qualcom.com.
3. "Amul: The Poster Boy of Rural IT." www.Expresscomputeronline.com/20020916/ebiz1.shtml.
4. World Watch, "State of the World, 2004," Chapter 3.
5. 4EPA. 2001 Municipal Solid Waste in The United States. www.epa.gov/garbage/facts-text.htm.
6. "Pots of Promise," *Daily News*, July 30, 2003.

3

BOP: A Global Opportunity

We have described the process by which large firms can create products and services that are ideally suited for the BOP markets. It is natural to ask whether the managerial energy required for these innovations is justified. Although there are opportunities for growth in BOP markets, are these opportunities attractive enough for large firms (including MNCs) to go through the changes that are required in their internal systems and processes? To challenge their dominant logic? Similarly, will the social and developmental benefits of such business growth be substantial enough for NGOs and community organizations to give priority to market-based approaches?

I believe the answer is an unambiguous "yes." Based on emerging evidence, we can identify four distinct sources of opportunity for a large firm that invests the time and energy to understand and cater to the BOP markets:

1. Some BOP markets are large and attractive as stand-alone entities.
2. Many local innovations can be leveraged across other BOP markets, creating a global opportunity for local innovations.
3. Some innovations from the BOP markets will find applications in developed markets.
4. Lessons from the BOP markets can influence the management practices of global firms.

The benefits of operating at the BOP, therefore, do not just accrue in local markets. We describe each one of these opportunities next.

Engaging the BOP

There are two ways in which large firms tend to engage the BOP markets. The traditional approach of many MNCs is to start from the business models honed in the developed markets—the top of the pyramid and their zone of comfort. This approach to the BOP market inevitably results in fine-tuning current products and services and management practices. There is growing evidence that this approach is a recipe for failure. MNCs and large firms must start from a deep understanding of the nature and the requirements of the BOP, as outlined in Chapter 2, "Products and Services for the BOP," and then architect the business models and the management processes around these requirements. This approach to the BOP market will not only allow large firms to succeed in local markets but will also provide the knowledge base to challenge the way they manage the developed markets. Let us consider some examples.

BOP consumers in Latin America are careful in their use of diapers. They use one or two changes per day compared to the five or six changes per day common among the top of the pyramid consumers. Because they can afford only one or two changes, they expect a higher level of absorbency in the diapers and an improved construction of the diaper that will accommodate additional load. This means that the firms have to technically upgrade the quality of their diapers for the BOP consumers compared to the products they currently sell to the rich in those markets. Needless to say, the new product built for the BOP market is higher in quality and provides a better price-performance proposition. Similarly, detergent soap, when used by BOP consumers in

India washing their wares in running water, becomes mushy. About 20 to 25 percent of the detergent soap can be lost in the process. Therefore, HLL developed a soap with a coating on five sides, which makes it waterproof. The coated soap saves 20 percent wastage even in a hostile user environment. The innovation is of interest to the rich as well. Access to clean water is a major concern at the BOP. Polluted water (particulate, bacterial, and viral pollutants) is common. Boiling water is the only current alternative to eliminating the bacterial and viral pollutants. A focus on solving this problem has to start with a cost target that is no more than the cost of boiled water. Further, the system has to create a quality level that is better than boiled water (removing sediments). The process is of interest to the rich as well.

The quality, efficacy, potency, and usability of solutions developed for the BOP markets are very attractive for the top of the pyramid. The traditional MNC approach and the approach suggested here—top of the pyramid to BOP and from the BOP to the top of the pyramid—are shown in Figure 3.1.

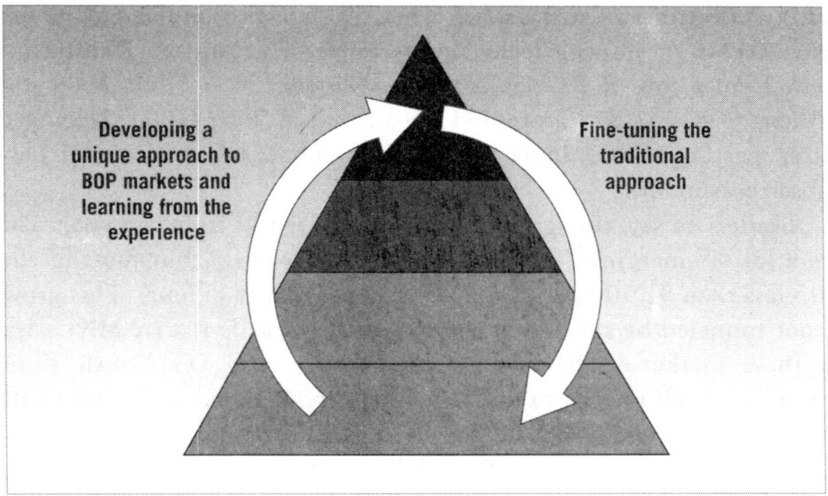

Figure 3.1 Learning from the BOP.

As the foregoing examples illustrate, the demands of the BOP markets can lead MNCs to focus on next practices. **The BOP can be a source of innovations for not only products and processes, but business models as well.** Let us start with the growth opportunities in local, stand-alone BOP markets first.

Local Growth Opportunities

Some of the local BOP markets are very large. A large population base is one indicator of the size of the market opportunity at the BOP, not necessarily the per-capita income. For example, China, India, Indonesia, Brazil, Mexico, Russia, South Africa, and Nigeria can potentially be large emerging BOP markets. If an industry or a firm finds the "sweet spot"—meaning the right business model and the right combination of products and services—these markets could have explosive growth. Consider growth opportunities in China, the world's largest producer of steel. The growth of the appliances, building, and auto markets has created an insatiable appetite for steel. China's steel capacity is estimated at 220 million tons compared to 110 million tons in Japan and 90 million tons in the United States. China has also an installed base of more than 250 million cell phones. That is larger than the installed base of the United States. China is also one of the largest markets for televisions, appliances, and autos. The growth spurt in China is without parallel. Similarly, India is at the early stages of a growth spurt in a wide variety of businesses such as two-wheelers (4.8 million during the fiscal year 2002–03), housing loans, and wireless. The housing loan business went from a low of Rs. 19,723 crores during fiscal 1999–2000 ($4.4 billion) to Rs. 51,672 crores ($11.5 billion) in 2002–2003. During the latter part of 2003, India was adding about 1.5 million telephone subscribers/month.

Needless to say, this growth was not all derived from the poor. There are a lot of emerging "middle"-class customers here, but most of them earn less than $1,500 per capita ($6,000 per family of four). This growth is not funneled by the top of the pyramid. What is it that MNCs learn in these markets? The lessons for Samsung and LG (South Korean suppliers of cell phones to India), not just for Reliance and Tatas (Indian providers of service), is that they have to adjust to rapid growth, not 2 to 5 percent per year, but perhaps 50 to 100 percent per year.

Learning to Grow

BOP markets can collapse the time frames taken for products, technologies, and concepts to diffuse in the system. Many of the drivers of change and market growth—deregulation, involvement of the private sector in BOP markets, digitization, ubiquitous connectivity, and the attendant change in the aspirations of people, favorable demographics (a young population), and access to credit—are simultaneously present in BOP markets. These drivers interact. The result is the challenge to the "S curve" that is the model for the diffusion of new products and services in the developed world. The changes that played out over 15 years in the developed markets are being collapsed into a short period of just three to five years in many BOP markets. M.S. Banga, CEO of HLL, suggests that the real challenge in BOP markets is that managers have to cope with the "I curve." The entire management process in most large firms is geared for slow growth, if at all. The I curve challenges the status quo. The S and the I curves, the two approaches to diffusion of innovations (products and services), can be conceptualized, as shown in Figure 3.2.

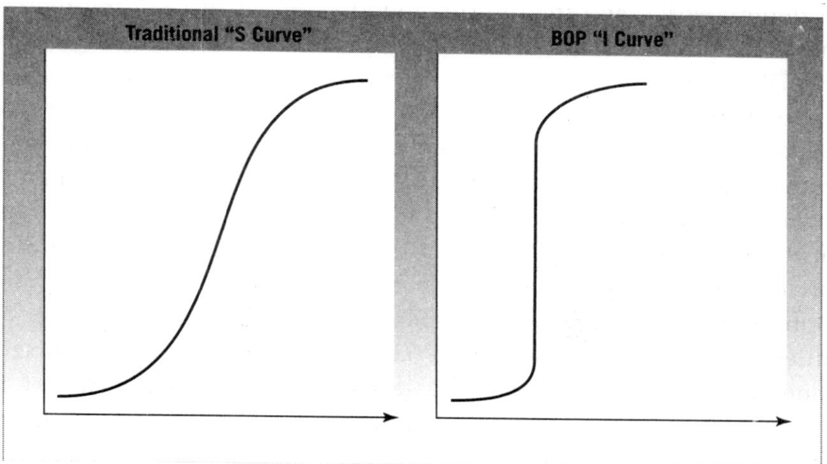

Figure 3.2 Traditional and BOP growth patterns. Source: M.S. Banga, CEO, HLL.

This is good news and bad news. A cell phone today is a telephone, a camera, a watch, a computer, and a partial radio and TV. Why would you need a traditional watch (other than as an ornament) if you had a cell phone? The I curve can rapidly propel some innovations and can equally rapidly destroy some traditional markets.[1]

Rapid growth can also make new demands on firms. For example, HLL wants to build a network of 1 million direct distributors. This means the recruitment and training of about 30,000 to 40,000 people every month. Evaluating applicants; identifying those who could make good HLL distributors; training them in products, business models, and the values of the company; and inducting such a large number into the system create new demands on the process of management. Few firms around the world have experience in inducting this many new recruits (independent distributors) per month.

Local Innovations and Global Opportunity

The micro encapsulation of iodine in salt to preserve the iodine in the harsh conditions of transportation, storage, and cooking in India has found market opportunities in Africa, especially in Ivory Coast, Kenya, and Tanzania. Iodine Deficiency Disorder (IDD) is common across the developing world, and the solution found in India has been transported across other similar markets with IDD by Unilever. Similarly, during the late 1980s, in response to the growing success of Nirma, a local entrepreneurial startup in the detergent business that created a new category, focused on the BOP markets, HLL launched Wheel, intended for the same market segment. Wheel today is one of the largest brands in the HLL portfolio in India ($150 million). The BOP market has grown rapidly. BOP markets in India account for a total of 1.0 million tons of detergents, compared with 300,000 tons for the top of the pyramid. More important, the lessons learned in India were not lost on Unilever. It wanted to protect BOP markets in countries such as Brazil, Indonesia, and China. It took the lessons from developing Wheel in India—from the formulation, manufacturing process, packaging, pricing, distribution, and advertising and promotion—to Brazil. It introduced a similar product oriented toward the BOP called Ala. The product was a runaway success. The product was available in 2,000 small neighborhood stores in less than three months. The detergent team that developed the new business model for the BOP in India also went to Brazil and China to help build the distribution systems that were critical for the success of the business. Today, India is seen as a laboratory for similar "India-like" markets within Unilever. Product ideas and concepts are tried out in India with a global BOP market in mind. Similarly, the idea of single-serve units has become a global phenomenon in the BOP markets. The growth in fast-moving consumer goods businesses in Bangladesh, Nepal, Pakistan, and China has been fueled by similar requirements.

The success of Grameen Bank in developing microfinance in Bangladesh as a successful commercial operation has led to global interest in the process. Grameen Bank was totally focused on BOP customers. The average loan size was less than $20 when it started. There are more than 17,000 microfinance operations that are variants of the Grameen concept around the world, including in the United States. The microfinance revolution now has its own global conference every year.

The success of Jaipur Foot is now exported to a wide variety of countries with similar requirements. The primary demand in all these countries for prosthetics is from BOP customers. They have been available in 19 countries, from Afghanistan to Vietnam. The Aravind Eye Hospital, in a similar vein, is training doctors to establish a low-cost, world-class delivery system for eye care in South Africa, Cambodia, and Vietnam. In an interesting twist of the traditional view of capabilities, the cost and quality advantages of cardiac care in India are allowing it to negotiate terms for the possibility of moving a portion of the patients from the National Health System in the United Kingdom to India. The total cost of the trip for the patient and an accompanying family member, the stays in India, and the cost of patient care will be less than the cost in the United Kingdom. More important, the quality of care is equally good or better. There are no delays in accessing care.

The Indian pharmaceutical industry had to learn to serve the BOP market. Prices were regulated by the government. Further, affordability of the public health system forced very low prices. It also forced them to develop methods for reverse engineering. Controversial as it is, the Indian pharmaceutical industry can deliver drugs coming off patents in the United States at a fraction of the cost charged by the established drug companies. However, the focus on the BOP has allowed these firms to invent cost-effective ways to manufacture, test, and distribute.

BOP Solutions for Developed Markets

In the rural areas of countries such as Peru, providing high-quality health care is difficult. More difficult is the surveillance of outbreaks of infectious diseases. These remote regions must be kept under constant surveillance to avoid the spread of disease, be it cholera or SARS. However, these locations are not well connected for constant communications. PCs are rare, and telephone lines are a luxury. The question for public health professionals in such a situation is simple:

How do we connect remote areas to a real-time surveillance system so that the spread of infectious diseases can be monitored using devices that are currently available on location (often simple telephones)? This implies that the system must be simple and device-agnostic. Remote locations must be connected to a central node so that planners and policymakers are fully informed. Such a system, originally developed for Peru, is finding successes in the United States. The system, originally created by Voxiva, was based on three premises:

1. The system, to be robust, must be based on any device that is available: telephone (landline or wireless) or PC. The local community must know how to use the device. The telephone is the most widely used device for communications.
2. The remote populations were either illiterate or just moderately literate. The system had to deskill diagnosis at the point of patient contact. The chances of having a trained and experienced doctor in remote regions in the Andes are low. However, the quality of the diagnosis must be world-class.
3. The system must be reliable and available in real time so that senior members of the health care system can react immediately to emerging problems of infectious diseases. Early detection of health problems and rapid response (reaction time) are critical components of the system.

The system was first deployed in the remote regions of Peru and was a success. Similar problems confront the United States. The CDC and the FDA have to prepare to remotely monitor outbreaks of diseases caused by terrorists or problems in food quality that must be traced rapidly. Blood banks have to be monitored for stock and quality. When the FDA and CDC were looking for a system to help them with remote, real-time surveillance, they found the Voxiva system to be the best. Both of them are now Voxiva customers. Further, as the U.S. Department of Defense was inoculating soldiers with smallpox vaccine as a preventive measure, it needed a system for monitoring soldiers for possible adverse reactions to the vaccine. Voxiva, with its capabilities, was the obvious choice. Voxiva has moved on to sell its platforms for the detection of SARS, HIV, and other public health problems. The underlying platform is low-cost, robust, and simple, needs few skills, and can be grafted onto an existing telecom network.

Lessons for MNCs from BOP Markets

The most interesting lesson for MNCs from operating in the BOP market is about costs—for innovation, distribution, manufacturing, and general "costs of organization." Because the BOP forces an extraordinary emphasis on price performance, firms must focus on all elements of cost. Shortage and the cost of capital force firms in BOP markets to be very focused on the efficiency of capital use. MNCs tend to impose their management systems and practices on BOP markets and find that it is hard to make a profit. The choices are simple: Change the management systems to cut costs or lose significant amounts of money. The lessons learned from BOP markets by MNCs are covered in the following sections.

Capital Intensity

The judicious use of capital is a critical element of success in BOP markets. For example, HLL works with negative working capital. It focuses on reducing capital intensity in plants and equipment. By focusing on a judicious mix of outsourcing to dedicated suppliers, it not only reduces its capital intensity but also creates several small- and medium-size enterprises that can conform to the norms and standards set by HLL. HLL, as the only customer to these suppliers, can and does influence their operations. Second, a senior management focus on logistics and distribution is critical for reducing the capital needs of the business. HLL serves 850,000 retail outlets in one of the most difficult distribution terrains. The sales data from every retail outlet is collected and processed in a central processing facility. All the retail outlets are serviced frequently. Finally, a focus on revenue management allows for reducing the capital tied up in receivables. HLL can collect revenues in real time as the goods leave the warehouses of their suppliers. The suppliers might provide credit to the dealers and retailers. HLL as a manufacturer can reduce its capital intensity. The results can be compelling. For example, the system for focusing on capital first initiated with the introduction of the detergent Wheel to the BOP provided evidence of how many more opportunities for value creation can be unearthed by serving the needs of the BOP. A comparison of the financial performance of Nirma (the local competitor), HLL in the top of the pyramid market with Surf, and HLL in the BOP market with Wheel is shown in Table 3.1.

Table 3.1 Economic Value Creation at the BOP

	Nirma	HLL (Wheel)	HLL (Surf)
Sales ($ Million)	150	100	180
Gross margin (%)	18	18	25
Return on capital employed (%)	121	93	22

Notes: The bottom line can be very profitable. Low margins/high unit sales. Game is about volume and capital efficiency. Economic profit versus gross margins.

Source: John Ripley, senior vice president, Unilever PLC.

It is important to separate gross margins from return on capital employed (ROCE). The real economic profit is in the effective use of capital.

A similar situation exists at the Aravind Eye Hospital. It uses the most modern equipment available in any facility in the world. Its costs are dramatically brought down by its capability to use the equipment effectively, as it specializes only in eye care, and every doctor and nurse team performs an average of 50 surgeries per day. Only 40 percent of its patients pay. A cataract surgery costs $50 compared to $3,000 to $3,500 in the United States. In spite of these differences, Aravind's ROCE is in the 120 to 130 percent range. Aravind is totally free of debt. The revenues for the year 2001–2002 were Rs. 388.0 million ($86 million) with a surplus (before depreciation) of Rs. 210.5 million ($46.5 million). This would be the envy of every hospital in the United States. The productivity and the volumes at Aravind are the basis for this level of profitability. Every doctor accounts for 2,000 operations per year, compared to a national average of 300 in India. The four locations in the Aravind system process more than 1.4 million patients (including 1,500 eye camps) and perform 200,000 surgeries. They operate with about 80 doctors and a total staff, including paramedics, counselors, and others, of 1,275.

With an ITC e-Choupal, it costs the company about Rs. 100,000 ($2,100) per kiosk installation. The company saves about Rs. 270 per ton on the acquisition of soybeans. The payback period can be as low as one full season. The recovery of that investment requires an acquisition target of about 4,000 to 5,000 tons from a single kiosk. (A cluster of villages is supported by the kiosk.) Adding additional services such as selling seeds, fertilizers, and crop insurance can enhance the profitability of the system. The economic returns can be significant.

Sustainable Development

BOP markets are a great source for experimentation in sustainable development. First, resources such as water, energy, and transportation are scarce and expensive. Automotive and two-wheeler manufacturers are learning that the BOP customers are attuned to the total cost of ownership and not just the cost of purchase. The miles per gallon—the efficiency of energy use—is a significant determinant of market success. Similar demands are imposed on water use.

BOP markets can also represent an emerging problem. Single-serve packaging is advantageous to create the capacity to consume at the BOP but can also lead to a major environmental problem. More than 13 billion single-serve packages are sold annually in India, and this trend is growing rapidly. Although plastic bags appear attractive, they are not biodegradable. MNCs involved in the BOP markets have the capability and the motivation to find solutions to the problem of packaging in emerging markets.

Innovations

As we discussed in depth in Chapter 2, the process of innovation for the BOP forces a new set of disciplines. First, the focus is on price performance. **Innovations must become value-oriented from the consumer's perspective. The BOP focuses attention on both the objective and subjective performances of the product or service.** Markets at the BOP also focus on the need for 30 to 100 times improvements in price performance. Even if the need is only for 10 to 20 times improvement, the challenge is formidable. The BOP can become a major source of innovations. Consider, for example, the need for user-friendly interfaces. Biometric authentication systems such as fingerprint and voice recognition are emerging from the BOP markets, as we saw in the case of PRODEM FFP in Bolivia and Elektra in Mexico. Logistics and distribution requirements are an integral part of the innovation process at the BOP.

Serving the BOP forces a new business model on MNCs. Management systems developed for a price performance level cannot be fine-tuned to cope with the demands of the BOP markets. Although MNCs are slowly adapting to the needs of the BOP, few have consciously focused attention on examining the implications of their own operations in the BOP for their global operations. So far the attention has been on outsourcing from the more cost-efficient locations such as China, Taiwan, Thailand, the Philippines, and India. A $50 CD player is not just about wage rates, but a totally different way of approaching manufacturing.

The I curve has different implications for scaling. The timing of investments, investment intensity, and the pace of market and distribution development become crucial, as is the rate at which costs must be brought down to fuel growth of the market.

The Costs of Managing

ICICI Bank manages, with 16 managers, a portfolio of 200,000 customers at the BOP. The entire network of management consists of a hierarchy, as shown in Figure 3.3.

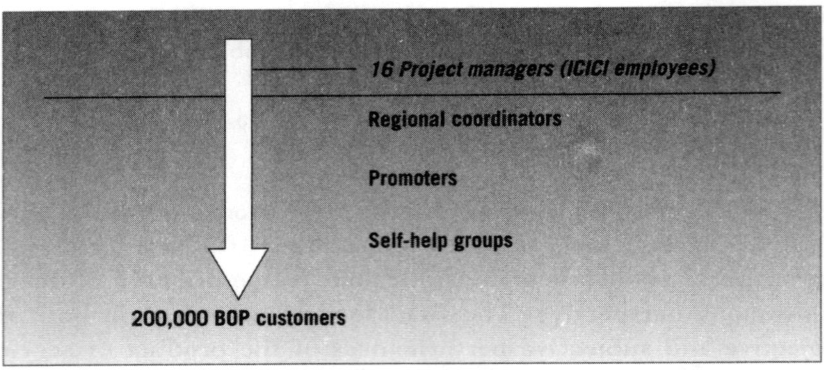

Figure 3.3 The cost of management.

There are only 16 managers (employees) from the ICICI side. Each project manager oversees the work of 6 coordinators. Coordinators are women who are experienced in the development of self-help groups. They are identified and are asked to be coordinators. They helped project managers in approval of loans and help develop new self-help groups (SHGs). The coordinator oversees the work of promoters. The primary responsibility of the promoters is the formation of new SHGs. She must form 20 groups per year. She is financially compensated for the successful formation of new groups. The promoters understand the village culture because they are part of it. They carry credibility because they have been part of a successful SHG. They speak the language of the groups that they deal with. They are also identified from the local communities. As a result, the organizational system that is built in this case is quite unique.

1. The basic unit of analysis is the SHG with 20 members. Loans are given to the SHG, and the group decides how to partition the money it receives as loans. The SHG is responsible for paying back the loan and the interest. The bank does not lend to individuals. As such, the credit-worthiness of the SHG depends on how well it can enforce compliance among its members. They all understand that what is at stake is the access to cheap and reliable capital, compared to all the alternatives including the local moneylenders. Therefore, the SHG does credit analysis, project evaluation, monitoring of the use of funds, collection, and reinvestment. The control is totally local and the SHG is empowered. From this perspective, ICICI Bank takes little risk.
2. Market development is also handled by SHG veterans. The promoters are from SHGs and their territories are clearly demarcated. As a result, the person promoting the idea is closest to the community that the bank wants to reach. The promoters are paid an incentive based on the number of SHGs formed by them in good standing.
3. The regional managers or coordinators are also from local communities in which they work. Their work is primarily focused on training and supervising the promoters and evaluating the quality of the SHGs as they are formed.
4. The concept of the structure and the management process is built from the bottom up. There is distributed leadership. The role of the company employees in the day-to-day running of the SHG is minimal. The general sales and administration costs of this system are about 5 to 10 percent of the costs of a typical bank. That makes the system cost-effective and makes small transactions profitable. Further, this also allows for rapid scaling. ICICI increased from 2,000 SHGs in 2002 to 10,000 in 2003.

The SHGs and the direct distribution system we have described, such as Shakti Amma, represent an extraordinary innovation that both cuts costs and risks for the firm and at the same time creates an empowered group of new entrepreneurs with sustainable, rising income opportunities. **Business management skills, technology, and contacts are pushed down to the local grassroots level.** The SHGs perform several of the functions that the firm would have handled in the traditional approach to managing. For example, the SHG, by validating the individuals who will get the loan, by checking the nature and viability of the project, and by taking responsibility for monitoring the progress of the project is, in essence, an extension of the traditional firm. The SHG helps co-create value for the firm—in this case, ICICI. The bank does not have direct contact with the individuals but monitors the loan indirectly through the SHG. This represents a new model of relationship between the firm and its consumers. The quality of the SHG is the guarantee of the investment. However, the SHG, being so close to its members—same village, same group, frequent meetings, visibility of progress of projects, and, most important, the ability to assess behaviors—is in a great position to alter the risk profiles of the loans. The large bank gains local responsiveness capability at low (or no) cost. The same is true of the Shakti Amma system. The local entrepreneur knows her village and its needs and can also influence the buying decisions of the villagers. She is at once the salesperson, the supplier, the trusted advisor, and the educator for the village. She is the one who can convince the villagers that iodized salt will be a healthy option for the family. HLL is now experimenting with connecting these individual distributors through an Internet network. The I-Shakti project will create the most dramatic opportunity for the BOP consumers to influence the firm and its decisions regarding product features, costs, availability, and the business model in general.

What we see here is the convergence of the traditional roles of the firm and the consumer and the distributor and the consumer. Functions such as advertising, credit management, risk analysis, and market development are assumed by the consumers-entrepreneurs and the consumer-entrepreneurial community (SHG). The boundaries of the firm expand beyond its legal parameters and begin to engage and empower the large and heretofore economically isolated segment of developing country societies known as the "informal sector." The resources that are available to the firm expand even more dramatically. Access to the 10,000 SHGs is, in its simplest form, a huge resource multiplier to the firm. Whether it is resource leverage through selective access, local knowledge, risk reduction, or reduction in capital needs, the firm benefits. This is at best a win-win situation. The local communities take charge of what they want. They make their own decisions and choices. They are accountable and, therefore, feel a sense of empowerment and self-esteem. They know they can deal with the large firm on an equal basis. Although the resources are limited for the SHG, the bank cannot unilaterally make decisions. In that sense, there is less asymmetry in power.

Learning to Live in a Network of Relationships

MNCs working at the BOP learn rapidly that they have to learn to live with a wide variety of relationships with a large number of institutions. For example, in the case of selling iodized salt, HLL learned fast that its efforts would impact public policymakers and officials in the health department. NGOs focus on local communities and in many cases conflict with industry practices. HLL had to learn to cope with the agendas of the various parties that might be involved and work with them effectively in a cooperative mode. The case of soap, intended to reduce diarrhea, was more interesting. HLL had to deal not only with state governments and NGOs, but also with the World Bank, which wanted to partly fund the program of education and distribution. It also wanted to be involved in the evaluation of results. As such, the firm had to learn to cope with the differing priorities, time scales, decision cycles, and perspectives of both the causes of the problem and the nature and efficacy of the solution. The reactions of the various groups can vary from open hostility toward the MNC to a willingness to cooperate. At the end of the day, however, MNCs learn how to transform their ideals of good corporate citizenship and social responsibility into their core business of delivering value on a day-to-day business basis. Social sector organizations learn how to scale their still-marginal efforts at "social enterprise" into viable business models serving a mass market.

BOP markets represent 80 percent of humanity. It is reasonable to expect that 4 billion people in search of an improved quality of life will create one of the most vibrant growth markets we have ever seen. Private-sector involvement in development can be a win for both the BOP consumers and the private sector. All of us can learn. The flow of ideas, knowledge, and innovation will become a two-way street—from the developed countries to the developing and the reverse. MNCs can help BOP markets to develop. They can also learn from BOP markets.

In the next chapter, we discuss how the large firm can create a private-sector ecosystem and act as a nodal firm. This ecosystem is a prerequisite for developing markets at the BOP.

Endnote

1. Paul Glader. "China Feeds Desire for Steel Abroad," *The Wall Street Journal*, March 31, 2004.

4

The Ecosystem for Wealth Creation

The need for building an ecosystem for wealth creation and social development at the BOP is obvious from the previous chapters. ICICI Bank with its 10,000 SHGs is an ecosystem. So is the HLL system with Shakti Ammas or ITC with sanchalaks in the e-Choupal. However, traditionally, the focus of both business and social developmental initiatives at the BOP has been on one aspect of the ecosystems for wealth creation at a time—social capital or individual entrepreneurs (the focus of so much of the microfinance efforts), small and medium enterprises (SMEs), or large firms (market liberalization or foreign direct investment). **There have been few attempts to focus on the symbiotic nature of the relationships between various private sector and social institutional players that can lead to a rapid development of markets at the BOP.**

Let us digress a moment to understand the thinking behind poverty alleviation and economic development. This thinking has influenced the pattern of private-sector involvement in development in many countries. We must start with the historical roots of the debate. The focus of public policy on the private sector as a possible instrument of poverty reduction is of recent vintage. Not surprisingly, there is no consensus on what "private sector" means. Public policy positions tend to shift from microfinance (individual entrepreneurs), to SMEs, to large domestic firms and MNCs. These trends tend to follow well-publicized successes in specific situations. The success of the Grameen Bank in Bangladesh, for example, spawned a spate of interest in microfinance. Similarly, there is a growing interest in SMEs fueled by the fact that they contribute a disproportionate percentage of jobs in poorer countries. The importance of SMEs correlates negatively with GDP per capita.[1] However, it is not clear why low GDP per capita coexists with SMEs. Is the dominant role of microenterprises and SMEs a result of an underdeveloped market system? Does the dominant role played by SMEs reflect poor enforcement of commercial contracts outside the neighborhoods in which they operate? Can an underdeveloped and poorly implemented legal system condemn countries to microprivate enterprises that cannot flourish beyond local communities? Development of SMEs cannot then become the sole basis for policy. The role of MNCs gets attention only as a vehicle for foreign direct investment (FDI). The role of the MNC (and large private-sector firms) in the development of solutions at the scale of the BOP neighborhood and the infrastructure needed for such a market economy are often not fully understood either by the MNCs or the development community.

Increasingly, the role of cooperatives is being debated. The successes of the milk cooperatives in India are a case in point. Cooperatives are an integral part of the private sector. They are inclusive. Amul, the showcase for the cooperative sector in developing countries, encompasses the poor farmer with two buffaloes and world-class processing facilities and a distribution system with a national and increasingly global reach. What cases like Amul and ICICI illustrate is the need for a more holistic understanding of the wealth creation process. Wealth creation at the BOP does not result from isolated public investment programs, from NGO self-help groups, or from FDI. Shifting the focus of debate from public investment to private sector, and vice versa, does not create the preconditions for wealth creation. Our cases demonstrate the fundamental role played by the private sector. **The private sector in the BOP context includes social organizations of different kinds that interact to create markets and develop appropriate products and services and deliver value. A business system is at the heart of the**

ecosystem for wealth creation. In this chapter, we want to change the focus of the debate from a preference for one form of private sector (say, SMEs) at a time to a focus on a market-oriented ecosystem that is a combination of multiple forms of private enterprises coexisting in a symbiotic relationship.

Market-Oriented Ecosystem

A market-based ecosystem is a framework that allows private sector and social actors, often with different traditions and motivations, and of different sizes and areas of influence, to act together and create wealth in a symbiotic relationship. Such an ecosystem consists of a wide variety of institutions coexisting and complementing each other. We use the concept of the ecosystem because each constituent in the system has a role to play. They are dependent on each other. The system adapts and evolves and can be resilient and flexible. Although there will always be distortions at the margin, the system is oriented toward a dynamic equilibrium. What then are the constituents of the market-based ecosystem? We can conceptualize it, as shown in Figure 4.1.

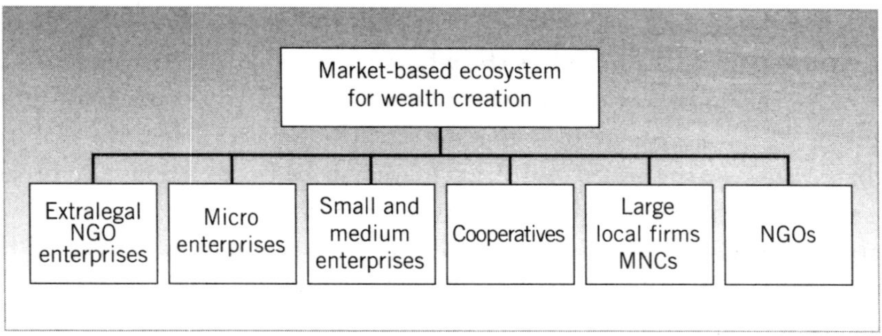

Figure 4.1 Components of the market-based ecosystem.

Every developing country has the components of this portfolio. However, the relative importance of the various components of the ecosystem is different across countries. For example, the extralegal (those who exist outside the legal system) vegetable sellers in the slums of Sao Paulo or Mumbai coexist with global firms such as Ford and Unilever. The chicken cooperatives and processors such as Sadia in southern Brazil and a local fast-food chain such as Habib's coexist with

Kentucky Fried Chicken and McDonald's. Whether it is Brazil, Mexico, South Africa, or India, a portfolio of these constituents of various ecosystems exists. Needless to say, if the portfolio is totally skewed toward extralegal entities, the economy cannot advance, and the private sector cannot contribute to poverty reduction. If it is skewed toward large local firms and MNCs, then it probably is a well-developed economy with a well-functioning private sector but is not oriented toward the creation of wealth among those living at the BOP.

Historically, the evolution of the large firm was a symptom of a maturing economy focused on system efficiencies through scale and scope. For example, the development of the large firms in the United States at the turn of the 20th century fueled by electricity, the telegraph, refrigeration, and the railroads is well documented. There is a paucity of similar studies that document the evolution of ecosystems in developing countries. We do not have good studies on the underlying driving forces that create different compositions of private-sector firms in various countries. Further, we lack systematic evidence of triggers that shift the composition of an ecosystem in any direction.

It should be clear that a focus on any one component of the ecosystem to the negligence or detriment of others is not desirable. The dilemma for public policymakers is clear: If we can't pick one sector for special attention, how do we mobilize the whole ecosystem? Alternately, how do we move the composition of the ecosystem toward large firms? Both are legitimate questions. This is the state of the debate. I believe that the debate must shift toward building market-based ecosystems for broad-based wealth creation. Only then can we tap into the vast, dormant, and trapped resources, purchasing power, and entrepreneurial drive at the BOP. This will allow for new growth opportunities for the large corporations and a better quality of life for those at the BOP.

Ecosystems for a Developing Country

The evolution of the U.S. economy during the late 19th and 20th centuries might not be a good basis for prescriptions on how Brazil or South Africa should evolve. The competitive conditions, the availability of new technologies, the nature of resource endowments, and the educational infrastructure are vastly different. Are there new models of ecosystem development that public and private policymakers must focus on?

Let us start with an understanding of a private-sector ecosystem by considering the fast-moving consumer goods (FMCG) industry in India. The largest FMCG firm in India is HLL, a subsidiary of Unilever. HLL is a Rs. 100 billion ($2.3 billion) company with a wide portfolio of personal care and food products. The ecosystem of HLL consists of six components:

1. HLL (MNC) operates 80 manufacturing facilities.
2. A dedicated supplier base of 150 factories (SMEs) that employs anywhere between 30,000 and 40,000 people.
3. Exclusive stockists (7,250) who distribute HLL products nationwide.
4. Wholesalers (12,000) and small retailers and shop owners (300,000) who are either SMEs or microenterprises.
5. A growing direct distribution system (HLL net) and a rural direct distribution system called Shakti that cover 250,000 individual entrepreneurs in urban and remote villages who sell HLL products. This number had grown to 1 million by 2005.
6. An advisory relationship with the government of the Indian state of Madhya Pradesh to help it brand local produce from villages and tribal areas, such as natural honey collected from forests in the state. It touches 35,000 to 40,000 tribals.

The ecosystem that this represents is shown in Figure 4.2.

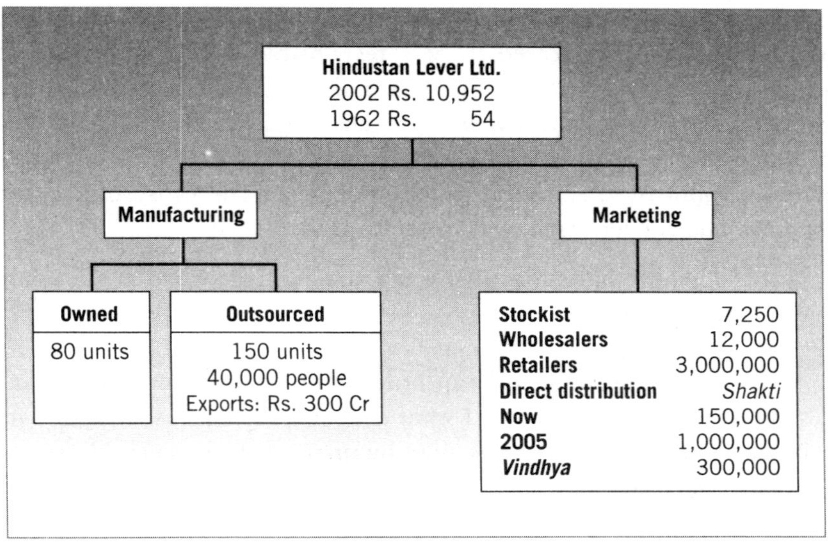

Figure 4.2 HLL's ecosystem for wealth creation.

HLL does not have legal control over the entire ecosystem, nor does it have direct influence on all the elements of the system. However, HLL provides the framework, the intellectual direction, and the processes by which the system is governed and operated. The Shakti Ammas are independent, but they must follow simple rules to be part of the system. In this sense, HLL is a *nodal firm* that facilitates the entire functioning of the network. Ownership is not the issue. Access and influence without ownership are more important factors, as are quality standards, mutual obligations, commitment to contractual relationships, and a shared set of values. As a nodal firm, HLL provides expertise and establishes technical standards for a wide variety of private-sector enterprises, from supplier factories to individual entrepreneurs in remote villages. Quality levels in the system are prescribed by HLL and are consistent with global standards and local needs.

What is the value of a private-sector ecosystem? Who benefits from the standards and quality requirements demanded by the nodal firm from the constituents to participate in the network? How does this transform the basis for commercial transactions within a developing economy?

Learning the Sanctity of Contracts

Underpinning this ecosystem is education across all levels. The individual entrepreneur in the village—the Shakti Amma, for example—is being educated to be a responsible entrepreneur. She is a wealth creator in her village. She learns about products, prices, returns, and being an advisor and helper to her customers in the village. When I interviewed one Shakti Amma, who had been an entrepreneur for less than six months, the impact of being part of the ecosystem became obvious. The conversation went something like this:

> Q: If you could have any wish you want granted, what would your top three wishes be?
>
> A: I want a telephone so I can order only the products that I can sell fast (inventory control). I want a scooter for my husband so that he can go and sell in villages close by (market expansion). I have no other wishes at this time.

Q: What is the biggest difference this job has made for you?

A: I am somebody now. People look up to me. They ask me for advice. I can help them.

The training she received from the representatives of the company on products and business certainly helped her. She and a million other entrepreneurs will help HLL get distribution reach to 200 million to 300 million people whom they could not cost-effectively reach through established distribution channels. This type of symbiotic relationship in the ecosystem creates a win for all. Better informed, educated, and financially successful, these independent entrepreneurs seek the same type of transparency and access to information on products and features (what is unique about these compared to similar products from other firms operating in the same market, with similar prices, promotional schemes, and advertising). For example, the Shakti Amma that I interviewed had clear and unambiguous answers to all questions about product features and benefits. Market-based ecosystems can be a source of informing the poor of the benefits of transparency in transactions. She is also learning to respect contracts, be they implicit or explicit with the company. The mutual obligation between her and the parent company, HLL, which is just a concept for her, is real. Respect for contracts binds her to the company and allows her to make a profit. She recognizes that violating the contracts will dry up the source of her economic and social success. Transparent transaction governance is an integral part of the ecosystem. She is a local entrepreneur. She is a one-person company, but she does not operate as an extralegal entity. She is bound to the national and global system and is less beholden to the local system of moneylenders and slum lords. The social collateral of open and honest entrepreneurship that the market-based ecosystem provides will be significant. The ecosystem can provide the tools for the poor and the disadvantaged to be connected seamlessly with the rest of the world in a mutually beneficial and nonexploitative way. It provides them with skills and opportunities that are often denied by the informal sector.

Reducing Inequities in Contracts

Consider ITC's initiative, the e-Choupal (literally, the "electronic village meeting place"). ITC is the Indian subsidiary of British American Tobacco. ITC has branched out of its traditional and primary focus on tobacco to include hotels, paper, and food. The International Business Division (IBD) of ITC was concerned about its capability to source soybeans from widely scattered and subsistence farmers in Madhya Pradesh, India. The traditional system focused on the *mandi*, the place where the farmers brought their produce to be auctioned. The buyers in the mandi aggregated the produce and sold it to firms like ITC for further processing. The farmers got a raw deal in the mandi, and the large processors like ITC were beholden to the intermediaries. ITC decided to use advances in digital technologies to reduce the inefficiencies in the system and to ensure a steady supply of good-quality soybeans for its processing plants. The approach depended on building a network of PCs in villages around the soya belt. ITC picked a successful farmer called the *sanchalak* in each village. He was given a PC that could be used by all the farmers in the village. The sanchalak took a formal oath in the village to be impartial and make access to the PC available to all the farmers in his area. The farmers could check the prices of soybeans in the neighboring mandis and decide when and where to sell their crops.

ITC decided to build a system that changed many of the existing practices. The farmers could check prices and decide at what prices they wanted to sell. They were not at the mercy of the auctioneers at the mandi on a particular day. The produce was weighed accurately, unlike the previous practice with the traditional aggregators in the mandi. Under the old system, farmers lost about two to three kilograms per ton in inaccurate weighing. Under the old system, farmers were also expected to pay for the bagging of their produce, about Rs. 3 per bag. IBD's system allowed for better and accurate weighing, immediate payment, and reduction of transportation and bagging costs for the farmer. The new system efficiencies compared to the traditional mandi system resulted in savings of Rs. 270 per ton for the farmer. The composition of the savings is shown in Figure 4.3.

ITC also saved Rs. 300 per ton. This is a win-win situation for both the farmer and the company.

The real benefits of the e-Choupal are more than cost reduction in the system. There were four sources of friction in the system:

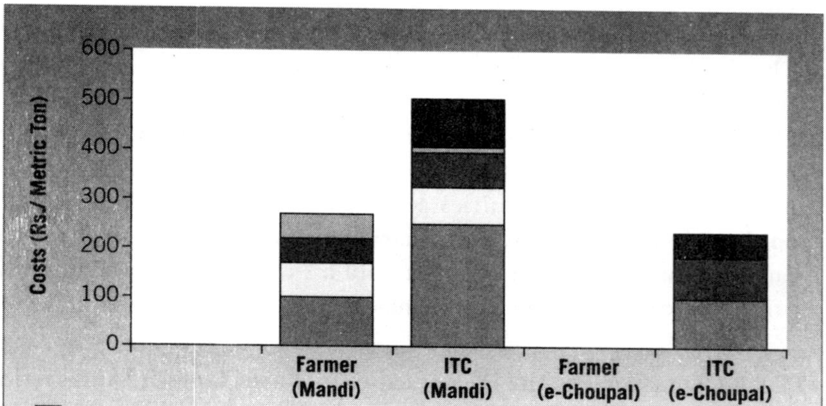

	Farmer (Mandi)	ITC (Mandi)	Farmer (e-Choupal)	ITC (e-Choupal)
Commission	0	100	0	50
Handling and transit losses	50	10	0	0
Labor costs	50	70	0	85
Bagging and weighing	70	75	0	0
Transportation	100	250	0	100

Figure 4.3 Savings for farmers compared to the traditional mandi system.

1. There was significant *asymmetry in the access to information* between the farmer, the traders in the mandi, small local processors, and the large processors such as ITC. By providing the farmer access to information about prices not only in his mandi but also around the world, the e-Choupal system dramatically eliminates the asymmetric information that confines the subsistence farmer to a helpless bargaining position.
2. There was an *asymmetry in choice* between the farmer and the trader under the old system. The new system reduces the logistical problems of moving soybean crops from the village to the mandi and the costs incurred by the farmer in doing so. The farmer also had to deal with the procedural requirements imposed on him by traders, such as paying the costs of bagging the produce. The inaccuracies in weighing the product are eliminated. These logistical and procedural inefficiencies (as seen from the farmer's perspective) were built into the traditional system. It reflected the lack of choice for the farmer. He was for all practical purposes a semi-indentured supplier to the mandi close by.
3. There was an *asymmetry in the ability to enforce contracts* under the old system. The moneylenders and traders had the upper hand. The farmer could not alienate them. Therefore, the traders could take

advantage of their strong bargaining position and delay payments. The farmers had no official recourse. The current system changes this dramatically.

4. Finally, under the old system, there was an *asymmetry in the social standing* of the farmer (the producer), the buyer, and the trader. Although all social inequities are unlikely to be solved, farmers do not have to face the indignity of a rigged auction in the mandi. They can be assured that what they get paid for their work is a fair market price that can be verified by them without any distortions.

ITC's e-Choupal takes the idea of explicit contracting and transaction governance capacity a big step forward. **By providing access to information that the farmers can independently obtain, the system changes the inequities that the extralegal and the quasi-legal systems impose on BOP consumers and producers in developing countries.** ITC still pays the taxes due to the government as if the trade did take place in the mandi. The government is happy with revenues. The traders are likely to be unhappy, as their ability to coerce farmers into selling at the price that they decided in the auction is getting eroded. The most telling comment was from a farmer captured on video by the researchers:

"I did not even know how to hold a mouse."

Four months later:

"Even if they take away the computer, we will buy one. We need Net connectivity."

That summarizes it all.

Building Governance Capabilities Among the Poor

There is a third phase of building transaction governance capacity. This entails building the capacity for self-governance. The Bank of Madura initiated a model of village development in southern India that has shown great promise. It was based on three assumptions:

1. Microsavings must precede microlending. BOP consumers must learn to save, and there were no institutions to support microsavings.
2. BOP consumers must start trusting themselves. They must be actively involved in solving their problems. Outside help (financial

and other) can go only so far. The village must break its cycle of dependency built by more than 40 years of subsidies and government handouts, NGO interventions, and the like. Private-sector development (in this case, banking based on commercial principles) and subsidies do not mix.

3. There is no dearth of latent leaders in the villages. Given the opportunity, they will emerge and will influence the start of a transparent and commercially viable system. This group will then become the custodians of transaction governance instead of lawyers or the local slum lords.

These were bold assumptions, but the work started with a clear position. Dr. Raj Thiagarajan, who was the CEO of the Bank of Madura, initiated this project in the rural areas of Tamil Nadu, India. He had difficulty, initially, getting the best managers to work in the area of rural development. When it became obvious to the bank employees that he was personally involved and it was going to be his initiative, the perceptions of the value attached to this work changed. There is a lesson for large firms here: Unless BOP work is seen as central to the firm, the best managers are unlikely to sign up. Carefully selected bank employees were assigned to villages where their primary focus was to build confidence and trust among local groups. They interviewed and picked a woman in each village who could be a potential leader. The SHG consisted of 20 women in each village who formed the core group. They had no prior familial relationship, no formal participation or experience with the financial sector, and no incentives to trust each other. All were from the same village but could be strangers. The officers of the bank continued to visit these SHGs, organizing them and creating a sense of cohesion. The women who formed the SHGs were taught the disciplines of holding a meeting, developing an agenda, writing the minutes, keeping records, and saving. The team had to jointly guarantee any financial dealings with the bank. The SHGs understood the basic dimensions of transaction governance capacity—transparency, access, explicit contractual obligations, penalties for violating contracts, the connection between the cost of capital and the track record of performance of contracts, and most important, the need to take charge of their community and protect their newfound access to capital at reasonable rates.

The Bank of Madura paid a lot of attention to the maturation of the SHGs. As they matured and became a working group with a clear understanding of each other's obligations and the process by which conflicts of interest and ideas would be settled, the bank progressed them to the next stage, making capital available as microloans for building a common village facility (for example, a toilet in the village) or expanding a member's agricultural operations.

The maturation model for SHGs is shown in Figure 4.4. The first three steps often took more than a year.

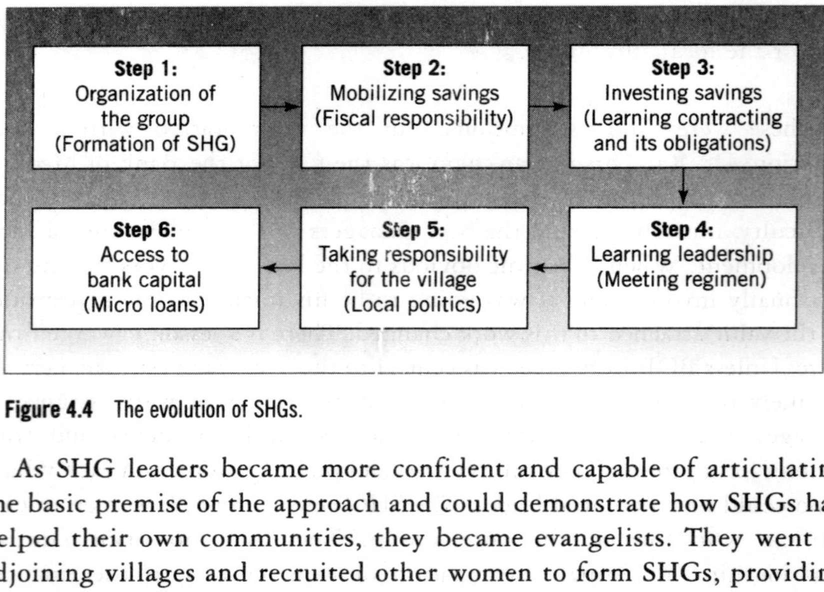

Figure 4.4 The evolution of SHGs.

As SHG leaders became more confident and capable of articulating the basic premise of the approach and could demonstrate how SHGs had helped their own communities, they became evangelists. They went to adjoining villages and recruited other women to form SHGs, providing both the motivation and the training.

At the time of the merger of the Bank of Madura with ICICI, the second largest retail bank in India, there were 1,200 SHG groups. During the next two years, the number expanded to 10,000 SHGs covering about 200,000 women and therefore 200,000 families. The default rates have remained, as of writing, at less than 1 percent. The model is scalable because the preconditions for the success of SHGs can be identified. The key criteria are as follows:[2]

1. Is the group between 15 and 20 members?
2. Are all of the members considered very poor?
3. Was there a fixed amount of savings collected each month?
4. Is there more than 20 percent literacy?
5. Have they used their savings for internal lending purposes?
6. Have the members kept a high level of attendance?

The second criterion is not critical. However, this was part of the policy adopted by the government of India. The concept of SHGs can work quite effectively with the other principles.

The lending from the bank is quite safe. The marketing ecosystem—the private sector—left to operate in a commercially responsible way, can create transaction governance capacity at all levels of society, from the very poor individuals in the villages to microentrepreneurs (like Shakti Ammas), to SMEs. Governments tend to overregulate the private sector (assuming that such overregulation will protect the poor) or tend to use public-sector corporations as a way of creating a culture of subsidies disguised as commercial operations (for example, loans from banks that are not returned and where no enforcement is possible). Nonperforming assets are not only a problem with large borrowers but also with small borrowers at the village level.

In this chapter, we tried to illustrate the three steps in creating a transaction governance capacity based on the marketing ecosystem:

1. Help the poor understand that there is a win-win situation for them and the firm by respecting contracts. The Shakti Amma wants to be within the system and can respect the contract with a large firm such as HLL. Respect for the contract must transcend people you see every day. A contract with another legal entity, large or small, seen or unseen, is critical.
2. The private sector can reduce the asymmetries in information, choice, ability to enforce contracts, and social standing. The use of information technology to build a network can create a powerful motivation to be part of the system. The farmers know the difference between the old system and the system introduced by the ITC e-Choupal. It is more than just a win in terms of savings. It provides a social basis for becoming an insider.
3. The ICICI-supported SHGs take it one step further. They start with understanding the rationale for the contacting system: how and why it reduces transaction costs and, therefore, reduces the cost of capital and increases access to capital. Further, governance cannot be just between ICICI and the individual. By creating a collective commitment to accountability to contracting conditions, SHGs continually reinforce in the local community the benefits of being within the system.

Ultimately, the goal in development is to bring as many people as possible to enjoy the benefits of an inclusive market. Transaction governance capacity is a prerequisite. The market-based ecosystem might provide us an approach to building the basic infrastructure for inclusion of BOP consumers. It also allows large firms to build new and profitable growth markets.

The impact of the market-based ecosystem and the role of the nodal company can be important in developing the disciplines of the market—respect for contracts, understanding mutuality of benefits, being local and at the same time getting the benefits of being national and global, and most important, recognizing the benefits of transparency in relationships. **The private sector, in its desire to leverage resources and gain market coverage, will invent new systems depending on the nature of the market. That is precisely what we need. We need the capacity to bring more people into the market system.** This means not only gaining the benefits of globalization, but also accepting the disciplines that it imposes. Opaque, local moneylender-based contract enforcement and participating in a national or regional private-sector ecosystem are not compatible. Again, this is a positive situation for both the large firm and the BOP consumers. MNCs and small-scale enterprises and entrepreneurs can co-create a market and the BOP consumers can benefit not only by the quality and choice of products and services available to them, but also by building local entrepreneurship.

In the next chapter, we address the ever-present but seldom openly discussed topic of corruption. Corruption and poverty go together. However, given the advancement of technologies, we can mitigate corruption rapidly. This is what governments can do to facilitate the rapid development of market-based ecosystems and the active involvement of large firms and MNCs in the BOP market.

Endnotes

1. Meghana Ayygari, Thorsten Beck, and Asli Demirguc-Kunt. "Small and Medium Enterprises Across the Globe: A New Database," World Bank, 2003.
2. NABARD. "Banking with Self-Help Groups: How and Why," p.5.

5

Reducing Corruption: Transaction Governance Capacity

The private sector, as we saw in the previous chapters, can be a major facilitator of poverty alleviation through the creation of markets at the BOP. Although managers might be convinced about the opportunity, it is likely that there are lingering doubts about the capability of large firms to operate in these markets. The primary source of this concern is corruption. In many cases, the impact of micro regulations and local customs that are opaque to MNC managers might be interpreted as corruption. For example, the criticality of relationships in Japanese and Chinese business, opaque to the Western MNCs, can appear to be corruption. So will local customs and the set of mutual obligations in rural societies. We must understand the difference between corruption and local practice. Alliances with local firms and NGOs can provide visibility to these "understood but not explicit" local practices. **Transaction governance capacity (TGC) is about making the entire process as transparent as possible and consistently enforced.** We must reduce the frictional losses in doing business at the BOP. The focus of this chapter, however, is overt corruption. Corruption in various forms adds to this cost burden and business uncertainty. In the previous chapter, we examined how MNCs and large firms (nodal firms) can create transaction governance capacity (TGC) within their ecosystems.

Most developing countries do not fully recognize the real costs of corruption and its impact on private-sector development and poverty alleviation. The capacity to facilitate commercial transactions through a system of laws fairly enforced is critical to the development of the private sector. I call this a nation's TGC as opposed to the TGC within an ecosystem we considered in the previous chapter. In this chapter, we examine the need for and the process by which countries can develop their TGC. Again, as in the last chapter, we digress and consider the accumulated thinking on corruption and poverty alleviation.

Are the Poor Poor?

Some basic assumptions have been at the core of the thinking on poverty reduction and developmental assistance during the past 30 years.

- First, poor countries are poor because they lack resources.[1] Aid was, therefore, seen as a substitute for locally generated resources.
- Second, aid from rich countries to the governments of the poor countries for specific projects (typically infrastructure) would reduce poverty.[2]
- Third, investments in education and health care might have the largest multipliers per dollar of investment in economic development. Therefore, aid must be skewed to these sectors.
- The record of aid and loans from the various donor countries and the World Bank, International Monetary Fund, and other institutions is at best mixed. More recently, the development community is paying attention to the role of the private sector in building markets.

There have been few voices of dissent to the dominant logic of the development community. Hernando de Soto, in his path-breaking book, *The Mystery of Capital*, challenged the assumption that poor countries are poor.[3] Poor countries could often be asset-rich but capital-poor. Assets cannot become capital unless the country guarantees a rule of law—

primarily the law of contracts—whereby the ownership of assets is clear; and because of clear legal title, these assets can be sold, bought, mortgaged, or converted into other assets. It is this concept of legal ownership that converts assets into capital. This is a compelling argument. De Soto also demonstrated in his work that the trapped resources—assets that cannot be converted into capital because of underdeveloped legal framework and institutions—can be significant. For example, he estimated that the trapped resources of Mexico are about $300 billion. In Egypt, the estimate is about $198 billion. This perspective suggests that poverty is, at least partially, a self-imposed problem in most of the world. Local capital formation and the functioning of markets are stymied by the lack of appropriate institutional arrangements.

We can derive several conclusions from this:

1. All forms of foreign investment in poor countries—whether aid, FDI by multinational firms (the private sector), or philanthropy—are but a fraction of the potential for capital that is trapped in these countries.
2. In the absence of enforceable contract law, local commerce is conducted by a vibrant extralegal or informal sector (or the black market). This is the primary face of the private sector in most developing countries.[4] These firms in the informal sector are unable to grow because they cannot attract capital. They remain small, local, and often inefficient.
3. There are contract enforcement systems that are local. Each slum might have its own unwritten but clearly understood rules. Enforcement might be the privilege of the local "strongmen."

This is the ultimate paradox. Poor countries might be rich if we consider trapped assets. They might have a vibrant private sector and a market economy, although this private sector is informal, fragmented, and local. Ironically, these economies tend to be high cost with poor access to credit and inefficient systems of management.[5] However, not all poor countries have a poor legal structure. Some merely lack the capability to enforce the laws. India, for example, is not Congo. In India, contract law is well-developed but enforcement mechanisms are not. What, then, is the problem?

The consultants from McKinsey & Company believe that the laws on the books are not enough. It is how laws are implemented at the ground level through a system of microregulations that matters. In a study jointly conducted with the Confederation of Indian Industries (CII), the McKinsey consultants found that the cost of microregulations in the areas of import-export, labor laws, and transactions involving land can be as high as 2 to 3 percent of GDP growth.[6] Microregulations result from bureaucratic interpretation of the laws. The proliferation of regulations can make the system opaque to anyone but the very savvy. De Soto argued that his country, Peru, enacts more than 28,000 pieces of legislation per year at the rate of more than 100 per day. No one can keep pace with that rate of change.[7] Interpretation of the regulations can compromise the timely execution of contracts and the clear establishment of ownership. As a result, corruption at all levels of bureaucracy can become endemic. The consequence of proliferation of microregulations can be the same as not having laws in the first place. An informal sector emerges outside the law of the land. The private-sector businesses remain small and local. For large firms, corruption becomes the cost of doing business.

Yet another variant of the same phenomenon is that the laws are underdeveloped. As a result, bureaucrats have a significant influence on the interpretation of the law (or the desires of the state). In spite of this, business can flourish. China represents a case in point. Oddly enough, in China, the bureaucrats are also the entrepreneurs. It is in the interest of the bureaucrats to guarantee a level of "certainty" in the interpretation of the contract—implicit and explicit. In the absence of laws and institutions that govern contracts, aligning the interests of the private sector and bureaucracy seems to have worked in building a vibrant economy in China. However, the poor in villages might be paying a price. For example, in the absence of institutions and laws, farmland can be appropriated by bureaucrats for other uses without a legal recourse for the farmer.

Given these variations, what is the secret for the evolution of a market economy in the BOP markets? What are the essential requirements for active private-sector involvement in development? I believe that the key lies in a nation's TGC.

Transaction Governance Capacity (TGC)

Fundamental to the evolution of capital markets and a vibrant private sector is the need for a transparent market for capital, land, labor, commodities, and knowledge. **Transparency results from widely understood and clearly enforced rules. Transactions involving these rules must be clear and unambiguous.** Ownership and the transfer of ownership must be enforced. Under such a system, assets can become capital. Investors will seek the best opportunities. TGC is the capacity of a society to guarantee transparency in the process of economic transactions and the ability to enforce commercial contracts. This is about reducing uncertainty as to ownership and transfer of ownership. Transparency in the process reduces transaction costs. Clearly developed laws, transparent microregulations, social norms, and timely and uniform enforcement are all part of TGC. My argument is that TGC is more important than laws that are not enforced.

BOP consumers live in a wide variety of countries with varying degrees of TGC. Consider the spectrum:

1. Countries that are arbitrary and authoritarian. Laws do not exist and the laws that do exist are not enforced. Congo is an example of this situation. Private-sector development, in the Western sense, is very unlikely here. The only FDI that is likely is focused on the extraction of mineral wealth.
2. Countries where laws and institutions of a market economy exist. The private sector is vibrant. Still, the country does not reach its potential. India is a case in point. Alternatively, the GDP growth is great, but the underlying legal systems are not fully developed. China is an example.
3. Countries with well-developed laws, regulations, institutions, and enforcement systems. The United States is an example.

We can look at the spectrum of TGC, as shown in Figure 5.1.

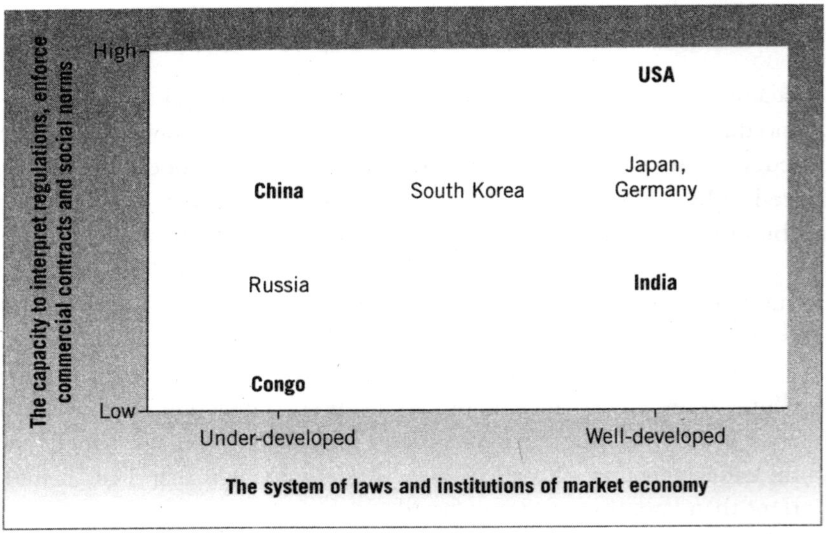

Figure 5.1 Transaction governance capacity (TGC).

TGC captures the dilemma that the BOP consumers and the private sector face. A country like Congo will have a long wait before an active private sector will propel the economy. However, both China and India are growing rapidly. They are the only two large countries showing more than 5 percent GDP growth over a decade. Both countries have significant corruption. Estimates of nonperforming assets on the books are as high as 50 percent of GDP for China and 20 percent for India. However, they have to travel different roads to become full-fledged market economies. As commercial transactions become large, complex, and multiyear, traditional approaches to bureaucratic interpretation and enforcement in China become problematic. China must develop laws and institutions. India must become more aggressive in enforcement. Political and bureaucratic intransigence will hurt investments and growth.

There is a need for us to recognize that economic growth fueled by the market economy around the world is not a single, monolithic problem. Each country has its own road to travel. Easy prescriptions that suggest that enacting laws will suffice are as naive as suggesting that contract enforcement even without laws provides adequate protection. The migration path toward the goal of a fully functioning market economy will be different depending on the point of departure for each country. Private-sector investors seek certainty—enforcement—over laws on the books. Enforcement allows firms to compute the cost of doing business in a system. That is the reason that most MNCs continue to prefer China over India: a clear preference for enforcement capacity over the legal system on the books. In China, corrupt as they are, the bureaucrats and politicians can enforce a contract. However, the corrupt in India cannot necessarily enforce contracts consistently. The checks and balances built into the Indian polity, especially the press and the multiparty political system, continually unearth corruption in contracts.

Building TGC

TGC is about creating transparency and eliminating uncertainty and risk in commercial transactions. The specifications for TGC are fourfold:

1. A system of laws that allows for ownership and transfer of property.
2. A process for changing the laws governing property rights that is clear and unambiguous. Democracies provide a safety net from idiosyncratic changes. For example, in the United States, the process by which new laws are enacted is clear and unambiguous. The process in democracies is arduous and open. This provides a share of voice to all the affected in shaping the laws.
3. As societies become more complex, a system of regulations that accommodates complex transactions.
4. Institutions that allow the laws to be implemented fairly, in a timely fashion, and with transparency.

TGC is more than laws or regulations. For example, de Soto found that there are 71 procedures and 31 agencies that are involved in legally acquiring and registering land in Egypt. The situation is no different in other developing countries. However, to come to the conclusion that microregulations are the problem would be premature. The United States is full of microregulations, as anyone who has tried to build a new factory can testify. The regulations are even more complex if it happens to be a chemical factory. In addition to regular procedures involved in building a factory, additional regulations for a chemical factory can add to the difficulty of getting a license. Microregulations are an integral part of any complex legal system.

TGC consists of laws, regulations, social norms, and institutions. We need to think of the various components of TGC as a portfolio, shown in Figure 5.2.

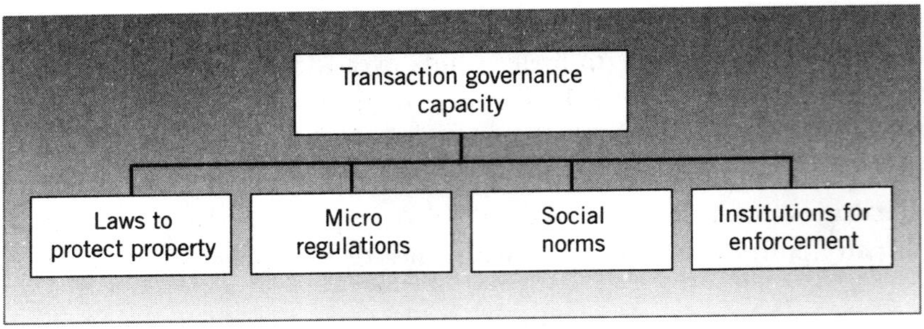

Figure 5.2 Components of TGC.

Each country and economy might need a different portfolio of the elements of the TGC: One size might not fit all. The goal is to increase the TGC of a society in such a way that a vibrant private sector can flourish. We need to recognize that each country is at a different starting point.

I believe that the real problem is how bureaucracies deal with citizens. Consider a farmer in India, a semiliterate person approaching government officials to register his land. He will be approached by "brokers," who are the facilitators of the transaction. They fill out the forms for the farmer, lobby with the authorities, and ostensibly make the process easy. The total cost of the transaction for the farmer consists of the fee paid to the broker for his services (an uncertain percentage of the value of the transaction), the registration fee, and the bribes paid to corrupt officials. The process is so opaque to the farmer that the broker and the officials have opportunities to be arbitrary about the quality of the title and the value of the land. More important, they have the ability to decide how long the process will take. They can give this particular case the level of priority that they think is appropriate. Corruption is about providing privileged access to resources and recognizing the time value of money. *Corruption is a market mechanism for privileged access.* Bureaucrats use microregulations to control access, transparency, and therefore time.

TGC is about eliminating the opaqueness in the system and providing ease of access. Changing laws and regulations does not help the ordinary citizen if the system is not transparent or if access is not easy. From the point of view of the citizen, TGC must fulfill four criteria:

1. Access to information and transparency for all transactions.
2. Clear processes so that selective interpretation by bureaucrats is reduced, if not eliminated.

3. Speed with which the processes can be completed by citizens.
4. Trust in the system (with its faults). Trust is a result of the first three criteria and is a crucial component of TGC.

I prefer to start with building ease of access and transparency, even before the regulations and the laws are changed to reduce selective interpretation. How?

The Andhra Pradesh e-Governance Story[8]

Let us look at one bold move by the Chief Minister of Andhra Pradesh, Nara Chandrababu Naidu. Andhra Pradesh is a state in India with 75 million people, 48 percent of whom are illiterate. Seventy percent are involved in agriculture. The GDP per capita is a low $600. Fifty percent have no electricity and 69 percent have no running water. Five distinct languages are spoken in the state. There are an estimated 15.6 million households and 2 million farms. Citizens depend on the state for a wide variety of services, from admission to schools to birth and death certificates, paying utility bills, taxes, driver's licenses, and registering property. The role of the government is pervasive. Therefore, a large bureaucracy has evolved to administer the various laws and regulations. There are more than 1 million government employees servicing 75 million citizens, a ratio of 13 to 14 government employees per 1,000 citizens. The system is opaque and the opportunities for corruption are high. This appears to be an unlikely place for a world-class experiment to develop good TGC.

Naidu decided in 1998 to make his state the model state in India. His approach was unique: He wanted to use digital technologies and the Internet as the basis for making his government responsive and citizen-centric. The goal was to reverse the process from an institution-centric civil service (citizens adjust to the requirements of the bureaucracy and government) to a citizen-centric system (a bureaucracy that is accountable to the citizens who elect the government). This concept was a 180-degree turn from the prevailing norm. The intended transformation is visualized in Figure 5.3.

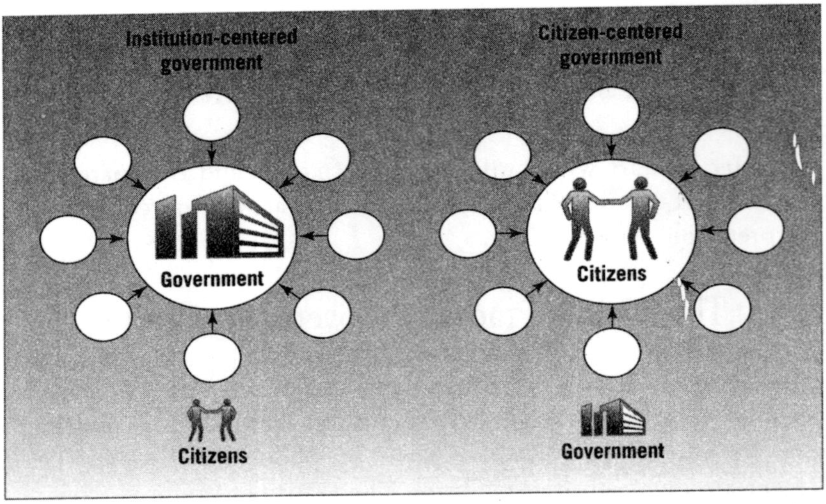

Figure 5.3 Intended transformation to citizen-centric governance.

Over a period of five years, a wide variety of governmental systems and services was brought online. Let us continue with the land registration process as an example. What has changed? The work flow has not changed. However, the quality of interaction between the citizen and the system has changed in the following ways:

1. All the steps that are required are now transparent and easy to access. The sequence of steps to be followed is also clear. All interdependent steps are completed automatically.
2. In the old system, the officials calculated the value of the land and the associated fees for registration. There were opportunities for selective value assessment. Now the entire process of calculation is automated with market value assessment algorithms built in. The documents are scanned and stored digitally, reducing the opportunities for them to be lost or misplaced.
3. The entire process of registration of land now takes one hour (from initiation to completion), compared to 7 to 15 days in the old system. Title searches over the past 20 years from 50 different offices can be done in 15 minutes versus three days. Certified copies of documents can be obtained in 30 minutes against the three days in the conventional system.

No laws have changed here and no regulations have been eliminated. However, the transparency, access, and time to transact business have changed dramatically. Andhra Pradesh has more than 2.8 million land records on digital files that can be accessed by citizens on the Internet from their homes or through Internet kiosks set up by the government.

Land registration is one of the key areas in which TGC can help. However, the transition to an all-digital, Internet-enabled system will not be without glitches. Actually, it might increase corruption before it reduces it dramatically as shown in Figure 5.4. The logic is fairly straightforward. E-governance[9] requires the education of the citizen as well as bureaucrats and politicians. Citizens who have grown up with a system of bribes to get things done are unlikely to believe that this is different. They need to experience the difference. Officials who recognize that this will dramatically alter their ability to wield power and extract "speed money" will extract bribes to get the records properly digitized. The opportunity for altering the records before digitizing is high. Finally, all officials do not see that the system will be reducing opportunities for corruption immediately. Some will persist and must be prosecuted. Therefore, in the initial stages of implementation of the system, we should not be surprised if the level of corruption increases. However, the shape of the corruption curve, over time, is not in question.

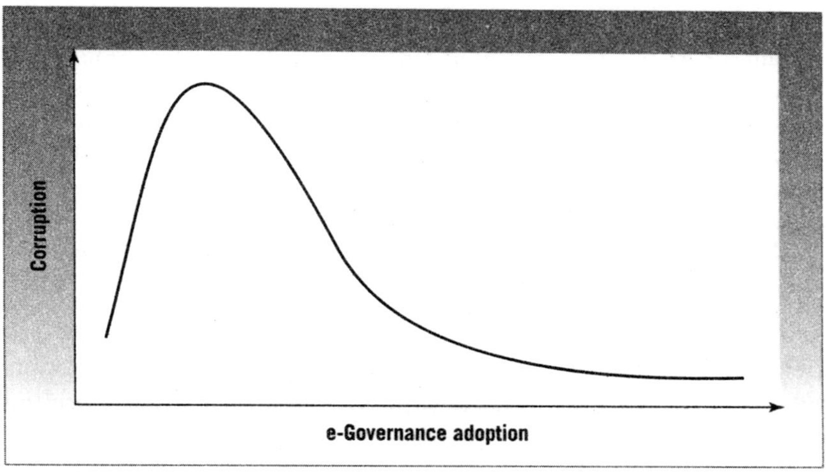

Figure 5.4 Corruption and e-governance.

This schematic is important to bear in mind as countries move toward e-governance as a way to improve the TGC. For example, the initial reaction to the e-governance in Andhra Pradesh is best captured in the following excerpt taken from the original case study:

> Using a sophisticated document management system with imaging technology, the land registration department digitized 2.8 million land records dated from 1983 onward and implemented the project in 387 offices around the state. A pilot was conducted in 1996 at a cost of $55,000. The project, which was launched in 1998, cost $6 million to implement. The department is integrating all 148 offices in the state, empowering the citizen to choose the location where he or she wants to transact with the government. A recent survey conducted by the Center for Good Governance (CGG), the think tank instituted by the government of Andhra Pradesh and the Department of International Development, uncovered disappointing insights into the current registration process. Eighty-seven percent (90 percent rural and 80 percent urban) of all those registering land went to the CARD office with the help of a document writer or a middle man. The average bribe paid was an additional 7.95 percent (2.85 percent urban and 25.81 percent rural) of the actual fees due. Eighty-three percent (60 percent urban and 94 percent rural) of citizens share the view that the registration officer is corrupt and 85 percent (64 percent urban and 96 percent rural) feel that the land department is corrupt. One hundred percent do not feel that the government of Andhra Pradesh has done anything to tackle corruption in the registration department. The study also observed that citizens and document writers consistently underdeclare the actual transaction price and real market values are far higher than those kept on the CARD systems. Rural transaction prices (Rs. 550,000) are underdeclared on average by Rs. 48,000 each. Urban transaction prices (Rs. 450,000) are undeclared by Rs. 36,000 each. This adds up to a potential annual revenue loss to the government of Andhra Pradesh of Rs. 4.5 billion. The think tank recommends privatization of the front office as one of the ways to reduce corruption. This would mean providing land registration services through the zero-corrupt Internet kiosk environment.

The survey confirms the logic of the corruption curve; corruption is bound to increase in the near time, peaking and then steadily declining to near-zero levels. After the system is fully operational, it is difficult to change the data in the system. Further, all entries will leave a trail, indicating who as well as when. This level of scrutiny and openness will reduce the opportunities for corruption.

TGC is not just about large, one-time transactions that people engage in, such as buying land or property. Every citizen depends on the government for much of his or her day-to-day existence. Paying utility bills, getting a license for opening a shop, and getting admission to a college using birth and caste certificates are all part of a citizen's dependence on government. That is where the government of Andhra Pradesh turned next.

eSeva

The government of Andhra Pradesh has now set up eSeva (literally, "e-service") to provide ease of access to services from the government and its agencies. eSeva centers are operated through a public–private partnership model. This is outsourcing of government functions to the private sector. The government of Andhra Pradesh is trying several models, including build-own-operate (BOO) and build-own-operate-transfer (BOOT).

eSeva can be accessed via the Internet or through the kiosks[10] set up by the government. Citizens can pay water and electricity bills through eSeva. They can get their driver's license. They can pay their property taxes. There are more than 45 integrated state and federal services currently available to citizens through this system. The list of services is given in the Appendix at the end of this chapter. Imagine the losses that this approach to government service can eliminate. It used to take a minimum of half a day for a worker to go to the Electricity Department and pay his or her monthly bill; 3.5 million bills are paid per month in the city of Hyderabad alone. If we compute the frictional cost at a meager wage rate of Rs. 50 per half day (U.S. $1.00) per person, it totals a staggering Rs. 2.1 billion per year. The cost to the citizens of just paying electricity bills is a staggering collective wage loss of about U.S. $45 million in one city. There is also a host of other bills to be paid and services that require the citizen to go to government offices and wait. Again the paradox is that the poor pay a heavy price for basic services. In the eSeva system, a citizen can, in one trip to the kiosk, transact all routine business with the state at the same time without "speed money."

A wide variety of ordinary citizens was interviewed for our research on what they thought of these services and they reacted favorably. Here are some citizens' reactions in their own words:

"There is absolutely NO corruption in eSeva."

"We needn't stand in long lines in the hot sun and waste time."

"All transactions are visible and it is easy for us to pay all bills in a single location."

"eSeva system is beautiful."

"We are not harassed anymore at the hands of government employees."

"I can get back to work to earn my hourly wages."

Unlike most government establishments, the eSeva centers[11] are clean and citizens receive the same levels of service regardless of their economic class. The services are used by an average of 1,000 citizens per day, ranging from 400 to 2,000 people. The software system is cleverly designed to prevent corruption and create accountability at every level. More important, every detail in a transaction is permanently recorded into a database in Telugu, the local language. Of the 750,404 transactions in March 2003, the number of transactions that had a rupee value below Rs. 100 ($2.00) contributed 11 percent (presumably the poor), greater than Rs. 20,000 ($400) about 1 percent, and the middle segment, Rs. 100 to Rs. 20,000, about 80 percent. Considering the amount collected during the period, the middle segment contributed 73 percent of the Rs. 4.3 billion.

It is important to recognize that an Internet-based system such as eSeva can be of great help to a large number of educated citizens, be they rich or poor. The educated can access their own records, pay their bills online, and get the benefits of the system. How about the illiterate and poor? By providing the urban poor with access to the kiosks and help from the kiosk operators, the long waits and trips to multiple agencies can be eliminated. The intermediary is still needed. He or she is not a broker but is the operator, a private-sector employee, in the kiosk. The satisfaction scores from the citizens with eSeva services are high, even with an intermediary, with no opportunity to be corrupt. The access to eSeva for the rural poor met the goal of the government of Andhra Pradesh of 100 percent access across the state by 2005.

Center for Good Governance

Although the governance initiatives set up by Andhra Pradesh are praiseworthy, it is important that the direction of change, the quality of implementation, and progress are measured. With this in mind, the government of Andhra Pradesh, in collaboration with the International

Development Institute of the United Kingdom, has set up an independent watchdog agency called the Center for Good Governance (CGG). The role of the CGG is to monitor the implementation of the ICT approach to citizen-centric governance and publish independent and periodic reports of how the entire process is proceeding. The CGG is authorized to challenge the government agencies. Further, it makes recommendations to the Chief Minister on what needs to be changed.

The CGG approach is based on the simple premise that power in a democracy is derived from the people and government must be accountable to them (see Figure 5.5).[12] Obvious as this is, the basic premise of an elected government is often lost in the bureaucratic and regulatory maze.

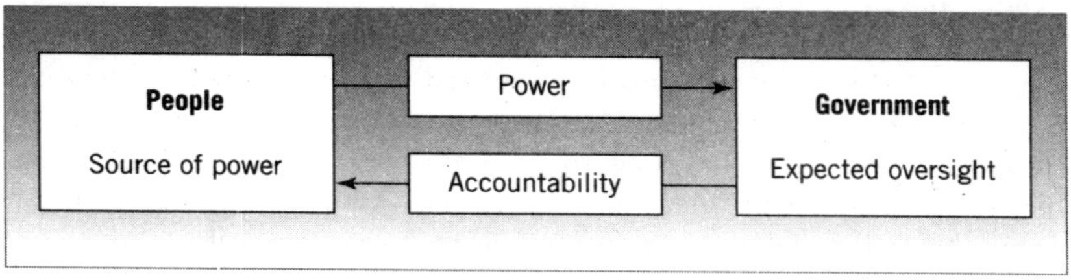

Figure 5.5 Good governance model.

Needless to say, good governance, as shown in Figure 5.5, cannot be achieved without a clear set of guiding principles, performance indicators and measurements, and constant attention to improvement of the underlying processes.

The guiding principles of CGG in Andhra Pradesh are listed in Table 5.1.

Table 5.1 Guiding Principles of the CGG in Andhra Pradesh

Guiding Principles	Explanation
Consultation	Public consulted regarding service level and quality.
Service standards	Educate public on level of service entitled.
Access	Equal access regardless of societal position.
Courtesy	Treat people with courtesy and consideration.
Information	Give public full and accurate information about service.
Openness and transparency	Inform public about government operations and budget.
Redress	Apologize and redress if promised service is not given.
Value for money	Public services provided economically and efficiently.

A performance management system (PMS) for the efforts of the government of Andhra Pradesh is introducing a citizen-centric view through a wide variety of schemes, including land registration (2.8 million records) and monitoring of public spending programs. The Chief Minister (who calls himself the CEO of the state) can directly access any village, bypassing the usual layers of bureaucracy that separated the ministers from their constituencies. The chief minister of Andhra Pradesh started town meetings (via videoconferencing facilities) with the villages randomly chosen. That further cemented the transparency and access available to ordinary citizens.

> According to Dr. P.K. Mohanty, Executive Director of the Center for Good Governance, the PMS was developed as a "hexagonal model." In other words, it can be used to rate a department on six variables: 1) relative performance compared to last year, 2) relative performance compared to peers now, 3) relative performance compared to peers last year, 4) relative performance to benchmarks, 5) relative performance to targets, and 6) relative performance compared to government as a whole. This model presents a complete picture of a particular department over time, allowing senior officials to get to the root cause of problems that arise.

How does the performance system work? Is the transition to the system smooth and without tensions? Do bureaucrats believe in the system? What is the role of political leadership in making this system work? TGC cannot be enhanced without a deep commitment from the top. The researchers witnessed the monthly meeting of the Chief Minister (CM) with the district collectors. These monthly meetings were one of the tools used to implement the system and identify problem areas. Here is an excerpt from the case study on the government of Andhra Pradesh:

> Researchers witnessed firsthand the PMS in action. The CM holds monthly, sometimes weekly, video teleconferences with all 26 district collectors. The CM is located in Hyderabad, and each district collector is located in his or her respective district headquarters. Each district collector was joined by 50 other personnel. Interesting to note was that the press was given full and open access to this meeting; in fact, they recorded the entire five-hour meeting.

> Various subjects were covered throughout the meeting, with the CM driving the discussions. Significant time was spent on the issue of drought remediation actions taken by the districts. The CM was using data from the PMS and forcing the district collectors to explain any negative trends. It was very evident when a particular employee was not familiar with the data that had been entered. What the reader needs to realize is that this was taking place live in front of more than 1,000 government employees across the state, plus the press. The pressure to perform in front of peers is a huge motivational factor for the district collectors.

The CM also used this forum to discuss public opinion numbers. Each district collector was again asked why things were going poorly in his or her area and what he or she planned to do about it. It was evident during the meeting that many of the figures that had been input in the system were not the "actual" numbers, but simply placeholders that were entered by the cut-off time, four hours before the meeting. Staff scrambled to present the CM with appropriate numbers, especially when the new numbers were better than the fictitious ones. Transparency such as this, in front of the press, is forcing government officials to embrace the PMS. Also, they must now pay attention to the citizens and perform only actions that are important.

During these meetings, the CM chooses a random subject to scrutinize. At this particular meeting, commodity prices were picked. The officer in charge of this was caught, and subsequently embarrassed, because he had entered data simply to enter data. Quite often his commodity prices were off by a factor of 10 or 100! There is no doubt this particular individual will input proper data from now on. No doubt seeing one's peers publicly embarrassed will encourage district collectors to make sure that proper data are input by their staffs.

Although the systems are in place, they are still works in process. E-governance increases the TGC of a society through increased transparency, accountability, speed, and accessibility. Such citizen-centric governance creates a better economic climate by reducing risk. However, the concept, the approach to implementation, and the initial results suggest that it can lead to improved TGC. Further, improved TGC can lead to development. Conceptually, the virtuous cycle is shown in Figure 5.6.

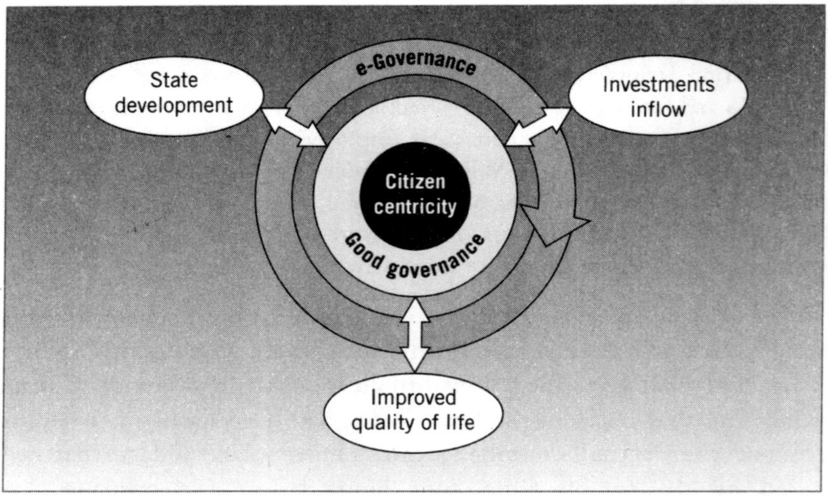

Figure 5.6 The virtuous cycle.

Impediments

One should not conclude that this experiment is a done deal. There are significant impediments to the entire process, the most important being the education of the citizen. For decades, the citizens associated corruption, sweat, long lines, and humiliation with government, so they are likely to look at these initiatives with skepticism. Only consistent performance can convince the skeptics. The bigger problem is with the employees—the functionaries within the government. Initially, they accepted these initiatives because no one was displaced by the e-governance initiatives. No changes were made to the underlying processes. As might be expected, in the initial stages, the potential for "speed money" was not severely compromised. However, in the second phase of implementation, this will start to change. The regulations and governmental business processes can be simplified. Interconnected systems can identify pockets of graft and corruption. Records cannot be easily altered or lost. The change will not come easily. It is the support of the citizens and the pressure from them for change that can reduce the political price for moving forward with these initiatives. The benefit of TGC is worth the risk.

Lessons from the Andhra Pradesh Experiment

There are several lessons to be learned from the experiment in Andhra Pradesh. Transformation of a well-entrenched system takes not only building an IT system, but also building trust. Citizens must feel that changes are taking place. The experience with eSeva is therefore critical. The services offered by eSeva allow citizens to experience streamlined services, not just once in their lifetimes (as in buying or selling land and property) but frequently (as in paying electricity and water bills every month). Furthermore, confidence-building requires that citizens experience a high quality of service with no corruption in a wide variety of services such as getting a driver's license or a birth certificate. TGC is about communicating a consistency in the behaviors of the bureaucracy and governmental institutions. Citizens must convince themselves that it is cheaper to be within the system than outside it. The shift from the informal sector to the formal sector will take place if ordinary citizens can be confident that:

$$\frac{\text{The cost of being } \textit{inside} \text{ the system}}{\text{The cost of being } \textit{outside} \text{ the system}} \leq 1$$

Ordinary people instinctively recognize that there are costs to being within the system. They have to declare their assets and pay taxes. They also recognize that there are costs to being outside the system. They have to be beholden to local politicians and a cruel system of enforcement of local practices with no legal recourse. The cost is high and difficult to predict. Bureaucratic corruption had made the cost of being inside the system too high for most citizens and the benefits too low. Poor access to the formal system and its lack of transparency compared to social norms force people to seek a higher cost option, but one where the rules are clear (even if cruel).

Corruption, as we said, is a market for privileged access. It thrives in a system that allows for opaque decision making. The cost of being inside the system will decrease only if governments tackle the issues of access and transparency and recognize the changes needed in both the regulations and the laws. The experiment in Andhra Pradesh is one example of how digital technologies can be used to creatively enhance TGC through better access and transparency.

Building TGC is not only the job of the government. It does play a significant role in ensuring that corruption is reduced, but market-based ecosystems that large firms can create, as we saw in Chapter 4, "The Ecosystem for Wealth Creation," can also increase TGC in a society. The combination of the two, with the use of digital technologies, can rapidly transform the TGC of a country.

Endnotes

1. Some would argue that development assistance was based on the belief that although resources might exist (for example, Nigeria), they might have a bottleneck in some of the critical ingredients to development. In this sense, development assistance was a "complement," not a substitute.
2. The focus of development aid has also shifted from infrastructure, education, and structural adjustments over the decades.
3. Hernando de Soto. *The Mystery of Capital: Why Capitalism Triumphs in the West and Fails Everywhere Else*. Basic Books, New York.
4. It is important to distinguish the informal, extralegal sector from the private sector even though the informal sector is about entrepreneurship under very hostile conditions.
5. C.K. Prahalad and Allen Hammond. "Serving the World's Poor, Profitably." *The Harvard Business Review*, September 2002.
6. CII-McKinsey Report on Learning from China to Unlock India's Manufacturing Potential, March 2002.
7. Hernando de Soto. Presentation at the World Economic Forum, Davos, Switzerland, 2004.
8. Supportive case written by Praveen Suthrum and Jeff Phillips under the supervision of Professor C.K. Prahalad. Copyright © The University of Michigan Business School, 2003.
9. The World Bank defines e-government as the use of information and communications technologies to improve the efficiency, effectiveness, transparency, and accountability of government (www1.worldbank.org/publicsector/egov/). I prefer to use the term e-governance, as it refers to a broader relationship between the political system and society. The terms e-governance, e-government, and e-democracy are used interchangeably in the literature.
10. Available only in towns and cities in Andhra Pradesh. Kiosks will cover the entire state in two years.
11. Our researchers visited three eSeva centers in Andhra Pradesh's capital city, Hyderabad, and one in the village of Nagampally.
12. This view is accepted in a vibrant democracy. How about countries that are not democratic (even if they hold "mock elections")? The idea of ultimate accountability to the citizen is fundamental to good governance.

Appendix: List of eSeva Services

Payment of utility bills Electricity Water and sewerage Telephone bills Property tax Filing of CST returns Filing of A2 returns of APGST Filing of AA9 returns of APGST Collection of examination fee Filing of IT returns of salaried class Sale of prepaid parking tickets Permits and licenses	Renewal of trade licenses Change of address of a vehicle owner Transfer of ownership of a vehicle Issue of driving licenses Renewal of driving licenses (nontransport vehicles) Registration of new vehicles Quarterly tax payments of autos Quarterly tax payments of goods vehicles Lifetime tax payments of new vehicles
Certificates Registration of birth Registration of death Issue of birth certificates Issue of death certificates	Reservations and other services Reservation of APSRTC bus tickets Reservation of water tanker Filing of passport applications Sale of nonjudicial stamps
Internet services Internet-enabled electronic payments Downloading of forms and government orders	Sale of trade license applications Sale of National Games tickets Sale of entry tickets for WTA Sale of EAMCET applications

Business to Consumer (B2C) services
Collection of telephone bill payments
Sale of new Airtel prepaid phone cards
Top up/recharge of Airtel Magic cards
Sale of entry tickets for Tollywood Star cricket
Sale of entry tickets for Cricket match (RWSO)
Filing of Reliance CDMA mobile phone connections

- Railway reservation
- Sale of movie tickets
- Payment of traffic-related offenses
- Payment of degree examination fees of O.U.

- Sale of I-CET applications
- Online reservation of Tirupati Temple tickets
- Collection of bill payments of Idea Cellular
- Collection of bill payments of HUTCH
- Issue of encumbrance certificate
- Market value assistance
- General insurance
- Reservation of tourism tickets for accommodation
- Reservation of tourism bus tickets
- Call center
- Indian Airlines ticket reservation
- Life insurance premium payment
- Issue of caste certificates
- Sale of Indira Vikas Patra
- ATM services
- Collection of bill payments of Airtel
- Renewal of drug licenses
- Issue of bus passes
- Collection of trade licenses of Labor Department

6

Development as Social Transformation

We have looked at the BOP as a viable and profitable growth market. We have also understood that treating the BOP as a market can lead to poverty reduction, particularly if NGOs and community groups join with MNCs and local companies as business partners. The development of markets and effective business models at the BOP can transform the poverty alleviation task from one of constant struggle with subsidies and aid to entrepreneurship and the generation of wealth. **When the poor at the BOP are treated as consumers, they can reap the benefits of respect, choice, and self-esteem and have an opportunity to climb out of the poverty trap.** As small and micro enterprises, many of them informal, become partners to MNCs, entrepreneurs at the BOP develop real access to global markets and capital and effective transaction governance. MNCs gain access to large new markets, developing innovative practices that can increase profitability in both BOP and mature markets.

National and local governments have an important role to play in this process. They have to create the enabling conditions for active private-sector involvement in creating this BOP market opportunity. TGC is a prerequisite. Governments now have new tools to create TGC in a short period of time. Further, new technologies and new approaches to reaching the BOP such as SHGs and direct distribution (creating millions of new entrepreneurs) can also create a respect for the rule of law and commercial contracts among the BOP consumers (for example, as they access credit through the microfinance route) and local entrepreneurs. **The capabilities to solve the perennial problem of poverty through profitable businesses at the BOP are now available to most nations, as we have illustrated. However, converting the poor into a market will require innovations.** The methodologies for innovation at the BOP are different from and more demanding than the traditional approaches, but so is the opportunity for significant profitable growth. Finally, BOP markets represent a global opportunity. Lessons learned at the BOP can transform MNC operations in developed countries as well. BOP can be the engine for the next round of global expansion of trade and good will. If we follow this approach, what impact will it have on the BOP consumers? How will their lives change?

Development as Social Transformation

We have come full circle. We have made three transitions in our thinking. First, we demonstrated that the BOP—the poor—can be a market. Second, when we accept the BOP as a market, the only way to serve that market is to innovate. The BOP demands a range of innovations in products and services, business models, and management processes. Third, these innovations must be accompanied by increased TGC, making the government accountable to the citizens and making it accessible and transparent. Market-based ecosystems can also facilitate the process of making transparency, access, and respect for commercial contracts a way of life. The intellectual transitions that are the substance of this book and its implications are shown in Figure 6.1.

How can these changes impact life at the BOP? **As BOP consumers get an opportunity to participate in and benefit from the choices of products and services made available through market mechanisms, the accompanying social and economic transformation can be rapid.** The reason for this is that BOP consumers are entrepreneurial and can easily imagine ways in which they can use their newly found access to information, choice, and infrastructure. Let us look at some examples.

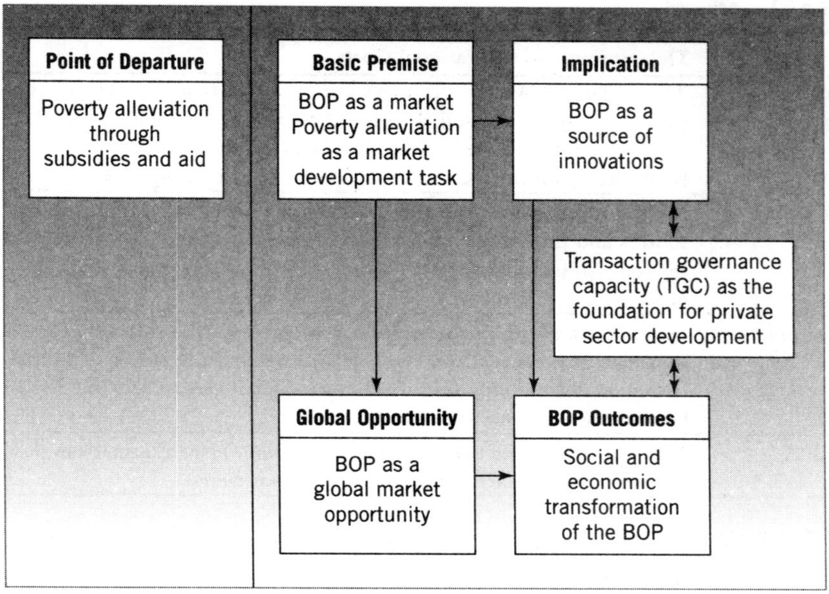

Figure 6.1 The private sector and the BOP: transitions.

The ITC e-Choupal infrastructure was created for farmers to have access to information regarding prices as well as agriculture-related information, as shown in Table 6.1. The system was configured to make them productive farmers and to make the supply chain for soybeans more efficient so that there was a win for both the farmer and ITC. That was the intent.

Table 6.1 Intended Uses of ITC e-Choupal System

Features	Description and Operational Goals
Weather	Users can select their district of interest by clicking on the appropriate region of a map. Localized weather information is presented on regions within a 25-km range. Typically, 24–72-hour weather forecasts are available along with an advisory. The advisories are pieces of information directly related to the farmer, which he can put to use. For instance, during the sowing season, a weather forecast for days following rains might include the advisory that instructs the farmer to sow when the soil is still wet. Weather data is obtained from the Indian Meteorological Department, which has a presence even in small towns and can provide forecasts for rural areas.

Table 6.1 continued

Features	Description and Operational Goals
Pricing	The e-Choupal Web site displays both the rate at which ITC offers to procure commodities and the prevailing mandi rates. ITC's next-day rates are published every evening. The prices are displayed prominently on the top of the Web page on a scrolling ticker.
News	For the soyachoupal Web site, relevant news is collated from various sources and presented. Aside from agriculture-related news, this section also includes current affairs, entertainment, sports, and local news.
Best practices	Here, best farming practices are documented (by crop). Here again, the information presented is actionable. For instance, in this section, the farmer would not only find what kind of fertilizers to use, but also how and when to use them.
Q & A	This feature enables two-way communication. Here a farmer can post any agriculture-related question he needs answered.

It took farmers fewer than three months to understand the strength of the Internet, and they started using the system for a host of other, nonbusiness-related and socially beneficial tasks. They found that they could connect with each other and chat about a whole range of issues, not just agriculture and prices. They found that the PC could be an entertainment device. It could be used to play movies, listen to songs, and watch cricket (a sport that is a national obsession in India). They could print out the classroom grades of their children. They also became sophisticated in tracking prices, not just at the local mandi or ITC prices, but also for futures at the Chicago Board of Trade. They correlated intuitively the futures prices with the prices they should expect in selling to ITC or others. They established a clear link between global price movements and the prices in remote villages of northern India. Just three months earlier, they were "hostages" to the vagaries of the local merchants in the mandi. They also became experts at e-mail and chat capabilities. The list of dominant, unplanned activities that evolved in three to six months among the villages connected by the system is shown in Table 6.2.

Table 6.2 Unplanned Activities at e-Choupal: The Social Transformation

News	Dainik jagran, Web Dunia
Market prices	One sanchalak actually followed Chicago Board of Trade prices for a month and arrived at a correlation with the local market prices. He used this information to help other farmers decide when to sell.
Entertainment	Movie trivia. Rent CDs to watch movies on the computer. Music downloads from the Internet.
Sports	Cricket-related news.
Education	Students use the Internet to check their results and grades online.
Communication	E-mail.
	The sanchalaks have e-mail accounts on Yahoo! Chat. Some sanchalaks frequent chat rooms and chat with other sanchalaks and ITC managers.
General interests/other	Information about cell phones.

Breaking Down Barriers to Communication

ITC worked hard to create interfaces in the farmers' native language, Hindi. It also provided software that made it possible to type Hindi characters using a standard English keyboard. The preferred language for writing e-mails and other electronic communication, however, is "Hinglish," or Hindi typed with English characters. The reason for this is that combining vowels and consonants to create Hindi letters is a cumbersome affair on a keyboard. It sometimes takes three keystrokes to render one letter. All the sanchalaks we spoke to agreed that this was the only aspect of computer usage they had not yet mastered.

Undeterred, the sanchalaks started to use the English keyboard to write e-mails in Hindi. They could move fast in building both the capacity to communicate with the outside world and the ability to make themselves understood. The creativity in building communication patterns can be illustrated by one of the e-mails between a sanchalak in a remote village in northern India and the researcher in Ann Arbor, Michigan. There appear to be no barriers. The student in the United States was educated, rich, sophisticated, and well traveled. The farmer probably never traveled beyond a cluster of villages, was poor and uneducated. All those boundaries were broken by the possibility of asynchronous communication through e-mail. We do not know how long it took to compose this e-mail, but suspect probably not long. It is straightforward and to the point. The e-mail is shown in Figure 6.2.

> Date: Sunday, May 18, 2003 11:01 PM
>
> From: arun nahar
>
> To: <sachinr@umich.edu>
>
> sachin ji namaste
>
> aapka mail padkar khushi hui aapki english meri samajh mae aati hai agribusiness mae jaivik khad(bio-fertilizer) ke bare mae aapke kyaa vichar hai present polution ko dekhate hua future plan ke bare mae socha ja sakta hai public chemical less product khana pasand karte hai aane wale 10 years organic product ke honge organic product bio-fertilizer se taiyar hote hai village mae organic product taiyar kiye ja sakte hai in product ko sahi market dene ke liye aap network bana sakte ho
>
> thanks

The English translation of this e-mail is as follows:

> Date: Sunday, May 18, 2003 11.01 PM
>
> From: arun nahar
>
> To: sachin@umich.edu
>
> Mr. Sachin, greetings
>
> I was delighted to read your mail. I was able to understand your communication in English. What is your opinion about bio-fertilizers in agro-business? Considering current pollution, we can develop trends. People prefer meals, which are prepared with "chemical less products." For the next 10 years, markets will be dominated by organic products. Organic products can be produced with bio-fertilizers in our village. ("We can do it"). In order to market this product, can you develop the distribution network?

Figure 6.2 E-mail from a sanchalak.

The use of the infrastructure in creative ways is not confined to the sanchalaks. Across the board, BOP consumers can use the systems they have access to in ways unimagined by those providing the systems.

What is the real change for those at the BOP? The real advantages of a private-sector network can be captured, as shown in Table 6.3.

Table 6.3 The Drivers of Social Transformation

Dimension of Social Transformation	Traditional	Emerging
Access to information	Limited	Unlimited; large firms, government, and bureaucracies in areas of interest to them.
Community	Locationally bound, typically a cluster of villages	Could be regional, national, and global.
Patterns of interaction and access to knowledge	Limited	Infinitely more; word of mouth "turbocharged."
Ability to make independent choices	Low	High and can get very sophisticated through dialogue and interaction.

The simple case of the ITC e-Choupal, if repeated 1,000 times, can transform a country. We find increasingly that women from different villages who have never met each other are in chat rooms discussing complex issues like interest rate fluctuations and political positions to take with respect to specific issues. They also use it for more family-oriented topics. In one chat room on the n-Logue network in southern India, the women were discussing the status of their grandchildren or other relatives living abroad. The newly found advantages are the building blocks of a market economy: transparency of information, universal access, dialogue among various thematic communities that form autonomously, and a discussion of the risks and benefits of various courses of action, such as "Should I sell my corn today or hold back?" These four building blocks are dialogue, access, risk benefits, and transparency (DART). These are the same building blocks that are leading to more consumer activism in developed markets.[1]

BOP Consumers Upgrade

Contrary to popular belief, BOP consumers are always upgrading from their existing condition. MNCs and large firms oriented toward the top of the pyramid sometimes look at what the BOP consumers use and think of it as downgrading from the products they are selling. These products are seen as cheap. On the other hand, for the BOP consumers, the newly found choice is an upgrade from their current state of affairs. For example, when Nirma, a startup, introduced a detergent powder in India, the established firms in that business—both MNCs and large Indian firms—considered the product as low end and not of interest to them. At that time, the total tonnage for high-end products was about 25,000 tons. Nirma was a new category, upgrading the BOP consumers from poor-quality, locally made soaps, and the brand built an impressive market of 300,000 tons. The lessons were not lost on the incumbents. The size of the market at the BOP is significant (300,000 tons versus 25,000 tons at the top of the pyramid), but more important, Nirma was a product uniquely fashioned for the poor who wash clothes under a tap or in a running stream rather than in a washing machine.[2] The same process is evident in a wide variety of businesses, including financial services. When the BOP consumers opt for a loan from a bank, as opposed to a local moneylender, they are upgrading. When they use iodized salt over the locally available unbranded salt, they are upgrading. When they get access to good-quality building materials and a design for how to add an additional room from CEMEX, they are upgrading. The examples can be multiplied. The message is simple: **For the BOP consumer, gaining access to modern technology and good products designed with their needs in mind enables them to take a huge step in improving their quality of life.**

Gaining Access to Knowledge

We have already examined the benefits of access and transparency and how that impacts the asymmetric information that was (and is) the norm in most BOP markets. However, when BOP consumers get access to digital technologies, the pattern of access to knowledge changes. For example, in the EID Parry Agriline example used in this book, the farmers had a concern about the quality of a particular crop: betelnut. They used their PCs and the attached cameras to send pictures of the affected leaves to a central agronomy center 600 miles away. They received advice from the agronomists at a remote location. That certainly improved their ability to solve the problem. Examples such as this one are proliferating by the day. It is becoming well accepted in some parts of India that telemedicine is the way to go to get remote diagnostics based on PCs. Shanker Netralaya, for example, brings world-class eye care to rural India. It has vans fitted with optometric equipment that connect via satellite hook-up to the hospital. Senior doctors can review complex cases on a two-way videoconferencing hook-up and discuss with the patients their problems. They can also offer a diagnosis based on images presented on a split screen. They can then recommend a course of action. This incredible access to high-technology solutions is changing the way we think about the BOP consumers. Increasingly sensitized to what is possible, they are also demanding high-technology solutions to their problems.

Identity for the Individual

One of the common problems for those at the BOP is that they have no "identity." Often they are at the fringe of society and do not have a "legal identity," including voter registration, driver's license, or birth certificate. The instruments of legal identity that we take for granted—be it a passport or a Social Security number—are denied to them. For all practical purposes, they do not exist as legal entities. Because they do not have a legal existence, they cannot be the beneficiaries of a modern society. Voter registration in vibrant democracies, such as India, provides one form of identity. Erstwhile communist regimes had a system of documenting everyone, including the location to which they belonged. In Shanghai, for example, all the migrant workers were undocumented for a long time. They did not officially belong to Shanghai and, therefore, could not participate in programs such as government-assigned housing.

This picture starts to change as a private-sector ecosystem emerges. The individuals in an SHG have an identity. They are recognized as legal by the ICICI Bank. They all have a name, a designation, a group to which they belong, and a scheme in which they participate. The same is true of the eSeva service provided by the government of Andhra Pradesh. Now all citizens who pay their utility bills or register births and deaths have an identity. In fact, many BOP consumers are elated to see their names on a computer screen. This is universal. The poor in Brazil, when they shop in Casas Bahia, get an identity. They get a card from the company, and that tells the world who they are. Consumers proudly display their Casas Bahia cards as proof of their existence and their creditworthiness. A similar situation exists in Mexico. When CEMEX organizes women, it not only gives them the tools and the materials required for them to build a kitchen; it also gives them a legal identity. The women are bound to the firm and vice versa. Neither party can break the contract without penalty. That is a proof of legal identity.

The importance of legal identity cannot be underestimated. Without it, BOP consumers cannot access the services we take for granted, such as credit. Hernando de Soto documented the problems of a lack of legal identity at the BOP. The status of a "nonperson" in legal terms can confine people to a cycle of poverty.

Women Are Critical for Development

A well-understood but poorly articulated reality of development is the role of women. Women are central to the entire development process. They are also at the vanguard of social transformation. For example, Grameen Bank's success is based on lending only to women. The entrepreneurs who used the micro finance made available were women. The Grameen phone "ladies" are the entrepreneurs. In the cases in this book, there is adequate evidence of the role of women in building a new society at the BOP. The SHGs at ICICI Bank are all women, as are the Shakti Ammas at HLL. These women are entrepreneurs responsible for saving and accessing credit. In the case of CEMEX, the company works only with women. Amul, a milk cooperative, depends on women for their milk origination in villages. Women also collect the "cash" for the milk and, therefore, have achieved a new social status. Access to economic independence can change the long tradition of suppression of women and denial of opportunities. The success of Avon, Mary Kay, and Tupperware in the United States and other parts of the world is also based on the role of women entrepreneurs. Although the evidence is overwhelming, little explicit attention has been paid to actively co-opting women in the efforts to build markets and lead the development process. MNCs and large firms will do well to keep this in mind in their efforts to create new markets at the BOP.

Evolving Checks and Balances

It is natural for us to ask, "If the involvement of the private sector in BOP markets can have such a significant impact on social transformation, do we need checks and balances?" Yes. **We need to make sure that no organization abuses its power and influence, be it corrupt governments or large firms.** Fortunately, checks and balances are evolving rapidly. The spread of connectivity—wireless and TV—makes it impossible for any group to abuse its position for long. Further, civil society organizations are always on alert. However, the most important protection is informed, networked, and active consumers. The evolution of the BOP consumer is ultimately the real protection.

The social transformation that is taking place in markets where the public and the private sectors have been involved at the BOP is quite impressive. BOP consumers have constantly surprised the elite with their ability to adapt and their resilience. As we described in this chapter, they do the following:

1. They adapt to new technology without any difficulty and are willing to experiment and find new and "unforeseen" (by the firms) applications for the technology. Nobody thought that the farmers from the middle of India would check prices at the Chicago Board of Trade.
2. Technology is breaking down barriers to communication. Given that BOP consumers can increasingly enjoy the benefits of dialogue, access, risk benefit analysis, and transparency (DART) and make informed choices, the chances of change in tradition will be improved.
3. BOP consumers now have a chance to upgrade and improve their lives.
4. By gaining access to a legal identity, they can participate more effectively in society and gain the benefits of the available opportunities. They do not have to remain marginalized.
5. Finally, the emancipation of women is an important part of building markets at the BOP. Empowered, organized, networked, and active women are changing the social fabric of society.

Taken together, these changes will lead to significant social change and transformation.

The Real Test: From the Pyramid to the Diamond

Although we have discussed the nature of social transformation that is possible at the BOP, the real test of the entire development process is poverty alleviation. How will we know it is taking place? Simply stated, the pyramid must become a diamond. The economic pyramid is a measure of income inequalities. If these inequalities are changing, then the pyramid must morph into a diamond. A diamond assumes that the bulk of the population is middle class. The morphing that we must seek to accomplish is shown in Figure 6.3.

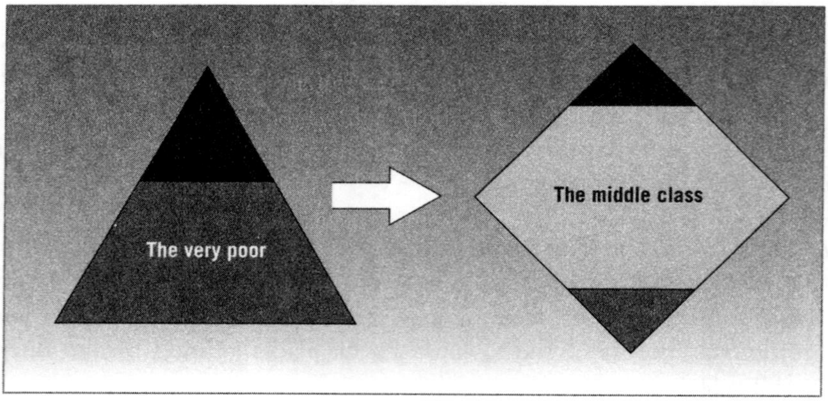

Figure 6.3 The morphing of the pyramid into a diamond.

There will always be "the rich," but a measure of development is the number of people in a society who are considered middle class. **More important, social transformation is about the number of people who believe that they can aspire to a middle-class lifestyle. It is the growing evidence of opportunity, role models, and real signals of change that allow people to change their aspirations.** Our goal is to rapidly change the pyramid into a diamond. To be confident that this transformation is occurring rapidly, we should, at a minimum, measure the changing patterns of income inequities in a society. This is a relative measure. We can also measure the income levels over a period of time. This is an absolute measure of change in that society. Needless to say, modeling this change requires reliable measures of income, appropriate sample size, and longitudinal data. These are hard to come by.

An interesting study by the National Council of Applied Economic Research (NCAER) in India suggests that there might be some weak but clear signal that this change is emerging. During the last decade, India has liberalized its economy, promoted private-sector development, and allowed each state to experiment. As a result, instead of one monolithic approach to economic development, there are multiple models of development being implemented. The various states are also growing at highly differentiated rates. NCAER modeled the changing patterns of income distribution by states and had projected the inflation-adjusted income pyramid for 2006–2007. It is easy to see that in some states such as Bihar and Orissa, the shape of the income distribution does not change. It is still the pyramid. However, in other states, such as Assam, Maharashtra, Gujerat, Haryana, and Punjab, the pattern is shifting noticeably. The projections of income distribution from NCAER are shown in Figure 6.4.

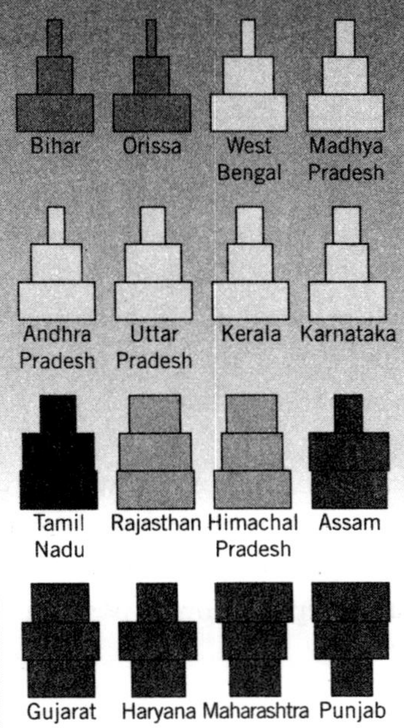

Contribution to agri GDP (%)		Index of number of households		
		Lower	Middle	High
8.1	Bihar	100	43	17
	Orissa	100	43	11
48.6	West Bengal	100	65	21
	Madhya Pradesh	100	60	26
	Andhra Pradesh	100	67	22
	Uttar Pradesh	100	74	30
	Kerala	100	59	36
	Karnataka	100	57	37
5.4	Tamil Nadu	100	96	44
5.3	Rajasthan	100	88	67
	Himachal Pradesh	100	76	64
22.8	Assam	100	106	38
	Gujarat	100	112	83
	Haryana	100	145	76
	Maharashtra	100	125	151
	Punjab	100	179	188

Figure 6.4 The shape of rural income distribution.

This pattern will repeat itself in both rural and urban India. This has several implications. First, we can measure the patterns of income distribution over time and can develop both relative and absolute measures of change. Second, the changing nature of the income distribution creates a virtuous cycle. The demand for products and services increases domestic economic activity, creating more jobs and wealth. The changing patterns of consumption of durables in India—in both rural and urban markets—are well documented.[3] Third, as the BOP morphs from a pyramid into a diamond, the distinction between the BOP consumer and the top-of-the-pyramid consumer disappears. There is only one consumer group.

The pattern of changes in income distribution seen in India is an early signal of what is possible. A measure of success is when the debate about BOP consumers becomes irrelevant as they become part of the mainstream market.

I have tried to depict a picture of the possibilities. I am sensitive to the fact that the illustrations that I provide are but islands of excellence in a sea of deprivation and helplessness. The important question for us is, "Do we see the glass as half full or half empty?" There is a long way to go before the social transformation leading to the elimination of inequalities around the world will be accomplished. The private sector, as shown by the examples we have examined, can make a distinct contribution. The changing patterns of income distribution, the increasing confidence of the BOP consumers, and their ability to become activists in changing their own lives through entrepreneurship give us hope. But the examples that we have examined challenge all of us, whether our primary obligation is boosting shareholder returns or reducing poverty and social injustice, to bring the resources and capabilities of the private sector to bear in pursuit of that goal.

Our best allies in fighting poverty are the poor themselves. Their resilience and perseverance must give us courage to move forward with entrepreneurial solutions to the problem. Given bold and responsible leadership from the private sector and civil society organizations, I have no doubt that the elimination of poverty and deprivation is possible by 2020. We can build a humane and just society.

Endnotes

1. C.K. Prahalad and Venkat Ramaswamy. *The Future of Competition: Creating Unique Value with Customers*. Harvard Business School Press, 2004.
2. "Hindustan Lever Limited: Levers for Change." Case study, INSEAD, Fontainebleau, France, 1991.
3. Rama Bijapurkar. "The New, Improved Indian Consumer." *Business World*, December 2003.

PART III

CEO Reactions to the Concept and the Book

In this part, we reproduce letters from CEOs and senior leaders of large global firms. The letters demonstrate their growing interest in embracing the opportunities in BOP markets and the innovations they foster. These letters from the CEOs reflect the voices of a wide variety of firms and, more importantly, individuals. It is our hope that these perspectives will motivate more CEOs.

List of Firms:

1. Microsoft
2. Bharti Airtel
3. Thomson Reuters
4. Royal DSM
5. ING
6. GlaxoSmithKline (GSK)
7. Unilever
8. Philips Electronics
9. University of Maastricht
10. Acumen Fund

Microsoft

Many of the ideas in *The Fortune at the Bottom of the Pyramid* are reflected in Microsoft's Unlimited Potential product-development effort. Designing and selling products targeting the Bottom of the Pyramid requires new thinking around market-opportunity sizing, relevant design, and nontraditional business ecosystems. But the results are proving to be quite exciting, not only in terms of the market impact in developing economies but also in seeing how innovations targeting the Bottom of the Pyramid can "trickle up" to the developed world.

A great example of this involves Microsoft's work around Windows Starter Edition and low-cost computing. This began as an effort to redesign a computer operating system's user interface, business model, and storage technology to meet the unique requirements of the world's poorest students. Millions of new customers later, we now know this approach can work in emerging markets. But we underestimated the speed at which the technology would be adopted in developed markets: Consider the netbook phenomenon, which uses many of these innovations and in 2008 became the fastest growing PC segment.

At an individual level, *The Fortune at the Bottom of the Pyramid* serves as a catalyst that helps our engineers and product managers rethink how they can help Microsoft prepare for its biggest, long-term opportunity. "Bottom of the Pyramid" and "Middle of the Pyramid" have become a core part of our company's vocabulary, and people here are excited to work on projects where business interests and social-development interests are so closely aligned.

Craig Mundie
Chief Technology and Strategy Officer
Microsoft Corporation

Bharti Airtel—Empowering the Villages of India

Over the last decade, the Indian telecom has witnessed transformation: a transformation from basic telephony being an elitist possession to mobile telephony being a means of empowering masses.

As recent as 2000, the bottom of the pyramid consisted of close to 95 percent of the Indian population deprived of basic telephony. It took nearly 5 to 10 years of waiting before getting a basic telephone connection in India. The big divide between "haves" and "have-nots" presented an unprecedented opportunity that Bharti Airtel recognized early on and took responsibility to bridge this divide. The efforts of the Indian telecom sector have made mobile telephony available and affordable to the Indian masses. Today, mobile telephony has become the gateway to the world and a means of enhancing productivity of the people of India.

The second phase of this revolution is underway. It is led by the large rural population of India that is the fortune at the bottom of the pyramid. India has around 70 percent of its population living in semi-urban and rural villages. This more than 700 million population is the largest single market opportunity in the world to any consumer-focused corporation today. In addition, this population is fast becoming aware of the choices that are available to them, thanks to the penetration of mass media like television and cinema. More than 75 percent of these villages also have the required purchasing power to afford branded products.

Bharti Airtel has recognized this opportunity well in time and has been investing heavily to cater to the demands of the rural customers. Today, even when 60 percent of the new customers are from rural India, this accounts for less than 30 percent of telecom penetration. The rural opportunity will continue to be the biggest strategic focus for years to come. Bharti Airtel is leading this revolution, conscious of the fact that "inclusive growth" is the only way ahead. Some of the innovations that we have led from the front include

- Massive rollout, both network and distribution, focused around rural market in 400,000 villages.
- Value added services specifically targeted to benefit the rural population. These include information on crops, weather, commodity prices, education, and telemedicine to name a few. This information is now made available on the mobile handset.
- Alliances with handset manufacturers such as Nokia targeted at the rural market. Initiatives like vernacular messaging, voice messaging to overcome the barriers of language.
- Alliance with IFFCO (India's largest fertilizer company) to reach out to the relevant population in an organized way. This alliance has shown superior results in terms of educating the rural population on telecom, sales, services, and in capturing the specific needs of the rural customers.
- Mobile commerce initiatives are underway targeting the rural population in an attempt to "financial inclusion." Less than 50 percent of the Indian economy is a cash economy, and through this initiative we will cover the unbanked people through our partner banks.

The Fortune at the Bottom of the Pyramid aptly captures the biggest opportunity not only in India but also in all emerging markets for corporations across the globe. It clearly describes the imperatives and business models for companies to be successful riding on the fortune at the bottom. Our company has derived immense value from the visionary thinking of C.K. Prahalad, which is extremely relevant in the market we operate in, and hence, we have obtained powerful results. I believe this book is a starting point for any corporation aspiring to grow in developing markets, where the biggest fortune still continues to be at the bottom of the pyramid.

Manoj Kohli
CEO and JMD
Bharti Airtel Limited

Reuters Market Light and *The Fortune at the Bottom of the Pyramid*

It was early 2006 when a tall Swede named Mans Olof Ors and his highly persuasive Indian colleague Amit Mehra first approached me with a passionate pitch about something called Project Market Light—an idea to sell information services on mobile phones to farmers in emerging markets.

Mans' vision, conceived while on a one-year sabbatical at Stanford University in 2004, was inspired directly by reading *The Fortune at the Bottom of the Pyramid.* At its heart was a simple idea: In India, where 60 percent of the population is dependent on agriculture, and where approximately eight million new mobile phone users were connecting each month, a vast farming community of 120 million cultivators lacked simple access to information to maximize their profits. So what was stopping us from providing them with the weather updates and market prices they so clearly needed? Reuters had historically provided the same sort of information to established financial markets to promote price transparency and fair trading.

All of us in the room were instantly energized by the scale and opportunity here. It was one of those eureka moments in business when you happen across an idea so innovative and right you know instinctively it's a home run.

Reuters Market Light (RML), as the product was named in April 2007, provides information that impacts the productivity of the Indian farming community, connecting farmers to buyers and helping to establish fair prices in local markets. Farmers receive crop prices from local markets, localized weather forecasts, and relevant news and advisory information in their local language via text messages to their mobile phones. This tailored information helps farmers make commercial decisions about their crops, such as when and where to sell, so they can maximize their profits.

The first time I read *Bottom of the Pyramid*—like Mans and so many others—I was struck instantly by the breadth, boldness, and clarity of its insights. In a company like ours, which operates in nearly all major centers around the world and opened its first office in India in 1866, C.K.'s book soon influenced our thinking about how to expand our global footprint to less-developed markets.

RML was looking to address the same urgent questions: How to reach consumers in developing countries and offer them innovative products that meet their needs? What opportunities arise as the 80 percent of consumers at the bottom of the pyramid start to exploit the benefits of information networks and show an appetite for advanced technology? Like C.K., I am a passionate believer that good business is consistent with a sensible development approach for societies, and nowhere is this more true than with RML. The links between the book and the project go even deeper. People with experience working for C.K. in his BOP consulting practice have given RML much sound advice.

More than a dozen trips right across India gave us the insights to build the business model, supplemented by secondary research in Africa. Some 1,500 Indian farmers took part in concept testing and prototyping. We also carried out ethnographic studies with a hand-picked group. April 2007 saw the scaled market trial with 7,000 farmers. The team, initially based in London, was relocated to Mumbai to be close to the customer during this key growth stage. At times, unexpected floods would spoil our on-the-ground research, but Amit and his team were hugely motivated by consistently positive customer feedback.

All this culminated in the formal launch of RML in October 2007 in Maharashtra. The fact that nearly 1,000 farmers were present, as well as the Indian Minister of Agriculture Sharad Pawar, spoke volumes about the excitement it generated. RML reflects Thomson Reuters' core strengths—accurate information, timely delivery, and unbiased analysis—in this case to a large, developing, often isolated audience.

The results in the months post-launch surprised even RML's biggest advocates and gave us a green light to enter a second state, Punjab, a year later. To date RML has already sold more than 100,000 3-month subscriptions. Some farmers have reported an extra 100,000 rupees (U.S. $2,090) when they sell their crops—an incredible rise for small businessmen whose average annual incomes are around $1500.

We've learned a lot in the process about how to provide products to Bottom of the Pyramid consumers. Most academic research suggests that large companies often fail at strategic innovation because of rigid structures, sluggish processes, and inflexible mindsets. RML confounded that stereotype and succeeded with a business model that is low price, high-volume, direct sales and distribution-led, and mobile-driven. We have the largest network for sourcing and creating localized and personalized content for farmers in India. On the critical dimension of distribution reach, we already have more than 500 retailers/dealers selling RML in the two states. Selling to rural customers is different from selling to our traditional professional customers. We got around this by spending the right amount of time on the ground with potential customers pre-launch. We also got it right back in the office with a solid management and wider project team, an experienced governance team, and top-level sponsors.

RML is making a difference to the lives of thousands of customers while at the same time achieving our financial and operational goals. It has garnered recognition in India and globally: The United Nations selected RML as one of six business initiatives for other businesses to follow in helping to deliver the Millennium Development Goals, which aim to slash global poverty, hunger, and disease by 2015. It has also been endorsed by the World Bank, and we're working alongside several agricultural research institutes, such as the Agarkar Institute and Cotton Research Institute of India. Recently, RML has signed a major partnership with Nokia to market and distribute RML on a special mobile application—exactly the sort of aspirational co-brand this book identifies as important to brand-conscious BOP consumers.

Having expanded into Punjab, the service will extend to Haryana in January 2009, and then to six other states across India by the end of 2009. Since illiteracy rates remain high among rural communities (the overall literacy rate for India is 61 percent), there are also plans to develop a voice-based system over the next year.

At the time of writing, I believe that RML is the only initiative of its kind in India (and possibly the world). It's exactly the type of innovation C.K. has written about so eloquently, and it is scalable and transportable across borders. Once the business model, technology, and partnerships are firmly established, Thomson Reuters will explore potential roll-out to Africa, South America, and Asia. By providing transparency, RML can help to create fair and efficient markets at the bottom of the pyramid.

Tom Glocer
CEO
Thomson Reuters

Royal DSM

C.K. Prahalad's book *The Fortune at the Bottom of the Pyramid* has had a significant impact on all its readers, including those of Royal DSM NV, headquartered in The Netherlands. DSM is a globally operating company of almost 10 billion Euro revenues and almost 25,000 people, active in life sciences and materials sciences, enhancing with its products the quality of life by nourishing people and protecting the world.

This visionary book elucidates how the world can become a better place for all, taking into consideration how society has evolved in the past decades.

DSM became inspired through the numerous examples and arguments that are brought forward in this inspiring book, opening up new avenues to create value in a sustainable manner for the less fortunate in our world, not forgetting that the real Bottom of the Pyramid need "just" humanitarian help as well.

DSM became convinced that there are indeed ways to jointly create economic value together with the less fortunate at the Bottom of the Pyramid, if one is willing to truly become engaged in their world, their daily challenges, and problems. In doing so, a wealth of innovation potential is uncovered that through co-creation and joint development can be brought toward economic fruition.

DSM is a life science and performance materials company and has among others a broad product and knowledge-base in animal nutrition. We have embarked on projects that aim to support rural farmers in India to create more value by providing performance nutrition services (a combination of diagnostic tools, training modules, basic farm management, and animal feed). In addition, projects are started to improve local biogas production, through the use of additives that assist in converting agricultural waste and manure in a local source of heat, cooking gas, and off-grid electrical power.

Trust among all partners, creative business models that allow financial benefits for all, and patience have proven to be key (and complex) in the development of the DSM programs.

As indicated in this book, this is by no means an easy and straightforward objective for any industrial party. We should almost learn again to truly listen to our new customers at this economic bottom. Only by reaching out and truly diving into their world, we will become successful and generate value for all stakeholders in society, including those who are now at the first rung of the economical ladder. We should be proud and honored with these visionaries that help us to shape our society into one that truly will benefit all inhabitants of the world.

Feike Sijbesma MSc, MBA
Chairman of the Managing Board and Chairman of
DSM Nutritional Products

ING

The influence of *The Fortune at the Bottom of the Pyramid* on ING's thinking and that of others in the financial industry cannot be overestimated. The book has challenged our ideas of how we look at markets and the customers we serve, as well as the delivery methods we use to reach them. ING prides itself on its multi-distribution capabilities and indeed some of the channels we employ can be—and, to some extent, are being—adapted to serve markets that fall outside of our traditional target markets.

We were fortunate enough to be able to have C.K. Prahalad as a speaker at our international conference for senior management in May 2008. At the conference, he challenged our ideas about markets and costs. Specifically referring to India, which is an important growth market for us, he posed the question: Are you willing to change the way you work and not limit your reach, or do you maintain the way you work and walk away from the opportunities?

C.K. Prahalad asked us to consider whether the way we work will allow us to reach the largest—and in aggregate numbers most valuable—consumer groups in Asia. He made it clear to us that we need to step outside of our comfort zone of the top earners of the country. We have come to realize that we are a part of a myriad of financial institutions, which together forms a patchwork of financial inclusion. As a large retail financial institution, we have a role to play in the mass retail market. Although the reality of developing markets may mean that we are not able to serve those who are all the way at the Bottom of the Pyramid, we have the ability to serve those in the tiers below the mass affluent groups; and we intend to use that ability.

As you can see from the examples mentioned here, we are indeed surveying different markets, experimenting with delivery methods and ways to work with customers that we are not accustomed to. One particular pointer that C.K. Prahalad gave us was that in order to serve lower income markets, we need to convert customers from the unorganized to the organized sector and be innovative. In the case of the biometrics card as described here, that point is well taken.

Key Business Initiatives

To illustrate ING's involvement in providing financial services toward the Bottom of the Pyramid, we focus on the case of ING Vysya Bank in India. ING is capitalizing on the shift of economic power to the East and has established retail banking in this market. A sizeable part of ING's business initiatives in India is associated with, but not limited to, micro finance. Taken together, these initiatives allow us to capitalize on growing retail and wholesale opportunities in a responsible way.

ING Vysya Bank

ING Vysya Bank, which is owned by ING for 44 percent, reaches out both directly and indirectly to micro finance entrepreneurs.

The direct way is by financing so-called Self Help Groups (SHGs) consisting mainly of female entrepreneurs. As of December 2008, ING Vysya's outstanding loan portfolio to SHGs amounted to EUR 10.3 million. In addition, micro deposits are collected through this channel. Furthermore, ING Vysya started a pilot to reach out to rural communities and offer organized banking services through a unique biometrics card. This example is described in the following case study.

ING Vysya also indirectly finances several millions of micro entrepreneurs by providing wholesale loans to micro finance institutions. As of September 2008, the total value of wholesale loans outstanding amounted to €42.8 million to 17 micro finance groups.

Monitoring and Additional Services

ING actively monitors its social performance in the micro finance area and reports on an annual basis in its Corporate Responsibility Report, which is based on the Sustainable Reporting Framework of the Global

Reporting Initiative. In addition to these business initiatives, ING also supports education through our Chances for Children program and offers technical assistance through ING Microfinance Support.

Case Study: Banking Services for the "Unbanked" Population in Rural India

In a pilot involving wage and pension distribution on behalf of the government, ING Vysya reaches out to rural communities and offers organized banking services. Establishing the identity of rural Indians through biometrics makes it possible for illiterate or barely literate people to become part of the banking user community.

In the area of Andhra Pradesh, ING Vysya Bank is working together with the government to disburse wages and pensions to rural residents. As an alternative to distribution via post offices, which are few and far between, ING Vysya employees now travel from village to village to identify the villagers with the help of the government offices and enroll them in the program. After the identification, a smart card, personalized graphically and electronically, is given immediately to the villagers. This smart card, on which the personal records will be listed, allows ING Vysya to pay out the periodic wages and pensions to the villagers.

"This card is really useful, no more forms to fill, finger imprints, and delayed pension; ING Vysya Bank people come to us on a specific day, we show them the card and get our money, and this is hassle free and extremely easy," said a villager under the scheme.

In the first pilot project, more than 55,000 people received an ING Vysya smart card. The total project will reach more than 100,000 people in 20 villages in the Andra Pradesh region. ING Vysya plans to expand the project to include the rest of the population in these and adjacent rural areas and introduce the smart card as a means for micro savings, investment, and insurance.

Eli Leenaars
Member of the Executive Board
ING Group

GlaxoSmithKline

C.K.'s book *The Fortune at the Bottom of the Pyramid* has been a catalyst, enabling us to look at our business in the Emerging Markets in new ways. In fact, unleashing the opportunity with this new emerging consumer class has become one of our four main growth strategies.

The case studies, and videos in particular, really helped inspire my management team—illustrating the opportunity and the importance that technology could play in delivering solutions for consumers at the Bottom of the Economic Pyramid.

GlaxoSmithKline markets a wide-range of consumer health-care brands in the Emerging Markets. Historically, many of these brands have been comprised of products that were developed with the Western consumer in mind, and as such, were relevant only to the consumers at the Top of the Economic Pyramid. To better understand the consumer at the Bottom of the Pyramid, or as we refer to them as the Emerging Consumer Class, we have launched an in-depth market research study.

To win the consumers at the Bottom of the Pyramid requires rethinking traditional approaches around the supply chain and encouraging the organization to face the realities of affordability and profit requirements. C.K. Prahalad's work has shown that turning the traditional value equation from price minus cost equals profit to price minus profit equals cost demands creative solutions.

I think the power of the book and the concepts therein will be in the longer-term impact on my organization. The book does not promote quick fixes, rather it establishes principles upon which longer-term programs and new ways of working can be built.

The consumer at the Bottom of the Pyramid—and the commercial opportunity they represent—now has a seat at the table as we set global strategies and priorities and allocate our resources, both financial and human.

As a global organization, our management focus will need to move increasingly from "West" to "East." We are placing greater importance on the application of standards as opposed to standardization and will demand intellectual leadership and a greater contribution from diverse cultures.

It is no coincidence that my organization is the fastest-growing division in GSK Consumer Healthcare worldwide at the same time as we are putting many of C.K.'s concepts and principles to work as we tap into the opportunity at the Bottom of the Pyramid. He has inspired us to be bold in our aspirations, and in many cases we feel we really contribute to GSK's mission—of helping people "do more, feel better, and live longer."

Ian McPherson
President
Consumer Healthcare International, GlaxoSmithKline

Unilever

Doing Good, Doing Well

"Doing business responsibly and successfully–or, if you prefer, doing good and doing well–are two sides of the same coin."

—Patrick Cescau, speaking at Business as an Agent of World Benefit, Cleveland, Ohio, October 2006

Corporate philanthropy enjoys a long and proud history. Unilever should know. And today, making charitable donations and supporting community activities remains an important way in which businesses can help to address social challenges. But in recent decades, the agenda has moved on, significantly. There is growing recognition that companies' responsibility to society at large goes well beyond making philanthropic gestures—no matter how generous. Social responsibility and environmental sustainability have become the watchwords for businesses wanting to make a wider contribution to the communities in which they operate. Many factors explain this change of emphasis. For one, there is a growing recognition that the social and environmental challenges facing us in the 21st century are so complex and so multidimensional that they cannot be solved by governments alone. Industry has to be part of the solution. But perhaps the biggest catalyst for change has been the increasing awareness within business itself that many of the big social and environmental challenges of our age, once seen as obstacles to progress, have become opportunities for innovation and business development. We have come to a point now where the agenda of sustainability and corporate responsibility is not only central to business strategy but has become a critical driver of business growth. In fact, I would go further: I believe that how well and how quickly businesses respond to this agenda will determine which companies succeed and which will fail in the next few decades. This is particularly true in the case of sustainability. As globalization accelerates, and as the limits of the planet's resources are reached, large companies and brands will increasingly be held to account on the sustainability of their business practices.

Patrick Cescau
Retired CEO
Unilever

Philips Electronics—Improving Health and Well-Being at the Base of the Pyramid

Since the publication of the first edition of this groundbreaking book, the recognition has been growing that businesses are an essential part of solutions to kick-start emerging and developing economies. Increasingly, we are also seeing practical examples of win-win situations where development of communities and value creation for companies go hand in hand. Of course, as a representative of the business community, I very much welcome this change of heart.

But even with business now accepted as a partner in the efforts to achieve a more just and sustainable world, the tasks remain daunting. Still, our world is characterized by a clear divide between those who have access to a decent income, to affordable health care, to education, to the fruits of the digital revolution, and those who have not. This divide is unsustainable, the have-nots should become haves as well, enjoying the fruits of our technological progress.

Business has the prime responsibility to come up with innovations in technology, products and services, business models, and management solutions that will help us to meet the sustainability challenges.

At Philips, we see exciting opportunities in emerging markets and apply our competence in health and well-being to address major economic, social, and demographic challenges; for example, the growing demand for better health care at lower cost and the need for energy efficiency and for sustainable development.

For instance, Philips is involved in several partnerships to develop energy-efficient lighting solutions for the base of the pyramid, addressing the fact that 1.3 billion people still use expensive and dangerous kerosene lighting today. In Ghana, we have developed new low-cost sustainable solar lighting products for rural areas. It's part of the Sustainable Energy Solutions for Africa public-private partnership agreement between Philips and the Dutch government relating to 10 sub-Saharan African countries.

Making health care available to patients in remote areas who currently lack any access is an even more important task. It is unacceptable that thousands of people die every week from diseases that could be easily diagnosed and treated. High-end patient monitors are out of reach for many small- to mid-sized clinics, forcing doctors and nurses to decide upon treatment based only on visible symptoms. Sometimes this means they must wait for a patient's condition to deteriorate before changing treatment. That's why we have developed an easy-to-use, affordable ultrasound system particularly meeting the needs of users in emerging markets. This will allow clinicians to observe a patient's vital signs and make more informed and timely decisions.

These examples also show that only cooperation between all stakeholders—industry, governments, national and international organizations, and NGOs—will lead to solutions that really work. That's why it is encouraging to see initiatives in this direction; for example, with collective micro financing of health care in various Asian countries. At Philips, we develop our business as much as possible with local partners, local expertise, and local products.

A good example partnership is that which we have with the Dutch government's ORET international development initiative to improve health care conditions in Zambia. The project has seen substantial improvements made to 71 hospitals across the country. It also has included the training of more than 200 local hospital staff, creating a sustainable skills base to ensure a brighter future for the provision of health care in the country. We will continue to maintain the equipment we installed and have implemented a train-the-trainer program to ensure that the project's benefits continue to be realized for years to come.

I am convinced that companies must realize that, in the long run, there will be a sustainable world with sustainable business, or there will be no world and no business at all. The corporate community must learn to see sustainability not as a nice add-on, but as an essential part of doing business. That's our ethical challenge, but also an exciting business opportunity where companies need to go beyond their commonplace thinking.

Gerard Kleisterlee
President and CEO
Royal Philips Electronics

University of Maastricht

Management Education for the Poor: The Maastricht School of Management Story

Higher educational systems in developing countries with substantial Bottom of the Pyramid markets have traditionally been poor in quality. Often there are hardly enough resources available for regular primary and secondary schooling of children in these countries. It is, therefore, not surprising that there is a scarcity of resources for quality higher education. In many countries in Africa, for example, management schools either do not exist or build on outdated western materials that are not relevant for students in such countries. These textbooks on management include examples of companies that most of the students are not familiar with or have never even heard of. Perhaps more significant is that many of the advanced theoretical approaches assume that a certain infrastructure and level of economic development have already been realized, as they are a given for their application in developing markets and countries. In many cases, even the minimum imaginable market infrastructure is often not yet present. It is clear, however, that education, and management education, in particular, is essential for developing the local business community (micro companies and local entrepreneurs). It is important that an appropriate link be made in management education between the perspective of young aspiring managers regarding Bottom of the Pyramid markets and their knowledge of their business and local markets and the practical and theoretical ideas from the Western World.

The Maastricht School of Management started in 1952 with short management education programs for managers from developing countries. In the 1990s, it developed the Outreach MBA to deliver MBA programs of top quality in developing countries. Today it serves more than 2,000 students. Currently, there are more than 400 students in programs in Africa in, for example, Namibia, Uganda, Tanzania, Malawi, and Rwanda. The mission of the Maastricht School of Management is *"to offer management education, international projects (institutional partnering) and research with a special focus on programs and participants from and in emerging economies and developing countries."*

MSM is providing world-class programs in countries with substantial BOP markets and is committed to offering these students the same high-quality education that is offered in other parts of the world. All MSM MBA programs have been accredited by the Association of MBAs. Only the top business schools with MBA programs in the world have this prestigious accreditation.

Providing world-class management education in developing countries with large BOP markets requires any management school from the Western World to rethink the delivery of such education. There are three unique challenges that need to be met effectively to achieve this goal:

1. To provide top of the line management education very cost-effectively
2. To provide relevant content to the programs in developing countries
3. To procure financial resources to finance a world-class education for students

MSM has addressed these issues in the following ways.

To Provide Top-Quality Management Education at a Fraction of the Cost of Comparable World-Class Management Schools

In order to develop and provide management education at a fraction of the cost at world-class standards, administrative, as well as teaching and research professionals, need to be educated.

Funding from International Donor organizations and the Dutch Government has made it possible for MSM to educate administrators and managers of management schools to enable them to run their schools according to international standards. At MSM, there is a special department implementing these capacity building projects in Africa and in other developing countries.

In addition, local faculty members in developing countries need to be educated to fulfill their role in the delivery system of education in their country. This is done in two ways at MSM: 1) The Doctoral and MBA programs of MSM in Maastricht are primarily focused on educating students from developing countries in the Netherlands and 2) MSM also offers Doctoral programs in developing countries to upgrade existing know-how locally.

A proper and fitting education for students from BOP markets could not be done without relevant research. The Sustainable Business Center of MSM links both Doctoral and Applied Research students from developing countries. One of the large projects is the Round Table Africa project combining the practical realities in many African countries (through discussions with the local business community) with research by Doctoral students from Africa and world class researchers from the global network of MSM (see the following graph).

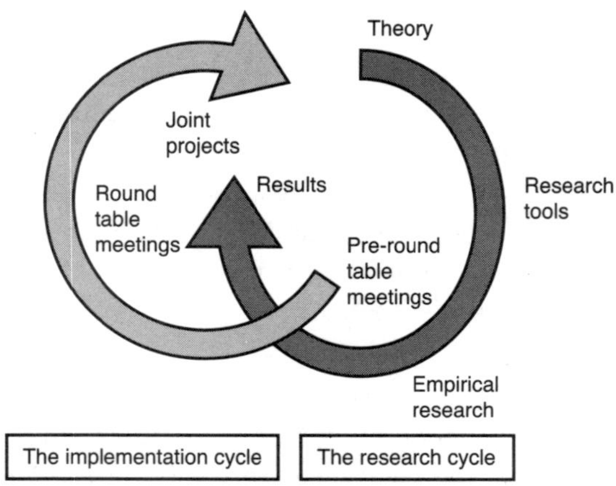

Source: Sustainable Business Center, MSM

To Provide Relevant Content to the Programs in Developing Countries

All MBA programs in Africa are jointly taught by MSM and local faculty members combining the knowledge of the local realities and an international dimension in each MBA program.

Recently, a book series has been written by MSM faculty members as an alternative to the typical business and management textbooks that are primarily focused on North America and Europe. Their frame of reference and examples are much more relevant for students from BOP markets. The *MSM Book Series* is a must-read for students. In developing the book series at MSM, a publisher was found who was willing to publish the book series at one-third of the cost to save students a substantial amount of money on the purchase of their books.

Financial Resources for Students' Tuition Fees

The international project department of MSM can often offer financing not just to individual students but also to whole cohorts of MBA students through funding awarded for various projects. These projects often include capacity building elements, as previously listed, but also finance tuition fees of students. This makes it possible to educate the most intellectually gifted students who do not necessarily have the funds to pay for their education. Providing them with a world-class education offers them opportunities they would not otherwise have, will make a contribution to their home country, and will link them to the international community.

Creative and new financial constructions for capacity building, faculty development in BOP markets, student tuition fees, and content development are all part of a new business model for reaching out to students in developing countries. The Maastricht School of Management has shown that this can be done in a manner that has been advantageous to the students and to the school.

Ronald Tuninga
Director, Dean, and Professor of International Business and Marketing at the Maastricht School of Management and Professor of International Management at the Open University of the Netherlands

Acumen Fund

Acumen Fund has great respect for Dr. Prahalad's work on serving people at the Bottom of the Pyramid through market-based approaches. Indeed, our work to bring affordable, quality services to low-income people in the developing world has resulted in the creation of more than 23,000 jobs and enabled tens of millions to avail themselves of the safe water, health care, housing, and energy they need to improve their lives. We agree with Dr. Prahalad that choice is where dignity starts and that the world will change only when we view truly low-income individuals as full participants in their local economies and communities, as producers and consumers, rather than as passive recipients of charity. I'm thrilled to read the updated version of this important book.

Jacqueline Novogratz
CEO
Acumen Fund

PART IV

Case Studies and CEO Comments

- Jaipur Rugs: Connecting Rural India to Global Markets (New)
- Casas Bahia: Retail for the Poor
- CEMEX: Homes for the Poor
- Hindustan Unilever: Lifebuoy Soap
- Hindustan Unilever: Iodized Salt (Annapurna Salt)
- Jaipur Foot: Prosthetics for the Poor
- Aravind Eye Care: The Most Precious Gift
- ICICI: Financial Services for the Poor
- ITC e-Choupal: Technology for the Poor
- Voxiva: Health Alerts for All
- E+Co: Energy for Everyone

In this section, we present detailed case studies of successful innovations at the BOP. These cases span a wide range of industries—health care, financial services, housing, energy, personal care, and agriculture. Each case details innovations in business models. They represent a wide variety of country settings: Peru, Brazil, Mexico, and India.

Global firms, large domestic firms, nongovernmental organizations (NGOs), and startups are all represented. This collection of cases is intended to demonstrate that the opportunities for innovation at the BOP are not limited to a locale, an industry, or a certain type of business entity.

These studies of innovation were written with three goals in mind. First, we want to give the reader enough information to make an assessment of how to innovate at the BOP. The studies, therefore, are rich in detail. Second, we want to demonstrate that there is no mystery to unlocking the potential of these markets. It requires vision, leadership, a new perspective, and a new approach. Finally, we want you to know the potential of this opportunity—how big it is. Each one of these innovations can be turned into a global opportunity. As you read these studies, think of the people behind the studies, their motivations, the innovations that allowed them to create new markets, the obstacles they had to face (and in some cases continue to face), and the social transformation to which they have contributed. Each case represents a "win–win" scenario: a win for the BOP consumer as well as for the firm. The relationship between the consumer and the firm at the BOP market is symbiotic. They co-create value.

New to This Edition

Jaipur Rugs is a new case study. For all others, which were part of the original version of the book, we have an update written by the CEOs of the companies/projects. These leaders and innovators at the BOP, in varied voices and styles, confirm the sustainability of these innovations. In fact, all of them have grown and moved beyond the original experiment. These updates reassert the basic premise of the book: It is possible to construct a "win-win" solution and market-based solutions can enhance the lives of those at the bottom of the pyramid.

Videos

The CD with the videos comes with this book. You can also download, for free, the videos at the following Web site: **www.whartonsp.com/Prahalad**

Jaipur Rugs: Connecting Rural India to Global Markets

Introduction

The Jaipur Rugs case explores how a company can benefit the poor by connecting them with global markets. Jaipur Rugs makes this connection by building and orchestrating a global supply chain on a massive scale—one focused on developing human capability and skills at the grassroots level, providing steady incomes for rural men and women in the most depressed parts of India and connecting them with markets of the rich, such as the United States. Thousands of independent workers are organized to produce consistently a very high quality product, on a complex decentralized basis through a system of organization that is unique. The company not only uses traditional weavers but also teaches, in remarkably short time, the craft to people who do not have a tradition of weaving. Raw materials are sourced from around the world, processed into rugs with traditional and new designs in rural India while maintaining quality control of end products. Jaipur Rugs provides a unique and dynamic example of how a profitable commercial connection between the poor and the rich—across the world—can be done.

The Grassroots of a Global Supply Chain

Figure 1 The Ali family at home in Sonbhadra district, Uttar Pradesh.

Mr. Sakir Ali was a weaver in Sonbhadra district, who had been working directly for Jaipur Rugs since 2006. Within his first 1.5 years of working for Jaipur Rugs, he bought two new double looms and said that he earned more income than he did previously when he worked for a middleman. His wife and two daughters were trained by Jaipur Rugs Foundation. He was happy that his two daughters were weaving because they could earn money in the home without having to work in the fields. His wife also said that she was happy because she could earn money for her family and work beside her two daughters.

The rugs made by Sakir Ali, his family, and thousands of people like them may wind up in a living room of a million dollar home in New York or Los Angeles or gracing a Soho loft in London. Such is the nature of Jaipur Rugs' knack for tapping the skills of people on the low end of the income scale to create a quality handmade product marketed to people at the opposite end of the income spectrum.

Company History and Description

Nand Kishore (N.K.) Chaudhary grew up in a small town in Rajasthan, a state in northwestern India. After graduating from the University of Rajasthan, Chaudhary began his career in his family's shoe shop. However, he wanted to do something on his own and heard that high-quality rug weaving was in demand. He bought two looms and installed them in his home and fell in love with the weaving business. He quickly learned the technical aspects of weaving from local weavers and expanded his business, adding six more looms in his house, and then more looms in six nearby villages.

Chaudhary's entrepreneurial drive ultimately led him to Jaipur, the capital of Rajasthan, to pursue a career in the rug export business. Chaudhary and his brother started exporting rugs in 1986. Both brothers remained in the rug industry but split up their business interests in 1999, and after several company name changes, Chaudhary registered his export company under the name of Jaipur Rugs in 2006.[1]

By 2008, Jaipur Rugs was the largest manufacturer and exporter of Indian hand-knotted rugs, with fiscal year revenue of USD $21.1M.[2] It was a profitable and fast-growing company, with a compound annual growth rate of 38 percent from 2005–2008. Jaipur Rugs produces handmade area rugs, including the hand-knotted, hand-tufted, and flat woven styles. The company prides itself on the design and quality of its finished products.

Jaipur Rugs operates with the help of a complex web of human resources:

Approximately 300 direct, full-time employees:

- 7 family members
- 226 headquarters employees
- 70 regional branch office staff, including 40 area commanders

Approximately 40,000 contractors (indirect employees):

- 28,000 weavers
- 12,000 other laborers involved in the manufacturing process

The Ecosystem of Jaipur Rugs

The Jaipur Rugs operation is divided into four different entities: Jaipur Rugs Company, Jaipur Rugs Incorporated, Bhoomika Wools, and Jaipur Rugs Foundation. All entities are held accountable by a member of Chaudhary's immediate family.

The coördination of activities across multiple legal entities gives Jaipur Rugs

- Access, but not ownership, to specific skills
- Influence, but not control, over key processes
- Decentralization of investment

Figure 2 is a diagram of the various Jaipur Rugs entities and how they interact:[3]

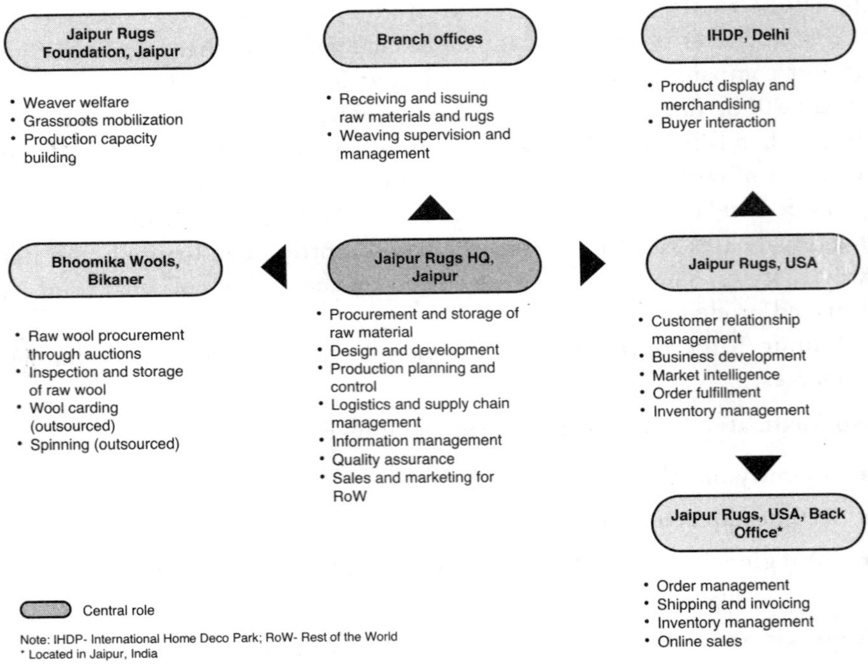

Figure 2 Diagram of Jaipur Rugs entities.

Jaipur Rugs Company (JRC)

JRC handles all the operations from raw material procurement to final sale for every market except the United States.[4] JRC is run by N.K. Chaudhary (CEO) and his eldest son, Yogesh (director). In addition to the JRC headquarters in Jaipur and a showroom for final products in International Home Deco Park (IHDP) in Delhi, there are 22 branch offices throughout northern and western India.

Jaipur Rugs, Incorporated (JRI)

JRI, headquartered in Atlanta, Georgia, handles distribution, marketing, and sales for the United States. JRI is run by Chaudhary's two eldest daughters—CEO Asha Chaudhary and COO Archana Chaudhary. As of July, 2008, the company employed 17 people, mostly in sales positions.

Bhoomika Wools

Bhoomika Wools facilitates the wool acquisition process solely for Jaipur Rugs. Bhoomika Wools is run by Chaudhary's brother-in-law, Navratan Saraf.

Jaipur Rugs Foundation (JRF)

Jaipur Rugs Foundation is a non-profit organization established in 2004 to encourage grassroots mobilization of weavers and to improve the welfare of the company's weavers and their families. In 2008, the Foundation was run by Chaudhary, with five employees based in the Jaipur Rugs headquarters and twelve field employees working with the communities where Jaipur Rugs has operations.

Business System Building Blocks

Four foundational building blocks allow Jaipur Rugs to profitably influence quality and rapidly adjust to marketplace demands, while executing the extremely complex process of handing over raw materials to an autonomous group of individual contractors.

Deeply Rooted Relationships

Chaudhary built Jaipur Rugs by emphasizing family ties and strong personal loyalties. This foundation allows Jaipur Rugs to efficiently operate a highly decentralized manufacturing and logistics system. Besides the five Chaudhary children that head up different areas of the company, many of the area commanders and entrepreneurs who own the businesses that are key parts of the production processes got their start as weavers for Chaudhary.

By treating his workers fairly, Chaudhary creates a feeling of loyalty, which, combined with investments in logistics and quality control systems, and even personalized training in some cases, positively affects the quality of all the key production processes that are outsourced to virtual employees.

Driven by Social Values

The company's social values are reflected in its commitment to provide the following:

- **Competitive wages**—Wages paid by the company give people options to have a better quality of life than the alternative work available in villages.
- **Investment in skills training**—The main activities of the Jaipur Rugs Foundation are to recruit and train new weavers for the company. Because of the social impact that Jaipur Rugs has on many regions of the country, the government subsidizes the cost of looms and training in certain regions.
- **Access to healthcare and education**—The Jaipur Rugs Foundation leverages alliances with other NGOs that provide health care and education to the weavers.
- **Opportunities for aspiring entrepreneurs**—When he recognizes contractors who do good work and have the right attitude, Chaudhary believes in giving them loans so that they can become key links in the overall production process. As a result of his recognition of their talents, many contractors see their incomes, social standing, and capabilities multiply.

Because Jaipur Rugs demonstrates strong social values, its contractors recognize the difference in working for Jaipur Rugs versus other companies. This recognition elevates the relationship between contractors and the company from a contractual agreement to one of multifaceted value for both. These strong relationships help Jaipur Rugs influence the quality of its products, despite utilizing such a highly decentralized production process.

Reducing Capital Intensity

Jaipur Rugs benefits from a business model focused on converting fixed costs into variable costs, which allows them significant flexibility:

- **Work is decentralized**—Rug production is done on a "pay for performance" basis, depending on the quality and the quantity produced. As a result, the company's largest costs—labor and raw material—are variable.
- **Investment is decentralized**—By using contractors for its manufacturing operations, Jaipur Rugs reduces its capital needs by not owning the key manufacturing assets, such as the dyeing, washing, machine carding, machine spinning operations, and most weaving looms.
- **Management influence over key functions is highly leveraged**—The company directly employs only 300 people, yet influences 40,000 artisans who act as entrepreneurs and contractors.

Technical Architecture

The company's technical architecture combines information technology (IT) infrastructure, human interaction, loyalty, and training. Jaipur Rugs' investment in IT infrastructure includes an Enterprise Resource Planning (ERP) system to optimize its geographically diverse supply chain, allow for the continuity of work, institutionalize quality control, and achieve scale. The company also focuses on creating well-designed communications networks to deliver raw materials, communicate with weavers, and track the progress of work in remote villages with no electricity. These communications networks are used by the company's branch office staff to effectively manage a highly human capital-intensive process.

One of the company's most interesting processes is the design and creation of the build sheets, known as "maps." The maps give the weavers, who generally have minimal education, easily understandable instructions on where to put each strand of different colored yarn. Because of the way the maps are designed, a weaver essentially needs no training to produce a new design on a given loom. This flexibility in Jaipur Rugs' business model means the company can prototype new designs very cheaply, and that its 28,000 weavers can respond fairly quickly to changing customer preferences and business needs.

Management Team

N.K. Chaudhary, Chairman

Figure 3 Mr. N.K. Chaudhary

At age 11, Chaudhary knew he would do something unique for society, beyond just working in business. However, at that time, he had no idea about the role his business would play for his eventual 40,000 direct and indirect employees, and for the rest of Indian society.

Chaudhary's philosophy about what successful businesses means for society evolved over the years, and includes empowering others, promoting entrepreneurship, and constant learning. Chaudhary described:

> There is a need to transfer more and more ownership to the grassroots level. The business is scaling up each year. We want to develop more good leaders who can make their own right decisions. They can take care of profits and take care of society. Profits mean more efficiency, and better systems.

Villagers often refer to Chaudhary as the Gandhi of the rug industry, an honor which he considers the highest form of respect he can receive.

Family

All five of Chaudhary's children chose to work within the family business, and they held many of the senior-level management positions within the company. Table 1 depicts each of their roles within the company.

Table 1 Chaudhary Children's Roles Within Jaipur Rugs

Name of Chaudhary Child, in Order of Age	Role Within Business	Educational Background
Asha	CEO, JRI	Bachelor's degree from Emory University
Archana	COO, JRI	Bachelor's degree from North Carolina State University
Kavita	Design Director, JRC	BA in Textiles from the Illinois Institute of Art
Yogesh	Wholetime Director, JRC	Two years at Boston College
Nitesh	Trainee, Jaipur Rugs. Nitesh planned to get one year of experience with the company before going to college.	Plans to attend Babson University in 2009

Field Management

Three types of employees work outside of the headquarters, either in one of the 22 branch offices, or in the field: branch managers, area commanders, and Jaipur Rugs Foundation (JRF) motivators:

- **Branch Managers**—Each of the 22 branch offices has one branch manager, most of whom were promoted from weaving and have been with the company for an average of 15 years. The minimum salary of a branch manager is Rs 8,000 per month (USD $174),[5] and as high as Rs 50,000 per month (USD $1,087), based on experience.
- **Area Commanders**—Responsible for maintaining communication with the weavers in a given area. In 2008, there were 40 area commanders, each responsible for an average of 200 looms.[6] Area commanders generally report to a branch manager, but in some cases, the area commanders doubled as branch managers.[7] The minimum salary for an area commander was Rs 5,000 per month (USD $109).

- **JRF Motivators**—Responsible for recruiting weavers; managing weaver training; educating weavers on various government schemes that provide health insurance, education, loans, etc.; and maintaining good relationships with the weavers and their families. One Jaipur Rugs Foundation motivator typically covers each branch region. A motivator earns between Rs 4,000–Rs 10,000 per month (USD $87–USD $217).

Production

The Jaipur Rugs production process is a complex system that begins with global sourcing of raw materials and ends with worldwide distribution of the finished products. In between, the rugs are produced by 28,000 rural artisans across seven states in north and west India, supported by more than 12,000 additional production workers and a comprehensive system of quality control and logistics.[8]

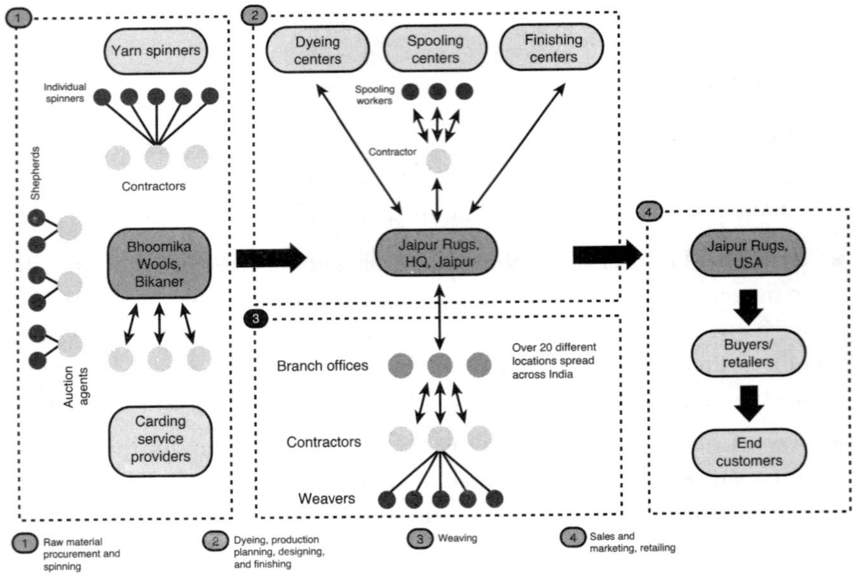

Figure 4 The Jaipur Rugs supply chain.

Table 2 provides a snapshot of the approximately 40,000 contractors, who contributed to the production of the rugs. The average income of these workers is compared to similar alternative employment that may be available to them. However, Jaipur Rugs contractors are ensured a steady income from Jaipur Rugs in contrast to the seasonality of many other employment options, and many earn additional income from seasonal agricultural work.

Table 2 Snapshot of 40,000 Contractors[9]

Production Activity	# of Workers	Average Monthly Income	Alternative Employment	Average Monthly Income from Alternative Employment
Initial sorting of raw wool	50-60	Rs 1050	Agriculture, Government schemes	Rs 300*
Raw wool washing	15-20	Rs 2500–3000	Work in similar factories	Rs 3000
Carding—machine	60	Rs 3000–4000	Salesperson	Rs 3000–4000
Carding—hand	Included in numbers for hand spinning	Rs 1100–1300	Agriculture, Livestock; Government schemes for rural employment	Rs 300
Spinning—machine	50-60	Rs 2500–3000	Work in similar factories	Rs 3000
Spinning—hand	10,000-12,000	Rs 1100–1300	Agriculture, Livestock; Government schemes for rural employment	Rs 300
Yarn washing	Included in raw wool washing	Rs 2500–3000	Work in similar factories	Rs 3000
Dyeing	35	Rs 3,000–Rs 20,000, depending on skills—Masters are the highest paid	Unskilled/ skilled labor in factory	Minimum Rs 3,000 for unskilled labor
Opening	200	Rs 1800	Jewelry making (in Sarai Bawri village)	Rs 1200–1400
Weaving	28,000	Rs 1300–3000	Handicraft making and agriculture	Handicraft: Rs 1200; Agriculture: Rs 300

Table 2 continued

Production Activity	# of Workers	Average Monthly Income	Alternative Employment	Average Monthly Income from Alternative Employment
Finishing	500	Regular workers: Rs 3000-3500 / Washers: Rs 6000	Similar work with other finishing centers/factories	Rs 3000
Transportation	40-50 (direct and indirect employees)	Rs 1155—up to Rs 8000 for company drivers	Similar transportation work	Rs 1155

* Agricultural work is seasonal, so the average monthly income figure has been normalized per annum.

Raw Materials Sourcing

The primary raw materials required by Jaipur Rugs Company are wool and silk. The wool is primarily sourced by partner company, Bhoomika Wools. Table 3 gives total procurement of wool and silk for FY 2007–2008.

Table 3 Procurement of Wool and Silk (Kgs) for Fiscal Year 2007–2008[10]

Company	Raw Wool Indian	Raw Wool Imported	Silk Indian	Silk Imported
JRC	0	347,383	2143	40,415
Bhoomika	746,759	195,307	0	0

Wool Processing

There are a number of steps involved in preparing the raw wool to be put on the looms for weaving, and these steps are highly decentralized. All of the work is outsourced, either by Bhoomika Wools or by Jaipur Rugs. Bhoomika Wools is responsible for all of the wool processing steps from procurement through transport to Jaipur for dyeing. By outsourcing all of these steps, Bhoomika is able to convert almost all of its costs into variable costs and dramatically decrease its fixed costs—the only fixed costs are Chaudhary's brother-in-law, Navratan Saraf's salary and the warehouse units. Jaipur Rugs is responsible for the remaining wool processing steps of dyeing and opening, both of which are also outsourced to partner companies.

Figure 5 Cleaning and sorting raw wool.

Raw Wool Cleaning, Sorting, and Blending

Immediately after the wool is purchased from the auction, it is taken to one of Bhoomika Wools' seven warehouses in Bikaner for sorting, blending, and storage. The women who work at these warehouses are paid on the basis of output.

Carding

Figure 6 Brush used for hand carding.

Carding is a process of brushing raw wool to prepare it for spinning. During the carding process, the fibers are separated, unwanted matter falls out, and then fibers align together. Although the process can be done by hand or by machine, Jaipur Rugs outsources the vast majority of their wool to an external machine carding company. However, hand-carded wool makes the best quality and is actually required for a rug to be "real hand spun."

For several years, Jaipur Rugs was the only company in India that used hand-carded wool, but by 2008, several other Indian companies had introduced some production with hand-carded wool. In 2008, Jaipur Rugs used hand-carded wool for 7 percent of its rugs, although the demand for hand-carded wool rugs was significantly higher. The Jaipur Rugs Foundation is addressing this supply-side constraint by trying to partner with local NGOs in Bikaner to mobilize more women to do hand carding. Jaipur Rugs is considering increasing the price paid for hand carding to give more women an incentive to do this activity. A small sub-set of the women who do the hand spinning also do the hand carding. Women earned Rs 19 per Kg (USD $0.41) for spinning and Rs 38 per Kg (USD $0.82) for carding and spinning, which takes double the time.

Spinning

After the wool has been carded, it is ready for spinning. In fiscal year 2007–2008, 57 percent of the wool spun by Jaipur Rugs was hand spun and 43 percent was machine spun.[11] The hand-spun wool was produced by women in villages near Bikaner—according to Chaudhary, much of the quality is lost with machine spinning. The spinners employed by Bhoomika Wools come mostly from very low castes and Muslim communities with a tradition of textile production. High-quality rugs require yarn of consistent thickness, and this is achieved by a good spinning technique. Chaudhary believes that the quality of the yarn depends largely on the passion and dedication of the spinners. He aims to develop women's groups among the spinners so they can discuss their problems—similar to the micro finance self-help group model. He believes that the biggest problem in the rural areas, such as the ones outside of Bikaner, is mindset. If you give people a purpose and help them understand the needs of the business and how they could contribute, you change their attitudes and uplift them.

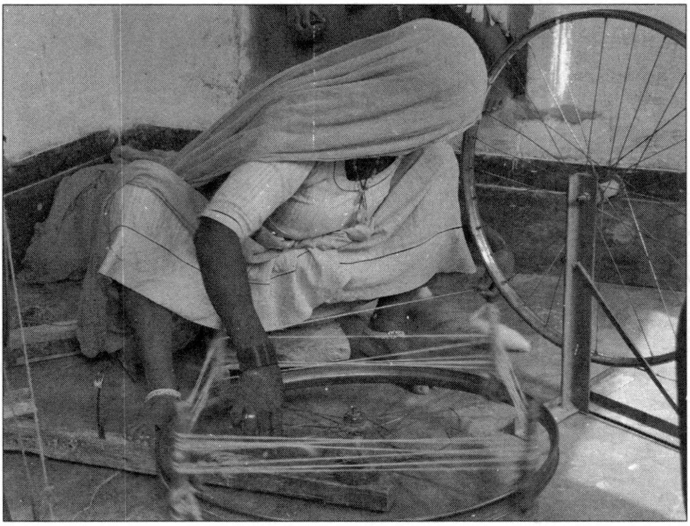

Figure 7 Hand spinning raw wool into hank.

It takes approximately one hour to spin one kilogram (Kg) of wool, for which a spinner is paid Rs 19 (USD $0.41). The spinner is required to deliver the spun wool to Bhoomika Wools in hanks—hank is a unit of yarn that is in a coiled form. The spinners walk to the closest

Bhoomika Wools branch office every other day to deliver a completed five to seven Kgs of spun wool (two days worth of spun wool) and pick up a new batch of raw wool. They are paid once or twice a month in cash by the branch manager, who is also responsible for checking the quality of the delivered yarn. Once a week, the hanks of wool are transported from the branch offices to the Bikaner warehouses by truck. In addition to spinning, the women usually earn other income from seasonal agricultural work.

Dyeing

In the early years, all hanks of wool yarn were sent from Bikaner to Jaipur for dyeing. To improve efficiency and meet the growing requirements for dyeing, in 2008 Jaipur Rugs established a relationship with a dyeing house 774 Km away in Bhadohi (in the central Indian state of Uttar Pradesh—the highest volume production region for Jaipur Rugs), so that some of the undyed yarn could be sent directly from Bikaner for dyeing, and then on to the weavers in this region. The dyeing process takes an average of two to three days, including transportation to and from the Jaipur Rugs office.

Opening

Opening is the process of making spindles from the hanks of dyed yarn. This process is required for both wool and silk. At Jaipur Rugs, the yarn is transported daily from the dyeing centers to the Jaipur Rugs headquarters to one of five opening centers. The company plans to make this process more efficient by sending the yarn directly from the dyeing centers to the opening centers.

One of the opening centers is in Sarai Bawri village, just north of Jaipur. As of May, 2008 there were approximately 140 women working at the Sarai Bawra Opening Center, earning a monthly average income of Rs 1800 (USD $40). Previously some of the women had made jewelry and some had been unemployed. Surendra Kumar Mahawar, who runs the center, trained the women and gave them each an opening machine free of charge, at a cost to him of Rs 300 (USD $6.50) per machine. Each worker can open approximately 15–20 Kgs of yarn per day. The women say they have more money to spend on their family's food and clothes and that they enjoy the opening work, primarily because it can be done in their own homes.

Weaving Locations

After the yarn has been made into spindles, it is kept in storage at the Jaipur Rugs office until it is transported (bundled in a bag with the design map) to one of the 7,500 looms across seven states in north and west India. As of June 2008, Jaipur Rugs had 22 branch offices in seven states. Production centers were concentrated primarily in three states with different locations producing specific products. The states were: Gujarat, Uttar Pradesh, and Rajasthan. From 2007 to 2008, four new "development" states had been added—states that do not have a tradition of rug weaving—but had very low initial production rates: Nagaland, Jharkhand, Orissa, and Bihar. Additionally, production was planned to begin in three more states by 2009: West Bengal, Arunachal Pradesh, and Maharashtra.

With very few exceptions, the artisans work in their own villages, either in their own home or in a neighboring home. In stark contrast to most employment opportunities in rural India, Jaipur Rugs provides steady, year-round income for its weavers. The 7,500 looms are always in use—as soon as a finished rug comes off the loom, the materials for a new rug are installed.

Finishing

After coming off the loom, all rugs are transported to one of four finishing centers in Jaipur, each of which is an independent entity but exclusively services Jaipur Rugs. At the finishing centers, techniques are employed to fix mistakes and accentuate highlights of the design. In addition, final cleaning and inspection takes place before the rug is prepared for export.

Weaver Engagement Models

Jaipur Rugs uses a number of different models to engage with weavers. The primary models include: direct relationships with weavers, indirect relationships with weavers through entrepreneurs, and indirect relationships with weavers through middlemen. In addition, there are several outsourcing partnerships. Table 4 provides data on the three primary models of engagement with weavers.

Table 4 Primary Weaver Engagement Models for Jaipur Rugs[12, 13]

Mode of Employment	# of Weavers	% of Weavers	Average Monthly Income (Rs)	Average Monthly Income (USD)
Direct contract with JRC	15,170	55%	1870–2970	40.70–64.50
Indirect via Entrepreneur	6,900	25%	1760–2800	38.30–61.00
Indirect via Middleman	5,500	20%	1320–1980	28.60–43.10

Independent Weavers

Jaipur Rugs is changing the traditional model of middleman-owned looms to enable weavers to own their own looms. They support weavers to obtain subsidies from the government that help finance 50 to 75 percent of the cost of the looms in some regions. For example, Jaipur Rugs began working in Sonbhadra district (in the Mirzapur region) in 2006. In this district, a number of weavers had transitioned from working on looms owned by middlemen to purchasing their own looms. It cost Rs 7000–8000 (USD $152–USD $174) for a locally-made loom, and Rs 16,000–20,000 (USD $348–USD $435) for a higher-quality loom. In this region, it is common to see double looms on which two sumak rugs can be made at the same time. Weavers can start with just half the loom at a cost of Rs 3000–4000 (USD $65–USD $87) and upgrade later to the full double loom. In some cases, the company loans looms to weavers until the weavers gain enough credibility to get a monetary loan to purchase their own looms.

Entrepreneurs

The entrepreneurs who work with Jaipur Rugs own multiple looms and employ local villagers to weave rugs on their looms. For instance, Rohitari is an entrepreneur in Sonbhadra district, who used to be a weaver. He used his own resources to purchase three looms and as of May, 2008, he employed 12 people. He produces rugs exclusively for Jaipur Rugs and uses the revenues to pay back his loom loans and reinvest in his business, which he plans to continue to expand.

MIDDLEMEN

Middlemen have historically been entrenched in India's rug industry, depriving artisans of their deserved income. A major goal of the Jaipur Rugs business model is to remove the middlemen to give more income to the weaver, either through direct relationships with weavers or through entrepreneurs. The main differences between entrepreneurs and middlemen is that entrepreneurs usually start out as weavers (and some continue to weave—middlemen generally do not weave) and are generally more closely aligned with the company's philosophy, passing due credit onto the weavers who work on their looms.

While Jaipur Rugs works hard to develop direct relationships with weavers who had historically worked for middlemen, in 2008 the company still relied on middlemen to reach approximately 20 percent of their weavers. On the outskirts of Bhadohi, a hand-tufted rug factory was one of the biggest middlemen that Jaipur Rugs worked with. This factory employed 500 male migrant workers from rural areas in Uttar Pradesh, Orissa, Bengal, and Bihar, where there are very few employment opportunities. All of the workers lived on the factory compound. Weavers were paid every 15 days at the rate of Rs 150 per square yard, and they could make 0.75–1.0 square yards per day for an average of Rs 2900 (USD $63) per month. The rug washers could earn up to twice as much because the work was physically strenuous. These incomes are significantly higher than those stated for weavers working via middlemen in the table at the top of this section, and the primary reason for the discrepancy is that hand-tufted rugs combine good margins with low production times.

In 2008, 50 percent of the factory's business came from Jaipur Rugs, and the owner hoped this percentage would continue to increase. The owner commended Jaipur Rugs for being very organized, for providing timely deliveries of raw materials and payments, and for understanding his business' problems and helping to solve them. He communicates with the local Jaipur Rugs area commanders every day, and communicates frequently with Chaudhary and his daughter Asha (CEO of Jaipur Rugs, Incorporated in the U.S.).

Jaipur Rugs is developing production areas in the very poor neighboring states (Bihar, Jharkhand, and Orissa) where many of the aforementioned factory's employees come from. These states traditionally have large numbers of migrant laborers who leave home because of the dearth of employment opportunities. Jaipur Rugs hopes that, in time, the expansion efforts into these areas will create new income generation opportunities that allow people to have employment options other than migration.

OUTSOURCING PARTNERS

In 2008, Jaipur Rugs was working with seven outsourcing partners for rug manufacturing to diversify its offerings in the market and align its product portfolio with market needs. Jaipur Rugs provides only the design maps—the raw material procurement, production, and finishing is handled by the partner company.

Jaipur Rugs started working with one outsourcing partner in 2007 as a means to begin sales of Indo-Tibetan rugs. Jaipur Rugs developed an ecosystem for Indo-Tibetan Rugs that ensured superior product quality and the integrity of its business model. Indo-Tibetan rugs were quick and easy to weave—a low-quality 8'x10' rug took 7–10 days to make, while a high-quality 8'x10' rug took 15-20 days (depending on the number of knots per square inch).

In 2008, Jaipur Rugs sourced 12,000–15,000 square feet of rug per month from this partner. The outsourcing partner stated that they liked working with Jaipur Rugs because it was more organized and professional than any other of the dozen companies with whom they worked.

Technical Architecture

Jaipur Rugs uses a combination of human and electronic networks and logistics infrastructure to institutionalize quality and maintain influence over its geographically dispersed employees, customers, and suppliers.

Production Process Logistics

Each rug produced by Jaipur Rugs passes through a geographically dispersed and complex supply chain. To manage this supply chain, the company uses both standardized and nonstandardized processes for assignment and movement of raw materials, works in progress, and finished goods.

Rug orders are received via fax, e-mail, or phone, and the production process begins after an order is generated by the Production Department. Next, the Central Control Room acts as an interface between the

Production and Design departments. Employees in the Central Control Room determine if a production order is for a design with an available, reusable map; a design that requires no modification but does require map printing; or a design that needs modifications such as resizing or recoloring. The Design Department, run by Chaudhary's daughter Kavita, is where the design and size is finalized, and the map is created.

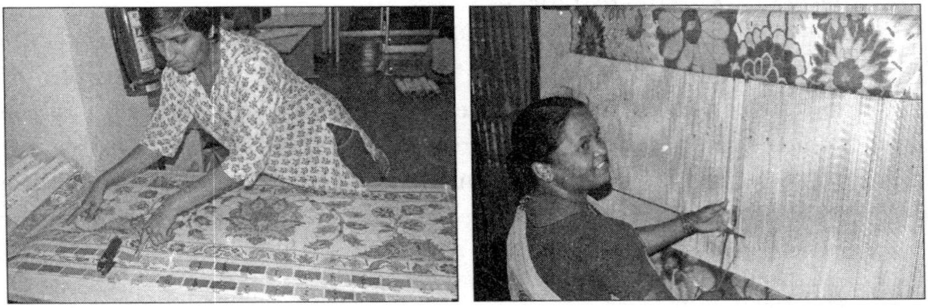

Figure 8 Left, Kavita Chaudhary explains the map production process. Right, a weaver making an Indo-Tibetan style rug keeps the map hung above her loom.

MAP PRODUCTION PROCESS

Creating the map is a human-capital intensive process. First, a Raw Material Card is matched with a design, printed, cut, then laminated for durability and pasted together. On the printout, instructions are handwritten to tell the weavers where to start weaving, and yarn samples are stapled to help avoid errors in color selection. Quality control is built into the process through several inspection points along the way. During an eight-hour day, approximately 120 maps are processed.

MATERIAL LOGISTICS

The Stores Department is responsible for stocking and moving raw material and works in progress. Staff in the Stores Department communicate with Design Department staff to find out what maps are in the pipeline, and for each new rug, they are responsible for stuffing a bag of materials to go to the weaver. The contents of each bag include a Raw Material Card, a map, and bundles of dyed yarn. The bags first go to the branch office and then ultimately to the weaver.

After weaving is completed, the Carpet Receiving Department receives the woven rug, leftover materials (if any), and the map. The rugs are sent to a finishing center, and the map is stored in the Design Department's Map Storage Room for future use. After finished rugs are received at the headquarters, the Shipping & Export Documentation Department is responsible for the shipping processes and making sure the products arrive to customers.

One difference between Jaipur Rugs and its competitors that the weavers say they appreciate is that the weavers are not responsible for picking up the raw materials and delivering back the woven rugs to the branch office. The Jaipur Rugs area commanders are responsible for ensuring that the bags of maps and materials are delivered from the branch office to the weavers' village, which saves the weaver significant time and money in transportation.

Weaver-to-Rug Matching Process

To match a rug order with one of the company's 28,000 weavers, the Production Department first determines the approximate geographic area in which the rug will be made (based on the type of rug and the quality required). Once the area is determined, the Production Department calls the area commanders from the nearest branch office to assign a weaver based on their loom availability, skill level, and weaving speed. Each area commander is responsible for knowing the skill level and speed of the weavers to which they are assigned. This knowledge is currently not formally recorded, although in the future the company hopes to incorporate this information into their internal computer systems.

Institutionalizing Quality

> *The main strength of the company is Mr. Chaudhary's strong technical knowledge. He knows how to make a good rug, whereas his competitors just buy raw materials and distribute to middlemen without knowledge.*
>
> –Deepak Sharma, Kanvic

It is this knowledge that Chaudhary uses to produce high-quality rugs in a supply chain with up to 30 product handovers. Because the company's overall goal is to decentralize many of the production processes without losing quality, quality control checks and standards are implemented at every step, from raw materials, to production, and to finishing. The avenues for feedback and enforcement throughout the production process are discussed next.

Inspection of Raw Material

Quality control staff at Jaipur Rugs headquarters check the counts and blends of raw wool. Cotton yarn, used for the rug foundation on the loom, is checked for strength and length. Both cotton yarn and silk are tested in the in-house lab.

Ensuring Quality of Wool after Spinning and Dyeing

Quality of hand-spun yarn is inspected at the Bhoomika Wools branch office (the point of collection), and the spinner receives immediate feedback. If yarn is rejected because it is too thick, it is returned to the spinner to be made thinner. If the yarn is too thin, it is carded again and re-spun. The first time that a spinner has a problem with quality, she is paid in full and educated by the branch manager about the importance of a high-quality product. If the spinner repeats the quality problem a second or third time, she is paid in full but does not receive new raw material.

Jaipur Rugs doesn't formally collect data on the number of quality issues related to spinning, but estimates rejections at 5 percent. Chaudhary said, "When we start up hand spinning in a new area, the number [rejected] depends on how long they have been working there. In the old areas, the number is almost nil—maybe one or two every month. In a new village, it may take some time."

After dyeing, the dyed yarn is checked at the Jaipur Rugs headquarters in the map section of the Design Department. There, the color either passes or fails. Figures from April–June 2008 from three key suppliers showed the rejection rate in dyeing between 7–10 percent.

Quality Control in the Weaving and Finishing Processes

The area commanders know how to weave, so they help correct and re-train the weavers during the weaving process if necessary. Once a rug comes off the loom, it is sent back to Jaipur Rugs headquarters for quality checking before being transported to the finishing center. At headquarters, inspectors in the Carpet Receiving area check for a variety of defects, including rug length and width in three different places on every rug.

To correct quality issues, the company occasionally brings weavers to the office for re-training, or they return the rug to the weaver. Based on data from April to June 2008, the percentage of unfinished rugs checked at headquarters and then returned to the weavers was 0.5 percent. This return rate is low considering the amount of decentralization in the weaving process. Reasons for the low return rate include the thoroughness of the quality control process and the fact that the most common quality problems can be repaired during the finishing process.

To ensure the quality of rugs through the finishing process, two Jaipur Rugs employees go to the finishing centers every day. Once a rug is returned back to Jaipur Rugs headquarters, the quality of the washing and repairing is checked. When necessary, finishing center representatives are called into the Jaipur Rugs headquarters to discuss quality issues with Jaipur Rugs management. Over a three-month period between April and June 2008, the percentage of rugs returned back to the finishing center was 4.6 percent (265 rugs out of total received 5742).

Future Changes to Quality Control and Enforcement

Jaipur Rugs wants to eliminate quality control checks of unfinished rugs at the headquarters and replace them with checks at the branch offices, requiring a greater amount of process consistency. They identified their first step as creating a standardized booklet for area commanders to record the status of each rug every time they visit a loom.

Achieving International Quality Standards

Jaipur Rugs management recognizes the importance of internationally recognized quality standards. In May 2008, Jaipur Rugs received ISO 9001:2000 certification as a way to help standardize the documentation of company processes. The company is also in the process of applying for ISO 14000 (an environmental audit) and SA8000 (a social audit) certification.

Information Technology

In anticipation of aggressive future growth, in 2005 the company decided to make a big investment in new IT architecture as a way to more easily tailor products to customer needs, track orders, manage inventory, and reduce order processing time. In order to move toward the goal of enabling its customers live access to all of its order information, and scale the business, Jaipur Rugs decided to purchase an ERP system. At the time, this kind of strategic investment in IT was uncommon among competitors in the Indian rug industry. ERP was being used at headquarters as of the beginning of 2008 and a full roll-out was planned for completion by 2009.

Human and Communications Networks

Despite the company's strategic investment in technology, in some areas where the company has weavers, there are no phone or Internet signals. The company uses its extensive network of branch offices and area commanders to visit regularly each loom and get progress updates.

Capacity Building and Social Issues

Jaipur Rugs is grounded in its commitment to the development of the rural communities in which it works, and to the cultivation of leaders throughout the organization. Chaudhary's philosophy on the role of business in society, discussed earlier, is the guiding force behind the company's strong social mission.

Promotion of Leadership and Entrepreneurship

Amongst Jaipur Rugs employees, its network of artisans, and the entrepreneurs who run the enterprises that support the production of the rugs, there are numerous examples of people who moved up the ranks into positions of leadership. Chaudhary believes in rewarding talent and this helps create a culture where people are motivated to work hard and be successful.

EXAMPLES OF UPWARD MOBILITY

- In 2008, the top 20-30 people in the field level of the company were earning Rs 15,000–30,000 (USD $325–USD $650) per month as quality controllers—20 years ago, they were weavers.[14]
- Mr. Rameswar, a branch manager in Gujarat, has worked for Chaudhary for 20 years. When he started, he was earning Rs 50 per

month, as a weaver. He was promoted from weaver, to map reader, to area commander, and finally to branch manager. In 2008, he earned Rs 50,000 (USD $1,087) per month. He was very happy with the progress he made and was particularly proud of the fact that all three of his children were receiving an education.

- Mr. Babu Singh, a finishing center owner, and Mr. Surendra Kumar Mahawar, an opening center owner, started as laborers in the rug industry and worked their way up the ladder to eventually run their own enterprises, employing 150–200 people each. Both men were supported by Chaudhary in their efforts to start their own enterprises.

LEADERSHIP DEVELOPMENT THROUGH EMPLOYEE INTERACTION

There are several activities within the Jaipur Rugs headquarters office, initiated by Chaudhary, to facilitate leadership development amongst employees:

- **Sunday night conversations**—Chaudhary spends one hour every Sunday night engaging in informal conversations with the approximately 50 employees who live at the Jaipur Rugs headquarters.[15] Chaudhary's goal is to teach the workers about the qualities of entrepreneurship and leadership while learning about the individual talents of the workers.
- **Book Share Program**—In 2007, Chaudhary established a library at the Jaipur Rugs headquarters, which houses 20–30 copies each of a handful of books with leadership, inspiration, and business management themes. The goal is to encourage groups of employees to read the same book simultaneously, and then share with each other what they learned and how those insights applied to the company.

Training

While training at the Jaipur Rugs corporate headquarters level is primarily informal, there are more formal training programs in place for weavers, particularly in new production areas where there is no tradition of rug weaving. All training is managed by Jaipur Rugs Foundation staff, and primarily conducted through an apprenticeship model. Master weavers, chosen as trainers by JRF staff, live at the training centers for the average six-month training period and are paid Rs 200 (USD $4.35) per day. Weavers-in-training are paid Rs 20–50 (~ USD $1) per day and receive free housing and food. However, the company faces many problems retaining trainers for consistent periods of time. It is common for trainers to run away from the training centers without warning, until they run out of money and subsequently return. In Sonbhadra District (Uttar Pradesh), the company is making a big effort to recruit and train female weavers in an area that has traditionally had male weavers. Jaipur Rug management believes that females are more tied to their household and village, and therefore less likely to leave for other employment opportunities.

Labor Practices

The company's official Social Accountability policy states:

> We provide all round development of all stakeholders with special emphasis on the economically and socially backward class of people of the society. We are committed to accomplish this by doing the following:
>
> - We are developing health and safety management for our stakeholders.
> - We very well know the rights of the employees and their freedom of association.
> - We do not discriminate people on any ground.
> - We provide fair remuneration on the basis of recognized job evaluation system.
> - We ensure that no child or forced labor exists in our company and with our suppliers.

The company has a clear policy of minimum working age for all weavers and employees. It conducts spot audits in the field to ensure policy implementation but sometimes finds it hard to enforce since carpet weaving is traditionally a family vocation and largely unsupervised in the context of the Jaipur Rugs business model. Jaipur Rugs wants to create a more rigorous system of contractors and weavers that do not recruit any child labor.

As of June 2008, the company was not a member of Rugmark or Care and Fair, two associations that work to prevent child labor in the rug industry. Jaipur Rugs adopted a different approach to deal with the issue of child labor by choosing to create the Jaipur Rugs Foundation, which deals with all aspects related to a weaver's life including education, healthcare, training, and awareness on social issues. However, the management team planned to get Rugmark certification in the near future for select products that were purchased by customers who were specifically requesting the Rugmark label.

Sales and Product Snapshot

Jaipur Rugs sells its products through a variety of channels across the globe. 98 percent of 2007 sales and 90 percent of 2008 sales were direct exports to either Jaipur Rugs, Incorporated (JRI) in Atlanta or other U.S. customers that Jaipur Rugs has had long-existing relationships with. 2 percent of 2007 sales and 10 percent of 2008 sales were through the Rest of World channel. This included direct exports to agents, representatives or direct retailers in Germany, Belgium, France, Netherlands, Japan, Australia, South Africa, Turkey, and the UK. As noted by the jump from 2 percent to 10 percent, the Rest of the World market for Jaipur Rugs is both growing and diversifying.

66.5 percent of Jaipur Rugs' sales were in the Hand Knotted product category, and within this, the 8/8 (64 knots) Wool was the most popular product at 22.5 percent of total sales. Hand Tufted rugs were 10 percent of Jaipur Rugs' total sales, and Flat Weave were 20 percent of total sales (~15 percent sumaks and ~5 percent dhurries). Approximately 3.5 percent of sales fell into the "other" category of custom made-to-order products. Below is a look at the cost build for some of Jaipur Rugs' most popular products:[16]

Table 5 Cost Build for Most Popular Jaipur Rugs Products[17]

Product Quality	8/8 W	10/14 W	10/14 WS	14/14 PS	Sumak-W	Tufted-W
Material	37%	25%	43%	31%	25%	43%
Labor	43%	52%	33%	39%	49%	35%
Overhead	16%	21%	13%	8%	19%	13%

Product Quality	8/8 W	10/14 W	10/14 WS	14/14 PS	Sumak-W	Tufted-W
Margin (average)	4%	2%	10%	22%	8%	9%

W = Wool; WS = Wool Silk; PS = Pure Silk
Material costs include cost of dyeing
Labor consists of weaving, finishing, map production
Overhead includes selling and distribution expenses
Figures represent percentage of selling price

Below is a chart detailing the life cycle of a typical Jaipur Rugs product from raw materials to end sale at a retail store. This example is for one 5'x8' (40 square feet) sumak rug and all costs and prices are quoted in terms of one square foot:

Table 6 Life Cycle Costs and Selling Prices of a Typical Jaipur Rugs Product[18]

Description of Process	Cost/Sq. Ft. (Rs)	Cost/Sq. Ft. (USD)	Capacity/ Time
Customer (large retailer) placed order with JRI			
JRI communicated order to JRC			
JRC forecasted and acquired raw materials (includes wool bought in Bikaner or imported from another country)	Rs. 22.71	0.49	15 days
JRC completed pre-production logistics (cleaned, prepared, and delivered wool to weaver with rug map)	Rs. 33.09	0.72	30 days
Weaving process	Rs. 100.5	2.18	32 days (@2 sq ft/day)
Post-production logistics (finished carpet returned to JRC and packed for shipment)	Rs. 26.62	0.58	3 days
Total JRC cost	Rs. 182.47	$3.98	
JRC wholesale price charged to JRI		$4.50	
Shipping cost (paid by customer)*		$0.25	45 days

Table 6 Life Cycle Costs and Selling Prices of a Typical Jaipur Rugs Product[18]

Description of Process	Cost/Sq. Ft. (Rs)	Cost/Sq. Ft. (USD)	Capacity/ Time
JRI wholesale price (charged by JRI to customer)**		$5.00	
Final retail price (charged by customer to end consumer)***		$12.50	

*Shipping cost is assumed to be freight and includes all customs fees, duties, and final transportation to customer. Shipments by air cost $1.5/Sq. ft. and are only for back-ordered products. JRI pays for the shipment in this case (approximately 15 percent of all shipments).

**This is the wholesale price. If a customer makes a purchase from the JRI warehouse rather than placing a bulk order, JRI will charge a higher price, typically $8/Sq. ft.

***A large retailer typically charges markup of 2.5x cost

According to this chart, the total cost of production for JRC was USD $3.98 per square foot, and JRC billed JRI USD $4.50 per square foot. Therefore, JRC's gross margin was USD $0.52 per square foot (11.5 percent). Since this is a special case of sumak rugs sold to a large retailer, the margins are low compared to higher-margin catalogue products and are compensated by the higher-volume orders these customers place. Jaipur Rugs makes it a priority to find ways to streamline processes and cut costs in order to keep up with the pricing demands of these large retailers.

Future Goals and Challenges

Jaipur Rugs aims to achieve $50 million in sales by 2011. To accomplish this, the company has outlined six strategic objectives:[19]

- **Keep the core, target more**—Jaipur Rugs aims to offer a full product line in area rugs, particularly in the hand-knotted arena where they have a specialized competency. As the company grows, there are plans to expand into other home furnishing products.
- **Country focus**—Continued focus on penetration of the U.S. market. Outside of the U.S., focus on seven high-potential countries: South Africa, Turkey, Italy, United Kingdom, United Arab Emirates, Japan, and Germany.

- **Capacity building**—Make design a core competence by attracting new talent and developing new creations based on customer insights. Furthermore, the company plans to build up organization capacity (in terms of production and suppliers) in alignment with this strategy.
- **Adaptive organization**—Redesign the organizational structure in order to better align activities with its respective functions.
- **Efficient supply chain**—Build distinct supply chains for low-end and high-end products by focusing on three key aspects: time, transparency, and trust.
- **Financial prudence**—Exercise financial prudence by monitoring important measures and building linkages to customers, employees, and processes. Some specific areas of focus include customer satisfaction, retention and profitability, employee training and development, and supply chain efficiency.

Dedicated and loyal people are needed throughout the organization: in middle management (to fill the gap between the family and the rest of the staff), in upper management (to start to plan for succession), and at the weaver and contractor level.

As Chaudhary grooms his son Yogesh to be his eventual successor as head of the company, he wants to make sure that Yogesh can replicate his model of building long-lasting relationships built on interdependence among employees and contractors at every level. He seeks ways to ensure that his son has a strong connection to people at the village level and believes that Yogesh should, at some point, live in a village two days per week.

Jaipur Rugs seeks to continually deepen relationships with and between its 40,000 virtual employees and its growing number of global customers. The company views the connection between its artisans and end-consumers as a key to sustainability and scalability. The challenge is to find the best ways to foster these connections.

EXTENDED VERSION AVAILABLE ONLINE

To read an extended version of this case study, visit **www.whartonsp.com/Prahalad**.

Endnotes

1. Jaipur Rugs overview presentation, May 12, 2008.
2. This figure represents combined sales revenue from Jaipur Rugs Company (India) and Jaipur Rugs, Incorporated (U.S.).
3. Jaipur Rugs overview presentation, May 12, 2008.
4. The terminology that Jaipur Rugs uses for sales in countries other than the U.S. is Rest of World (RoW) sales.
5. The exchange rate used throughout this case study is: USD $1.00 = Rs 46.
6. Jaipur Rugs overview presentation, May 12, 2008.
7. E-mail from Deepak Sharma, October 12, 2008.
8. Approximately 70 percent of the weavers are female, and 30 percent are male.
9. Data provided by Jaipur Rugs Company.
10. Ibid.
11. In fiscal year 2007-08, 385,135 kgs of wool were hand spun and 292,139 kgs were machine spun. The sum of these numbers is less than the total quantity of wool procured in 2007-08. All procured wool could not be spun into yarn because the company did not have enough hand-carding/spinning capacity and they met the demand for machine-spun wool.
12. Data provided by Jaipur Rugs Company.
13. The range in monthly incomes was in part due to the construction (quality) of the carpet produced and in part due to variations in output across weavers.
14. Quality controllers were either area commanders or branch managers.
15. These employees were laborers who came from other states and did not have any family with them in Jaipur.
16. Data provided by Jaipur Rugs Company.
17. Ibid.
18. Ibid.
19. Kanvic, Jaipur Rugs Strategic Plan 2008-11.

This case study was written by Jennifer Anderson, Nina Henning, Marion Ntiru, and Shara Senior under the supervision of Professor C.K. Prahalad. This case was developed solely as the basis for class discussion. Cases are not intended to serve as endorsements, sources of primary data, or illustrations of effective or ineffective management. Partial funding for this case was provided by the William Davidson Institute.

Casas Bahia: Retail for the Poor

Companies as savvy as Sears and Wal-Mart have sought to do business in Brazil but failed. Casas Bahia, though, successfully developed a model that serves the Bottom of the Pyramid in that country. The company succeeded in serving the large, lucrative market represented by the poor through innovation and the right financial approach.

Casas Bahia is a family-owned business started more than 50 years ago by Samuel Klein. After surviving two years in a Nazi concentration camp, Klein left his homeland in 1952 to start a new life in Brazil. To support his family, he sold blankets, bed linens, and bath towels door to door in São Caetano do Sul. That business transformed through the years into the largest retail chain in Brazil, selling electronics, appliances, and furniture. With a 4.2 billion real (the Brazilian currency) annual revenue, 330 stores, 10 million customers, and 20,000 employees, Casas Bahia has established itself as a successful and sustainable business serving Brazil's poor.

In 2003, the population in Brazil was 184 million, more than 80 percent of whom were at the Bottom of the Pyramid. The Bottom of the Pyramid, though, represents significant purchasing power in Brazil's economy (specifically, 41 percent of the total spending capacity). This R$124 billion accounts only for the formal reported economy. According to some estimates, the informal market in Brazil for the Bottom of the Pyramid reaches an additional 50 percent. In Brazil, 45 percent of total appliance and furniture spending is done by the Bottom of the Pyramid. Of particular interest is the high penetration of major appliances, such as television sets and refrigerators, at the Bottom of the Pyramid in

Brazil. It is not uncommon to find households with a television or refrigerator yet lacking basic infrastructure, such as toilets and telephone lines. Those at the Bottom of the Pyramid in Brazil spend based on their needs. In a tropical climate, a refrigerator is a necessity. Everyone, regardless of class, feels the need for entertainment. For the poor in Brazil, that comes in the form of television or radio.

> *The Bottom of the Pyramid, though, represents significant purchasing power in Brazil's economy (specifically, 41 percent of the total spending capacity).*

For the market to connect with the products, though, some innovation was needed because 70 percent of Casas Bahia customers have no formal or consistent income. These customers are primarily maids, cooks, independent street vendors, and construction workers whose average monthly income is a bare minimum wage, whereas many do not declare an income at all. Yet this large portion of the population still wanted and needed appliances. Casas Bahia took an innovative approach and devised a unique financing model to serve this market. Part of the solution is the now famous *carnê*, or passbook, that allows its customers to make small installment payments for the merchandise. Payment schedules range from 1 to 15 months. The passbook is available only at Casas Bahia stores, and every month consumers must enter a store to pay their bill. The method also maintains relationships with clients. Financed sales represent 90 percent of all sales; 6 percent are cash payments and 4 percent are via credit card.

> *Casas Bahia took an innovative approach and devised a unique financing model to serve this market.*

All customers who want to finance a purchase must submit to an SPC credit check. If the customer has a negative SPC score, Casas Bahia cannot complete the transaction until the customer resolves the credit problem. If the customer has a positive score, there are two alternatives. If the merchandise costs less than R$600, no proof of income is required; a valid permanent address suffices. Casas Bahia developed a proprietary system to evaluate prospective clients when merchandise costs more than R$600. Clients receive a credit limit based on total income, both formal and informal, occupation, and presumed expenses. This "scoring" process takes less than one minute. If the system approves the prospect, the salesperson can continue with the sale. Clients rejected by the system are directed to a credit analyst for further evaluation. This is where the importance of building a relationship is prominent. Based on training, the credit analyst asks a series of questions to determine a client's creditworthiness. The entire process typically is finished in 10 minutes or less.

The proprietary system that determines the creditworthiness of new clients also evaluates existing clients for potential new purchases. Based on the same factors previously noted, in addition to payment history, the system automatically produces a new credit limit. This ability is key in the cross-selling process. When the customer comes into the store to pay a monthly installment, the Casas Bahia salesperson sees that a new credit limit is available for the client. This salesperson has the opportunity to make a tailored cross-sale in the amount of the new credit limit.

Many outsiders argue that Casas Bahia simply exploits the poor and charges them exorbitant interest rates because the poor do not know any better. Quite the opposite seems to be true.

Many outsiders argue that Casas Bahia simply exploits the poor and charges them exorbitant interest rates because the poor do not know any better. Quite the opposite seems to be true. To maintain low default rates, salespeople must "teach" consumers to buy according to their budget. For instance, a customer enters the store and wants a new 27-inch television. A salesperson sits down with the customer (a Casas Bahia regional manager mentions you always discuss price sitting down so that it is harder for the customer to walk away) and discusses multiple payment options. If it becomes clear the customer cannot afford the 27-inch television, the salesperson works with the customer to "tweak" the dream to temporarily include a 20-inch TV.

The consumer education process is a key component in Casas Bahia's default level of just 8.5 percent. To put it into perspective, the average for the entire retail sector, which serves all income levels, is 6.5 percent. Casas Bahia's competition at the Bottom of the Pyramid has a default rate that reaches 16 percent.

The credit analyst plays a vital role in the success of Casas Bahia. Therefore, the company has devoted significant time and resources to train its credit analysts. With an average of 750,000 customers requesting financing every month (1.4 million in December), Casas Bahia's 800 credit analysts are the lynchpin, not only in maintaining a default rate below the industry average but also in fraud detection. In 2002, 35,000 cases of fraud representing R$440 million were averted.

Many at the Bottom of the Pyramid have never applied for or been granted credit, rendering the formal SPC system useless. Without a steady or reported income and with a personal economic status that can change daily, the credit analyst must decide whether the customer is honest, sincere, and able to make the necessary payments. Every customer has a unique situation. The training the analysts receive prepares them to make decisions that enable the continued success of Casas Bahia.

> *Without a steady or reported income and with a personal economic status that can change daily, the credit analyst must decide whether the customer is honest, sincere, and able to make the necessary payments. Every customer has a unique situation.*

Training is a combination of classroom and informal techniques. The first step takes place in the classroom. Employees learn the basics, ranging from the importance of personal grooming to the necessity of having a positive attitude toward customers. In the classroom, Casas Bahia employees begin to understand the importance of building a long-lasting relationship with customers. When people, especially the poor, walk into the store, they want a friendly face, someone who they can talk to about their day. Customers want to ensure the person they talk with understands their background and can help them fulfill their dream. Many customers "come in as a client and leave as a friend."

> *When people, especially the poor, walk into the store, they want a friendly face, someone who they can talk to about their day.*

The relationship between the analyst and customer creates a virtuous cycle. For instance, a customer enters Casas Bahia in need of an oven to replace her current oven that is no longer working, yet she is currently unable to pay. Based on either an existing relationship or one that is developed in the short time she is in the store, a credit analyst can approve the loan even if the customer does not currently have the necessary proof of income. The customer is grateful the analyst is taking a chance and trusting she will make the payments. Then, when things turn around for the customer, she is willing to buy more from Casas Bahia, and she also tells family and friends about the experience.

It is also in the classroom where analysts learn the importance of asking the right questions. Analysts are taught to inquire, depending on the store location, which can represent varied income levels and backgrounds, about a customer's primary livelihood. In addition, analysts are taught to discretely "size up" customers. For example, if a customer comes in and says he is a construction worker, the analyst will notice whether the customer has calluses on his hands or wrinkles around his eyes from working outside all day. The analyst might also ask a few technical questions (perhaps in the context of a project the analyst purportedly has going on at home). This interaction serves two purposes: It begins to filter out fraud potential, but more important, it helps build a relationship with that customer. Analysts are taught to always ask questions and be creative in trying to understand the customer.

After completing classroom training, new employees "shadow" an experienced employee for two weeks in a store. Trainees learn firsthand how to implement classroom teachings and the importance of cross-selling at Casas Bahia. Cross-selling is an important part of the company's success; after all, fully 77 percent of clients who open an account make repeat purchases.

Another important aspect of Casas Bahia training is teaching the analyst the art of saying "no" to the customer. An estimated 16 percent of customers applying for credit are denied. What is a seemingly basic concept has a long-lasting importance to Casas Bahia customers. When customers enter a Casas Bahia store, they hope to fulfill a dream. When you tell a potential customer "no," you effectively destroy that dream. Samuel Klein has fostered a culture where this is unacceptable. Analysts always work to maintain the relationship. The customer should be viewed for long-term potential, as a lifetime customer. Although a customer might not be able to afford something right now, that customer's situation might improve, and then he or she can buy that new TV, for example.

The customer should be viewed for long-term potential, as a lifetime customer.

Rejection is sometimes necessary and appropriate. The main reasons for rejection are threefold: negative SPC rating, credit limit, and third-party acquisition. With a negative SPC rating, there is nothing Casas Bahia can do. The analysts state that if it were up to Casas Bahia, they would do business but cannot because of the score. They apologize and mention that as soon as the "little problem" is resolved, they will welcome the customer back and finish the transaction. An insufficient credit limit is handled with offers of similar products or different brands or models. Third-party acquisition is when the customer has a bad credit rating or cannot afford the merchandise, so he or she has another person purchase it. The customer then pays the third party. However, this arrangement usually leads to default. First, there is a reason the customer could not afford the merchandise in the first place; second, the third party who purchased the merchandise has no vested interest in paying Casas Bahia. Third-party purchase is the leading cause of default at Casas Bahia. The second is unemployment, and the third is simply spending beyond one's means.

Casas Bahia's dependence on banks is low. Brazilian law does not permit Casas Bahia to fund the interest portion of its consumer loans. Therefore, that portion is packaged and sold to banks or *financeiras*. Casas Bahia used to have its own *financeira*. The company dissolved this entity because it was not the core business for Casas Bahia. Now, the company's policy is to borrow as little as possible and finance the customer while funding the expenses internally.

Additionally, Casas Bahia does not hold external currencies. This is especially important in the Brazilian economy, where local currency devaluations have caused prices to increase dramatically. Casas Bahia believes that because they do business in Brazil, the company's currency and exposure should be within Brazil. Moreover, minimal exposure to banks for external debt is beneficial.

> ***In Brazil, bottom-of-the-pyramid customers desire the same merchandise as top-of-the-pyramid customers. They want the dream they see on TV, not a cheapened version of that dream.***

Casas Bahia carries and sells top-quality brands: Sony, Toshiba, JVC, and Brastemp (Whirlpool). There is a misconception that because customers are poor, they do not desire quality products. In Brazil, bottom-of-the-pyramid customers seek the same merchandise as top-of-the-pyramid customers. They want the dream they see on TV, not a cheapened version of that dream. The difference is that individuals at the

Bottom of the Pyramid cannot afford to walk into a store and pay R$500 cash for a new refrigerator. They can, however, afford to make small installment payments to pay for that new refrigerator.

Unlike its competitors, Casas Bahia does not strictly focus on streamlining the supply chain, minimizing working capital, or increasing its inventory turnover ratio. Casas Bahia differentiates itself by placing a large emphasis on the supplier negotiation process. The company strives to make the best possible deal with its suppliers, negotiating huge volumes at low prices. Casas Bahia claims this strategy works best both financially and in terms of customer service. For example, Casas Bahia typically sells 1,000 units of an item per month, and a supplier comes with a great offer on 6,000 units. For the right price, the deal will be executed. One reason why Casas Bahia has built the largest warehouse in South America (also one of the largest in the world) is to give management the freedom to make deals the company deems good for business. The large warehouse also allows Casas Bahia to hold large inventory positions. This can be important because the supplier and production system in Brazil can be much less reliable than in more developed countries. Casas Bahia cannot afford to be out of stock.

Marketing always has been important to Casas Bahia and is one of the key components to its success. Casas Bahia always strives to be foremost in the mind of its population because potential customers tend to research prices at one of the chain's stores prior to making a purchase. Fierce competition in the retail industry has increased the importance of marketing. Because most products do not differ significantly, competition is fierce. The lack of product differentiation reinforces the importance of marketing within the retail sector. Casas Bahia invests approximately three percent of its revenues in advertising. It maintains one of the largest advertising budgets in Brazil.

Casas Bahia's main advertising venue is television, which reaches more than 90 percent of all Brazilian households. Because there is little product differentiation, sales are often made on the basis of emotion, leveraging famous singers, actors, and television "anchors." More recently, Casas Bahia used a campaign with client testimonials for the first time, intending to show the emotional relationship between the company and its customers.

TRADITIONAL VALUES MEETS MODERN IT SOLUTIONS

Samuel Klein's two sons, Michael and Saùl, manage the day-to-day operations at Casas Bahia. Michael is responsible for finance, stores, distribution, fleet, technology, and employees. His brother, Saùl, oversees suppliers, customer sales, and marketing. Although Samuel no longer visits stores, because of security concerns, he is always at the headquarters and considered the "mind of the company." Staying a family-owned business has helped the company stay close to the culture by reflecting and supporting the communities they serve.

Casas Bahia has leveraged its traditional ideals with modern concepts. All stores are linked and monitored in real time. It has developed a system that can analyze data from multiple points of view: individual store; groups of stores; region or city; and even by product category, individual product line, or SKU (stock keeping unit). From his desk, Michael can track the results of the six million people who enter his stores every month. Those customers generate an average 900,000 new sales per month, 7 percent of whom take advantage of a cross-selling opportunity. The people comprising this 7 percent have an aggregate owing balance of R$11.7 million and purchase an additional R$31 million. The percentage of cross-selling seems relatively low because customers are eligible to make additional purchases only after they have paid at least 50 percent of the original purchase.

One important aspect of the Casas Bahia customer relationship is that every month customers must enter the store to pay their bills.

One important aspect of the Casas Bahia customer relationship is that every month customers must enter the store to pay their bills. Until 1995, customers and salespeople would complete a form by hand and then turn it in to the credit department to have it typed. In addition to errors, customers were forced to wait for extended periods of time.

The first significant change came in 1995, when Casas Bahia developed a system that printed the passbook from a computer. The company also decided to make it easier on the customer by sending the bill directly to the customer's home. The speed and accuracy of the customer ticket increased dramatically, and the waiting time decreased. However, the customer default rate and associated costs increased dramatically. Disturbed and surprised by the two negative side effects, Casas Bahia quickly began to investigate the root cause.

The problems stemmed from two simple issues. First, the new computer generated a passbook that could not fit into a shirt pocket. Until then, customers carried the passbook in their pocket as a reminder to pay their bill. Now, customers simply forgot to pay their bills. Customers also claimed they never received the passbook or it took too long to arrive at their house. Although some customers actually did not receive the book, others were tempted to default. Within a year, Casas Bahia developed a new system that solved these problems. The new passbook fit into a shirt pocket, and people remembered to pay. Also, all paperwork was completed at the store, and the customer provided a signature confirming receipt of the passbook and an understanding of the terms. Moreover, costs decreased (as postage and handling costs fell). With the modifications in place, default rates returned to their normal levels.

The new system significantly increased customer satisfaction. Every time a customer made a new purchase, that customer's information was already in the system. Effectively, no waiting time was associated with receiving a passbook. This system saved Casas Bahia more than R$4 million in annual labor and printing costs.

Every time a customer made a new purchase, that customer's information was already in the system.

The next evolution of this idea is currently in process. All customer-related materials will be optically scanned and digitized. Casas Bahia will examine any information by customer, store, contract number, credit analyst, and so on at the source document level. With an average of 800,000 tickets printed per month, any incremental efficiency has a significant impact.

Looking forward, there are several challenges to maintain the success. In the short run, the introduction of credit cards poses a threat of losing the important

In the short run, the introduction of credit cards poses a threat of losing the important client relationship and decreasing cross-selling opportunities.

client relationship and decreasing cross-selling opportunities. General acceptance of credit cards with C, D, and E customers forced Casas Bahia to accept credit cards in September 2002. Casas Bahia was the last major retailer in Brazil to accept credit cards. In six months, credit card sales have reached four percent of Casas Bahia's total sales. On a positive note, when the credit card sale is made, the risk of default transfers to the credit card company. Credit card companies in Brazil offer an installment payment option without interest on a product-by-product basis. There is some concern that an increase in credit card sales might decrease customer loyalty (based on the lack of in-store traffic). Currently, all customers must come in every month to a Casas Bahia store to make their monthly payment. This is the main traffic that facilitates the 77 percent cross-selling capability. As the Brazilian economy recovers and as the financing market evolves, Casas Bahia will need to continue to contend with the issue of loyalty. Little by little, banks are targeting the Bottom of the Pyramid in Brazil with accounts and credit cards; Casas Bahia must prepare for competition.

This case study was written by Sami Foguel and Andrew Wilson under the supervision of Professor C.K. Prahalad. This case study is intended to be a catalyst for discussion and is not intended to illustrate effective or ineffective strategies.

Update: Casas Bahia

By Michael Klein, CEO

Casas Bahia continues to grow. In 2003, the company operated 343 stores with a revenue of 6 billion reals. By the end of 2008, the progress was considerable: We ended the year with 534 stores and revenues of 13.9 billion reals. The increase in our customer base kept up with this evolution: We came from a base of 12 million people to 31 million people in December 31, 2008.

Another aspect that deserves further analysis is related with the number of credits cards. In November of 2005, Casas Bahia made a deal with bank Bradesco for making available private label credit cards. From November 2005 to January 2009, we issued 5.7 million credit cards with an activation index of 65 percent, considered one of the highest levels in the private label credit card market. The credit card Casas Bahia/Bradesco has some advantages:

- It can be used for shopping in Casas Bahia's stores or in any other commercial place that accepts Visa credit cards.
- It's the only one to parcel out the payment of products of Casas Bahia in 24 payments with interest.
- This credit card targets clients with low incomes.

The expansion of the company through these years also includes the beginning of operations in two new markets in Brazil: Espírito Santo (ES) and Mato Grosso do Sul (MS). In 2009, Casas Bahia discovered the northeast's market, launching Casas Bahia's first stores in Salvador (Bahia). In the same region, in the city of Camaçari, we will build a new Distribution Center to guarantee the delivery of products to this new market.

Also in 2008, the chain was the first retail company to open up a store inside of a *favela* (slum); the details are described in the following text.

Chain Launch Store in Paraisópolis

In November 12, 2008, Casas Bahia launched a store located in the community of Paraisópolis, a southern area of the city of São Paulo. It's the first store of the company inside of a *favela*. Paraisópolis is considered to be the second biggest favela of São Paulo and the fifth largest of Brazil.

Paraisópolis includes 21 thousand houses. Unfortunately, many social problems coexist there: unemployment, analphabetism (people who cannot read/write in their own languages), low literacy, and others. According to the Union Community, there are approximately five thousand local businesses, among micro, small, and big companies. Casas Bahia arrived to be part of this ecosystem and to serve this population facilitated by access to credit.

The store's team, consisting of 50 employees, has two-thirds of this number of people selected from the community. They have job positions such as salespeople, office assistants, and people responsible for the cleaning, and others. The chain received 1,600 resumes from local people.

The unusual launch of a Casas Bahia's store in a favela had an international repercussion. The journalist Jonathan Wheatley, from the main business and finances newspaper from Europe, the *Financial Times*, joined the party of inauguration and published a big article about it. He highlighted the entrepreneurism of the chain of stores, the joy of the community in hosting the store, and the mission of Casas Bahia of always fulfilling consumers' dreams, facilitated through access to credit.

Virtual Store

On February 2, 2009, Casas Bahia launched its virtual store (www.casasbahia.com.br). It is the first store of the chain that works 24 hours a day, and took an investment of 3.7 millions of reals and has the potential to answer for 2 percent of Casas Bahia's invoicing in its first year of operation. The virtual store has its own identity and works 7 days a week, 24 hours a day, during the whole year with total guarantee of availability of the system.

"The goal of the virtual store is to offer the best prices in each category and to take care of all social classes that can access the Internet and are open to search and buy in the Web." That includes the C-D-E (lower) classes of people who in the last years started to have access to computers with prices and payment conditions that were doable for their domestic income. "Casas Bahia has five million private label credit cards in partnership with Bradesco. We built this base in three years, giving opportunity to the lower classes to have their first credit card. In this way we also helped, somehow, the access to this group to do online shopping."

The market data confirms this strategy. These days, 97 percent of the companies are connected to the Internet, 20 percent of the houses are also connected to the Web, and Brazilians spend, on average, 23 hours/month connected to the Internet.

CEMEX: Homes for the Poor

The ability to build and finance a quality home has been beyond the means of most of the world's impoverished. These people are often ignored by major corporations because it is thought they have too little money and are too difficult to reach. CEMEX,[1] the largest cement manufacturer in Mexico, second-largest in the United States, and third-largest cement company in the world, has through innovation found a profitable and empowering means of housing the poor for profit, instead of leaving that to governments or not-for-profit organizations.

> *CEMEX, the largest cement manufacturer in Mexico, second-largest in the United States, and third-largest cement company in the world, has through innovation found a profitable and empowering means of housing the poor for profit, instead of leaving that to governments or not-for-profit organizations.*

During the Mexican economic crisis in 1994 through 1995, CEMEX experienced a huge drop in domestic sales. Part of this stemmed from legal barriers that broke down, paving the way for international competition. Quick analysis of where revenues were specifically hemorrhaging most led to an astute observation that involved taking a closer look at the Bottom of the Pyramid[2] market.

CEMEX analysts knew sales were down, but a key *awareness* was that whereas sales were down by as much as 50 percent in the formal market, sales in the less-wealthy segment informal self-construction market were down by only

10 percent to 15 percent.[3] The company realized the high level of dependency on the formal segment left it vulnerable to the business cycle swings in Mexico. According to an estimate made by CEMEX, the do-it-yourself segment accounted for almost 40 percent of cement consumption in Mexico and has a market potential of $500 to $600 million annually. However, that segment also represented a portion of the population existing for the most part in a state of poverty. The company realized the key difference between the formal segment and the informal segment was in the average revenue per customer. Though fewer big-ticket customers could generate most of the company's revenues, the situation is reversed for low-income customers (see Table 1). It is estimated that 60 percent of the population in Mexico earns less than $5 per day. CEMEX figured that by converting the low-income population (that forms a majority) into customers, the steady revenues from this segment could be impressive.

The company realized the key difference between the formal segment and the informal segment was in the average revenue per customer. Though fewer big-ticket customers could generate most of the company's revenues, the situation is reversed for low-income customers.

Table 1 Comparison of Formal and Informal Market Segments

Attributes	Formal Segment	Informal Segment
Sales	Higher revenue per customer	Low revenue per customer
Payments	Financing generally not required	Financing important
Demand	Depends on economy	More or less steady demand
Price sensitivity	Driven by bargaining power	Convenience driven (such as credit, delivery, and so on)
Brand equity	Recognized and trusted	Should build trust to deliver as promised
Growth	Slow growth	High potential for growth
Customer location	Usually located in places of easy access	Mostly located in remote areas
Relationships	Stops at the distributor-level	Requires close ties with end customers

Part of CEMEX's awareness involved considering the obstacles of reaching this market in an effective, efficient, and sustainable way. Clearly, hard work and innovation would eventually be needed, but getting a clear big picture first was vital. Headed by Francisco Garza Zambrano and a consulting team from Business Design Associates, CEMEX performed in-depth market research to gain a good understanding of this low-income market in Mexico. The team conducted a three-month study based on various demographic factors—social, religious, political, and financial. The study also analyzed the various construction practices and methods, brand perception, and image of various cement brands.

Part of CEMEX's awareness involved considering the obstacles of reaching this market in an effective, efficient, and sustainable way.

The team realized that financing was the foremost and most difficult challenge to overcome for low-income customers. Unless the poor obtain access to credit, it would be difficult to sell the idea of constructing a complete house in the near future. The second challenge was that most families employed local semi-skilled or unskilled masons who built rooms without any planning. The lack of technical expertise resulted in a lot of raw material waste. Often, the masons did not order the right amount of material, and families did not have a safe place to store the excess raw materials. They had to leave the material outside their houses to the mercy of nature and theft. The team identified three keys areas of improvement/change for CEMEX:

1. Identify ways to provide access to credit for the poor before selling cement.
2. Improve the brand perception of CEMEX as a socially responsive company to earn trust in the people, especially the poor.
3. Change/improve distribution methods and construction practices to make it cost-effective for CEMEX, its distributors, and the low-income customers.

Saving money is not a standard practice of most low-income families; when it occurs at all, it takes the form of *tandas*—a local neighborhood, family, and network of friends who pool money if and when they have any money left to save. Once a week (or at some predetermined interval), one of the members bids for the pool by deep discounting or might win the pool through a lottery. Typically, this pool is used for unanticipated family emergencies, education, and sometimes for housing. The only factor that enforces discipline in the tanda system is the social capital—the trust, reputation, and participation in the community. However, the tanda system is not nearly as effective for housing. Even before money found its way to such pools, families (usually the men) spent it on various other nonprimary activities—drinking, partying, and so on. Also, there were too many members in pools, and it was difficult to manage and enforce discipline.

Saving money is not a standard practice of most low-income families; when it occurs at all, it takes the form of tandas—a local neighborhood, family, and network of friends who pool money if and when they have any money left to save.

CEMEX realized, too, that women are the key drivers of savings in families. In the Mexican society (and most other societies), women are entrepreneurial in nature, and they actively participate in the tanda system. Regardless of whether they are homemakers, outside-the-home workers, or small-business owners, they are responsible for any savings in the family. Research conducted by the Patrimonio Hoy team revealed that 70 percent of those women who saved were saving money in the tanda system to construct homes for their families. The men in the society consider their job done if they bring in their paycheck at the end of the day. The women actually manage expenses with the limited "allowance" that they receive per day from the men. They have to find creative ways to allocate money from the allowance as savings to build a house, spend on children's education, and so forth.

The poorest people in the city live in settlements made of raw cinder blocks, and in worse cases cardboard and corrugated sheet metal. Most houses have one or two rooms per family, and the size of a family ranges from 6 to 10. The homes are overcrowded, and this overcrowding has its own set of social problems, including friction within the family and children taking to the streets.

The key to the innovation needed was that the team had to work with a different mindset that did not include the sale of cement as the sole objective of the program.

As a bold cultural *innovation*, CEMEX modified the existing tanda system within the Mexican communities and called it *Patrimonio Hoy*, revolutionizing the idea of savings by changing the basic spending pattern of the poor in Mexico. In this system, poor people not only save their money, but also obtain access to credit based on their savings and payment discipline—a new model that moved away from a savings-only or a credit-only system to a savings-credit system. Recognizing the inefficiencies inherent in the original tanda system, Patrimonio Hoy has strict rules and standards for the program.

As a bold cultural innovation, CEMEX modified the existing tanda system within the Mexican communities and called it Patrimonio Hoy, revolutionizing the idea of savings by changing the basic spending pattern of the poor in Mexico.

- **Socios/partners**—Socios are the actual customers who enroll in Patrimonio Hoy. The socios get together and form a group, restricted to three people. The reason for such a small group size is that it is easier to enforce payment discipline in a smaller group, and the group tends to form stronger relationships to help each other out during an emergency.
- **Promoters**—Promoters play a key role as ambassadors for Patrimonio Hoy. Ninety-eight percent of the promoters are women. They work on a commission basis that depends on the number of socios they help enroll and on the duration of the stay of the socio within the program.

The creation of Patrimonio Hoy to replace the tandas also had distribution implications. Traditionally, the company has "pushed" its products and services through the distribution channels, and hence it was a price-driven market. Distributors operated on a 15 percent average margin from sale of building materials. However, under the new business model, Patrimonio Hoy manages the distributor relationships on its own. Although it works with the existing CEMEX distributor network, the margins in the new channel differ slightly. Distributor margin on sale of building materials sometimes drops to 12 percent. But the slight drop in margins is more than offset by a steady demand for cement and other high-margin raw materials, such as sand and gravel (for which the margin can be as high as 45 percent). Patrimonio Hoy has effectively created a pull for cement, and CEMEX on the supply side pushes it, enabling the push-pull strategy for cement sales. Patrimonio Hoy has seen an enthusiastic response from distributors who are willing to participate in this program.

In a traditional distribution network and supply-chain model, bargaining power and market dominance play a key role in the determination of prices and selection of distributors. The distributors primarily care about prices and discounts. The industry is driven by price wars. However, the new model took a different approach. Not all the traditional distributors were part of Patrimonio Hoy. In fact, a new methodology was adopted to select distributors for this program. Certain prerequisites were established for distributors and resellers:

- Good understanding and appreciation of the new business model
- Excellent delivery capabilities with trucks to deliver to the local neighborhoods with not-so-accessible roads and infrastructure
- Capacity for storage of raw material inventory
- Exclusive relationship with CEMEX

Nearly one tenth of the distributors qualified under the rigorous selection process. For example, in the Mesa Colorada neighborhood in Guadalajara, of the 30-odd distributors that sold CEMEX, 10 distributors sold only CEMEX products; among the 10, three to four distributors were selected to participate in the project.

CEMEX chose Guadalajara, in the southwestern province of Jalisco, as the first city in which to implement the program. CEMEX chose this test market for a variety of reasons. First, the social/economic profile of low-income communities was representative of most of the populated areas in Mexico. More than 50 percent of the population live in homes that hug a network of pitted, unpaved roads in unplanned settlements surrounding the city and blending into the countryside. Second, CEMEX was gradually losing its stronghold in the second-largest city in Mexico. Nearly all the houses appear to be under construction. The third (and subtle) reason was that the construction methods in Guadalajara differ from that of other places. Traditionally, for every 100 pesos that were spent on construction raw materials, 52 pesos were spent on cement. In Guadalajara, only 22 pesos were spent on cement. Instead, clay and limestone were used in the construction of houses. So, CEMEX had to find new opportunities for growth in Guadalajara.

A special research team set out to explore neighborhoods in and around the city of Guadalajara to identify high-growth opportunities. In a broad sense, the team identified potential pockets or cells based on income, construction progress, housing development, concentration of poor people, distributor network, and population growth.

The team identified target communities where the average family (five or six people) earned between 50 and 150 pesos ($5 to $15 approximately) per day. The target population for Patrimonio Hoy is not the absolute bottom of the economic pyramid (for whom the average per-capita income is less than $5 per day).

After a neighborhood was identified, Patrimonio Hoy set up a cell for that neighborhood. A typical cell targets a customer base of 5,000 or a community with a population of 50,000 to 100,000 (or 20,000 families). Each cell has one to four employees—a general manager (or chief), an engineer, a technical advisor (or an architect), a supplies manager, and a customer service representative (administrative clerk).

The chief works to identify promoters within the community who sell (to the poor) door to door the new savings-credit idea. The supply manager works closely with corporate CEMEX in the negotiation of prices for raw materials, interacts with the distributors for the delivery, and monitors the quality of suppliers and distributors in terms of delivery time, customer treatment, quality of materials, and so on.

Savings and credit are the key drivers for the business model of Patrimonio Hoy. The enrollment of a socio ensures a consistent and steady source of revenue in the pipeline (for x number of weeks) for Patrimonio Hoy and the distributors. The predictability of revenue has huge implications across the value chain from the suppliers to the end customers.

Savings and credit are the key drivers for the business model of Patrimonio Hoy.

When a socio group is formed, the group goes to the nearest cell and completes an application. This application is completely informational and does not require any credit history or collateral. Also, the prices of raw materials are "frozen" throughout the payment period. The only requirement is a commitment from each socio in the group to pay 120 pesos per week for a definite period of time (at least 70 weeks).

After enrollment, each socio in the group sets up an appointment with the technical advisor/architect (for a low fee) for an interview. Through an interactive process, the technical advisor helps the socio decide the following:

- Types and quantities of the materials needed for the first room
- What the next room will be in his/her home, and its placement in the current layout
- The sequence of the following rooms to be constructed

The personal visits of architects make the socios feel like important customers and have helped Patrimonio Hoy build trust among the socios.

Each socio in the three-member group takes a turn every month to collect money from the other two members and remits a weekly payment of 360 pesos (120 pesos per head). For every 120 pesos a partner pays per week, Patrimonio Hoy charges 15 pesos as a membership fee per socio.

- **Phase 1 (first 10 weeks)**—Each socio pays 105 pesos (120 pesos net of 15 pesos) for the first five weeks, totaling 505 pesos. At the end of the fifth week, Patrimonio Hoy makes its first delivery of raw materials for construction worth 1,050 pesos (equivalent of payment for 10 weeks). By advancing five weeks' worth of raw materials, Patrimonio Hoy is effectively extending credit to its customers. The extension of credit by delivering raw material to partners in advance helps Patrimonio Hoy establish credibility with the socios by proving that it has lived up to its promise of delivering raw materials. This phase also serves as a pilot to test the commitment of the socios.
- **Phase 2 (11 to 70 weeks)**—If socios stay committed beyond the first phase, they gain from the program even more. During the subsequent phases, socios receive raw materials worth 10 weeks at the end of the second week (that is, an advance worth 8 weeks). They receive raw materials worth 10 weeks at the end of the twelfth week. Deliveries are made during the weeks of 12, 22, 32, 42, 52, and 62.

CEMEX offers socios two delivery choices: receive delivery right away for immediate construction, or receive a delivery voucher now that can be exchanged for raw material delivery at a later time when construction is ready to commence. However, they never receive cash in hand, unlike the original tanda system wherein pool members could receive cash.

If the partners choose to receive their raw material, Patrimonio Hoy coordinates with its distributors to arrange for delivery of the material. If partners choose to receive delivery vouchers for delivery at a later date, the inventory is stored at the distributors' warehouses.

Interviews with socios revealed the first delivery made after just five weeks of payment and consistent on-time delivery played a big role in earning the trust of the partners. The supply managers also play a role of an audit manager, ensuring the distributors deliver good-quality material on time and provide good service to the socios.

The objective of Patrimonio Hoy is to serve not only a social cause, but also make it a profitable self-sustainable business. Patrimonio Hoy also recognizes that volume is important for it to be a success and, hence, has based its revenues on a per-transaction basis. These revenues are in addition to the sale of cement by CEMEX. The revenue streams are as follows:

The objective of Patrimonio Hoy is to serve not only a social cause, but also make it a profitable self-sustainable business.

- Membership fee of 12.5 percent per socio per payment of 120 pesos
- Intermediation fee in the form of a 7 percent margin from distributors

The average initial investment per typical cell is 400,000 pesos. The operational cost per cell, including salaries, is approximately 85,000 pesos per month. An average cell needs approximately 700 enrolled socios to break even on operations. According to Patrimonio Hoy's general manager, the program generates approximately 125,000 pesos in cash flow from operations. The goal of this program is to operate as a standalone break-even unit because the initial objective is to increase customer awareness, change consumer behavior, and establish a competitive position in the market.

The traditional methods of marketing communication, advertising, and promotion are not effective in this operating model. Patrimonio Hoy realized early on that mass-media advertising through television, newspapers, and so forth would not convey a personalized message or help build trust among low-income people.

After its first three years of operations, Patrimonio Hoy had 36,000 customers and more than $10 million in credit. It operated through 49 cells in 23 cities across 19 states in Mexico. The customer base is growing at 1,500 to 1,600 per month.

It might be too early to use financial profits as a measure of success. As a standalone operation, Patrimonio Hoy might not be generating as high a margin as corporate CEMEX is through the sale of cement, but the project has strategic implications for CEMEX. According to the general manager of Patrimonio Hoy, the operation is generating positive cash flows from operations of one million pesos per month as of April 2003.

The more important and critical factor is that Patrimonio Hoy has successfully created, with *sustainability*, an entirely new channel for selling cement and other construction materials. Patrimonio Hoy has helped CEMEX triple its cement sales in places where the operations of Patrimonio Hoy are set up. This has increased from 2,300 pounds of materials consumed once every four years per family, on average, to the same amount being consumed in 16 months.

Patrimonio Hoy has helped CEMEX triple its cement sales in places where the operations of Patrimonio Hoy are set up.

By offering a complete and comprehensive solution for housing, Patrimonio Hoy has made it difficult for consumers to let go of this opportunity and has fundamentally changed consumer behavior, even if on a small scale. As part of its effort to maintain sustainability, it has introduced various innovations around Patrimonio Hoy, such as Patrimonio Hoy Escolar, Patrimonio Hoy Te Impulsa, Patrimonio Hoy Calle Digna:

- *Patrimonio Hoy Escolar* (School) is a variation of the original program in that it helps improve infrastructure of the local schools. Four percent of the membership payment of socios is allocated toward improvement of school facilities.

- *Te Impulsa* is an accelerated version of the original program, where raw materials are delivered to customers earlier. The materials are delivered in three installments—weeks 6, 14, and 22 in 30-30-40 percent. By the twenty-second week, 100 percent delivery is promised to the socios, although they make their usual weekly payments until the seventieth week. This program is available to returning socios who have established credibility by making regular payments on time the first time they enrolled in the program.
- *Calle Digna* (Worthy Street) was created in response to the request of socios who wanted to move on from building their homes to improving infrastructure in their neighborhood. This is a classic example of how Patrimonio Hoy has changed the consumer outlook and how it has changed those consumers from people in despair to people with hope. This project brings the people even closer to work together for the cause of their communities.

Patrimonio Hoy has partnered with the Mexican government to work on public infrastructure projects. Many projects that local governments had yet to implement, for various reasons, have been implemented by collaborating with Patrimonio Hoy. The local government provides drainage facilities; Patrimonio Hoy provides material to pave the streets. The payment structure differs slightly. The weekly payments are 150 pesos for x number of weeks, depending on each family. Patrimonio Hoy provides ready-mix or raw materials starting on the eighteenth week of the payment cycle.

Patrimonio Hoy has partnered with the Mexican government to work on public infrastructure projects.

Though customer enrollment is increasing at a rapid pace, customer retention is a huge problem for Patrimonio Hoy, not because of poor quality of products and services but because of the nature of the business. After a room is done, the probability of returning customers to build another room is not 100 percent. Many take a break from the rigors of payment. The biggest challenge for Patrimonio Hoy is to retain those customers for a longer period of time and motivate them to return for additional rooms or other expansions.

In many cases, the socios cannot afford weekly payments for raw materials and mason fees for construction at the same time. So, they first buy raw materials over 70 weeks, build houses later, and then may return to save for the next room. To facilitate the continuity of the socios with the program, Patrimonio Hoy has established masonry training facilities for "self-construction," where socios can obtain technical training to build homes on their own. The socios not only get to build their own homes, but they also gain a new competency.

Construmex is one more way in which CEMEX seeks sustainability. Having successfully launched Patrimonio Hoy in Mexico, CEMEX turned to another possibility. It was obvious that a large number of Mexican immigrants live and work in the United States. They send remittances home every week. These remittances in aggregate total approximately $10 billion. Although the size of the average remittance transfer is miniscule—$200 to $300—in the world of international finance, the cumulative sums are significant. Further, an estimated 10 percent of these funds is intended to build additions to immigrant families' homes.

CEMEX saw an opportunity to capture a share of the remittance market to Mexico. This would further its business of helping the poor build good-quality houses.

CEMEX knew a significant portion (approximately 10 percent) of remittances to Mexico is used for construction of houses. Most of these people remit money using traditional money transfer companies like Western Union. This process is fraught with inefficiencies:

- The money-transfer firms (oligopoly) charge high flat fees for transferring money.
- The exchange rate offered is less than the market rate.
- Relatives back home can spend a significant portion of the remittance, meant for building the house, on other purposes.
- There is a risk of theft when collecting money from counters of money-transfer agencies in Mexico.

CEMEX identified the need for an easier and cheaper way to help the Diaspora build houses back in Mexico. A subsidiary, Construmex, was formed to serve this need. Following small-scale market research, Construmex set up its first experimental office in Los Angeles in July 2001. The significant Mexican population of Los Angeles made it the natural choice for trying out this business model. In short, Construmex allows Mexicans living in the United States to send their money directly to cement distributors in Mexico. Distributors receive the order and the money and deliver cement and other building materials to the site of the person's future home or business.

Broadly, there are two types of customers:

- Individuals remitting money for building their homes in Mexico
- Home town associations (HTAs) remitting money for public service projects in their hometowns in Mexico

The express purpose of Construmex is to channel as large a share of the remittance flows to CEMEX as possible. It is not a profit center and has little revenues. Hence, the primary activities of Construmex center around generating customer awareness, customer education, and trust building in the Mexican community. Its reputation spreads through word of mouth and working with HTAs to capture a share of the HTA remittances. Not surprisingly, 60 percent of Construmex's budget is dedicated to marketing.

Construmex offices typically have one to two sales representatives. These sales representatives are multifunctional in that they do the following:

- Answer customer queries
- As trained Mexican architects, consult with customers about the architecture and plan of the house
- Estimate building material requirements based on the house plan
- Help customers do price comparisons and choose the best distributors
- Register customers in the Construmex database

Dolex is the money-transferring agency that transmits the money from the customer to the Construmex account in Monterrey, Mexico. The money is transferred in dollars, and there is no exchange of currency. Construmex is still trying to define the perfect business model according to its general manager, Luis Enrique Martinez. However, it has tried two variants up to this point:

1. The Construmex sales office has a Dolex counter within it. When a customer comes into this sales office, he has the option to remit money through Dolex or to send building materials through Construmex (for example, Broadway office, Linwood office, Fresno office, Santa Ana office).

2. Construmex sets up a simple kiosk explaining the value proposition in a Dolex sales office. The customer has the option to send building materials through Construmex instead of remitting cash (for example, the Huntington Park office).

Dolex started its U.S. operations in 1998 and is still a young player in the money-transfer business. Dolex has 600 sales offices in the United States, and Construmex wants to scale up its operations by using this existing network. Construmex will try out the second model in Chicago, where Dolex has around 25 counters. There will be one Construmex sales office to answer any questions and provide consultation. The lean cost structure in the later model is obviously appealing to an organization that has no revenues and for whom controlling costs is critical, because that is the only variable under its control.

The Construmex office in Mexico does the following:

- Selects distributors for the Construmex program
- Receives money from Dolex and processes the accounting of the money transferred
- Transfers the order to distributors
- Verifies delivery of material to beneficiary
- Releases money to the distributor

According to the general manager of Construmex, the quality of service provided in the United States and Mexico is critical for generating trust and acceptance. Because of this, Construmex carefully selects distributors for its program. The different criteria applied are (1) accuracy of materials delivered, (2) adhering to the five-day delivery guarantee, and (3) prompt service. Until now, 1,600 of the 6,000 CEMEX distributors are part of the Construmex program. They cover all states of Mexico except Tijuana. These distributors are typically known to the beneficiaries and, hence, help in building trust with the clientele. They are happy to work with Construmex because this means more business for Construmex. In 2002, a team from CEMEX Philippines visited Los Angeles to study the operations of the Construmex program. CEMEX Philippines has a strong interest to replicate this model; their program has great potential because they send much more money back home than Mexicans.

Patrimonio Hoy and its sustaining programs have helped CEMEX gain a good understanding of the low-income population. It has helped CEMEX clear the misconception it originally had about the poor, and realize they could indeed form a good and profitable segment of the market. CEMEX also learned the traditional methods of operation would not work. However, it remains to be seen whether CEMEX can continue to provide housing for the poor to serve a social cause and at the same time remain profitable in the long run by expanding this program globally.

Patrimonio Hoy and its sustaining programs have helped CEMEX gain a good understanding of the low-income population. It has helped CEMEX clear the misconception it originally had about the poor and realize they could indeed form a good and profitable segment of the market.

Endnotes

1. The company has operations in four continents and recorded global revenues of $6.54 billion in 2002 with a gross margin of 44.1 percent.
2. Prahalad, C.K., *The Fortune at the Bottom of the Pyramid: Eradicating Poverty Through Profit*. Wharton Business School, 2004.
3. www.vision.com—Media Coverage 2002: Enabling the poor to build housing: Pursuing profit and social development together.

This case study was written by Ajit Sharma, Sharmilee Mohan, and Sidharth Singh under the supervision of Professor C.K. Prahalad. The case study is intended to be a catalyst for discussion and is not intended to illustrate effective or ineffective strategies.

CEMEX Update: Patrimono Hoy

By Israel Moreno Barceló, General Manager for the Patrimonio Hoy program—CEMEX and Henning Alts

Present Modus Operandi

Patrimonio Hoy (PH) is an initiative of CEMEX that allows low-income families to obtain access to services and building materials on credit through a well-planned savings scheme. The overall objective of Patrimonio Hoy is to improve the quality of life of low-income families (Bottom of the Pyramid) by empowering them through a market-based solution to address their housing needs. This represents a win-win situation, whereby the company makes profits and customers receive improved access to products and services, which contributes to their economic and social inclusion.

Main Features

1. **Technical assistance**—PH provides *individual technical advice* to meet the needs of those families who are interested in improving their housing conditions, defining a quality building plan (distribution of the housing project, calculation of required materials, and determined time schedule).
2. **Materials**—The building plan is fragmented into packages of materials that are *delivered according to the beneficiaries' needs.* The acquisition of these packages is eased by means of micro financing.
3. **Credit**—Customers pay 20 percent of the materials needed for completing the construction project, and credit is granted *without the need of any income prerequisites* for the remaining 80 percent. The weekly installment per family is 200 Mexican pesos (ca. USD14.50): MXP165 (ca. USD12) covers the cost of the materials, and the remaining MXP35 (ca. USD2.50) covers the following services:

    - Access to technical consultancy
    - Fixed prices guaranteed for 70 weeks (typical duration of projects)
    - One year of materials storage

- Home delivery of materials packages
- Financing for 80 percent of the value of the materials received
- Improvement of public schools' infrastructure located in the area
- Self-construction training
- Patrimonio Hoy Escolar[1]

The program creates a collaborative network within the community: families in need of better housing conditions, CEMEX distributors based in the regions, and CEMEX, which provides families directly with financial services, technical advice, materials, and all the logistical organization. Furthermore, the program has important social impacts, which will be outlined here in greater detail but that can be exemplified through one in particular—PH hires community-based promoters: These are women who get empowered through their work and are the key factor for trust-building within the community and for generating commitment within the participants.

Achievements

By the end of December 2008, a total of 220,000 Mexican families had benefited directly from PH, which has an impact on the living conditions of more than 1 million people and has improved the infrastructure of 518 public schools. In fact, 122,000 ten-square meter rooms have been built through PH in the participating communities and credits for more than 110 million USD have been granted, with an on-time repayment rate of more than 99 percent.

In 2007, the first substantial partnership was signed with the Federal Mexican Government to distribute efficiently public housing subsidies. Since August 2007, PH has delivered more than 27,500 subsidies, and it is worthy to mention that PH is one of the few institutions that deliver 100 percent of the subsidies *in material* to secure that they are really invested in housing.[2]

Coverage

After having celebrated its 10th anniversary in 2008, PH is now present in most of Mexico, working in 22 of 32 federal states and in 45 cities.

Figure 1 Coverage of Patrimonio Hoy in Mexico.

In addition, the program has been successfully implemented in Colombia, Venezuela, Nicaragua, and Costa Rica, and 15,000 families have benefited from the program so far. The aim is to assess the potential replication of Patrimonio Hoy in additional markets where CEMEX operates and where the socio-economic conditions could make possible its financial feasibility.

The long-term goal is to launch PH in the markets where CEMEX is located and that present housing shortages, thus enabling millions of low-income families around the world to benefit from the program.

Impacts and International Awards

Besides the improvement of housing, PH has important impacts at the individual and local level, which lead to empowerment, ownership, and local economic development:[3]

- **Living standards**—Family members have more space and privacy, which has important social benefits: People, children in particular, can develop better. This results in greater harmony and responsibility within the house and better learning conditions for children.
- **Empowerment**—PH grants to families access to finance and gives them the possibility to build their house with their own abilities

and resources. This has impact at the personal level and results in a higher self-esteem, in the will to go beyond, and it finally changes personal attitudes (for example, learn to save and take control of their own lives).

- **Gender mainstreaming**—Ninety-five percent of the community-based promoters are women and 51 percent of them had no previous working experience. These women are empowered through training, recognition within the community, and work; differently put, they are enabled to develop abilities for making more strategic life choices, having their own independent income.
- **Public schools**—The delivery of material destined to improve school infrastructure (that is, new classrooms, sport courts, protection walls, and bathrooms) ensures the *active* participation of the school stakeholders (parents, neighbors). This increases children's security and improves their learning conditions.
- **Access to finance**—Sixty percent of the participants confirmed that they would not have been able to build their own house without the help of PH, which, it is important to stress, requires no specific income prerequisites. In addition, PH allows the family to build three times faster at one-third of average costs. This results in better economic opportunities for the less privileged members of society.
- **Local economic development:**
    - Fifty-five percent of the participants hire local masons. This has the potential to increase the employment rate in the area.
    - CEMEX's local material retailers increase their business volume (that is, they have a higher demand of materials from PH participants) and gain new customers with the potential of generating new local jobs.
    - Twenty-nine percent of the participants use the new built space to start or develop their own business. This makes the local economy more dynamic.
- **Building assets**—Participants have the opportunity to increase the value of their houses through affordable credit, and a larger house surface allows them to generate more income through business activities (for example, shops, garages, snack bars, or renting rooms). This increases the overall personal assets of PH participants.

The participation in PH leads to a progressive, efficient, and self-sustainable improvement in the quality of life of its participants. In other words, PH is not a sheer construction program, but it also helps consistently in reducing the multidimensional[4] state of poverty of its participants (BOP), which has led to the international recognition of PH and CEMEX's sustainable development strategy.

International awards and indices that recognize CEMEX's social contribution through PH include the following:

- **World Business Award in support of the Millennium Development Goals 2006**, granted by the International Chamber of Commerce (ICC) in association with the United Nations Development Program (UNDP) and the International Business Leaders Forum (IBLF).
- **Corporate Citizen of the Americas Award 2007** granted by the Organization of American States (OAS).
- **Socially Responsible Enterprise (ESR) 2004**, awarded by CEMEFI—*Centro Mexicano para la Filantropía* (Mexican Philanthropy Center).
- The Opportunities for the Majority Office of the Inter-American Development Bank (IDB) and Innovest Strategic Value Advisors have developed the **Opportunities for the Majority (OM) Index** of publicly traded firms operating in the Latin American and Caribbean (LAC) region for investors. CEMEX was ranked in fifth position in 2007.[5]

Challenge—Partnerships

According to several consultancy findings, international experts, and PH's own experience, the main challenge and opportunity in an increasingly competitive environment is not only to be innovative, but to be also, and above all, able to build sustainable partnerships with the private, social, and public sector.

Aware of large opportunities to make an impact in the medium-term (2 years to 10 years) at the national and international level with PH, CEMEX aims to be continuously innovative and creative. This means enriching the program with additional services through partnerships, enabling PH to cover each time more of the many faces of poverty, and therefore providing a higher quality of life to its customers and securing sustainable growth for the program.

The main objectives for building partnerships follow:

1. Higher **coverage** and faster **growth**, to assist more low-income families and reach rural low-income families (Bottom of the Pyramid).
2. Cover more **needs** of the customers to prevent their drop-out and to enable them to improve their quality of life *with* PH (multidimensional poverty, inclusion).
3. **Capacity building**, which facilitates the achievement of PH's objectives and moreover empowers PH's customers through respective educational training.

Current Achievements and Opportunities

The following brief description gives an overview of the efforts made by PH to seek sustainable partnerships to cover the above-mentioned objectives.

Academic Partnerships

PH implemented an internship program with the Columbia Business School funded by the International Development Club (IDC) and the Social Enterprise Program (SEP), which provides pro bono consulting teams of three to five MBA students each semester.

- PH will receive four MBA-students from the University of Michigan to carry out internships.
- PH maintains collaboration for the development of business cases, PhD studies, and other academic activities with the following institutions:

MEXICO	Instituto Tecnológico y de Estudios Superiores de Monterrey (ITESM) Escuela de Graduados en Administración y Dirección de Empresas (EGADE) Universidad de Monterrey (UDEM) Universidad Panamericana Instituto Panamericano de Alta Dirección de Empresa (IPADE)

USA	Harvard University Stanford University University of Michigan Cornell University University of North Carolina Northwestern University University of San Diego
OTHER COUNTRIES	Universidad Adolfo Ibáñez (CHILE) IESE Business School (SPAIN) University of Kassel (GERMANY) *Freie Universität* of Berlin (GERMANY)

PARTNERSHIPS WITH THE PRIVATE SECTOR

PH signed an agreement with Banamex, the Mexican subsidiary of Citigroup, for promoting financial literacy within the BOP.

PARTNERSHIPS WITH THE GOVERNMENT

- "Mejora Tu Calle" and the CPAs are working with several local municipalities.
- PH has been recognized by the Mexican Government as a reliable institution that efficiently delivers public housing subsidies to low-income families since 2007. However, PH is granting subsidies only to committed customers (during their affiliation to the program) as an additional support to their building plans, taking extreme care of its goal of empowering people through their own efforts.

PARTNERSHIPS WITH NATIONAL AND INTERNATIONAL DEVELOPMENT INSTITUTIONS

- "Mejora Tu Calle" has signed an agreement with the *Inter-American Development Bank (IDB)* that aims to facilitate the implementation and to improve the efficiency of the program.
- PH has designed with *German Technical Cooperation (GTZ)*[6] a Public Private Partnership (PPP) project to implement energy-efficient appliances with the aim to raise awareness among low-income families on climate change and enable them to save.

- PH is further developing a PPP-project with *Capacity Building International (InWEnt)*[7] to implement a sustainable training program for the *promotoras*, achieving higher skilled and more empowered promoters.
- PH also communicates with *Ashoka*, *the World Bank*,[8] *Acción International*, *UN-Habitat*, *the Swedish International Cooperation Development Agency (SIDA)*, and the *French Development Agency (AFD)* in efforts to build potential partnerships.

Although PH has achieved international recognition and established several partnerships so far, its main challenge of scaling up, by reaching more low-income families, is still a medium-term goal. By assessing this strategy at the national level, it will be possible to design a model that will be replicated at the international level.

CEMEX's Progress

In the quest of creative, innovative, and sustainable projects, which always intend to combine business with the improvement of the living conditions of the BOP, CEMEX has developed several new initiatives that are detailed here.

Mejora Tu Calle—Improve Your Street

Description

The program promotes partnerships between communities and governments to improve the streets and sidewalks' conditions of their neighborhoods through technical, financial, and social-oriented designed solutions by CEMEX. The principal target group is low-income families (BOP) who have suffered a lack of infrastructure for decades.

Implementation

- Each neighbor in the street to be renovated contributes by paying for the necessary hydraulic ready-mix concrete required to improve the street in front of their house, according to individual budgets prepared and presented by CEMEX.

- After the project is approved by the community, neighbors are provided with individual loans. The government guarantees 25 percent of such loans through a trust fund.
- Authorities collaborate with the design of dimensions, earthworks, introduction of services, and placement of the concrete.
- CEMEX determines individual affordable quotes, supplying the material at preferential prices and managing debt collection.

Benefits

- Community and the government work together in a mutually beneficial effort.
- Neighbors benefit from the direct sale price and the financing of hydraulic concrete.
- The community raises the living conditions and achieves increased value for their houses.
- The members of the community become supervisors of the construction works.
- By getting neighbors to collaborate, the government's budget can be used to carry out other public works.

Achievements

Having started as a pilot scheme in 2002 in the state of Jalisco, the program took off formally in 2006 with a large roll-out in the city of Reynosa, where more than 5,300 families signed-up for the paving of 230,000 m^2. In total, the program delivered 360,000 m^2 so far, benefiting 8,600 families.

What's Next?

CEMEX's goal is to implement the program among Mexican municipalities that present viable conditions for implementing the program. In 2009, the goal is to launch "Mejora Tu Calle" in four to six additional cities.

IMPACTS[9]

Mejora Tu Calle has proved to be sustainable. Depending on climate circumstances, it produces important sustainable development impacts, which are presented in Figure 2.

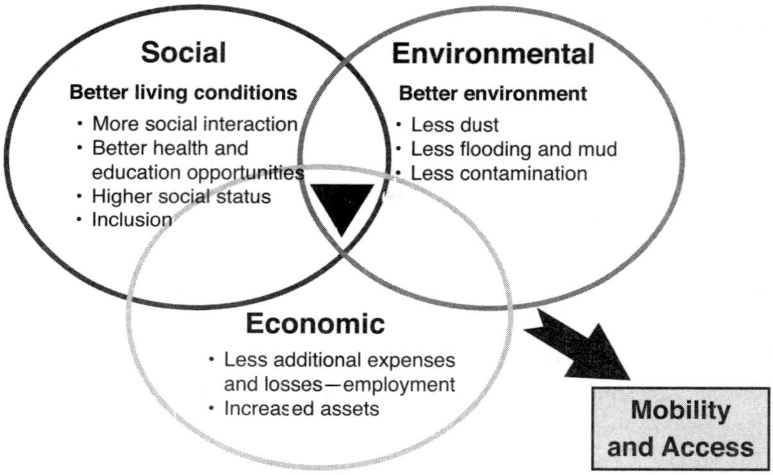

Figure 2 Mejora Tu Calle—sustainable development.

TESTIMONY

"Before, when it rained, the school transport couldn't pick up the children, nor could the public transport service. There were days when, if it rained too much, the children didn't go to school and classes were suspended. Now there is a big difference. I'm very happy with my new concrete street; I never thought I'd see my street like that. Children can now play without getting dirty. We don't get muddy any more when it rains and everything is clean because there is no dirt." (Rosa Guajardo, Gomez Farias Street, Reynosa, Mexico)

Microempresarios—Micro Entrepreneurs

Since 2007, CEMEX has engaged in a small-scale pilot program in Jalisco that supports low-income manufacturers of clay bricks to become producers of concrete bricks.

On the one hand, small manufacturers suffer several negative impacts due to the clay brick production: First, the traditional production process and the producers are not environmentally friendly because they use any kind of flammable material like garbage, tires, and so on in the brick-baking process; second, there is a high risk of explosion, given the use of hazardous materials.

On the other hand, the production process is highly inefficient and interrupted during the rainy seasons, which does not allow for a sufficient income generation, and fosters the poverty cycle.

Furthermore, new legislation forces these producers to invest in equipment adaptation that these low-income families cannot afford.

Therefore, CEMEX in cooperation with the *Inter-American Development Bank (IBD)* designed a pilot project to offer a sustainable market-oriented business solution. Its general objectives follow:

1. Investing in the training of producers to enable them to develop proper sustainable business activities and get formally included in the economy and society.
2. Guaranteeing that the new business generates sufficient income to improve significantly the living conditions of the family (health, nutrition, and education).
3. Eliminating the negative impacts on environment and personal health through the transfer of new technology and knowledge.
4. In the long-term: reaching a competitive advantage for CEMEX in a new market segment, empowering the BOP.

Centros Productivos de Autoempleo (CPAs)
Productive Centers for Self-Employment

Another recent socially oriented initiative is the *productive centers for self-employment (CPAs)*, which started in 2006 and so far has been implemented in 11 Mexican municipalities.[10]

Until December 2008, 1,200 low-income families have benefitted from the self-employment centers, which consist of all necessary equipment and machines—offered for free by CEMEX—to produce concrete bricks. The participants have produced 550,000 concrete bricks and have built 1,800 rooms of $10m^2$.

Low-income families use the CPAs to produce basic materials for their self-construction process or for housing improvements. Thus, participants produce their own concrete blocks for free. This means that the contribution of participants is their labor. What CEMEX asks of them is 50 percent of their production that will be used in two different ways:

By the terms of an official agreement, the local government buys the remaining concrete blocks to improve local infrastructure.

CEMEX sells the remaining part and reinvests the revenues in the centers: This allows for self-sustainability.

Therefore, CPAs present another opportunity for low-income families (BOP) to improve their housing and, hence, living conditions. In addition, the fact that there is a place where all neighbors meet strengthens the community cohesion and raises awareness on other necessary improvements. CEMEX achieves its objective to improve the living conditions of the BOP while producing additional income sources.

Conclusion

This brief survey of new initiatives related to the Bottom of the Pyramid demonstrates the awareness and willingness of CEMEX to go beyond the achieved programs and goals and find new ways to reach the Bottom of the Pyramid. At the same time, the financial crisis that began in late 2008 has had a negative impact on the business activities of the construction materials industry. However, evidence suggests that in times of worldwide financial crisis, a program like PH should not be reduced or abandoned, one reason being that the initiative is self-sustainable and underpinned by a robust social responsibility approach.

For instance, CEMEX conducted research on the Bottom of the Pyramid after the Mexican economic crisis in 1995–1996. One finding was that the informal sector (Bottom of the Pyramid) is less affected by crises of this nature than the formal one.[11]

CEMEX, as the founder company of Patrimonio Hoy and of the other mentioned programs, is aware of these circumstances and has demonstrated its long-term social and economic commitment to continuing its social responsibility efforts even in these difficult times.

Annex

Opportunities for the Majority Index: Analysis of Corporate Performance in Latin America and the Caribbean

Final Report (2007) prepared by Innovest Strategic Value Advisors prepared for the Inter-American Development Bank

Table 2 OM Leadership Index. Those companies that scored in the top tier (above 4.0) form the OM Leadership Index.

Number	Company Name	Country	Sector	Overall Score
1	Bradesco (Banco Bradesco, SA)	Brazil	Finance	4.85
2	Grupa ACP	Peru	Finance	4.80
3	Paralife	Mexico	Finance	4.70
4	Unibanco (Unibanco-Uniao de Bancos Brasileiros S.A.)	Brazil	Finance	4.68
5	CEMEX, S.A.B. DE C.V.	Mexico	Homebuilding	4.62
6	Caja Rural de Ahorro Y Crédito del Sur S.A.A.—Cajasur	Peru	Finance	4.43
7	Desarrolladora Homex, S.A.B. DE C.V.	Mexico	Homebuilding	4.38
8	Grupo Nueva	Chile	Homebuilding	4.33
9	Farmacias SIMI	Mexico	Consumer Goods/Retail	4.12
10	Unilever	Mexico	Consumer Goods/Retail	4.07
11	Promotora Ambiental, S.A.B. DE C.V.	Mexico	Infrastructure	4.02

Update Endnotes

1. Part of the membership fees cover the improvement of local public schools (PH Escolar), to which PH delivers material and offers technical assistance.
2. Furthermore, the executing institution—Consejo Nacional de Vivivenda (CONAVI)—has ranked PH on the first position with an approval of 99 percent of its operations.
3. PH realized in 2007 a six-month participatory research with the aim to measure and better understand positive impacts, to avoid negative impacts, to identify best practices, and to include them in its business model. As a result, now PH also collects data about impacts in its monitoring system.
4. It is an international consensus now that poverty is multidimensional. The theoretical framework used is developed by the Development Assistance Committee (DAC), which defines five interactive dimensions of poverty and well-being: human, economic, protective, socio-cultural, and political, which are also interrelated with gender and environment (DAC 2002).
5. "Over 70% of the population of the LAC region lives on less than $3,260 a year. This 'majority' of the population is both deprived of access to opportunities for wealth creation and underserved by the products and services that effective markets provide. Throughout the region, moreover, the wealthy have benefited more from the economic growth of the past decade than have the poor." See in detail annex: *Opportunities for the Majority Index*—Innovest Final Report (2007).
6. The GTZ is an international cooperation enterprise for sustainable development with worldwide operations. Its corporate objective is to improve people's living conditions on a sustainable basis.
7. InWEnt—Capacity Building International, Germany, is a nonprofit organization with worldwide operations dedicated to human resource development, advanced training, and dialogue. InWEnt is commissioned by the German Federal Government, the German business sector, and the German Federal States.
8. See the article published in the *World Bank Institutes* magazine Development Outreach (June 2008).
9. Likewise for Mejora Tu Calle, PH conducted in 2008 a three-month participatory research with the aim of measuring and better understanding positive impacts, avoiding negative impacts, and identifying best practices that could be be included in its business model.
10. Boca del Río, Linares, Mazatlán, Puerto Peñasco, Hidalgo, Huichapan, Mérida, Tamuín, Tepeaca, Valles, and Zapotiltic
11. The low-income segment has traditionally been an important cement market segment demanding about 30 to 40 percent of the bagged cement produced in Mexico. During the 1995–1996 economic crisis, the cement demand of the formal sector decreased by 50 percent; meanwhile, the demand of the informal sector was reduced by less than 20 percent.

Hindustan Unilever: Lifebuoy Soap

"Every time a diarrheal episode takes place, and for a poor family this could be two to six times a year, there are treatment costs, there are medicine costs, there are doctor costs. And so there is a spectrum of savings that is amassed."

—Yuri Jain

Diarrhea is the third-highest cause of death in the world in the category of infectious diseases, behind only acute respiratory infections and AIDS. It accounts for 2.2 million deaths annually.[1] The paradox of diarrheal disease is that the solution is known and inexpensive, but it is difficult to reach and educate the poor about the need to wash their hands with soap. Diarrheal disease is particularly prevalent in the developing world and takes a tremendous toll on the public health, especially among the poor and children.

The paradox of diarrheal disease is that the solution is known and inexpensive, but it is difficult to reach and educate the poor about the need to wash their hands with soap.

India alone accounts for 30 percent of all diarrheal deaths in the world.[2] In fact, in India, 19.2 percent of all children suffer from diarrhea. Access to safe water and sanitation facilities and instruction on better hygiene practices represent relatively simple preventive measures, yet getting the message to the poor was a hurdle that in India took an innovative approach combining the efforts of Hindustan Level Limited (HLL), the largest soap seller in India and a subsidiary of Unilever, in a public-private partnership for a solution—marketing a common consumer good: soap.

Hands are the main vector of diarrheal pathogens, transferring them from surface to surface and person to person.

Human excreta is the main source of diarrheal pathogens.[3] A lack of adequate sanitation facilities for disposal of excreta and poor hygiene practices results in the diarrheal disease pathogens being carried throughout the human environment. Hands are the main vector of diarrheal pathogens, transferring them from surface to surface and person to person.[4] Hands are used to feed children and prepare food, and in an Indian context, people do not typically use knives and forks.

A lack of sanitation facilities is also widespread throughout India. The majority of India's population is poor, with approximately 83 percent of the population (885 million people) earning a median household income of less than 2,000 rupees ($43) per month.[5] Almost 35 percent of the country is living below the poverty line.[6,7] Hand-washing habits also differ between urban and rural areas. Twenty-six percent of urban Indians (173 million) and 74 percent of rural Indians (492 million) do not wash their hands with soap every day.[8] Although the penetration of soap in Indian households is actually high, with 95 percent of Indian households owning soap, 665 million Indians do not use soap every day. Others use substitute products such as clay, ash, or mud. After visiting the toilet and before and after every meal, 62 percent of the population used water plus ash/mud, 24 percent used water alone, and only 14 percent used soap and water.[9]

Hand-washing habits also differ between urban and rural areas.

If a solution to diarrheal disease is simply washing hands with soap, why is this problem still stunningly pervasive? Historically, this issue has been approached as a public-health issue that could be solved through large infrastructure projects, a timely and costly proposition for governments in developing countries. In addition, three other reasons are ascribed for the persistent incidence of diarrhea.[10] First, the disease fell into the multiple domains of Ministries of Public Health, Water, or Environment. However, no group ever assumed full responsibility for the disease. Second, attention has been focused on "hot" issues such as HIV that command more public attention, leaving diarrheal disease to be "championed by no one." Third, behavior programs to address diarrheal disease are difficult to design and implement, and are "more complex and problematic than expected."

Changes in consumer beliefs and behavior are especially difficult to engineer in India. First, a deep understanding of the current practices, motivations, and hindrances preventing the use of soap and hand washing is required. This understanding is difficult to obtain in a country dominated by local cultures. India's billion citizens are spread across 25 states and 7 union territories. They speak more than 15 official languages and 325 different dialects, many of which are so different they are only understandable to those in a small geographic area.[11] Second, messages on health and hygiene to create behavior change are difficult to communicate to dispersed populations. Many rural parts of India are "media dark" areas, where citizens have little to no access to mass-media channels.[12] Only 22 percent of the population has a TV, and only 43 percent has a radio.[13] This lack of a mass-communication venue adds complexities and costs to education campaigns, requiring targeted messages distributed through unconventional means.

> *Changes in consumer beliefs and behavior are especially difficult to engineer in India.*

HLL is the largest soap and detergent manufacturer in India, with $2.4 billion in sales, 40 percent of which is from soaps and detergents.[14] In recent years, the CEO's increasing focus on differentiating HLL's products based on a health platform has pushed employees to delve deeper into consumers' needs and behaviors in an effort to find opportunities to make their products become imperative to a family's health and safety. Currently, HLL accounts for 60 percent of all soap sales in India. Other large competitors include Nirma, with 11 percent of the market, Godrej Soaps with 6.2 percent, and Johnson & Johnson with 1.6 percent.[15]

> *In recent years, the CEO's increasing focus on differentiating HLL's products based on a health platform has pushed employees to delve deeper into consumers' needs and behaviors in an effort to find opportunities to make their products become imperative to a family's health and safety.*

Only 5 percent of all soaps come from the small-scale sector. The market is subdivided into several segments, including discount, popular, premium, and super premium, with the discount segment currently the largest segment in India.

HLL sought out initiatives that connect the use of soap to health and hygiene behaviors, including hand washing. In the fall of 2000, as part of its research centered around hand washing, HLL learned of a public-private partnership (PPP) being developed between the World Bank, the Water and Sanitation Program, the London School of Hygiene and Tropical Medicine, UNICEF, USAID, and the Environmental Health Project. The PPP envisioned a large-scale hand-washing intervention that used lessons learned from pilot projects to promote the approach on a global scale. They entitled the initiative the Global Public-Private Partnership for Handwashing with Soap (later to become Health in Your Hands—A Public Private Partnership).

The structure for the program was based on the successful Central American Handwashing Initiative, a public-private partnership that united four private corporations (La Popular, Colgate-Palmolive, Unisola [Unilever], and Punto Rojo), the USAID, and UNICEF.[16] Before the program was initiated, diarrheal disease caused "19 percent of under-five mortalities in Honduras, 23 percent in Nicaragua, 20 percent in El Salvador, and 45 percent in Guatemala." The initiative developed hand-washing education messages that each private partner incorporated into its own marketing campaigns. The hand-washing program resulted in a "30 percent increase in hygienic hand-washing behavior in mothers and an estimated 1,287,000 fewer days of diarrhea per year for children less than five years of age in the two lowest socioeconomic groups."

The initiative developed hand-washing education messages that each private partner incorporated into its own marketing campaigns.

At the same time HLL was trying to expand the soap market through the PPP, one of its oldest and most successful soap products, Lifebuoy, was losing top-line growth at the rate of 15 percent to 20 percent per year, starting in 1999.[17] The Lifebuoy brand team was trying to determine appropriate next steps to revive the ailing brand and began to look toward hand washing. As a means of countering sales declines, the Lifebuoy brand looked to HLL's work on the PPP for new ways to attract and win customers.

The team decided to leverage the historical brand platform of health by tying soap usage to the eradication of family health problems. HLL also linked the data demonstrating how soap can help eliminate common health problems, such as diarrhea, to Lifebuoy, finding that members of families often experience stomach infections (diarrhea), eye infections, and infected sores. As described by Yuri Jain, this results in a significant loss of time and disposable income for an Indian family: "Every time a diarrheal episode takes place, and for a poor family this could be two to six times a year, there are treatment costs, there are medicine costs, there are doctor costs. And so there is a spectrum of savings that is amassed."[18] The team also changed the target audience from men to entire families, to expand its audience for the health message and to cater to the increased influence of women on household purchases. HLL hoped this revitalized health platform would create relevance for the new Lifebuoy target consumers and reassure existing customers that it was still health soap.

To address the health needs of one billion Indians, the team created a reformulation that was relevant, accessible, and affordable to the mass market. HLL replaced the carbolic smell with a more fragrant smell to better appeal to families and women. The team also changed the manufacturing process from "hard" soap production to milled soap production, a change that made Lifebuoy longer-lasting and produced more lather.[19] Its new positioning was now targeted at the entire family's health.

In addition to these changes, HLL wanted to ensure it could differentiate its product on a health platform. The team decided to add Triclosan, a common antibacterial agent, to strengthen the antibacterial power of the soap. In Europe and the United States, Triclosan has been the center of the antibacterial controversy. Dr. Laura McMurray at Tufts University School of Medicine found evidence that bacteria could develop resistance to Triclosan and propel the creation of more dangerous forms of bacteria.[20] Despite these criticisms, HLL believed the use of an antibacterial agent was critical in producing the health impact of eradicating and preventing germ regrowth. They named the ingredient Active-B as a cue to the consumer that Lifebuoy provided additional health benefits over other soaps.

The team also had to ensure Lifebuoy was still affordable for its consumers. HLL Chairman Manvinder Singh Banga explained: "Lifebuoy is priced to be affordable to the masses.... Very often in business you find that people do cost-plus pricing. They figure out what their cost is, and then they add a margin and figure that's their selling price. What we have learned is that when you deal with mass markets, you can't work like that. You have to start by saying I'm going to offer this benefit; let's say it's germ kill. Let's say it's Lifebuoy. You have to work out what people are going to pay. That's my price. Now what's my target margin? And that gives you your target cost—or a challenge cost. Then you have to create a business model that delivers that challenge cost."[21]

As a starting place, the Indian state of Kerala was chosen for the pilot program. Despite higher levels of education and sanitation access, research studies in Kerala found that only 42 percent of mothers used soap after using the toilet, 25 percent used soap after cleaning up a child, 11 percent used soap before eating, and 10 percent used soap before preparing food. The Kerala results also showed those who did not wash with soap were five times more likely to have diarrhea than those who washed with soap.

Based on this data, the PPP designed a program that tried to link the hand-washing initiative to life-changing events or times when new behaviors are most likely to be adopted (such as the arrival of a new baby or vaccination).[22] The complete program was to include four main pieces: a direct-contact campaign, a mass-media campaign, evaluation, and communications development. The first piece was a direct-contact program for women when they visited health or social service institutions. The PPP also designed a direct-contact program in schools, consisting of four health hygiene education days per year and the creation of a mandatory lunchtime hand-washing program for children ages 6 to 11. Finally, the plan included a mass-media campaign.

Calculations for Kerala suggested that through this program, "Seventy percent of households would be reached 43 times a year via mass media, and 35 percent of households would be reached 9 times a year through the direct-contact program."[23] The initial cost estimate for Kerala was a little more than $10 million spread over three years to cover the whole state. Per-person costs were estimated to be $.10 per year.[24] Program administrators estimated that savings in health-care costs would cover total program costs after two years.

The Indian government agreed to fund the mass-media campaign, while the Kerala government and UNICEF agreed to pay for the direct contact program.[25] The World Health Organization took charge of the evaluation function, and the private sector agreed to fund the communications research and message development. This allocation of costs among partners allowed each party to achieve a larger objective while only bearing a portion of the costs each year. The private sector committed to take on one-third of total program costs. These costs were further divided among all participating companies (primarily HLL, P&G, and Colgate-Palmolive). HLL agreed to bear the majority of the private-sector costs because it is the largest player in the market. However, this funding model might change. In total, HLL planned to contribute almost $776,000 per year (15 percent of total program costs) or $.027 per head per year.[26]

For HLL, it was an opportunity to stimulate demand for soap through education campaigns. The health sector and development agencies sought to leverage additional resources and expertise in designing and implementing education campaigns. The government sought to reduce costs and gain professional communication skills and resources in tackling the general health issues associated with diarrheal disease.

For HLL, it was an opportunity to stimulate demand for soap through education campaigns. The health sector and development agencies sought to leverage additional resources and expertise in designing and implementing education campaigns. The government sought to reduce costs and gain professional communication skills and resources in tackling the general health issues associated with diarrheal disease.

Program design and implementation plans progressed until the spring of 2002, when nonprofit groups and political opponents started speaking out against the initiative in Kerala. Environmental and antiglobalization activist Dr. Vedana Shiva, director of the Research Foundation for Science, Technology, and Natural Resource Policy, wrote, "Kerala has the highest access to safe water, highest knowledge of prevention of diarrhea because of high female literacy and local health practices such as the use of jeera water and high use of fluids during diarrhea. The World Bank project is an insult to Kerala's knowledge regarding health and hygiene. It is in fact Kerala from where cleanliness and hygiene should be exported to the rest of the world. People of Kerala do not need a World Bank loan for being taught cleanliness."[27]

Others accused the Kerala government of side-stepping the real problem: proper toilets and sanitation facilities.[28] This opposition soon spread to politicians such as Mr. V.S. Achuthanandan, leader of the opposition in the state assembly, who began speaking out against the initiative.[29] The criticism generated by adverse press began to hinder the PPP's efforts. The World Bank asked the government of Kerala to respond to the criticism, but the state refused. Meanwhile, the state cabinet had not yet approved the proposal, bringing the initiative to a standstill. Final negotiations for the effort are under way, but as an alternative, the PPP has downsized the initiative from $10 million over three years to $2 million for one year[30] and begun to discuss options of moving the initiative to other states in India.[31]

Moving forward with the downsized pilot, the PPP hired the Indian Market Research Bureau to conduct studies on hand-washing habits in Kerala. To reach its rural consumers, HLL had to first understand rural behaviors and preferences. HLL researched hygiene and hand-washing practices and the trigger points for using soap. HLL found that while attention to cleanliness has been increasing over time, most customers still associate cleanliness with the absence of dirt as opposed to the eradication of bacteria. For example, focus group and observational interview participants in rural areas often described their hands as being dirty if they were sticky, oily, discolored, or smelled badly. However, if their hands looked and felt clean, consumers considered their hands to be clean. Through this research, HLL determined the trigger for a consumer to wash his or her hands was to remove unpleasant contaminants, not to kill germs that cause infections. They also found this perception of "visual clean is safe clean" leads to infrequent hand washing and limited use of soap.

Focus group research showed similar results in that only 5 of 13 people washed their hands before eating, and only 10 of 18 washed their hands before preparing food.[32] Moreover, if consumers did wash their hands, they most often used water or a proxy product for soap such as mud or ash. The same study found that after handling cow dung, 5 of 7 interviewees rinsed their hands with water, one washed with mud, and one used soap. Consumers were not using soap because they did not believe they were dirty or did not perceive that soap had added benefits over water or other materials. Therefore, HLL decided it would have to educate customers on germs and the consequences of germs on health to increase soap usage as a means of deterring bacterial infection.

HLL teamed up with the rural India outreach arm of Ogilvy & Mather to design a behavior change education campaign focused on uniting the health attributes of Lifebuoy soap with health messages of germ eradication. First, HLL and Ogilvy & Mather brainstormed a way to communicate the negative effects of "invisible" germs in an easily understandable and relevant message to the rural consumer. They also decided to highlight the unique attribute of Lifebuoy soap, Active-B. HLL and Ogilvy & Mather outlined the following key messages:

HLL teamed up with the rural India outreach arm of Ogilvy & Mather to design a behavior change education campaign focused on uniting the health attributes of Lifebuoy soap with health messages of germ eradication.

- Invisible germs are everywhere.
- Germs cause diseases common to rural families, including painful stomach, eye infections, and skin infections.
- Lifebuoy soap with Active-B can protect you from germs.
- Wash your hands with Lifebuoy soap to prevent infection.

HLL titled the program Lifebuoy Swasthya Chetna (Lifebuoy Glowing Health). HLL hoped to change the trigger for washing hands from "visual clean is safe clean" to a social convention of frequent hand washing.

Through strategic selection of villages, Swasthya Chetna has maximized use of limited funds to reach targeted demographics to increase Lifebuoy sales. This not only results in cost-savings and efficiencies, but also might be more effective than an unbranded campaign in creating behavior change. Research shows that use of a brand can help strengthen the health messages being delivered by conveying quality, increasing consumer confidence, and ensuring that messages are delivered in a nonpatronizing or nondemeaning tone.[33] By reaching out to poor populations with strong brands and building habits involving their brands, HLL can create an unshakable hold on consumers' wallets. Conversely, the PPP seeks overall market sales, which might or might not directly benefit HLL.

At the same time, promotion of a branded product can leave the company open to criticism. Therefore, it is important that the campaigns have a solid science-based foundation and are transparent. The Lifebuoy Swasthya Chetna campaign meets this criteria. As explained by Harpreet-Singh Tibbs, "We're not shying away from the fact that Lifebuoy is going to benefit or we're trying to get soap consumption up. We're being upfront about it. But we're also telling them that we're doing something for the good of the community, and it's there for you to see yourself. And that's the reason we're actually going into schools and schools are giving us permission to go in. Because they believe that what we're saying is actually making sense.... I'm trying to develop the category because I believe soaps can reduce diarrheal incidents by 40 percent. And if you believe it's true, there's no reason why you should dispute this program."[34]

A central challenge in "selling" health is the development of successful partnerships between private business and public-health offices and organizations. Both groups need to invest together to create the market for a product. Private organizations contribute competencies around behavior change and delivery of low-cost products, while public organizations provide access to consumers, in effect the channels to deliver messages and extend product reach. Both groups are investing in and addressing a common problem but are evaluated on producing two different results: NGOs and governments are interested in an increased quality of life, while private businesses seek increased earnings.

A central challenge in "selling" health is the development of successful partnerships between private business and public-health offices and organizations.

These different motivations produce an inherent tension in the public-private partnership model. This tension is apparent in the status of the highly publicized Global Handwashing Initiative PPP, where political roadblocks have slowed down the program and thus impacted HLL's plans to deliver health education and expand the soap market. Yet, these lessons have helped HLL to transfer knowledge from the Global Handwashing Initiative PPP to improve its own branded health education program, Swasthya Chetna. Working with more localized partners, in this case village schools, HLL is rapidly scaling its program throughout rural India. By learning how to build partnerships and work in PPPs, even if toward seemingly different ends, HLL has gained a competitive advantage. HLL can leverage its experience accessing public-health channels to sell products as health solutions, while increasing its market share both in India and abroad.

Endnotes

1. Curtis Valerie, "Health in Your Hands: Lessons from Building Public-Private Partnerships for Washing Hands with Soap," October 2002, globalhandwashing.org/Publications/Lessons_learntPart1.htm.
2. Water and Sanitation Program. "Hand Wash India presentation," www.wsp.org/english/activities/handwashing/vbehal.pdf, April 28, 2003.
3. Curtis, Valerie. Op. Cit.
4. Curtis, Valerie. Op. Cit.
5. Water and Sanitation Program. Op. Cit.
6. The World Bank. *India: Achievements and Challenges in Reducing Poverty*. Washington, D.C., June 1997.
7. This World Bank study defines someone living below the poverty line as anyone with a per capita monthly expenditure lower than 49 rupees (rural) and 57 rupees (urban) at 1973–1974 all-India prices. This corresponds to a per-capita expenditure sufficient to provide basic nonfood items and a caloric intake of 2,400 calories per day for urban Indians and 2,100 calories per day for Indians.
8. Water and Sanitation Program. Op. Cit.
9. Ibid.
10. Curtis, Valerie. Op. Cit.
11. Kolanad, Gitanjali. *Culture Shock! India, Graphic Arts Center Publishing Agency*. 2001.
12. Water and Sanitation Program. Op. Cit.
13. Gwatkin, Davidson R. et al. "Socioeconomic Difference in Health, Nutrition, and Population in India." HNP/Poverty Thematic Group of the World Bank, May 2000.
14. HLL, Annual Report, 2001. All figures have been converted from rupees to U.S. dollars based upon an exchange rate where $1 is equal to 46 rupees.
15. India InfoLine, www.indiainfoline.com/comp/vade/mr02.html, March 20, 2003.
16. "Public-Private Partnerships: Mobilizing Resources to Achieve Public Health Goals the Central American Handwashing Initiative Points the Way," globalhandwashing.org/Publications/BASICS.htm#private, April 28, 2003.
17. Interview with Aasif Maalbari, March 26, 2003.
18. Interview with Yuri Jain, HLL, March 26, 2003.
19. Interview with Gurpreet Kohil, HLL, March 27, 2003.
20. Fox, Maggie. "Common disinfectant could breed superbugs." August 19, 1998, www.nutriteam.com/triclo.htm, April 24, 2003.
21. Interview with HLL Chairman Manvinder Singh Banga, HLL, March 29, 2003.

22. "Clean Hands, Clean State. Kerala 'handwash with soap' program." January 2002. www.wsp.org/english/activities/handwashing/kerala.pdf, April 28, 2003.

23. Curtis, Valerie. Op. Cit.

24. Ibid.

25. Water and Sanitation Program. Op. Cit.

26. This figure is calculated by dividing total project costs of $10.48 million by three years to get an annual cost per year of $3.49 million. This figure is then divided by three to ascertain private-sector costs. The resulting $1.16 million is then multiplied by two-thirds to get an estimated annual cost per year for HLL of $776,000. The original $10.48 million figure is from the Handwash India presentation, www.wsp.org/english/activities/handwashing/vbehal.pdf, April 28, 2003.

27. Shiva, Vandana. "Saving lives or destroying lives? World Bank sells synthetic soap & cleanliness to Kerala: the land of health and hygiene." *AgBioIndia*, September 23, 2002.

28. Devinder, Sharma. "So(a)ps for Unilever." Indeconomist. October 30, 2002, www.indeconomist.com/301002_health.html, April 24, 2003.

29. Kurian, Vinson. "'Hand wash' campaign in Kerala raises a stink." Business Line. November 6, 2002.

30. London School of Tropical Medicine and Hygiene. "Health in Your Hands PPP-HW. LSHTM Progress Report. August 26, 2002–June 30, 2003." www.globalhandwashing.org/Globalpercent20activities/Attachments/lshtmreportyear2.pdf, December 10, 2003.

31. "Meeting on Public-Private Partnership Initiative to Promote Handwashing with Soap, November 25-26, 2002," Washington DC, global handwashing.org/Globalpercent20activities/Attachments/PPPHWpercent20Meetingpercent20Report percent2011-25,26-02.doc, April 28, 2003.

32. Probe Quality Research. "Project Glove: A Triggers and Barriers Study on Handwash Habits." Prepared for HLL. Not dated.

33. Harvey, P. *Let Every Child Be Wanted: How Social Marketing Is Revolutionizing Contraceptive Use Around the World.* Westport: Greenwood Publishing Group, 1999.

34. Interview with Harpreet-Singh Tibbs, HLL, March 26, 2003.

This case study was written by Mindy Murch and Kate Reeder under the supervision of Professor C.K. Prahalad. The case study is intended to be a catalyst for discussion and is not intended to illustrate effective or ineffective strategies.

For the update on HLL, see the "Hindustan Unilever Case Updates" section at the conclusion of "Hindustan Unilever: Iodized Salt (Annapurna Salt)."

Hindustan Unilever: Iodized Salt (Annapurna Salt)

Iodine deficiency disorder (IDD) is the world's leading cause of mental disorders, including retardation and lowered IQ. Research indicates that 30 percent of the world's population is at risk of IDD. Well-balanced diets provide the required amount of iodine, making the poor particularly susceptible to this condition. A beggar on the street with a prominent goiter on his neck is one visible sign of IDD. Children living in iodine-deficient areas have an average IQ 13 points less than that of children in iodine-sufficient areas. The most severe form of this disease is hypothyroidism and is prevalent among young children in remote areas where the daily iodine intake is less than 25 micrograms (mcg).[1] Hypothyroidism causes cretinism, gross mental retardation, and short stature. In India, almost 90 percent of the population earns less than $3,000 per year;[2] over 70 million are already afflicted with IDD, and another 200 million are at risk.[3]

Because even the poorest people eat salt, it is globally recognized as the best vehicle for supplementing diets with iodine. However, many still do not receive the required amount of iodine from salt because

- Only about 25 percent of edible salt in India is iodized.
- Many consumers are not educated as to the human body's requirements for iodine, despite the availability of iodized salt in the marketplace.
- Even those who understand the importance of iodine might be reluctant to pay the premium for iodized salt over the cost of noniodized salt.

- Traditionally, iodized salt loses a significant amount of iodine in storage, transportation, and Indian cooking. Even consumers who purchase iodized salt for its health benefits might not actually receive the recommended daily allowance of iodine.

The paradox of IDD is that the solution is known and is inexpensive. The issues are how to reach and educate the poor while, at the same time, getting salt producers to innovate inexpensive methods to guarantee a minimum level of iodine concentration in salt.

The paradox of IDD is that the solution is known and is inexpensive. The issues are how to reach and educate the poor while, at the same time, getting salt producers to innovate inexpensive methods to guarantee a minimum level of iodine concentration in salt. In developing countries, such as India, traditional methods of iodizing salt are no guarantee that the salt will retain its iodine content as it reaches the consumer.

Nongovernmental organizations and governmental organizations are traditionally called on to solve problems pertaining to the poor and public-health crises such as IDD. Conversely, multinational corporations typically limit their involvement with the poor to corporate social responsibility. Although many multinational corporations have tapped into India's wealthy, urban populations, few have attempted to reach the poor. Yet multinational corporations have a greater breadth of key capabilities, such as technological know-how, distribution networks, marketing experience, and financial backing that enable them to combat public-health problems such as IDD at a profit. The key to tackling epidemics such as IDD is the collaboration between nonprofits and multinational corporations.

Unlike other parts of the world, mineral salt only comprises 5 percent of the Indian salt market because India's topography does not lend itself to salt mines. Ninety-five percent of Indian salt is obtained by "salt farming," a lengthy evaporation process whereby seawater is pumped and stored in man-made inland pans. The salt market attracts a large number of producers, despite its being a low-unit-price business. Salt margins can be quite high, and although the absolute values of revenues and profits are not as high as some consumer products, such as soaps and detergents, the return on capital employed makes for an attractive business. India's salt market is dominated by more than 300 local players producing unbranded products of varying quality. A few branded manufacturers produce 500,000 to 600,000 tons per year, whereas most local producers sell less than 1,000 tons.[4] Because it is virtually impossible to differentiate refined salt on the basis of taste, smell, or color and because honest packaging laws are inadequately enforced, Indian consumers face unique challenges:

- Imitation brands such as Captain Hook in place of Captain Cook or Tota for Tata lead confused consumers to purchase the wrong product.
- Many manufacturers print "iodized salt" on packs when, in fact, the salt is not iodized.

Under pressure from the world health community, China (1995) and India (1997) banned the sale of noniodized salt. India's Universal Salt Iodization law mandated that all salt manufacturers add at least 15 parts per million (ppm) of iodine to edible salt.[5] The law was hailed as a positive step by the health community. However, it was vehemently protested by independent salt producers who accounted for nearly one-third of India's salt production that was consumed by 200 million people. These producers argued they could not afford the additional cost of purchasing iodine, machinery, and packaging to iodize salt.[6] Salt industry employees continued to consume noniodized salt. (This population is now afflicted with some of the highest incidences of IDD.) Succumbing to intense lobbying by the producers, many of whom operated manual 10-acre coastal plots that were leased from the government, the government of India repealed the Universal Salt Iodization law in July 2000. Although a few manufacturers voluntary added iodine, most uneducated consumers continued to purchase the lower-priced uniodized salts, perpetuating IDD. Since 2000, a few individual states, including Gujarat, have reversed the federal government's repeal and forced manufacturers to iodize salt.

Environmental factors such as air moisture, high temperatures, poor quality of raw salt, impurities in salt, low environmental pH, and time before consumption can all exaggerate the instability of salt iodized with potassium iodate, resulting in excess iodine loss. Most Indian salt is farmed in desert areas near India's coastline and must be transported long distances to reach consumers, adding storage time and exposure to external conditions. According to the National Institute of Nutrition (NIN) in Hyderabad, India, "Under Indian climate and storage conditions, iodine loss in fortified salt has been observed to be 25 percent to 35 percent in the first three months and 40 percent to 70 percent by one year."[7]

Indians' unique cooking style leads to further iodine loss. Traditional Indian cooking calls for salt to be added before food is fully heated, boiled, fried, or cooked; this contrasts with most Western cooking, in which salt is added for taste after food has been completely cooked. In addition, the varying pH levels of Indian spices interact with salt and result in further iodine loss. "The loss of iodine in Indian culinary practices ranges from 20 percent to 70 percent."[8] The cumulative effect of heat, storage, and cooking can result in an almost complete loss of iodine by the time the consumer eats salt. Because salt is the primary carrier of iodine and a typical adult consumes 10 grams of salt per day, iodized salt must deliver 15 ppm of iodine upon consumption to achieve the recommended daily allowance of 150 milligrams of iodine per day. Acknowledging that iodine is lost during storage and transport, the Indian Prevention of Food Adulteration law of September 2000 mandated that manufacturers of iodized salt add at least 30 ppm of iodine to ensure that 15 ppm are delivered to the consumer at retail. This law, however, did not take into account the iodine lost during "Indian cooking."[9]

The cumulative effect of heat, storage, and cooking can result in an almost complete loss of iodine by the time the consumer eats salt.

A few national players dominate the Indian salt market, which is also saturated with numerous local players. Although many brands of salt are also iodized, Annapurna, a product of Hindustan Lever Ltd. (HLL), was the first to be marketed based on the iodized and healthful platforms. As the government of India and the International Council for the Control of Iodine Deficiency increased attention on the problems of iodine deficiency and the role salt could play to combat IDD, HLL seized the opportunity to become the first to market salt on an iodized platform. Though other branded salts were iodized, none were advertised as such. HLL became the first corporation to address IDD-related health concerns such as mental retardation and goiters and, subsequently, earned an endorsement from the International Council for the Control of Iodine Deficiency.

HLL became the first corporation to address IDD-related health concerns such as mental retardation and goiters and, subsequently, earned an endorsement from the International Council for the Control of Iodine Deficiency.

When determining which part of the salt market to enter, HLL considered which segments offered the greatest potential. HLL created the Annapurna brand for its new line of salt and atta (milled wheat flour). Annapurna (an means food or grain; purna means to prepare) is also the name of the Hindu goddess of abundance. In 1995, after considering input from brand managers and executives, Gunender Kapur, director of foods division, led his team to enter the refined salt market with the primary goal of upgrading the 75 percent unrefined market (Bottom-of-the-Pyramid consumers) to Annapurna and the secondary goal of converting branded consumers to Annapurna.

The 1997 launch of Annapurna salt forced HLL to compete at the lowest price point of any product in the history of HLL; the brand team realized the need to differentiate the commodity in the increasingly competitive salt market. After the launch, sales and market research indicated consumers were more interested in the appearance and taste of salt than its chemical properties.

HLL made sure its product actually was more effective in conveying iodine. Its research lab developed a proprietary product, K15, a stable iodine released only in an acidic environment such as the human stomach, which ensures that as much iodine as possible gets into human systems instead of being lost in the cooking process. The salt team believed all mothers are motivated by the same dreams of bright, healthy children. As a result, all Annapurna's subsequent advertisements conveyed this message. During the 2001 relaunch of Annapurna with K15, HLL aired a puppet show

Its research lab developed a proprietary product, K15, a stable iodine released only in an acidic environment such as the human stomach, which ensures that as much iodine as possible gets into human systems instead of being lost in the cooking process.

about IDD on Doordharshan, an Indian government-run television network, sharing costs equally with the network. The infomercial was extremely successful. According to HLL market analysis, the target group viewed Annapurna advertisements an average of four times. Although the long-term retention is unknown, the immediate recollection of the advertisement's message was about 90 percent.

Transport times can be long because of India's poor road infrastructure. HLL also had to look to getting its product to market swiftly. Because the shelf life of salt is only one year, minimizing storage time in the *godowns* (storage areas), decreasing transport distances, and increasing the number of consumer purchase points are vital. The Annapurna salt supply chain varies significantly from region to region and takes between one and a half to six months from natural evaporation of sea salt to a customer's purchase, the bulk of which is during the salt farming stage. In response to these concerns, HLL successfully executed a salt supply-chain innovation in the beginning of 2001. HLL began to use rail, mitigating some of the problems with trucking and earning an edge on competitors.

HLL also recognized the Bottom of the Pyramid's inability to pay for large packages of salt. Annapurna responded by introducing 200g and 500g low-unit-price packs to appeal to these consumers. Although the proportionate cost of manufacturing low-unit-priced packs is currently higher than that of the 1kg bag, HLL is researching technologies that would drive the cost down. Another way HLL aims to increase consumer demand for Annapurna salt is by aggressively increasing volumes in retail outlets. Although stockists educate retailers on HLL brand differentiation, most retail outlets are driven primarily by margins and schemes (promotions). Most dealers sell brands from a variety of companies, many of which offer competitive schemes. Annapurna salt successfully penetrated many retail chains and converted shopkeepers with superior promotions. These schemes have spawned price wars among manufacturers and resulted in even less brand loyalty from store owners.

The company also had to develop means beyond standard mass marketing to reach India's poor. As Vindi Banga, chairman and CEO, HLL, says, "One of the greatest challenges with rural India is that the media only reaches 50 percent of the population. This leaves over 500 million people that don't see your message. The population lives in 600,000 villages, and over half don't have motorable roads, so we needed unique means to communicate to them. This challenge is the same in other emerging markets." This awareness led to Project Shakti. *Shakti* (meaning strength in Sanskrit) is a direct-to-consumer initiative targeted at individuals in the Bottom of the Pyramid in rural India.

Project Shakti utilizes women's self-help groups (SHGs) for entrepreneur development training to operate as a "rural direct-to-home" sales force, educating consumers on the health and hygiene benefits of HLL brands and nurturing relationships to reinforce the HLL message. This direct-to-consumer initiative is expected to not only stimulate demand and consumption to earn huge profits for HLL, but also to change the lives of people in rural India, something that mass marketing alone cannot accomplish.

Project Shakti utilizes women's self-help groups (SHGs) for entrepreneur development training to operate as a "rural direct-to-home" sales force, educating consumers on the health and hygiene benefits of HLL brands and nurturing relationships to reinforce the HLL message.

A Shakti dealer or Shakti amma (mother) works as an HLL direct-to-consumer distributor, selling primarily to individuals from her SHG. She also relies on smaller distributors, retailers, and consumers in six to ten satellite villages to supplement her business. Most training is in a market setting (versus a classroom) with dealers learning selling, business, and record-keeping skills. Although sharing success stories with other dealers in a classroom could be beneficial, HLL has found the logistics difficult to manage.

The Shakti *pracharani* or communicator is a person hired on a fixed monthly sum and typically earns less than a Shakti dealer. An ideal pracharani is confident and outspoken, with excellent communication skills. Unlike the dealer, whose travel is limited to her village and a few satellite villages, the pracharani must travel throughout the district. She is paid bonuses for attending more than her required number of SHG meetings. At such meetings, she facilitates games and tests members' knowledge with questions such as how to identify Annapurna salt from an imitation product. True to HLL's vision...

- A picture of a laughing sun (the universal symbol for iodine) is printed on all Annapurna salt packaging so that those speaking other languages or even the illiterate can recognize the symbol and identify Annapurna salt.

- The Pracharani distributes pamphlets and other educational material on IDD during SHG meetings.
- Other educational marketing initiatives such as a two-week Annapurna salt drive and Iodine Day (as a part of World Health Day) further the stable iodine message in rural markets.

From the corporate perspective, Shakti's greatest challenge is distribution with India's underdeveloped infrastructure. For the sales managers on the front line, training rural women to work on their own for the first time poses the primary hurdle. For dealers and pracharanis, educating rural consumers about the quality of HLL products continues to prove difficult because most villagers are accustomed to less-expensive, unbranded, local products. Even if they are convinced of HLL's marketing message, many imitation products cloud the market and confuse consumers.

> ***HLL is demonstrating that for multinational corporations, the Bottom of the Pyramid can serve as a profitable impetus of innovative technology and marketing savvy, and that corporations together with nongovernmental organizations can address social problems at affordable costs.***

HLL is demonstrating that for multinational corporations, the bottom of the pyramid can serve as a *profitable* impetus of innovative technology and marketing savvy, and that corporations together with nongovernmental organizations can address social problems at affordable costs. Annapurna salt's K15 technology is uniquely positioned to combat IDD, a worldwide health problem, while delivering substantial profits to HLL. Similarly, Project Shakti is proving to be a repeatable model that can empower the Bottom of the Pyramid to enhance their quality of life and help pave a road from the bottom of the neglected social strata to a sought-after market. Although these accomplishments are admirable, several questions still remain. It is unclear whether Annapurna consumers truly appreciate the breakthrough technology embedded within the salt and purchase it *because of* K15, or whether most sales are a result of margin-driven shopkeepers who push Annapurna over other brands. HLL has not yet determined whether consumers are willing to pay a price premium for Annapurna based on the technology alone. Only time will tell; until then, HLL is working to decrease costs, which in turn can lead to a price decrease of Annapurna salt if the market demands it.

Should HLL keep the K15 technology proprietary? If K15 alone is not a differentiator in the sale of the product, would HLL earn higher profits by licensing the technology to other salt manufacturers and, at the same time, battle the IDD endemic on a larger scale?

HLL acknowledges that for Project Shakti to be a significant part of the company's rural penetration, dealers and communicators must be well trained. It is unclear how dealers will perform in an expanded infrastructure. Also, HLL needs to determine whether the Project Shakti model is repeatable in other countries. Indian family structure and village interaction provide a unique diffusion mechanism that is an effective vehicle for Shakti. Whether this model would succeed in Africa, South America, or other parts of Asia (considering the cultural differences in village structures) must be further explored.

Even though these questions remain unanswered, HLL has developed an innovative model that other corporations can examine to determine how they might utilize the Bottom of the Pyramid to enhance their bottom line.

Endnotes

1. Venkatash, M.G., and Dunn, John (1995). Salt iodization for the elimination of iodine deficiency.
2. Economic Intelligence Unit, India Country Indicators 2003.
3. International Council for the control of Iodine Deficiency Disorder, www.iccidd.org.
4. Interview with Ram Narayan, HLL, March 31, 2003.
5. Ministry of Health and Family Welfare, Notification, September 13, 2000.
6. Kurlansky, Mark (2002). Salt: A world history, 387.
7. HLL internal report, "The benefit of iodine to human beings and Iodine Deficiency Disorder (IDD), 2001.
8. Ibid.
9. Interview with Dr. V.G. Kumar, HLL, April 5, 2003.

This case study was written by Anuja Rajendra and Tej Shah under the supervision of Professor C.K. Prahalad. The case study is intended to be a catalyst for discussion and is not intended to illustrate effective or ineffective strategies.

Hindustan Unilever Case Updates

By Nitin Paranjpe, CEO & MD Hindustan Unilever Ltd. &
Executive Vice President Unilever South Asia

I. Project Shakti

Hindustan Unilever's (HUL) Project Shakti is a rural initiative that targets small villages populated by less than 2,000 individuals. It is a unique win-win initiative that catalyzes rural affluence even as it benefits business.

Project Shakti makes an impact on society in two ways—the Shakti Amma (mother) Entrepreneur program creates livelihood opportunities for underprivileged rural women of direct-to-consumer distributors of products like iodized Annapurna Salt and the Shakti Vani (the voice of Shakti) program improves quality of life by spreading health and hygiene awareness by women trained to communicate on those issues.

Project Shakti benefits business by significantly enhancing Hindustan Unilever's direct rural reach, and by enabling Hindustan Unilever's brands to communicate effectively in media-dark regions.

The Shakti Entrepreneur program recognizes that while micro credit plays a key role in alleviating poverty, its capability to do so depends on the availability of investment opportunities. Shakti contributes by creating profitable micro enterprise opportunities for rural women. Armed with micro credit, rural women become Shakti entrepreneurs: direct-to-home distributors in rural markets. This micro enterprise offers low risks and high returns. The products distributed are some of the country's most trusted brands of consumer goods and include a range of mass-market products especially relevant to rural consumers. Moreover, Hindustan Unilever invests its resources in training the entrepreneurs, helping them become confident, business-savvy professionals capable of running their own enterprise.

Shakti entrepreneurs typically earn between 600 Rupees (R.) to Rs 800 per month. Because most of these women are from below the poverty line and live in extremely small villages (with a population between 2,000 to 5,000), this earning is significant and often doubles their household incomes.

Poor hygiene practices are the single largest cause of common diseases, such as diarrhea. Lack of awareness of basic health and hygiene practices kills more than 500,000 children every year in rural India. The Shakti Vani Program educates the rural community about basic health practices. Rural women are appointed as Vanis (communicators) and trained to communicate in social venues, such as schools and village get-togethers. The Vani program covers areas including pre- and post-natal care, infant nutrition, sanitation, good hygiene practices, and the prevention of common diseases. By the end of 2007, the Vani program had covered more than 50,000 villages, reaching out to more than 50 million people.

Various central and state government agencies, including the governments of Andhra Pradesh, Karnataka, Madhya Pradesh, Chhatisgarh, Uttar Pradesh, and Orissa have extended support to Shakti. More than 300 NGOs are actively involved in the project. A national MOU (memorandum of understanding) has been signed with CARE India, covering the fields of health and hygiene awareness and functional adult literacy.

Shakti's impact on society is far-reaching. The Shakti entrepreneur program creates livelihood opportunities for underprivileged rural women. It has already improved the lives of more than 45,000 families of Shakti entrepreneurs, Vanis, and iShakti kiosk entrepreneurs. The Shakti Vani program works to improve the quality of life in rural India, by spreading awareness of best practices in health and hygiene. The iShakti community portal empowers rural community by creating access to information.

Shakti operates in fifteen states: Andhra Pradesh, Karnataka, Tamil Nadu, Gujarat, Madhya Pradesh, Chattisgarh, Maharashtra, Uttar Pradesh, Punjab, Haryana, Rajasthan, West Bengal, Bihar, Jharkhand, and Orissa. There are more than 45,000 Shakti entrepreneurs covering more than 135,000 villages across 15 states. The Vani program has covered more than 50,000 villages.

Since 2007, Hindustan Unilever has also started several new initiatives to help the Shakti entrepreneurs get additional sources of income. Hindustan Unilever has made a tie-up with an affiliate of USAID that is piloting a project to sell ORS (Oral Rehydration Salt) to villagers. Directionally efforts are planned to create a larger community of Shakti Entrepreneurs that will work together to develop themselves.

II. The Challenge of Safe Drinking Water

A major source of disease in the developing world is poor-quality drinking water—in fact, 80 percent of all diseases are water-borne, and this burden is most acute among the poor. As an example, it is estimated that every year, there are four billion episodes of diarrheal disease, with two million child fatalities. In this context, the World Health Organization (WHO) has established that water purification inside the homes will reduce diarrheal and enteric diseases substantially, even in the absence of other hygiene measures.

Given this context, Hindustan Unilever has embarked on a mission to provide safe and affordable drinking water through in-home water purification. Unilever scientists have worked for many years to develop a range of technological breakthroughs that have led to the creation of Pureit, which is an affordable in-home water purifier that provides water that is as safe as boiled water, thereby providing children and families complete protection from all water-borne diseases including diarrhea, jaundice, typhoid, and cholera.

Pureit's germ-kill performance meets the criteria of the Environmental Protection Agency (EPA)—the toughest regulatory agency in the USA. This ensures that consumers are protected even with the most severe germ contamination that they might come across in their drinking water. The Pureit technology is the only one in the world that provides this level of safety without dependence on electricity, pressurized tap water, or cooking gas, thereby making safe drinking water both accessible and affordable to urban and far-flung rural families. What is remarkable is how affordable Pureit is—at a price of just 24 paisa per liter of water, with an upfront cost of Rs 2000.

The Government of India's premier health assessment agency, the National Institute of Epidemiology (NIE) has conducted a year-long scientific study on the impact of Pureit on diarrheal disease in the slums of the tsunami affected southern Indian city of Chennai. The NIE scientifically established that homes using Pureit had a 50 percent lower incidence of diarrhea. Notably, this health benefit was delivered even in the absence of any other health, hygiene, or sanitation intervention.

In 2008, Hindustan Unilever completed the launch of Pureit throughout India. More than five million people have already been protected by Pureit. The company is working with leading national and international social and nongovernment organizations to bring the benefit of safe drinking water to the needy.

Reflective of growing external recognition, Pureit has received the following awards in 2008: i) the Water Digest award supported by UNESCO for the best domestic nonelectric water purifier; ii) the Golden Peacock innovative product award; and iii) the innovation award in India from the United Kingdom Trade and Investment organization.

Based on the high consumer acceptance of Pureit, Unilever has an ambitious vision of bringing safe water to many millions more. This ambitious vision would, in turn, make a significant contribution in helping to achieve the United Nations' Global Millennium Development Goals.

III. Lifebuoy Swasthya Chetna—Health and Hygiene Education

Lifebuoy Swastya Chetna (LBSC) is a rural health and hygiene initiative that was started in 2002. LBSC was initiated in media-dark villages (in Uttar Pradesh, Madhya Pradesh, Bihar, West Bengal, Maharashtra, Orissa) with the objective of spreading awareness about the importance of washing hands with soap.

The need for a program of this nature arose from the fact that diarrhea is a major cause of death in the world today. It is estimated that diarrhea claims the life of a child every 10 seconds, and one-third of these deaths are in India. According to a study done by the London School of Hygiene and Tropical Medicine, the simple practice of washing hands with soap and water can reduce diarrhea by as much as 47 percent. However, ignorance of such basic hygiene practices leads to high mortality rates in rural India.

Being India's leading personal wash health brand, Lifebuoy saw a role for itself in propagating the message of hygiene and health in villages. Hindustan Lever launched its Lifebuoy Swasthya Chetna initiative with this in mind.

LBSC is a multiphased activity that works toward effecting behavior change among the rural population it touches. It demonstrates that "visible clean is not really clean," thereby proving the importance of washing hands. It targets children because they are the harbingers of change in society and mothers because they are the custodians of health.

The campaign has been divided into various phases. In the initial phase, a Health Development Officer (HDO) and an assistant initiates contact and interacts with students and influencers of the community (Key Opinion Leaders)—that is, village community representatives, medical practitioners, school teachers, and so on. A number of tools such as a pictorial story in a flip chart format, a "Glo-germ demonstration," and a quiz with attractive prizes to reinforce the message are used. The "Glo-Germ demonstration" is a unique tool to make unseen germs visible and emphasize the need to use soap to wash hands and kill germs. Each phase of the activity is customized to the needs of the respective group, interactive games for kids and mothers, and such. The various stages reinforce the message, which is crucial to affect awareness and behavior change in favor of hand wash hygiene.

The program involves meeting the local Panchayat bodies—especially Anganwaadi workers—and seeks their help in implementation at the village level. The program was working closely with government bodies such as NRHM and also UNICEF (2008) for Initiatives on Hand Washing programs.

The Indian postal department released a special postal cover on Lifebuoy Swatshya Chetna on the occasion of World Health Day (April 7) in 2006.

The Department of Posts has a long history of honoring great personalities, institutions, and monuments through commemorative postage stamps. A few events are commemorated by the Department of Posts through the issue of a Special Postal Cover. Special Postal Covers are of great importance and philatelic relevance that have emerged as a vehicle to accord symbolic recognition to past and present events and to honor individuals, institutions, and organizations. Lifebuoy is the first and the only brand to receive this honor and recognition in India.

The impact of LBSC is as follows:

- Increase in awareness of germs among the population covered in this campaign from 52 percent to 83 percent.
- Increase in association of germs with disease in the population covered from 35 percent to 57 percent.
- Since 2002, the project has touched 50,676 villages and 120,000 million people. In 2008, LBSC had contacted 15,000 villages in Uttar Pradesh, Madhya Pradesh, Maharashtra, Bihar, and Karnataka.

Jaipur Foot: Prosthetics for the Poor

At age fourteen, Sudha Chandran, an aspiring dancer, lost her right foot and part of her leg in a car accident. Devastated and convinced she would never walk again, let alone dance, she spent several months on crutches. Then one day in 1984, she read about Jaipur Foot.

A prosthetic foot in the United States costs on average $8,000. This cost is far beyond the means of the poor in developing countries,[1] and even many of the poor in the United States.[2] As many as four billion people, in India and the rest of the world, live in poverty on less than two dollars per day. When someone loses a limb, the inability to work is catastrophic, often for a whole family. The Jaipur Foot is tailored specifically to the lifestyles of the poor and costs only about $30—affordable to all, and it is often given away free to many of the handicapped poor who have lost a limb. Here is a working model of a nongovernmental, nonreligious, and nonprofit organization able to financially sustain itself while helping the world's disabled poor.[3]

The Jaipur Foot is tailored specifically to the lifestyles of the poor and costs only about $30—affordable to all, and it is often given away free to many of the handicapped poor who have lost a limb.

There are 10 to 25 million amputees in the world, a figure that grows by approximately 250,000 each year. People in developing countries are particularly susceptible to the loss of lower limbs[4] from disease (70 percent), trauma (22 percent), congenital or birth defects (four percent), and tumors (four percent). In developing countries with recent war-torn histories, such as Afghanistan, land mines account for a significant number—approximately 300,000 children are severely disabled because of land mines, with an additional 15,000 to 20,000 new victims each year.[5] In Afghanistan alone, there are nearly 10 million land mines.[6] Diseases such as diabetes and even polio are the cause of even more of the amputees.

The Jaipur Foot was first developed in 1968 by Ram Chandra, one of Jaipur city's finest sculptors. Concerned by the inadequacy of performance and the cost of imported artificial limbs, he began work on a rubber foot,[7] which he refined with the help of Dr. P.K. Sethi, an orthopedic surgeon, Dr. S.C. Kasliwal, and Dr. Mahesh Udawat into what became known as the Jaipur Foot. To facilitate the spread of the foot, its creators decided not to patent it. Their society, Bhagwan Mahaveer Viklang Sahayata Samiti (BMVSS), was organized in 1975 to treat amputees and to distribute the product at as low a cost as possible, or for free when necessary.

The Jaipur Foot was designed to simulate normal foot movements and provide a quality solution for the masses that also allowed the poor to continue to earn a livelihood. Aspects specific to the cultural and working needs of the poor included being suitable to activities such as squatting, sitting cross-legged, walking on uneven ground, and barefoot walking. Other constraints the designers had to consider included the following:

- **Poverty**—The cost of fabrication, with the possibility of adjustments and alignments, had to be low (while creating an effective product).
- **Closed economy**—Limited import of foreign materials in India meant the foot had to be fabricated from readily available local materials.
- **Work lifestyle**—Most amputees work hard and long hours in an agricultural economy. Days spent without limbs threaten livelihood and sustenance, which is reason to seek an acceptable prosthesis that could be fitted quickly.
- **Cultural issues**—The everyday lifestyle involved sitting cross-legged, walking barefoot on uneven ground, and squatting.
- **Limited training manpower**—Lack of skilled labor relative to the huge demand for prostheses necessitated a simplified manufacturing process that could be performed with limited training.

The distribution of the Jaipur Foot occurs at BMVSS sites (of which there are seven in India, two in Jaipur alone) and at camps, including camps in 19 countries, including Afghanistan, Bangladesh, Dominican Republic, Honduras, Indonesia, Malawi, Nigeria, Nairobi, Nepal, Panama, Philippines, Papua New Guinea, Rwanda, Somalia, Trinidad, Vietnam, Zimbabwe, and Sudan. At a main site, such as one in Jaipur, a full-time doctor is on staff; other doctors contribute time to ensure the proper prosthetic fit and follow-up. Each foot is fitted by a technician, an artisan who makes the equivalent of $1,200 annually, about twice the per-capita income in India. The actual cost of materials used for an above-the-knee prosthetic foot is about $7.68, which includes the Jaipur Foot itself and the simulated joints for a below-knee limb. The most expensive piece of equipment used in a prosthetic fitting is the vacuum-forming machine used to get an exact replica of the mold of the patient's remaining limb (stump). These run about $4,000 and last from five to seven years.

About 60 patients each day obtain prostheses from Jaipur Foot's main facility in Jaipur, India. Remarkably, unless other medical conditions intervene, each patient is custom fitted with a prosthesis in one day—usually within three hours. The goal is to return the patient to his or her profession and an independent life after the patient's first visit to the clinic. The society's services do not just include a speedy fitting of a prosthesis. The operating process also attends to psychological needs, and there are on-site meals and overnight accommodations for patients at no cost. Free meals and accommodations are also provided for the patient's family members who can therefore provide on-site support and comfort.

BMVSS has laid down extremely simple procedures for reception, admission, measurement taking, manufacturing, fitting, and discharge of patients. Unlike in all other medical centers all over the word, patients are admitted as they arrive without regard to the time of day. In addition, patients are provided boarding and lodging facilities at the centers of BMVSS until they are provided with limbs, calipers, or other aids. In most orthopedic centers around the world, patients must come back several times for a custom fit. This process can take several weeks. Such a system is unsuitable to poor patients who find it extremely difficult, both in physical and financial terms, to come back a second time from long distances. Jaipur Foot is custom fitted on the same day (in fact, in less than four hours). Most significant, the prosthetics, orthotics, and other aids and appliances are provided totally free of charge to the handicapped. But for this policy, more than 90 percent of the patients would have remained deprived of artificial limbs, calipers, and other aids and appliances. The setting up of patient-oriented value and management systems was an equally important innovation.

BMVSS has ten branches in India. In addition, approximately 60 workshops fabricate or fit the Jaipur Foot in India. The society also has aided the establishment of several centers abroad. Funded by the Indian government and philanthropic groups, BMVSS and similar organizations offer medical care, room, board, and a prosthetic at no cost to the patient. It also has helped launch free clinics in more than a dozen countries.

The determination was made at the outset that the Jaipur Foot prosthesis would be provided at a low cost, or free when necessary, which necessitated a nonprofit framework. The prospect of no (or little) incoming funds for prostheses fitted forced administrators to focus on containing costs. In particular, emphasis was placed on the cost of the materials used to construct the Jaipur Foot, the capital equipment required to fabricate the foot, and the method by which the foot was fitted to a patient to make the prosthesis widely available.

Cost-efficiency is reflected in Jaipur Foot's annual expenses. Jaipur Foot's expense breakout for the 2002 fiscal year underscores the efficiency of expense and underpins the society's effort to serve as many patients as possible given its financial resources. About 90 percent of the company's expenses in the 2002 fiscal year were directly related to the cost of producing and fitting prostheses for the poor. Another 7 percent of the company's expenses went toward other forms of charitable assistance. Only 4 percent of its expenditures went toward administrative and overhead expenses.

The number of limbs fitted every year by Jaipur Foot is about 16,000. Between March 1975, when BMVSS was established, and March 2003, the society fitted 236,717 limbs in India (and 14,070 others around the world). BMVSS is still finding innovative ways to help the poor. With all of its innovations in technology and management, and understanding the needs of its patients, BMVSS has developed a unique business model. This model spreads the Jaipur Foot technology that allows *rickshaw-wallah* (pedicab operators) amputees to perform their job, farmer amputees to be farmers, and in the case of fourteen-year-old Sudha Chandran, classical Indian dancer amputees to be classical Indian dancers.

Endnotes

1. http://www.jaipurfoot.org.
2. According to Mark Taylor, from the University of Michigan Prosthetics Department, because of insurance company policies and high costs, only 50 percent of patients in the United States receive the prosthetic medical care they require.
3. Bhagwan Mahaveer Viklang Sahayata Samiti (BMVSS) fabricates and fits approximately 16,000 patients annually with the Jaipur Foot.
4. www.mossresourcenet.org/amputa.htm.
5. U.S. Centers for Disease Control, cited at www.openroads.org.
6. United Nations data.
7. A variation of the Solid Ankle Cushion Heel (SACH) foot developed in 1956 at the Biomechanics Laboratory at the University of California, Berkeley, which had become the most popular prosthetic foot.

This case study was written by Scott Macke, Ruchi Misra, and Ajay Sharma under the supervision of Professor C.K. Prahalad. The case study is intended to be a catalyst for discussion and is not intended to illustrate effective or ineffective strategies.

Jaipur Foot Update

By D.R. Mehta, founder and patron, Bhagwan Mahaveer Viklang Sahayata Samiti (BMVSS), Jaipur

Bhagwan Mahaveer Viklang Sahayata Samiti, the nongovernmental, voluntary society in India for helping the handicapped started in 1975, has expanded its reach. By the end of March 2008, the number of beneficiaries getting artificial limbs, calipers, wheelchairs, hand-paddled tricycles, crutches, and other aids and appliances has been in the millions. Of these, the number of persons getting artificial limbs was more than 3,300,000. Approximately 2,800,000 people got calipers. The other aids and appliances numbered 4,200,000. By the end of March 2009 (the end of the financial year), the total number of beneficiaries was approximately 10,900,000.

Since the first edition of *The Fortune at the Bottom of the Pyramid* BMVSS's position as the world's largest prosthetic provider continues with a further increase in the number of beneficiaries. In the financial year April 2007 to March 2008, the total number of beneficiaries of BMVSS was 66,181, of which the number of beneficiaries provided with artificial limbs was 20,181.

A comparison with the International Committee of Red Cross (ICRC) that runs a program called Special Fund for Disabled validates BMVSS as being the largest providers of aids and appliances to the Bottom of the Pyramid amputees. According to the Report of the International Committee of Red Cross Special Funds for Disabled for the years 2007 and 2008 drawn from the Internet provides the following points:

- In 2007, Special Funds for Disabled provided support for the handicapped in 28 countries through 58 projects in association with nongovernmental organizations.
- In 2007, Special Funds for Disabled contributed to the rehabilitation of approximately 15,000 persons worldwide, including the fitting of 8,970 artificial limbs and 9,752 calipers.
- In 2008 Special Funds for Disabled, the figures of the disabled rehabilitated has not been given, but it is mentioned that SFD was operated in 29 countries through 61 projects in association with nongovernmental organizations.

The first edition of *The Bottom of the Pyramid* mentions that the Jaipur Foot fabricated and fitted by the BMVSS costs less than $30 compared to $8,000 for a comparable prosthesis in the United States. Now, the cost of a Jaipur Foot is $40, while the comparable figures of the U.S. limbs are not known. But, considering the price increase of various raw materials and labor, the price might not be less than $12,000.

Despite the mass customization on such an increased scale, Jaipur Foot continues to be given free of cost to the amputees.

Whereas, at the time of the first edition, Jaipur Foot was in 16 countries, now 22 countries (including India) are covered by BMVSS in Asia, Africa, and Latin America.

BMVSS held camps in 19 countries. This figure has increased to 22 countries.

The number of branches of BMVSS in India was only 10. This number has gone up to 19 now (including two branches in Jaipur, one each in Delhi, Mumbai Chennai, Ahmedabad, Hyderabad, Bangalore, Indore, Patna, Srinagar, and Ambala, and seven more in the State of Rajasthan at Kota, Bikaner, Udaipur, Jodhpur, Pali, Bharatpur, and Ajmer). Further apart from helping other nongovernmental organizations to set up Jaipur centers in various countries, in 2007, BMVSS set up one artificial limb fitting center in Colombia-Madeline as a joint venture. BMVSS also became a technical partner in two artificial limb fitting centers in Pakistan (Karachi and Islamabad).

BMVSS not only supports the setting up of new artificial limb fitting centers by other organizations to help benefit more handicapped, it also has increased its own centers from 10 in 2002 to 19 by 2008 and was planning to cover all the major states of India within three years of that.

Jaipur Foot seeks constant technical improvement. BMVSS's effort as a social organization is to combine sentiment with science. The philosophy of BMVSS is that poor patients will be helped properly only if the artificial limbs, even though given free of charge, should be constantly made into better and more lasting products. Toward this end, it has established links with world-renowned technology institutions like Stanford University and MIT in the United States and with the Space Research Organization (ISRO)—India's topmost and one of the world's leading scientific institutions. It is also establishing contact with IIT—Madras and Malviya Regional Engineering Deemed University—all for the improvement of existing devices and development of new devices.

Stanford University and BMVSS signed a letter of understanding in the beginning of 2008 for the development of a new knee joint for above knee prosthesis. In highly costly "above knee" prostheses, getting an efficient and cost-effective knee joint is a problem. After detailed computerized studies at Stanford, several visits of experts of Stanford to the center of BMVSS at Jaipur, and feedback from the patients provided by BMVSS, a new four-bar linkage knee joint has been developed. It is simple in design; however, it is very efficient. Field trials of this joint are under way at Jaipur Foot. The feedback up until now is very positive. Yet, the cost of this joint is only $25.

MIT has developed and given BMVSS a different prototype toward a different type of final product.

Further product development includes cooperative work with DOW Chemicals, a world-renowned chemical and polymer company, which is helping by providing better material and technical advice. Approximately 1,000 polyurethane foot pieces based on modified design of ISRO with material support and advice of DOW Chemicals have been put on field trials. The results so far are very positive.

In addition, BMVSS has signed a nonexclusive manufacturing agreement for the manufacture of special wheelchairs of the Whirlwind Wheelchair organization. These are light, sturdy, and safe. They will be exported all over the world.

BMVSS is also getting the hand-paddled tricycles and crutches of the Indian Standard Institute (ISI) certification. ISI joints for calipers are also underway.

In the workshop, special alignment systems have been imported from the United States, UK, and Germany for ensuring proper fit and gait.

Special emphasis has also been placed on training and repeated training of the technical staff, also available to the technicians of the other organizations making the Jaipur Foot, both in India and abroad. Bhagwan Mahaveer Viklang Sahayata Samiti is continuing its effort for its mass customization in India and abroad. Constant ongoing efforts are connecting with some of the best technology institutions in the world to improve the quality and reduce the cost so that the major problem of affordability of the standard products, in the disability segment of the health sector, is addressed even more effectively. The objective is "Jaipur Foot—that all may walk." On the other hand, the patient-centric value system and humane management continues unabated. All these efforts and arrangements are ultimately for the goal: mobility and dignity.

Aravind Eye Care: The Most Precious Gift

For an estimated 45 million people worldwide, and nine million in India, the precious gift of sight has been snatched away, most often quite needlessly. One man, seized with a passion to eradicate needless blindness, decided to do something about it.

In 1976, Padmashree Dr. G. Venkataswamy, popularly referred to as Dr. V, retired from the Government Medical College, Madurai, as the head of the Department of Ophthalmology. Rather than settling for a quiet retired life, Dr. V was determined to continue the work he was doing at the Government Medical College, especially organizing rural eye camps to check sight, prescribe needed corrective glasses, do cataract and other surgeries as needed, and advise corrective and preventive measures: in short, provide quality eye care. This was to be provided to the poor and the rich alike. His vision was simple yet grand: Eradicate needless blindness at least in Tamil Nadu, his home state, if not in the entire nation of India.

His vision was simple yet grand: Eradicate needless blindness at least in Tamil Nadu, his home state, if not in the entire nation of India.

Dr. V. started a modest hospital with his personal savings and with partial government support[1] for cataract surgeries done on poor patients from eye camps. From the beginning, a policy was put in place—there would be paying as well as free patients. The paying patients would be charged only moderately and not more than comparable hospitals in the city charged. There were to be no "five-star" customers to cross-subsidize the poor patients. Dr. V was certain that high productivity and volumes were necessary if the hospital were to be viable and generate a surplus to provide expansion funds.

Indeed, the hospital generated a surplus from the beginning, and using such surplus it was possible to open a 30-bed hospital within a year, in 1977. A 70-bed hospital meant exclusively for free patients was built in 1978. The existing paying hospital building was opened in 1981, with 250 beds and 80,000 square feet of space over five floors. The initial focus was on cataract surgery, but other specialties such as retina, cornea, glaucoma, pediatric ophthalmology, neuro-ophthalmology, uvea, low vision, and orbit were gradually added. No compromises were ever made on the equipment; they were of the best quality, and many were imported. However, the rooms (including those of doctors), waiting halls, and examination rooms were utilitarian. In 1984, a new 350-bed free hospital was opened to cater exclusively to free patients in Madurai. In stages, the number of beds increased to the present 1,468 beds (1,200 free and 268 paying) in the hospitals in Madurai.

The initial focus was on cataract surgery, but other specialties such as retina, cornea, glaucoma, pediatric ophthalmology, neuro-ophthalmology, uvea, low vision, and orbit were gradually added.

In addition, other hospitals in other towns in Tamil Nadu were being opened. In 1985, a 100-bed hospital at Theni, a small town 80 kilometers west of Madurai, was opened, mainly to cater to additional eye camp patients. A hospital with 400 beds was opened at Tirunelveli, a town 160 kilometers south of Madurai, in 1988. In 1997, an 874-bed hospital was opened in Coimbatore, the second-largest city of Tamil Nadu, to cater to the needs of the population in that area. In 2003, a 750-bed hospital was opened in Pondicherry (a Union Territory but within the geographical area of Tamil Nadu) to cater to the people living in northern Tamil Nadu. In total, the five Aravind Eye Hospitals (AEH) had 3,649 beds, consisting of 2,850 free and 799 paying beds.

Though the initial focus was on building hospitals and reaching out to the poor to do cataract surgeries, it was soon clear to Dr. V that to reach their goal of eradicating needless blindness, several other activities had to be put in place. Thus, over the years, these activities were added, and Aravind Eye Hospitals evolved into the Aravind Eye Care System, with its many divisions: Aurolab, the manufacturing facility set up primarily for manufacturing intraocular lenses; a training center named Lions Aravind Institute of Community Ophthalmology (LAICO); a center for ophthalmic research named Aravind Medical Research Foundation; a research center for women and children named Aravind Centre for Women, Children and Community Health; and an international eye bank named the Rotary Aravind International Eye Bank. All the activities of these divisions relate to the core mission of eradicating needless blindness.

Eye camps represented a popular way to reach out to rural communities. These camps were formed in different villages, with prior publicity in the form of posters, loudspeaker announcements from vehicles, and pamphlets. Charitable trusts or individuals sponsored the eye camps and contributed to the publicity necessary to get people to the camps. The government and institutions such as the World Bank covered the costs of surgery and treatment. The eye camp checkups and subsequent treatment were free for the patients. On the day of an eye camp, patients were examined, and those requiring surgery were advised of such. In some camps, surgeries were done *in situ* in makeshift tents. AEH believed this was neither hygienic nor productive, so it performed the surgeries only in its base hospitals. Follow-up checks and prescriptions for glasses were made in subsequent camps or during patients' visits to hospitals.

Eye camps represented a popular way to reach out to rural communities.

The cost (for a sponsor) of an eye camp varies with the nature of the camp. A "small" camp with 300 outpatients (leading to about 60 patients for surgery) costs about 6,700 rupees, whereas a large camp, with 1,000 outpatients and 200 surgeries, can cost up to 42,500 rupees. Finding sponsors is not a problem. Generally, local NGOs, Lions and Rotary clubs, local industrialists, and businessmen and philanthropists sponsor the camps. Sponsors also cover publicity expenses (posters, pamphlets, banners, megaphone announcements from vehicles, and so on) and expenses related to the organization of the camps (usually in a school or public place).

Other community outreach programs at eye camps include a diabetic retinopathy management project that screens nearly 12,000 people per year, a community-based rehabilitation project supported by Sight

Savers International that is aimed at rehabilitating incurably blind persons through community-based support, and an eye screening of school children that helps train teachers to detect eye defects so corrective measures can be taken early. (In 2002, for instance, 68,528 children in 80 schools were screened, and 3,075 children were given glasses to correct refractive errors.) The Aravind Medical Research Foundation coordinates ongoing research, such as clinical, population-based studies and social and health systems research conducted using the data readily available in the hospitals and the community outreach programs.

Despite having a majority of patients as free patients, the Aravind Eye Care System has always been financially self-supporting. Even from the beginning, it did not depend on government grants or donations (except for the support given by the government toward eye camp patients), and until recently it had not applied for any other government grants for service delivery. Dr. V, now in his 80s, stresses the point that not only is the Aravind Eye Care System self-sufficient in terms of operational income and expenditure, but it also takes care of capital expenditure for all expansion and new units. Said Dr. V: "You management people will tell me, why don't you go to the banks, take loans, and grow faster? Cost of debt is low. But we, as a policy, will not go to the banks for loans, since it will compromise our freedom." Each new hospital is not built until enough surplus has accumulated.

Despite having a majority of patients as free patients, the Aravind Eye Care System has always been financially self-supporting.

Aravind Eye Care System's purchase of the best equipment available includes an IT system that tracks all patients, regulates workloads, and closely monitors postoperative complication rates. The contrasting utilitarian rooms for doctors and staff confirm that the emphasis is placed on quality care for patients. Doctors and staff work longer and harder than in other health-care programs, in large part driven by the spirit of Dr. V's original commitment. The dedication of the earliest doctors and staff of the system extends itself with training and recruitment programs, among which is the Aravind Eye Hospital (AEH) & Post Graduate Institute of Ophthalmology, initiated in 1982, which had admitted around 30 resident doctors as of 2003. All admissions are based strictly on merit, and no admission or capitation fee are collected; the going rate in 2003 at other private teaching hospitals was about 1.5 to 2 million rupees.

Doctors are crucial at AEH, and most were recruited as residents. A doctor explained, "We do commit ourselves totally to the cause of eradication of avoidable blindness. That means we have to do a certain number of surgeries every day. (Each doctor does about 2,600 surgeries per year; the all-India average is about 400.) We have a unique culture based on service. All the doctors speak softly to patients and nurses. No shouting here. If a doctor behaves in an unacceptable manner, word goes around the hospital in no time, and the doctor will be in trouble. We believe in mutual respect as a core value." The system also recruits and trains its own ophthalmic assistants (900 on staff each year, and 99 percent of those trained stay in the system). Nurses, like the doctors, are there because they want to be. As one nurse said, "I work more than the government hospital nurses do; I get paid a little less or at par with them, but I get much more respect in the society. When I go in the bus, someone will recognize that I work in AEH and offer me a seat or be nice to me. I really feel happy about it." The staff strength of the Aravind Eye Hospital, Madurai, as of February 2003, was 762. For about 113 doctors, there were 307 nurses, 38 counselors, and 304 other staff. The pattern of staffing in other units is broadly similar.

Each doctor does about 2,600 surgeries per year; the all-India average is about 400.

"When I go in the bus, someone will recognize that I work in AEH and offer me a seat or be nice to me. I really feel happy about it."

The driving culture of the Aravind Eye Care System is that of giving as much time and effort as they can toward the organizational mission of reducing needless blindness. Dr. V's leadership style is that of "leading by doing." Dr. V and other top staff pick up pieces of paper lying on the hospital floor and hand them over to the next sweeper they see. They do not shout or get upset with the sweeper but by their action demonstrate the value of cleanliness and humility. Dr. V has reason to be pleased with his achievements, but he looks to the future beyond the Aravind Eye Hospitals with the urge to develop other

Dr. V has reason to be pleased with his achievements, but he looks to the future beyond the Aravind Eye Hospitals with the urge to develop other sustainable systems that better utilize doctors and heighten their productivity.

sustainable systems that better utilize doctors and heighten their productivity. Despite all their efforts, only about seven percent of the target population comes to the camps, and he hopes to increase that percentage. Also, he hopes to improve the skills of all doctors who perform eye surgeries, which will reduce recuperation time and increase the subsequent ability of patients to earn a living. Even better postoperative care and counseling are part of his ongoing efforts to ever improve the vision of everyone, while in his small way he spends every day making a difference.

Endnotes

1. "Partial" in the sense that although the government paid an amount for each surgery performed on poor patients from eye camps, this fell quite short of the total cost of the operation.

Compiled by C.K. Prahalad from a more detailed case study prepared by S. Manikutty and Neharika Vohra of the Indian Institute of Management, Ahmedabad, 2003.

Update: Aravind Eye Care

By R.D. Thulasiraj, Executive Director, Aravind Eye Care System

The Aravind Eye Care System at present is comprised of five hospitals; a manufacturing wing that produces intraocular lens, suture needles, cataract kits, pharmaceuticals, and instruments related to eye care; an institute for training; an institute for research; an international eye bank; four managed care hospitals; community outreach; and well-structured IT systems.

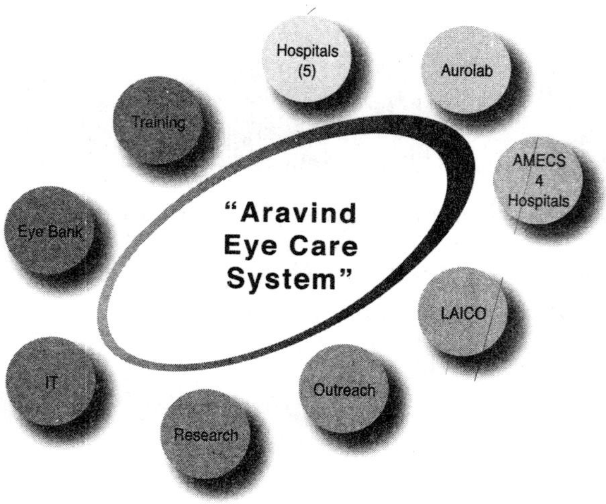

In the financial year 2007 to 2008, the Aravind Eye Care System screened 2,396,100 outpatients and performed 285,745 surgeries, making it the largest eye care provider in the world (in terms of volume). The consortium of nine hospitals, including Aravind Managed Care Hospitals, performed one million eye surgeries each year. The nine hospitals worked with at least 100 hospitals each in their regions to deliver quality and affordable eye care. The Aravind Eye Hospital is now working with 249 hospitals in the country and abroad.

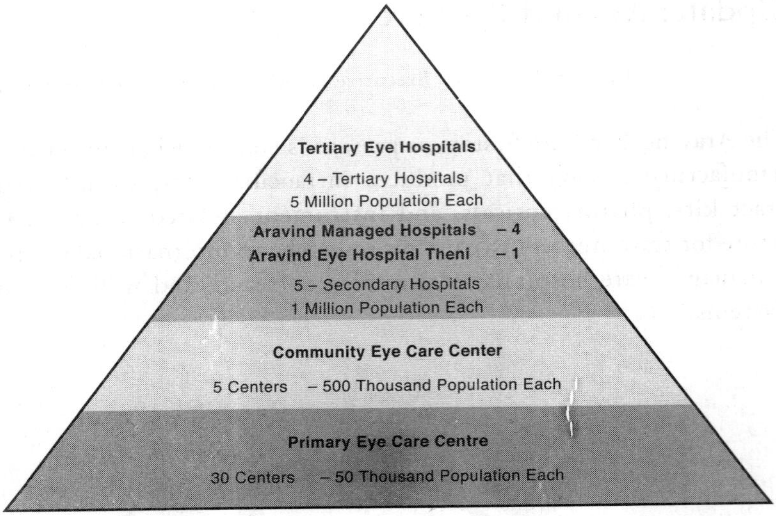

An average day at Aravind Eye Hospital network includes

- 6,000 outpatients in hospitals
    - 4 to 5 outreach screening eye camps
    - Examining 1,500 people
    - Transporting 300 patients to the hospital for surgery
    - 850 to 1,000 surgeries
- Classes for 100 Residents/Fellows and 300 technicians and administrators

This makes Aravind the largest provider of eye care services and trainer of ophthalmic personnel in the world.

Aravind is known the world over for its innovative approaches, which have become a replicable model ensuring efficient service delivery.

Community outreach, a cornerstone of Aravind's high-volume work, is one such approach that encourages active involvement of the community in providing eye care services. This approach, complemented with appropriate systems and processes at all levels of the organization, enables it to perform high-volume, high-quality, and affordable eye care services.

But the current reality is as shown in the following figure.

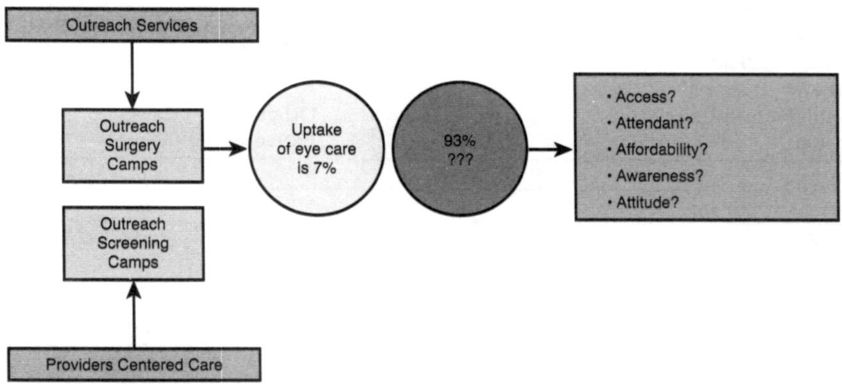

With nearly 70 percent of the Indian population residing in the rural areas, it is natural that a significant proportion of blindness and ocular morbidity is concentrated in these areas. Unfortunately, these are the areas that remain outside the mainstream of eye care services.

Vision Centre with a focus on primary eye care was designed to remove the barrier of access. Each Vision Centre is designed with the capabilities to do comprehensive eye examination and carry out basic intervention, including provision of glasses for refractive errors and rehabilitation for the blind. Each Vision Centre covers a population of 50,000.

- The Vision Centre is linked to the base hospital through low cost tele-connectivity with adequate bandwidth facilitating face-to-face interactions between the patient and the ophthalmologist.
- Persons identified with cataract, squint, diabetic retinopathy, glaucoma, and other ocular problems are referred to the base hospital for further surgical and procedural management. Aravind always focuses in developing sustainable and replicable models/approaches, thus benefiting the general public at large globally. Sustainability of the vision centers will be attained by collecting a nominal fee of Rupees 20 (50 cents) per OP consultation; the sale of spectacles at an affordable cost ranging from Rs 200–300 (U.S. $4–6). In addition to this, other services like blood tests to identify or monitor diabetes will also be provided for a small fee. The vision centers serve as a replicable model to be put up in any part of the country. This initiative has ensured sustained access to basic eye care to the community unlike the approach of screening eye camps that is proven to be cost-intensive and provider-dependent.

Economic Impact for Each Patient to the Hospital (in Rs)	No.	Transport	Other Expenses	Lost Wages	Total
Patient	1	25	50	100	175
Patient attendant	1	25	50	100	175
Total		**50**	**100**	**200**	**350**
to the Vision Centre					
Patient	1	20	20	50	80
Patient attendant	0.5	5	10	25	40
Total		25	30	75	130
Rupees saved	**Rs 220 (roughly Rs 50 lakhs for the 25,000 patients)**				

Impact in Service Delivery in the First 12 Months of Existence	No.	Per 50,000	%	Acceptance Rate
Number of Vision Centres	6	1		
Population covered	399,924	50,000		
20% may have eye care needs	79,985	10,000		
New patients seen	23,213	2,902	29%	
Patients referred for surgery	1,686	211	7%	59%
Other patients referred to hospital	2,080	260	9%	84%
Refractive error prescriptions	4,931	616	21%	92%

Diabetic Retinopathy Screening Through Mobile Van

- Diabetes is a major health problem in industrialized countries and a rapidly emerging problem in urban areas in developing countries. In developed countries, the prevalence of diabetes is approximately 5 percent. The implications for the provision of eye care are evident because everyone with diabetes will eventually develop diabetic retinopathy if they live long.

- Aravind developed a "Mobile Clinic for Advanced Eye Screening" powered by VSAT connectivity with the support of World Diabetes Foundation (WDF) and Indian Space Research Organization (ISRO).
- The main objective of the mobile van screening is to screen diabetic patients through digital imaging with tele-transmission for further diagnosis by the retina consultant.
- This screening unit is definitely helping the diabetic patients as an expert opinion is made available immediately without the need for the patients to travel to the tertiary center or the specialist.
- Experiences from this initiative have shown that only 20 percent of the patients needed further examination by the ophthalmologist, thus avoiding unnecessary travel for the rest of the diabetic patients. At the same time, awareness levels on the impact of diabetes-related eye problems improved.

Mobile Van DR Screening Camp Performance (Mar 07–Apr 08)	
Camps	51
Patients screened	13,062
Diabetics identified	2,449
DR patients identified	532

School Screening Camps

- Children constitute 3 percent of the world's blind population; childhood blindness has not been given its due importance during allocation of resources.
- The major causes for needless blindness—either preventable or avoidable—are refractive errors, lens anomalies (cataract 0.05 percent), and retinopathy of prematurity.
- Screening of school children done mainly to detect and treat refractive error, amblyopia, and rarely other diseases.
- Aravind Eye Care has developed a unique process where the school teachers are given training at the base hospital, and they do the basic screening before the ophthalmic team examines the children with an extended human resource.

- Aravind Eye Care intends to cover special schools for the visually impaired and integrated school in this area.

Scaling up Services by Developing Business Models and Extending to the Northern Part of India

AMECS—Aravind Managed Eye Care Services

- Aravind eye hospitals located in Tamilnadu and Pondicherry contribute to 42 percent of the cataract surgeries performed in the State of Tamilnadu and 5 percent of the overall national performance.
- This scale of operations is made possible by adopting innovative approaches and strategies: standardized systems and processes, innovations in human resources management, compassionate patient-centered care, and backward integration for the supply of critical resources like human resources and consumables.
- Aravind has now developed the approach of Managed Eye Care as a strategic direction to address the basic issues of providing eye care in the underserved regions.
- The goal is to perform 500,000 surgeries annually through 25 eye hospitals by the year 2015.
- This process involves working with local partners who are socially conscious individuals/organizations wanting to invest in eye care.
- While the partner organization invests in capital expenditure and local liaisons for the seamless implementation of the project, Aravind will carry out complete turn-key solutions starting from planning, operationalizing the project, implementation, and monitoring.
- Aravind is currently working with four such like-minded organizations in the states of West Bengal: Madhya Pradesh Birla group, Uttar Pradesh-Rajiv Gandhi Charitable Trust, Gujarat-Sun Pharma Group, and Rajasthan-Narotam Sekhsaria Foundation.
- Aravind has currently opened three hospitals in places like Kolkatta (West Bengal), Amethi (Uttar Pradesh), Lucknow (Uttar Pradesh), and Amreli (Gujarat).

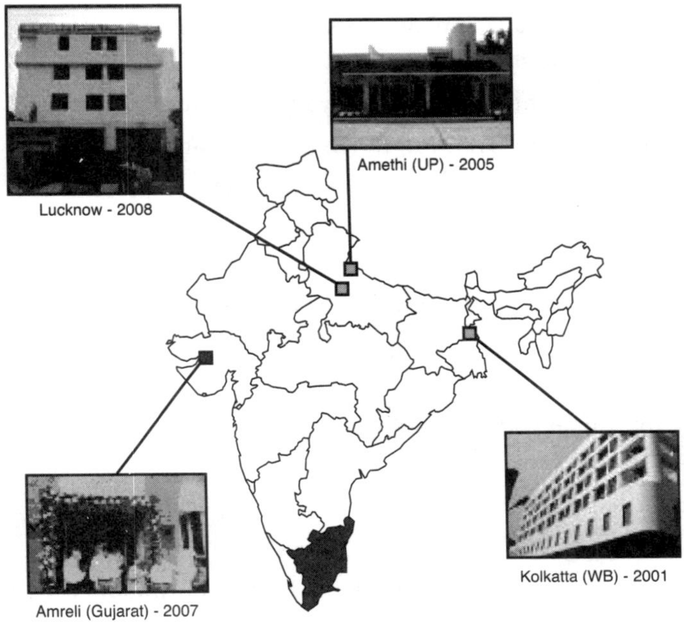

LAICO—Lions Aravind Institute of Community Ophthalmology

- A major part of LAICO's activities centers around enhancing the capacity of existing and new eye hospitals worldwide for comprehensive organizational development through sharing the best practices in eye care. It works in collaboration with international voluntary organizations such as the Lions Clubs International Foundation, Sightsavers International, Christian Blind Mission, International Eye Foundation, Right to Sight, Seva Foundation, ORBIS International, Lavelle Fund for the Blind, and the World Health Organization.
- Consultancy is carried out in phases.
    - Needs assessment visits
    - Vision building workshops
    - Follow-up visits and monitoring followed by a final situation analysis visit
- Until December 2008, LAICO has provided this service to 249 eye hospitals spread across the country and in other developing nations.

- The following management and skills development courses on eye care services are offered at LAICO:
    - Management Priorities in Eye Care Delivery
    - Management Training for Eye Care Program Managers
    - Management Training and Systems Development for Hospital Administrators
    - Community Outreach
    - Fellowship in Eye Hospital Management
    - Training in Eye Hospitals Operation Project Management Training for Eye Care
    - Instrument Maintenance and Training

Aurolab

- On September 30, 2007, Dr. Allen Foster, president, Christian Blind Mission, inaugurated the new facility.
- The new facility is located in a sprawling campus amid the lush grounds of Aurofarm that sets the atmosphere for dedicated work, while the beautiful design of the building inspires employees to do even better than what Aurolab has been doing for the past 16 years.
- Aurolab has commenced operations in the new facility, and each division is expanding its capacity and upgrading its technology to take advantage of the available space.
- The factory is a 110,000 square-foot operating area including the 20,000 square feet of clean rooms. The new facility is constructed as per the international regulations, like Schedule M, USFDA, and UK MHRA.

Dr. G. Venkataswamy Eye Research Institute

From the initial days of performing large-scale operational studies on barriers of service delivery, research at Aravind has grown all areas of research in ophthalmology—basic, clinical, operations research including community outreach and, with the establishment of Aurolab, product development. To integrate all these, the Dr. G. Venkataswamy Eye Research Institute was formed to be the nodal body.

The research activities at Aravind reflect Aravind's commitment to finding new ways to reduce the burden of blindness. The combination of high clinical load, extensive community participation, and access to a large network of eye hospitals provide ideal opportunities for conducting clinical, laboratory, population-based studies, and social and health system research.

Numerous randomized, controlled trials have been made possible by virtue of the high patient load. The integration of the manufacturing arm of the Aravind Eye Care System, the Aurolab, helps the clinicians to work in close tandem with engineers and designers to develop and evaluate new instruments and allied gadgets. Now, with the establishment of Centers of Excellence within Aravind's specialty clinics, along with its continued emphasis on academic rigor and its recent thrust on developing comprehensive service delivery models in areas like Diabetic Retinopathy, Glaucoma, and Pediatric ophthalmology, and its rapid strides in the field of tele-ophthalmology with remote consultation and teleconferencing between hospitals, Aravind is poised as never before to take on new challenges in research.

Training

Aravind Eye Care System with the support of the Indian Space Research Organisation has established a Virtual Academy for teaching and training ophthalmologists, eye hospital managers and administrators, and midlevel ophthalmic personnel through an online system. Initially it will cover the five centers of Aravind, and later the network will be extended to 30 to 40 partner hospitals out of 227 hospitals LAICO is currently working with.

So far, 10 percent of the ophthalmologists from India have undergone some sort of clinical training at Aravind.

Aravind is also a recognized center for MRCO (Member of Royal College of Ophthalmology) and ICO (International Council of

Ophthalmology) examinations. It has been recognized by The Tamilnadu Dr. MGR Medical University to offer postgraduate courses in ophthalmology and postdoctoral programs in clinical ophthalmology.

LAICO (Lions Aravind Institute of Community Ophthalmology) is recognized by the Indian Institute of Technology (IIT) Madras to offer a doctoral program in healthcare and biomedical engineering.

Eye Bank

Rotary Aravind International Eye Bank, started in 1998, is one of the six accredited eye banks in India that has received accreditation from IFETB (International Federation for Eye and Tissue Banks) and is also a lifetime member in the EBAI (Eye Bank Association of India).

IT Services

Aravind Computer Department was started in 1983 with two Apple computers for patient statistics and report generation. A LAN was set up in 1990, and online system patient care management was implemented in March 1991, with 11 computers at Madurai. In Tirunelveli, an online system was implemented in 1995, and in Theni, it was implemented in 1997. Coimbatore and Pondicherry hospitals were started in 1997 and 2001, respectively, with online systems from day one. More recently this has also been deployed in our managed hospitals.

Recent developments include

- Implement "EyesTalk" software in other hospitals for ophthalmologists/physician/eye care providers in any part of the globe to consult with Aravind Eye Hospitals ophthalmologist
- Aravind Virtual University: a facility to conduct classes, discussion, and sharing thoughts over satellite connectivity
- Wireless PDA applications in patient care and facility maintenance
- Aravind Diabetic Retinopathy Screening software, a simple and valid tool to assist in the detection of sight-threatening retinopathy and could supplement dilated fundus examinations (diagnostic procedures that employ the use of mydriatic eye drops to dilate or enlarge the pupil to obtain a better view of the internal surface of the eye) by ophthalmologists on patients to detect diabetic retinopathy
- Provision of primary eye care services to 30 centers across Tamilnadu through Aravind Tele-ophthalmology network.

ICICI: Financial Services for the Poor

The world's poor traditionally are trapped in the dilemma of having neither money nor the means to borrow any. Micro financing to the level of their needs has not been part of the agenda of formal banking, until now. For the poor in India, particularly in rural areas, ICICI Bank, the second-largest banking institution in the country, is beginning to convert the poorest of the poor into customers and, thus, at the same time empower them.

Ms. Pundiselvi, in the village of Nahramalaiphur, for instance, procured a bank loan to lease a small parcel of land to raise chilies for cooking and flowers for decorative purposes. The cost of the land was 10,000 rupees ($200) for the season, and the seeds cost a few thousand rupees. So far, Ms. Pundiselvi has paid back 7,000 rupees ($140), or 70 percent of the loan, from income generated from her land. In the same village, Ms. Saraswathi owned and operated a small grocery shop with a small inventory and limited selection of goods. With a 10,000 rupees ($200) loan, she expanded her existing shop and now enjoys a boost in monthly income. Ms. Saraswathi has never missed a monthly payment and has paid back 6,000 rupees ($120), or 60 percent of her loan. One enterprising woman pooled the money from a loan with other family assets and dug a new well for her village. She charges other farmers and villagers 25 rupees ($.50) per hour to pump water for irrigation purposes. The irrigation system the pump feeds has also increased the yield of her own nearby fields.

The number of people living on less than $1 per day in India is significantly greater than the entire population of the United States.

The number of people living on less than $1 per day in India is significantly greater than the entire population of the United States. From a social perspective, this is a humanitarian pandemic. From an economic perspective, these people represent the Bottom of the Pyramid. From a commercial perspective, these people, given their miniscule individual purchasing power, are usually not considered a viable market.

Traditionally, banking in India has focused on upper-income groups, principally in urban areas. With a rural population of 741.6 million in India, the rural penetration of banks is as low as 18 percent.[1] Micro financing, even in the formal sector, has existed for some time, but it usually has been characterized by its nonsustainable donor-led model. The primary focus of micro finance institutions has been access to credit, a capital-intensive process. Micro finance institutions have generally ignored the other plank of banking: savings. Also, most micro financing lending goes to people who are not at the bottom of the economic pyramid (the poorest of the poor).

The poor of India, in the absence of formal institutions, often must resort to the informal sector, which is characterized by monopolistic practices and exorbitant interest rates—at times even in the form of human capital. "Informal systems may be inefficient and even exploitive due to their monopoly power. Interest rates in the informal market vary from 3 percent to 10 percent a month. Vegetable vendors are known to borrow at even 10 percent a day to finance their daily working capital needs."[2] Yet formal financial intermediaries, such as commercial banks, typically do not serve poor households. The reasons include the high cost of small transactions, the lack of traditional collateral, geographic isolation, and simple social prejudice.

Informal systems may be inefficient and even exploitive due to their monopoly power.

The government of India has been aware of and sensitive to the asymmetric access to banking. "Of the 428 million deposit bank accounts in the country, 30 percent are in the rural areas. With a rural population of 741.6 million, the rural penetration of banks...is as low as 18 percent."[3] The Reserve Bank of India, through the Rural Planning and Credit Department and National Bank for Agriculture and Rural Development, has instituted several policies to encourage rural banking and the extension of credit to the rural hinterlands. The first was an initiative that required banks to open one rural branch for every three urban branches opened. As stipulated in Section 22 of the Banking Regulations Act of 1949, "Private sector banks...are required to open a minimum of 25 percent of their total branches in Rural/Semi-Urban areas as a condition of the license issued to them...."[4]

The Reserve Bank of India, also through the National Bank for Agriculture and Rural Development, started a pilot project in 1991 for purveying micro credit to the rural poor by linking self-help groups (SHGs) with banks. "A healthy micro finance sector leads to a healthy finance sector in general. This mutual link has to be established by the micro finance institutions/nongovernmental organizations and realized by the policymakers."[5] This pilot project was initiated because, despite having 150,000 rural banking outlets, a 1981 Reserve Bank of India survey found that 36 percent of the rural poor still utilized informal sources of credit. The project, the *SHG-Bank Linkage Program*, encouraged state banks with rural branches to give loans directly to SHGs as opposed to leaving the onus of Bottom-of-the-Pyramid credit to micro finance institutions.

Government initiatives, though great for the development of the Indian countryside, were viewed by most banks as developmental and, thus, nonprofitable. Providing credit to poor farmers and opening costly rural branches were seen as loss-making or break-even propositions at best. ICICI, however, viewed these reforms as an opportunity. K.V. Kamath, CEO and managing director of ICICI Bank, stressed that ICICI "...wants to lend in a *sustainable* way to rural India."[6] ICICI took a proactive approach when entering the retail banking sector, not only to satisfy the Reserve Bank of India regulations, but also to go above and beyond. "In the true ICICI style, we said if we have now acquired this initiative, let us see in what way we can actually make this initiative truly scalable."[7]

Government initiatives, though great for the development of the Indian countryside, were viewed by most banks as developmental and, thus, nonprofitable.

As a commercial entity with shareholders to satisfy, ICICI Bank could not enter this market aggressively unless it was convinced it could be done profitably. "At the ICICI Bank, we were very clear we would not restrict this initiative to be a mere marginal experiment. We decided we wanted to actually develop a model that not only is scalable, but is low cost and commercially viable."[8] Thus, the management of ICICI entered this market fully convinced it could be a profit-making venture. With this market in mind, ICICI outlined three strategic goals: to increase banking penetration in rural areas through innovative ways of defining distribution points, to prepare rather than react to the increasingly important rural market, and to support the downtrodden as a good corporate citizen.[9] All these goals were aimed at enabling the poorest of the poor to "...become active and informed participants in socioeconomic processes as opposed to passive observers."[10]

ICICI was well situated to take the lead in rural banking. ICICI was a universal bank providing a wide range of banking services and was technologically driven. For example, ICICI was the first bank in India to launch a Web site (1996), the first bank to launch Internet banking (1997), the first bank to launch online bill payment (1999), and the only bank in India with more than one million online customers. ICICI's channel usage reflects this technological approach toward banking. "If you are going to gain sustainable competitive edge, you have to leverage technology in a big way. Our aim was to move from physical branch banking to virtual banking. Block by block, we slowly built up a clicks-and-mortar strategy."[11] This progressive and imaginative use of technology was a vital key to ICICI's capability to serve the Bottom of the Pyramid profitably.

ICICI was also a new entrant to retail banking. ICICI started retail banking under a new and changing regulatory regime that was decidedly more market-based than before. As a new player in this environment, ICICI was not burdened with legacy thinking and could attack the issue with fresh ideas. Additionally, ICICI was not hampered with a large physical branch network and was, therefore, well positioned to introduce low-cost banking channels. In contrast, the State Bank of India, one of the oldest and largest banks in the country, had to financially support a network of more than 13,000 branches.[12]

As ICICI oriented the banking operations toward the bottom of the economic pyramid, they began looking at entering the micro financing field because there certainly was, and still is, a vast unmet demand for credit in rural areas. "In rural areas, only one million households have received access to micro credit from micro finance institutions."[13] Yet the competitive situation was relatively crowded. "India currently boasts more than 500 micro finance institutions."[14] However, the incumbents in this space were all struggling to turn profits because they were used to working as donor-funded and -supported institutions. This dependence often affects scalability and sustainability. Additionally, these micro finance institutions were experiencing low savings-to-credit ratios, liquidity problems, high "capacity building" costs, and general inefficiencies. ICICI saw a real opportunity in this area, believing that many of the problems/risks with micro financing could be alleviated by the capital, expertise, scale, and reach of a major bank. By entering the micro financing field, ICICI has taken on the role of social mobilization and financial intermediation.

In addition to looking at micro financing, ICICI wanted to increase its banking presence in rural areas. To do this, the bank needed to rapidly proliferate its points of presence (or distribution points). However, the traditional brick-and-mortar approach to expansion is prohibitively expensive given the vast and varied landscape of India. Additionally, it is difficult to staff rural branches with competent bankers because educated urbanites do not want to live in these areas, and often there is a dearth of qualified locals. To minimize the costs associated with expanding rapidly and to gain qualified rural staff, ICICI decided to partner with nongovernmental organizations and micro finance institutions currently in the field. By "piggybacking" on the established network of these rural-oriented players, ICICI believed it could gain knowledge about the market it intended to serve and eventually increase its banking presence. ICICI has combined the social mobilization strength of nongovernmental organizations and micro finance institutions with the financial strength of the bank.

ICICI developed two innovative models geared toward serving the bottom of the economic pyramid:

- **Direct-access, bank-led model**—Catalyzed by the merger with the rural banking institution Bank of Madura, this model utilizes the power of ICICI to promote and grow SHGs and to increase dramatically the scope and scale of rural savings and lending.
- **Indirect-channels partnership**—This model leverages the relationships, knowledge, and rural network of organizations in the field to avoid the costly brick-and-mortar expansion process and thus helps efficiently cultivate ICICI's banking presence.

Upon entering the new millennium, ICICI's executive team had identified three areas as the next sectors of growth: international, urban retail, and rural retail. With the rural sector targeted as an important driver of growth, ICICI began looking for a suitable partner. They identified the Bank of Madura as a profitable, well-capitalized private-sector commercial bank in operation for 57 years. The main advantages for ICICI were the addition of 1.2 million customers and the Bank of Madura's rural branch network. The Bank of Madura's most-significant presence was in the southern states, with 77 branches in the rural area of Tamil Nadu. The Bank of Madura was especially strong in small and medium-sized corporate banking, which would help ICICI expand its corporate business. An additional strength was the Bank of Madura's micro financing initiative. ICICI made it clear it intended to aggressively grow this initiative. The Reserve Bank of India approved this merger on March 10, 2001. With the merger, ICICI Bank became one of India's largest private-sector banks.

Earlier, the Bank of Madura, familiar with the Grameen Bank model in Bangladesh (providing small loans to clients below the poverty line), believed the efforts in Bangladesh could be replicated in India. In 1995, it developed and implemented the Rural Development Initiative, focused on economic empowerment of the poor in rural areas. To begin, it had to find the right people. Word spread quickly throughout the organization of the new and prestigious program. The Bank of Madura had reversed the negative perception of the rural managerial positions by creating a lengthy interview process for what was previously deemed a marginal job. Applicants were turned down if they expressed the slightest hesitation regarding the demands of the job or the time frame for the post. In addition, existing personnel in the rural branches were reviewed, and those who did not match relevant profiles were weeded out. The applicants had to have the desire to help the poor and become personally involved with their economic development.

The interview process produced a team of 325 individuals and a core executive team of 15. The bank also initiated a new policy that stipulated that any individual working in the rural sector could request a transfer at any time. This was a perk for the rural field agents and added to the allure of the position. Then, the team had to learn the intricacies of micro financing and how to make it successful. They began a serious study of micro financing with experts around the country; after all, many nongovernmental organizations and academics were already active in this area in India.

After a number of consultations with outside experts, the core team held a two-day retreat and decided the strategic and organizational directions the bank would take next. The program was placed under certain restrictions: no additional expenditures, including for new staff; operating costs to remain the same. Over the course of the retreat, the team decided that the clients, bank, and program would be better served with its own unique program. Of course, it drew upon many important lessons it had seen in the field from other players; however, with the financial backing of the savings institution it represented, it saw a new opportunity. The essential strategic design of its program was to form, train, and initiate small groups of women into formal savings, banking, and lending groups. The vehicle conceived for this was the Self-Help Group (SHG).

> *The essential strategic design of their program was to form, train, and initiate small groups of women into formal savings, banking, and lending groups. The vehicle conceived for this was the Self-Help Group (SHG).*

The Bank of Madura's conception of the SHG was as follows:

- A group of 20 women from the same village whose individual annual incomes placed them below the poverty line. Multiple groups could be formed in the same village.
- The members did not participate, as of yet, in the formal banking sector.
- Leaders should be selected from within the group to bear responsibility for collecting the savings, keeping the accounts, and running the monthly meetings.
- Upon formation of the group, the bank would undertake to educate these women as to the basic concepts of banking and encourage them to begin a savings program for themselves, thereby creating new customers for the bank.

After one year of training and monitoring the regularity of meetings, loans were dispersed to the group in the average amount of 10,000 rupees ($200) per member. This was a considerable loan, above the amount normally given for consumption purposes, to begin a small business or expand an existing operation in agriculture, for instance. The loans were given based on need, not in ratio to existing savings deposits.

The Bank of Madura's SHG vehicle allowed for many other positive intangible changes in the participants' self-esteem and confidence as they were allowed to decide on and influence events in their own homes and villages. The maturation of an SHG followed the general pattern shown in Figure 1.

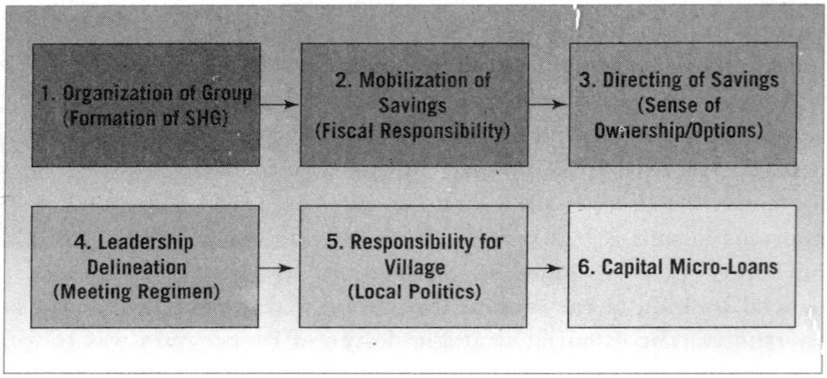

Figure 1 Maturation of an SHG.

At the time of the merger between ICICI and Madura Bank in 2001, there were 1,200 SHGs already formed; a social vehicle with considerable power had been created. Women participating in the SHGs found themselves becoming more articulate, confident, and empowered. The focus of the SHG movement was on the maturation of the individual and thus the group as a whole by enforcing a strict meeting schedule and savings regimen. Ultimately, federations were formed, representing large numbers of SHGs that included thousands of members. The rapid spread was due in part to the training structure the Bank of Madura provided.

The greatest difficulties the SHG program had to face first were intangible. How would a bank raise the confidence and motivation of a group of women without familial relation, without incentive to trust one another, without any formal participation in the financial sector? Further, a stigma was attached to formal banking, that it was not a trustworthy institution. This mistrust was based on prior experiences some of the women had with bank loan officers who demanded bribes and wrapped the entire savings and loan process in obscurity to confuse the locals.

Further, a stigma was attached to formal banking, that it was not a trustworthy institution.

The potential candidates for the SHGs, of course, understood their needs very well but had not been actively seeking alternatives. The answer to developing the group dynamic lay in the composition of the groups so that a feeling of mutual dependence was immediately created, not merely financial but also psychological. Additionally, the framework that created a joint guarantee for the loan of all the members was vital. This joint guarantee encouraged interaction between women who formerly would not have had any (or very little) reason to engage with one another. Eventually, a small number of groups began forming, and the members soon felt the benefits, initially in the form of increased confidence, the mutual benefit of cooperation, and other externalities of a diverse and established support network. Concepts of citizenship were developed; that is, members began to recognize their duty to the communal setting in which they played a role. As time passed, established groups and their most proactive members were trained to form new groups, which spread the SHG movement at an accelerating pace.

To date, there have been many instances of total transformation, not only of the individual's self-confidence, but also of village politics, ethics, and social norms. The SHG units began to develop a fierce identity both for themselves and within the context of the larger SHG network. Members of the SHGs adopted a certain color and style of sari to demonstrate their solidarity. The hustle and bustle at the local bank offices has become a flurry of blue, maroon, and yellow robes as the women go about their daily business. Songs and ceremonies have emerged celebrating the SHG unit and are offered at the commencement of each meeting to bring the members together in thought and act.

When ICICI inherited the Rural Development Initiative from the Bank of Madura, the SHG program was still not financially sustainable. To reach profitability, the number of SHGs had to expand exponentially without increasing ICICI's costs of managing these groups. ICICI developed a simple three-tier system. Under this system, the highest level is *a bank employee called a project manager.* Project managers oversee the activities of *six coordinators*, approve loan applications for the area manager, and help with the development of the SHGs. The coordinator is an SHG member with a contractual relationship with the bank. She overlooks the actions of *six promoters*. The promoters' primary responsibility is the formation of new groups. Within a year of election to promoter, promoters become *social service consultants* (SSCs) and must form 20 groups within the next 12 months. If the groups are formed, the

SSC is financially compensated by the bank and becomes part of the pyramid structure of creating and monitoring the SHGs.

Under the ICICI model, SHGs form and expand in a pyramid structure. In early 2001, at the time of the merger, 1,200 SHGs had been formed under the Bank of Madura structure. By March 2003, more than 8,000 SHGs had been formed. The acceleration and success of the program depended on training and empowerment of the women participating in the existing SHGs. At a certain degree of maturity, existing members who have demonstrated leadership ability are trained by the bank to become SSCs. The SSC's primary responsibility is to form new SHGs in neighboring villages and thus expand the SHG network. ICICI provides a small financial incentive of 100 rupees for each new group formed, and the Social Service Consultants must fulfill certain quotas to retain their status. The SSC must travel to villages within a 15-kilometer radius and form five new groups within 2 months and 20 groups within 12 months. ICICI has set strict guidelines for potential membership: All members must be from the same village; they must be married (to ensure a family receives the benefits, too); they must be between the ages of 20 and 50; SHGs must focus on the illiterate and those existing below the poverty line.

The National Bank for Agriculture and Rural Development created a list of questions to determine the poverty level of a family and to assess eligibility for SHG participation:

- Is there only one source of income for the family?
- Are there any permanently ill members of the family?
- Do you regularly borrow from moneylenders?
- Do you live far from your drinking-water source?
- Do you belong to a scheduled caste or scheduled tribe?[15]

Those who answer yes to three or four of the questions are considered good candidates for the SHG. After a series of visits with multiple families, plans for the group formation begin. The most successful groups have members who share some sort of similarity (perhaps they are from the same caste or have had a similar experience of poverty, for example). Before the first SHG meeting, the Social Service Consultant meets again with the village elders and gets their permission to work on a more significant level with the village to aid its development.

The National Bank for Agriculture and Rural Development estimates that the process of group formation can take five to six months. In the first few meetings, it is not unusual for members to leave and new members to arrive. When a core set of members has been established, a leader must be selected along with two animators. These three women are agreed on by all members and share the duties of running the group and keeping the accounts. The animators keep the minutes book (which details the proceedings of the meetings), the savings and loan register, the weekly register, and the members' passbooks. Proper documentation of the activities, especially of the internal lending, helps the approval process from the bank. The preliminary meetings also include Basic Awareness Training given by a Social Service Consultant (SSC), coordinator, or project manager. The SHG also must agree on the meeting times, penalties for missed meetings, and repayment guidelines.

The motto of the SHG becomes *Savings First—Credit Later*. They are taught that the savings habit is crucial to their rise out of poverty, in that savings reduce their vulnerability to consumption and medical emergencies. After the group has gone through training and begins to gather its own momentum, the SSC leaves to form new groups but is still responsible for a degree of monitoring and training assistance. After the Social Service Consultant has formed 20 groups, she earns 2,000 rupees ($40) from ICICI Bank and then becomes a promoter. During this process, she reports her activities to her coordinator. In the SHG hierarchy, a coordinator overlooks the activities of six Social Service consultant/promoters who have fulfilled their quota of forming 20 groups within one year. Similar to the Social Service Consultants, promoters are selected on the basis of talent and skill. With each promoter in charge of 20 groups, the coordinators overlook the activities of 120 groups. ICICI provides them an annual salary of 2,400 rupees ($48) for the 120 groups or some proportional piece thereof depending on how many are formed. The coordinators and the promoters work closely with the bank personnel who support their efforts. They are not considered official employees of the bank but

The motto of the SHG becomes Savings First—Credit Later. They are taught that the savings habit is crucial to their rise out of poverty, in that savings reduce their vulnerability to consumption and medical emergencies.

as contracted agents who perform a particular function. These women have passed through various levels of election and are considered to be the most talented and motivated members. Of course, they began as members within a particular SHG and continue with their duties to that original vehicle. Within the official hierarchy of ICICI, managerial positions support the efforts of the SHGs and their various executives, as shown in Figure 2.

The SHG process is oriented toward building new disciplines and capabilities. Collective responsibility and group pressure act as social collateral. Toward this end, the process has three essential steps:

1. Learn to save.
2. Learn to lend what you have saved.
3. Learn to borrow responsibly.

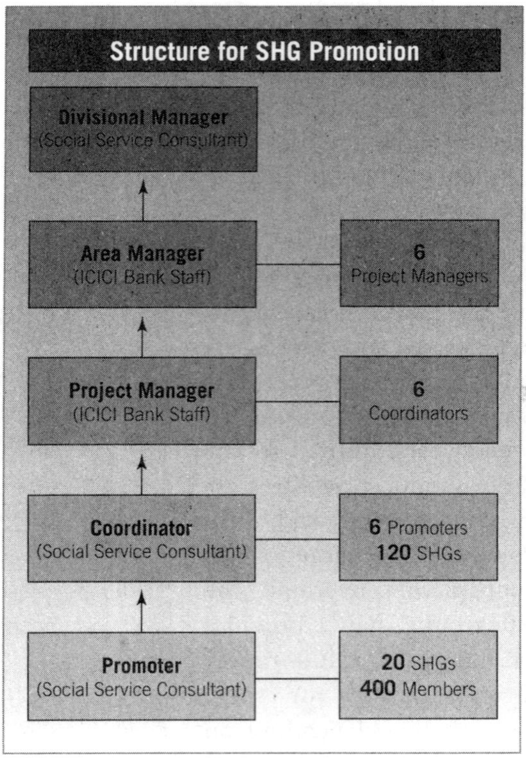

Figure 2 SHG management structure.

In the first monthly meeting, each member must bring 50 rupees ($1) to contribute to a joint savings account with the other members. The leader and representatives are responsible for collecting this money and opening up the savings account for the group. Instructions have been issued by the Reserve Bank of India to all commercial banks to allow registered and unregistered SHGs to open savings accounts in their group's name. It is imperative that each woman contributes and participates each month. This begins to build the momentum of savings that ICICI believes is essential for greater economic independence.

After six months, they have amassed 6,000 rupees ($120) plus interest. At this point, the idea that they are contributing to something that can expand beyond their individual means is evident. The savings are converted into a fund. The group can access this fund and use it for emergency lending to an individual within the group. This marks the first step in a transition to formal lending and a departure from the dependence on the local moneylender. Emergency lending is available for immediate payment of a medical emergency, short-term borrowing for consumption purposes, or other health-care reasons. This emergency loan is short term, and the women pay an interest rate of 24 percent per annum to the account. The members know, even if they have little or no education, that these loan terms are desirable compared to dealing with moneylenders. They compare the internal rate of the SHGs with the informal rate, which can be as high as 10 percent a day.

Often, monthly meetings take on a completely different agenda. Generally, the activity revolves around the needs of the village and other concerns of the women. In Tamil Nadu, water availability and purification, transportation, and electricity were the most highly debated topics. The SHG allows women to stand together as thousands, and local politicians take them seriously. Chanda Kochhar, the executive director of Retail Banking at ICICI, related stories of women who had rarely stepped out of their homes before joining the SHG. Through working with their peers, they gained such a degree of confidence and esteem that they began debating with local politicians on such issues as the construction of a dam and the digging of a well. SHGs also focus on literacy training.

One year after the formation of the SHG, the women are ready to submit a loan proposal to a bank manager, a relatively paper-intense process. Key supporting documents are required, including loan agreements signed by each member of the SHG, an updated family survey, a *No Due* certificate that guarantees that no outstanding loans are owed by any member, and a *Letter of Sanction* approved by the area manager. The size of the total loan to the SHG is 250,000 rupees ($5,000), with a distribution of 12,500 rupees ($250) to each member. Activities that can be funded with this amount include the purchase of livestock, the leasing of land for agricultural purposes, the opening of a small tea shop, candle manufacturing, and the purchase of a home. *These loans are noncollateralized. The savings account cannot be held as collateral against the loan, because the bank wants to continue encouraging the internal lending process. However, the SHG as a whole is responsible for each member's loan*, which builds a strong degree of social collateral. This social collateral has proved able enough to achieve a repayment rate of 99.99 percent, making the rural sector one of the most creditworthy in the banking industry. To fulfill the repayment terms, each member must pay 400 rupees ($8) to the bank for 43 months, an effective annual interest rate of 18 percent. Within India, this is higher than most home loans, which are in the area of 9 percent, and other commercial lending at 12 percent. ICICI charges this rate to cover the training costs and salaries of the promoters and coordinators who make this operation sustainable.

The National Bank for Agriculture and Rural Development has correlated high repayment rates with certain characteristics of SHGs, as follows:

- Is the group between 15 and 20 members?
- Are all members considered very poor?
- Was a fixed amount of savings collected each month?
- Is there more than 20 percent literacy?
- Have they used their savings for internal lending purposes?
- Have the members kept a high level of attendance?

If the SHG meets a certain number of these criteria, the loan officer is instructed to grant the loan immediately. If the SHG is lacking in many areas, the loan application is suspended, and they are granted four to six months to improve their operation. The officer is also encouraged to examine the books of the SHG and determine their accuracy and appropriate depth of content. Though the accounts are relatively small, the small savings of many SHGs grow into valuable large accounts. Cost-savings occur because, although the savings account and loan represents 20 people, only the three elected officers interact directly with the bank officers, saving time and labor of the bank. In addition, because there is internal monitoring for repayment, the bank incurs little cost in loan appraisal and monitoring. Further, the bank's reputation increases its social base of recognition within the village and attracts more business from other sectors.

In subsequent monthly meetings, individual members report on the progress of their various business enterprises. The members also bring their personal monthly loan payment. These payments are collected by the animators, recorded in each member's passbook, and taken to the bank the next business day. If a member misses a payment, the SHG assesses a penalty against that member, the amount of which is added to the shared savings account. If the first round of lending is successful, the SHGs can approach the bank for a second round, with an increased credit line of 15,000 rupees ($300) per member.

ICICI's dedication to the SHG program has a dual inspiration. The first is that ICICI believes the rural sector will be the next area of growth for India and that the SHG movement, if properly scaled and managed, makes good business sense. The bank expands its customer base and receives new deposits while reducing the cost of single transactions with the use of the animators and SHG leaders. The second aspect of the SHG program comes from ICICI's sense of corporate social commitment to the development and enabling of the rural poor.

The indirect-channel partnership model is another approach ICICI is taking in its effort to increase distribution points and cost-effectively serve the bottom of the economic pyramid. The model looks to leverage the current infrastructure and relationships that micro finance institutions and nongovernmental organizations have in place to deliver banking services to the rural poor. By "piggybacking" on this network, ICICI does not have to implement a costly brick-and-mortar expansion model. Also, ICICI can learn from these organizations, whose sole focus is to serve this customer class, and thus minimize its learning-curve costs.

ICICI found that giving grants and loans to micro finance institutions to spur the rural poor's credit activities was too passive, so the bank developed a more commercial partnership role in which ICICI provides micro finance institutions with a line of credit to meet a cash flow deficit for three years. In the fourth year, the micro finance institution begins to repay the loan (and in total within the ensuing two to three years). ICICI also developed partnerships by making equity investments and creating technologies that would help penetrate the rural areas. The first steps in this indirect-channel partnership model were as follows:

- The development of the Humane Action Foundation in Karnataka, a regional nongovernmental organization that assists the poor in micro credit, in researching the idea of kiosks, and in looking at "...rural information and communication technology projects that seek to bring emerging technologies like low-cost computing and Internet access to rural households."[16]
- Professional Assistance for Development Action in Jharkhand, providing loans so it could expand its SHG lending and, in the process, learn about setting up women's savings and credit groups.
- Credit and Savings for the Hardcore Poor in Uttar Pradesh, an association of Grameen Bank Replications in Asia, in the form of an equity investment, to catalyze the micro finance institution movement and to learn from the innovative Grameen model.
- ICICI has set up additional partnerships with EID Parry, n-Logue, ITC e-Choupal, and BASIX to take advantage of the rural kiosk network each has established. The partnerships were designed to build on the unique strengths of each organization and on the context in which they are working.

Though ICICI has already made a significant impact by providing credit to the bottom of the economic pyramid, its effort is still in its nascent stages. ICICI constantly strives to cost-efficiently serve this customer class by developing innovative technologies; novel distribution models; and new initiatives, such as rain insurance, venture capital, mobile ATMs, and derivatives. One of the key challenges for the future is how to create more convenient and low-cost access points for rural customers. Most important, ICICI has made profitable inroads into serving the bottom of the economic pyramid. "Banking with the poor has undergone a paradigm shift. It is no longer viewed as a mere social obligation. It is financially viable as well."[17]

Endnotes

1. Duggal, Bikram, and Singhal, Amit. (2002). *Extending Banking to the Poor in India*, ICICI Social Initiatives Group, 2.
2. Duggal, Bikram, and Singhal, Amit. (2002). *Extending Banking to the Poor in India*, ICICI Social Initiatives Group, 2.
3. Duggal, Bikram, and Singhal, Amit. (2002). *Extending Banking to the Poor in India,* ICICI Social Initiatives Group, 2.
4. Master Circular on Branch Licensing, Reserve Bank of India—www.rbi.org.in/index.dll/14?opensection?fromdate=&todate=&s1secid=1001&s2secid=1001&storyno=0&archivemode=0.
5. Bhatt, Ela. *Microfinance for Infrastructure: Recent Experiences*, 4.
6. Kamath, K.V. CEO/managing director of ICICI Bank. Personal interview. Thursday, March 27, 2003.
7. Kochhar, Chanda. Executive director of ICICI Bank. Personal interview. Thursday, March 27, 2003.
8. Kochhar, Chanda. Executive director of ICICI Bank. Personal interview. Thursday, March 27, 2003.
9. Gopinath, M.N. General manager of ROG & RMBG. Personal interview. Monday, March 17, 2003.
10. www.icicisocialinitiatives.org.
11. www.openfinancemag.com/spring03/story9.html.
12. www.tcs.com/0_downloads/source/press_releases/200210oct/sbi_ctf.pdf.
13. www.digitalpartners.org/planet.html.
14. www.digitalpartners.org/planet.html.
15. NABARD, *A handbook on forming self-help groups*, pg. 4.
16. edev.media.mit.edu/SARI/papers/CommunityNetworking.pdf.
17. NABARD. Self-Help Group—Bank Linkage Program, 1.

This case study was written by Todd J. Markson and Michael Hokenson under the supervision of Professor C.K. Prahalad. The case study is intended to be a catalyst for discussion and is not intended to illustrate effective or ineffective strategies.

Update: ICICI Bank

By Mr. K.V. Kamath, who was Managing Director and CEO at ICICI Bank until April 2009. In May 2009, he took over as the Chairman of the Board of Directors of ICICI Bank.

ICICI Bank's approach to reaching the Bottom of the Pyramid has evolved from the following three drivers: (1) acquisition of the Bank of Madura, which had significant linkages with rural Self-Help Groups

(SHGs) in Tamil Nadu; (2) meeting priority sector and rural lending requirements set by the Reserve Bank of India; and (3) micro finance activities through our social and nonprofit initiatives.

ICICI's strategy toward providing financial services to the Bottom of the Pyramid focuses on creating an ecosystem that serves the following purposes:

- Facilitating universal access to basic financial services
- Providing access to markets by bridging the gaps
- Creating complementary and facilitative infrastructure
- Improving the efficiency of financial systems

In this context, initiatives to cater to this market include

- The micro credit and business correspondent model
- Farmer financing
- Micro insurance and Micro Systematic Investment Plan products
- Formation of the ICICI Foundation to expand the scope of our developmental work in this area

1. The Micro Credit and Business Correspondent Model

One of ICICI's micro credit strategies has involved offering liquidity to micro finance institutions, which in turn are best equipped to reach out to the poor. When ICICI ventured into this segment in early 2000, micro finance institutions were in general highly capital-constrained and faced significant difficulty in scaling up. In 2004, ICICI pioneered the Partnership Model, an innovative financing structure for micro finance institutions. This scaled up ICICI's micro finance portfolio rapidly as ICICI became the largest supplier of funds to micro finance institutions in the industry. Between 2003 and 2008, ICICI lent more than $3.5 million to micro finance borrowers through this model. The key social benefit of this financing structure has been to enable smaller micro finance institutions to rapidly scale up operations at a time when most of the industry faced severe constraints. Today, the micro finance institution landscape in India has transformed significantly with external funding available through private equity and venture capital firms. In light of these new developments, ICICI Bank's strategy has also accordingly undergone changes and is now focused on commercial lending to micro finance institutions.

With a view to expanding access to financial services, Reserve Bank of India established guidelines for banks to work with certain entities under the business correspondent model for the delivery of financial services. As per the Reserve Bank of India's guidelines, business correspondents can undertake services such as collection of small value deposits; receipt and delivery of small value remittances and other payment instruments; sale of third-party products such as micro insurance, mutual funds, or pension products; disbursal of small value credit; and the recovery of principal and collection of interest.

With the enabling business correspondent framework in place, ICICI Bank has actively pursued financial inclusion through this channel. The business correspondent model has enabled us to offer easy savings facilities to the poor where ICICI has focused on a technology-driven model. ICICI delivers a zero-balance savings facility using state-of-the-art technology provided by Financial Information Network & Operations Ltd.

FINO SMART CARDS

Financial Information Network and Operations (FINO), a technology solutions company, provides innovative technology solutions to enable financial providers to reach millions of under-served people. One of FINO's key solutions is a biometric-enabled, multi-application smart card and a portable point-of-sale terminal, which combines with back-end software. The smart card forms the basis for ICICI Bank's micro savings product. ICICI Lombard is also using Financial Information Network and Operations' biometric cards to lower costs of enrollment and claims processing in the micro health insurance scheme. In partnership with Manipal Group of hospitals, smart cards have been piloted for some clusters, where enrollment stations have been established equipped with laptops for online enrollment of members into the health insurance program. The card will also be used for premium collection in the near future.

Through this technology, customers transact using a personalized e-passbook, which provides biometric authentication when used with an authentication device. Apart from this savings account, ICICI also offers recurring and fixed deposits to enable customers to avail higher return on their savings. ICICI currently works with 41 business correspondent partners in 13 states and union territories. These partners serve more than 91,000 customers through 105 business correspondent branches.

ICICI expects mobile banking to emerge as a major channel for expanding access to banking in rural areas. The rapid spread of mobile telephony and its low cost provides an opportunity to significantly scale up delivery of banking services through this channel, with appropriate regulations and safeguards.

2. Farmer Financing

ICICI Bank has sought to introduce several new products to meet the farmer's need for credit. Soon after harvest, prices for all commodities are at their lowest. The smaller and marginal farmers are most likely to succumb to a low price because their need for realization of funds is more acute. Realizing that the availability of finance at the right time strengthens a farmer's inventory holding capacity, ICICI launched a warehouse receipt-based financing product. This allows a farmer to avail of a loan against the produce stored in a warehouse. ICICI has also focused on enhancing credit to farmers by leveraging on corporate partnerships. For example, ICICI has partnered with various dairies to provide financing to farmers for purchase of milk cattle. This lending strategy has also been successful in the sugar and poultry industry.

3. Micro Insurance (Health and Nonhealth) and Micro Systematic Investment Plans

In addition to the Bank, ICICI's subsidiaries are also actively involved in reaching out to this segment of the population. Risk mitigation is an important service for the poor considering the uncertainties in their income cycle, which increases their vulnerability to economic shocks. Providing insurance products to the poor thus becomes important, and an effective way to deliver such insurance products is to bundle them with micro credit. In this respect, ICICI's subsidiaries are actively involved in the provision of insurance products to the poor.

- ICICI Prudential Life Insurance has promoted financial security among the rural poor and through its life insurance product. The total number of lives insured annually increased from 64,700 in 2003 to about 561,600 during April 2008 through December 2008, an increase of 770 percent in five and a half years. This scale up was aided by affordable premiums for rural policies as low as 25 cents for every U.S. $25 sum assured. In the provision of such products, ICICI Prudential Life Insurance is one of the first insurance companies in India to use innovative processes such as call center support in five local languages, financial awareness through audio-visuals, and simple application forms available in eight regional languages.

- In addition, ICICI Lombard General Insurance provides a range of nonlife insurance products, including health, weather, and cattle insurance to help mitigate the impact of other contingencies such as illness or crop failure. Micro-health Insurance is a significant part of ICICI Lombard's health portfolio targeted at financial inclusion of the Bottom of the Pyramid. Total lives covered under the micro health insurance program increased from 5.5 million lives in the fiscal year 2007 to 9 million lives in fiscal 2008. By November 2008, ICICI Lombard had extended its weather insurance products to cover 33 crops in 50 districts in 12 states covering about 316,000 farmers.
- ICICI Prudential Asset Management Company recently launched India's first Micro Systematic Investment Plan, a mutual fund targeted to the poor. The minimum investment amount for this plan is as low as $1. Although the product requires some policy support before it can be mainstreamed, the Micro Systematic Investment Plan offers a real opportunity for the poor to tap into returns offered by the Indian equity markets.

4. The ICICI Foundation

Considering the broad array of work that is involved in an effective financial inclusion endeavour, the ICICI Group has facilitated the creation of the ICICI Foundation for Inclusive Growth. The ICICI Group will provide a part of its annual profits to the Foundation and work with it closely to help achieve its mission of improving social, economic, and human development outcomes at the national level.

The Foundation's focus areas follow:

- Facilitating better access to markets for low-income households
- Promoting the development of better human capacity among the lowest-income households through interventions in education and health
- Promoting environmental sustainability and growth of a strong civil society

The Foundation seeks to focus on the preceding areas by actively mentoring institutions that work in these areas. For instance, the Foundation has facilitated a private equity fund (the Network Enterprises Fund) to invest exclusively in rural supply-chain companies. These specialized supply-chain interventions are required to expand lending to a variety of business enterprises in rural India. Its approach involves building channels that deliver financial and other services in rural remote locations nationwide, and creating Network Enterprises that invest across the supply chain in sectors like processed foods, handicrafts, energy, rural retail, dairy, housing, and so on.

Another focus area of the Foundation includes direct micro financial services to individuals via 200–300 micro finance institutions that it intends to establish across the country. To meet this goal, the ICICI Group is working through its following specialized entities:

- The Social Initiatives Group and Development strategy group within ICICI Bank to develops channels, products, and a facilitating policy environment for financial inclusion.
- The micro finance institution Strategy Unit that works with micro finance institutions whose volumes require stronger planning and processes at different levels to expand or consolidate their operations and manage an increasing inflow and outflow of funds.
- The Emerging Micro Finance Institution Team that is involved in micro finance institutions incubation and building micro finance institutions and identifying and developing organizations or individuals to take up micro finance as a viable business.

In addition to these, ICICI Bank is also involved in developing infrastructure to cater to the Bottom of the Pyramid population. These efforts include technology development through a partner Financial Information Network and Operations and multiple research and development centers through the Institute of Financial Management and Research. ICICI has also been supporting entities such as GIVE India, the MITRA Foundation, Governance Matters, and InfoChange to support the growth of civil society organizations and nongovernmental organizations to serve the Bottom of the Pyramid.

ITC e-Choupal: Technology for the Poor

Most people would agree that information technology has changed their lives—linked them to the global community, enabled them to share vital business data, and even provided entertainment and opportunity. For the rural poor, in countries such as India, this "connection of the times" to the world has been denied and has been far out of their reach, until now.

Picture, though, an agricultural village where a farmer goes to a computer and does something as simple as check the weather. In the past, unreliable weather information might result in prematurely planted seeds being washed away by early rains. Other farmers exchange information about crops and agriculture, mutually investigating approaches that allow them to compete in the outside world, not just locally. Or the village of Khasrod, where 2,000 local students printed out their report cards, saving them days of waiting or a long trip. Children also now use computers for schoolwork and even games. Like youngsters everywhere, those in the villages use computers to investigate the latest movies, cell phone models, and sports news. Some even explore their aspirations for the future in a world now within reach. They are, for the first time ever, connected.

This communication miracle—the empowerment of India's agricultural poor—began simply enough as a company's effort to reengineer the process of more efficiently and fairly getting the farmers' soya crop to market.

This communication miracle—the empowerment of India's agricultural poor—began simply enough as a company's effort to reengineer the process of more efficiently and fairly getting the farmers' soya crop to market. The ITC Group, one of India's foremost private-sector companies, with a market capitalization of approximately $4 billion and annual revenues of $2 billion, had to initiate challenging social changes in addition to business changes to make this miracle happen.

ITC made a commitment in mission and resources to change the system in a way that would be fair to the farmers and yet profitable to ITC.

The innovation—placing as many as 2,000 computer kiosks in rural agricultural villages as part of information centers (*e-Choupals*)—required ITC to address an existing traditional system governed by the Agricultural Products Marketing Act (1937), which had led to the establishment of a marketing channel through *mandis*, delivery points where farmers bring their produce for sale to traders and to be taxed Inefficiencies, and corruption, had led to an outdated monopolistic system that unfairly restrained the farmers. *ITC made a commitment in mission and resources to change the system in a way that would be fair to the farmers and yet profitable to ITC.*

E-CHOUPALS

The e-Choupals, information centers containing a computer linked to the Internet, represent an approach to seamlessly connect subsistence farmers with large firms, current agricultural research, and global markets. The name is derived from the Hindi word choupal, meaning a traditional village gathering place. The network of these, each operated by a local farmer in each community called the sanchalak, allows for a "virtual integration of the supply chain" and significant efficiencies over the traditional system.

Traditional *mandi* trading was conducted by commission agents called *adatiyas* (brokers who buy and sell produce). They are of two types, as follows:

- *Kachha adatiyas* are pure purchasing agents and buy only on behalf of others.
- *Pukka adatiyas*, on the other hand, finance the trade as representatives of distant buyers and sometimes even procure on their own account.

All the adatiyas belong to the Agarwal and Jain community, which manages grain trade across the entire country, an amazing fact considering the vast cultural and social diversity across the nation. It challenges the assertion that rural India is culturally unfathomable.

Three commercial channels exist for agricultural products: mandis, traders for eventual resale to crushers, and producer-run cooperative societies for crushing in cooperative mills. Traditionally, farmers keep a small amount for their personal consumption and have the produce processed in a small-scale, job-shop, crushing-plant called a *ghani*.

The lack of professional competition combined with the communal stranglehold on rural trading has made commission agents extremely wealthy. One commission agent, who belongs to a medium-size mandi, talked casually of assets and incomes in *crores of rupees* (millions of dollars). This counters the notion that there is no money in rural India. The adatiyas established the soya industry and grew it on the basis of familial and community trust, not professional norms. Buying and selling was based on oral agreements, mutual understanding, and community norms. Their network within this industry and their financial knowledge made them a formidable presence.

The mandi system reflected the heavily regulated government intervention in days of production shortfalls, controlled land ownership, input pricing, and all aspects of product marketing.

The mandi system reflected the heavily regulated government intervention in days of production shortfalls, controlled land ownership, input pricing, and all aspects of product marketing. Produce could only be sold in government-recognized locations to authorized agents. Processing capacities, private storage, forward trading, and transport were restricted. The result was corrupt, ineffectual, and archaic systems.

Typical inefficiencies and sources of unfairness of the mandi system from the farmers' perspectives include the following:

- The farmer does not have the resources to analyze or exploit price trends.
- When the mandi opens in the morning, farmers bring their trolleys to display areas within the mandi. Buyers inspect the produce by sight. There is no formal method of grading the produce, and the only instrument used is the moisture meter. Formal testing for oil content is not performed, and neither are global safety checks performed.
- After potential buyers have inspected the produce, a mandi employee conducts the auction in which commission agents place bids. The farmers have a largely negative opinion of the auction for nonfinancial reasons. They feel a systematic loss of dignity in the auctioning process. The fact that their lifework is auctioned off is seen as an insult. The final indignity is that the farmer cannot refuse the sale at the auctioned price. The agents belong to a close-knit community that is socially and economically distinct from the farming community. Although they might not collude in pricing, they do collude in establishing the practices of the trade. These practices uniformly exploit the farmer's situation.
- Mandi laborers bag and weigh the produce. A traditional compensation of these laborers is the sale of spilled produce. They, therefore, ensure that some portion of the produce is spilled in the weighing area, and then gather and sell this grain at the end of the day.
- The exploitative tone of interaction also runs through the payment process. The farmer is never paid in full at one time. Payments are stretched over time. The farmer often travels many hours to get to a mandi. Repeating the trip costs him time and money. The farmer bears all the cost of bagging and any overnight-stay costs. The farmer is also at the agent's mercy because the grain has already been delivered. Apart from the multiple trips to the agent's office, the farmer gets no interest for the delayed payment and bears the cost of the time and travel. In addition, crushers pay agents usurious rates for the privilege of delayed payment.

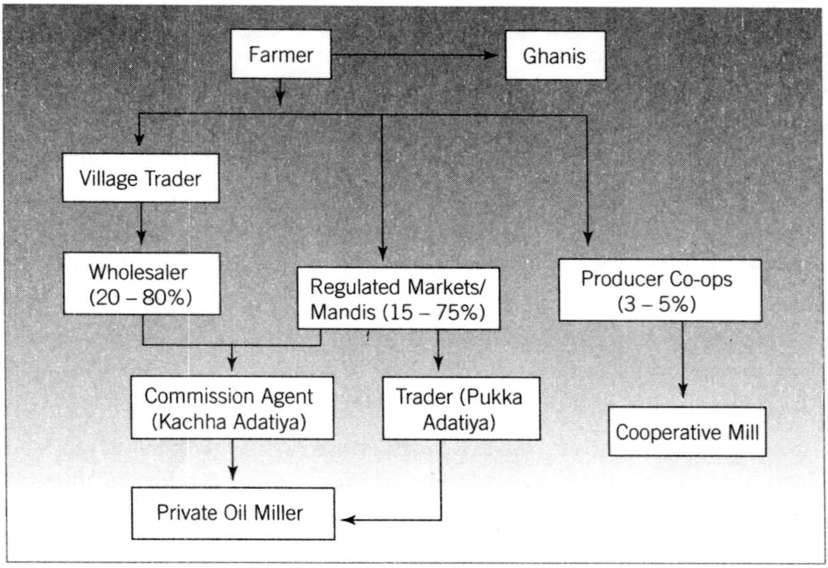

Figure 1 Marketing prior to the e-Choupal.

When ITC entered this industry, produce was bought and crushed by small crushers who were also traders. The company soon realized it needed a greater presence in the chain to better understand product dynamics. ITC then began renting processing-plant time and buying soya from mandis. ITC's procurement has grown rapidly since, and its initiative has seen the introduction of professional practices, transparency, and formal contractual relationships between agents and buyers. A unique set of tactical, strategic, and social imperatives drove ITC to conceive the e-Choupals and reengineer the entire value chain by deploying them. The mandi was clearly not an optimal procurement channel. Agent commissions would seem to be a source of inefficiency, but this sum is comparable to the salary paid to an employee for rendering similar services. The real sources of inefficiency were the *price and quality distortions* due to the agents' stranglehold on the market and ITC's distance from the farmer. Some examples of this are as follows:

A unique set of tactical, strategic, and social imperatives drove ITC to conceive the e-Choupals and reengineer the entire value chain by deploying them.

- **Distance from farmer**—ITC had no direct interaction with the farmer. This gap created a range of supply-chain issues. ITC's knowledge of its crops and suppliers (and therefore supply risks) was limited. ITC's capability to improve the quality and quantity of its supply by bringing modern agricultural practices to the farmers was also limited.
- **Daily price inflation**—The agent purchased grain through the day on ITC's behalf. Some produce of good quality would command a premium. Some of poor quality would sell at a discount. The agent purchased a range of qualities through the day at a range of prices. He mixed them at the end of the day and charged ITC a single price near the higher end of the spectrum.
- **Seasonal price inflation**—A corollary effect was that high-quality produce was used to make an entire lot of lower-quality produce acceptable. Agents, therefore, paid an inflated premium for high-quality produce. This drove up the high mandi price for the day. Few farmers actually got this price, but this price acted as the benchmark for the next day's pricing, thereby inflating the mandi price over a length of time. This created a distortion that inflated the overall *seasonal procurement prices* for ITC.
- **Capture of intra-day price shifts**—Mandi prices are fluid and vary within the day. ITC provided the agent a price range for the day to buy within. If the agent's average buy price within the day was lower than the ITC price, the agent sold the grain to ITC at the ITC price and pocketed the difference. If the average buy price was higher than the ITC price, the agent would still buy the produce but tell ITC that because its price was not high enough, no grain could be bought. He would store the grain and sell it to ITC the next day when ITC raised its price to make up for the previous day's procurement shortfall. Commission agents, therefore, captured the entire benefit of intra-day price shifts.

The agent never lost. Officially, the agent's commission is one percent of ITC's price. In reality, ITC estimated the agent's operating margin is approximately two and a half percent to three percent. The other insight is that the auction process is transparent in name only. The market is created, manipulated, and managed by the agents. The e-Choupal is an ideal vehicle to communicate directly with the farmer and thereby bypass the inefficiencies arising out of agent intermediation.

While the inefficiency in the supply channel was causing ITC to look inward, a changing landscape was forcing it to look outward. The agricultural commodity trading business was small compared to international players. By 1996, the opening up of the Indian market brought in international competition. These established and large companies had better margin-to-risk ratios because of wider options for risk management and arbitrage. To replicate their operating model would require a massive expansion of horizontal and vertical presence.

By 1996, the opening up of the Indian market brought in international competition.

ITC devised a strategy to systematically deploy information technology to change the game. An existing horizontal integration deficiency was addressed through customer-relationship, management-based solutions used to identify and provide for the nonstandard needs of customers in an industry where the basic services had been standardized. Customized information technology application and realignment of business goals and processes were deployed to manage risk and build the organization's knowledge base. The e-Choupal network was conceived to achieve "virtual vertical integration: by extending ITC's engagement all the way to the farmer in the field."

The e-Choupal network was conceived to achieve "virtual vertical integration: by extending ITC's engagement all the way to the farmer in the field."

THE ITC GROUP

The ITC group is one of India's foremost private-sector companies, with a market capitalization of approximately $4 billion and annual revenues of $2 billion. ITC has a diversified presence in tobacco, hotels, paperboards, specialty papers, packaging, agri-business, branded apparel, packaged foods, and other fast-moving consumer goods (FMCG) products. Spurred by India's need to generate foreign exchange, ITC's international business division was created in 1990 as an agri-trading company with the goal to "offer the world the best of India's produce." Today, that division is a $150 million company that trades in commodities such as feed ingredients, food grains, coffee, black pepper, edible nuts, marine products, and processed fruits. When ITC entered this industry, produce was bought and crushed by small-scale crushers who were also traders. ITC began with buying and exporting DOC (de-oiled cake, as that from soya). In a year, it realized it needed a greater presence in the chain to better understand product dynamics. ITC then began renting processing-plant time and buying soya from mandis.

The social agenda is an integral part of ITC's philosophy. ITC is widely recognized as dedicated to the cause of nation building. Chairman Y.C. Deveshwar noted, "ITC believes its aspiration to create enduring value for the nation provides the force to sustain growing shareholder value." This vibrant view of social conscience allowed ITC to recognize the unique opportunity of blending shareholder value creation with social development. The social impact of the e-Choupals as envisioned by ITC ranges from the short-term provision of Internet access to the long-term development of rural India as a competitive supplier (and buyer) of a range of goods and services to the global economy. The sustainability of the engagement comes from the commitment that neither the corporate nor social agendas will be subordinated in favor of the other.

Implementing and managing e-Choupals is a significant departure from commodities trading practices in India. Trading is not capital intensive because processing is outsourced and commodities are traded for margins that come through arbitrage of knowledge, time, or location. On the other hand, the e-Choupal model required significant capital outlays. Getting concurrence from the ITC board for such a venture and the diligent management of its progress required clarity of vision and an understanding of revenue streams and operations. Through its tobacco business, ITC dealt for decades with Indian agriculture, from research to distribution. ITC's translation of its strategic, tactical, and social imperatives into a business model demonstrates a deep understanding of both agrarian systems and modern management methods. Some of the guiding management principles included the following:

> ***Implementing and managing e-Choupals is a significant departure from commodities trading practices in India.***

- **Reengineer rather than reconstruct**—The conventional view of transforming established business systems begins with the failure of the current system and means to change it. ITC looked at what was good with the current system and, therefore, what they could build on. ITC not only kept efficient providers from the existing system but also created roles for some inefficient providers from the previous system. This philosophy has two benefits. First, it avoids reinventing the wheel in areas where ITC could not add value through its presence. Second, it co-opts members of the rural landscape, thereby making their expertise available to ITC while foreclosing the same from ITC's competition. A good example of this in action is the role created for the commission agents (as discussed later in this chapter).
- **Address the whole, not just a part**—The farmer's universe consists of many activities, ranging from procuring inputs to selling produce. Today, the village trader services the spectrum of the farmer's needs. He is a centralized provider of cash, seeds, fertilizers, pesticides, and marketing. In doing so, the trader enjoys two competitive benefits. First, his intimate knowledge of the farmer and village dynamics allows him to accurately assess and manage risk. Second, he reduces overall transaction costs by aggregating services. The linked transactions reduce the farmer's overall cost in the short term but create a cycle of exploitive dependency in the long term. Rural development efforts thus far have focused only on individual pieces rather than entire needs. Cooperatives have tried to provide agricultural inputs, rural banks have tried to provide credit, and mandis have tried to create a better marketing channel. These efforts cannot compete against the trader's bundled offer. Functioning as a viable procurement alternative, therefore, requires eventually addressing the gamut of needs, not just marketing.

From the conception of the model, an information technology-driven solution was recognized as fundamental to optimizing effectiveness, scalability, and cost. Information technology is 20 percent of all the effort of the business

From the conception of the model, an information technology-driven solution was recognized as fundamental to optimizing effectiveness, scalability, and cost.

model, but it is deemed the most crucial 20 percent. The two goals envisioned were as follows:

1. Delivery of real-time information independent of the transaction. In the mandi system, delivery, pricing, and sale happen synchronously, thus binding the farmer to an agent. The PC was seen as a medium of delivering ITC and other rates prior to the trip to the mandi, thus giving the farmer an empowered choice.
2. Facilitate collaboration between the many parties required to fulfill the spectrum of farmer needs. This goal follows from the need to address the whole, not just the part.

It is a tribute to ITC's understanding of rural value systems that it did not hesitate to install expensive information technology infrastructure in places where most people might think twice. It is a tribute to rural value systems that not a single case of theft, misappropriation, or misuse has been reported from among the almost 2,000 e-Choupals.

Profitable reengineering requires the unambiguous understanding of value provided, the circumstances in which they are applicable, and the revenues they are capable of generating. Three sources of payback were expected:

- **Crop-specific intervention**—ITC recognized that agrarian systems vary by crop. This means the sources of inefficiency in the supply chain, the correction required from the e-Choupal, and the magnitude and timing of the resulting efficiencies will differ by crop. For example, the systems, and consequently the e-Choupal models and payback streams, for coffee and shrimp differ significantly from that of soya. ITC's goals for the soya intervention reflected this nuanced analysis, and the project was targeted with recovering the entire cost of infrastructure from procurement savings. This is in contrast with the coffee and shrimp efforts, where the source of e-Choupal value is such that the investment recovery horizon is much longer.
- **Low-cost last mile**—The same system of physical and information exchange that brings produce from the village can be used to transfer goods to the villages. Because infrastructure has already been paid for by procurement, it is available at marginal cost for distribution. This ties in nicely with ITC's larger goal of transforming the e-Choupal network into a distribution

superhighway. ITC's current channels reach areas with populations of 5,000 and more. The e-Choupals allow penetration into areas with populations less than this. Products such as herbicides, seeds, fertilizers, insurance policies, and soil-testing services are, for instance, being sold through e-Choupals.

- **Intelligent first mile**—After the notion of consumerism and service has been established in the minds of the village farmers, their creativity and intimate knowledge of rural needs can be used to conceive the next product to be sold in villages. Thus, the farmers are transformed from being consumers to participants in the process of product design. This helps broaden the ITC offering and further bolster payback.

When the e-Choupals were conceived, they faced a fundamental regulatory obstacle. The Agricultural Produce Marketing Act (1937), under whose aegis mandis were established, prohibits procurements outside the mandi. ITC walked the government through the spirit of the Agricultural Produce Marketing Act as opposed to the letter and convinced them that e-Choupal procurement was in line with the goals of the act. Because ITC would not be using the mandi infrastructure for its procurement and it would have to incur its own costs on the e-Choupal infrastructure, the government offered to waive the mandi tax on the produce procured through the e-Choupal. ITC recognized the tax was a major source of revenue for the government and local mandis. Also, because ITC's competition was also subject to it, the tax itself was not making ITC uncompetitive. ITC, therefore, chose to continue paying the tax rather than risk relationships with the government and the mandi.

ITC walked the government through the spirit of the Agricultural Produce Marketing Act as opposed to the letter and convinced them that e-Choupal procurement was in line with the goals of the act.

The e-Choupal, which physically consists only of a computer with an Internet connection, is established in a village. A local farmer, called the *sanchalak* (coordinator), runs the village e-Choupal, which resides in the local sanchalak's living room. In keeping with the philosophy of modular increments based on proven results, ITC experimented with a variety of village conditions before developing a checklist for attributes it looks for in the selected village. The goal that ITC is working toward is to saturate its operating areas so that a farmer has to travel no more than 5 kilometers to get to an e-Choupal. ITC expects each e-Choupal to serve about five to seven villages in this 5-kilometer radius. Today, e-Choupal services reach out to more than a million farmers in nearly 11,000 villages through 2,000 kiosks across four states (Madhya Pradesh, Karnataka, Andhra Pradesh, and Uttar Pradesh). Of the e-Choupals in Madhya Pradesh, the one in Khasrod services about 500 to 700 farmers in 10 villages, and another one in Dahod services 5,000 farmers in 10 villages. The average seems to be about 1,000 farmers per e-Choupal.

ITC manages the geographical and cultural breadth of its network by channeling communication through a local farmer called the sanchalak. Recruiting a farmer as sanchalak from the community served several purposes:

- For generations, the Indian farmer has been betrayed by institutions, individuals, and even the weather. Trust is the most valuable commodity in rural India. No transaction will happen without trust, regardless of the strength of the contract. The sanchalak is selected to provide this vital ingredient to ITC's message.
- ITC did not have to invest in building and securing a physical infrastructure such as a kiosk for housing the computer.

  The sanchalak is trained in computer operation and can act as a familiar and, therefore, approachable human interface for the often-illiterate farmers and other villagers.
- ITC expects to leverage the power of the small-scale entrepreneur.

The sanchalak receives a commission for every transaction processed through the e-Choupal. Working as a sanchalak also boosts his social status, an important aspect of rural Indian life.

ITC insists that at no time should the sanchalaks give up farming, because this would compromise the trust the sanchalak commands. The fact the sanchalak works on commission could undermine his credibility. ITC mitigates this by projecting the role as a public office as opposed to a profitable venture. This is one reason he holds a title (sanchalak). This image is reinforced by a public oath-taking ceremony, where in the presence of a gathering of the local villagers, the sanchalak takes an oath to serve the farming community through the e-Choupal.

The sanchalak undergoes a training program at the nearest ITC plant. The training includes basic computer usage, functions within the e-Choupal Web site, basic business skills needed to function as a sanchalak, and quality inspection and pricing. For the sale of products through e-Choupal, the sanchalak receives product training directly from the manufacturer, with ITC involved only in product design and facilitation. In reality, the sanchalak gets most of his training on the job, which makes selecting sanchalaks with a natural drive all the more important.

"Virtual vertical integration" can work only if there is a continuous flow of information between the e-Choupals and ITC. Because of the numbers and geographic spread of the e-Choupals, this communication must be initiated by the sanchalaks. If their motivation to communicate with ITC diminishes, the channel will still function for procurement, but lack the vitality to manage supply risk, distribution, or product design. Maintaining continuous commercial flow keeps the sanchalak motivated to spend time and money in calling the ITC representative to ask about new products, convey village demand, and provide local updates. An example of the power of local information was seen early in e-Choupal implementation. A competitor tried to divert produce coming to the ITC factories by stationing motorcycle-riding representatives on the roads leading up to the plant. This person would stop farmers and offer them a premium over the ITC rate to divert their trolleys to the competitor's plants. Information about this came to ITC from alert sanchalaks, and ITC could take necessary measures.

ITC maintains commercial volumes (and therefore commission checks) flowing through e-Choupals by intelligently sequencing procurement and sales year round. Purchases and sales have been arranged so that *kharif* (crop season coinciding with India's monsoon, July to October) procurement, *rabi* (winter crop season in irrigated areas) inputs, rabi procurement, and kharif inputs sequentially maintain a steady stream of revenue for sanchalaks.

The previous day's mandi closing price determines the benchmark fair average quality price at the e-Choupal. The benchmark price is static for a given day. This information and the previous day's mandi prices are communicated to the sanchalak through the e-Choupal portal. The farmer brings a sample of his produce to the e-Choupal. The sanchalak inspects the produce and based on his assessment of the quality makes appropriate deductions (if any) to the benchmark price and gives the farmer a conditional quote. The sanchalak performs the quality tests right in front of the farmer and has to rationalize any deductions to the farmer. The benchmark price represents the upper limit on the price a sanchalak can quote. These simple checks and balances ensure transparency in a process where quality testing and pricing happen at multiple levels. If the farmer chooses to sell his beans to ITC, the sanchalak gives him a note bearing his name, the village, particulars about the quality tests (foreign matter and moisture content), approximate quantity, and the conditional price. The farmer takes the note from the sanchalak and proceeds to the nearest ITC procurement hub, ITC's point for collection of produce and distribution of inputs sold into rural areas.

The farmer bears the risk of transportation until the produce is delivered and the sale completed. The transportation costs he incurs are reimbursed by ITC. This reimbursement was initially based on the distance of the issuing e-Choupal from the processing center. This gave farmers the incentive to travel to a far away e-Choupal with their samples to get a higher transport reimbursement. ITC, therefore, did away with differential compensation and replaced it with a system of uniform compensation. Much of the procurement hub-related logistics are managed by the samyojak. Their responsibilities include the following:

- Labor management at the hub
- Bagging and baggage handling
- Storage management
- Transportation from the hub to processing factories
- Payment processing and cash management
- Handling mandi paperwork for the grain procured at the hub

For his services in the procurement process, the samyojak is paid a 0.5 percent commission.

Farmers' gains from the e-Choupal approach include the following:

- **Better information**—Prior to the e-Choupal, the farmer's information was incomplete or inaccurate. The only sources of information were the village grapevine and the commission agent. The e-Choupal gives farmers access to prices at several nearby outlets. Some e-Choupal sanchalaks have taken this a level further.

They have begun accessing external pricing indicators such as prices on the Chicago Board of Trade Web site to track global trends and determine the optimum timing of their sale.

- **Better use of time**—An indicative price was available only when the farmer traveled to the mandi, incurring costs that he could ill afford. The final price of the transaction was available to the farmer only upon the completion of the auction, at which time there was no backing out of the transaction. At the e-Choupal, the farmer has access to price choice prior to his trip.

  Both of these preceding factors work together to provide the farmer a better price for his crop.

- **Transportation cost**—The farmer bears the cost of transporting the crop to the mandi for a sale. ITC compensates its sellers for their transportation costs.
- **Transaction duration**—The mandi process can stretch into several days from arrival to full payment. Most farmers have traveled long distances to come to the mandi and incur costs of overnight stays or multiple trips. The sale to ITC takes no more than a few hours. (ITC targets two hours; farmers spoke of two to three hours. Our observation is that it probably takes two to three hours, possibly more in the peak season, but far less than a day.)

  Both of these preceding factors result in a lower logistics costs for the farmer.

- **Weighing accuracy**—The mandis' manual scales are inherently inaccurate, easily manipulated, and subject to manual errors. ITC's electronic scales are accurate and impartial.
- **Granularity of weighing**—The manual scales require that the produce be first transferred into bags. This intermediate bagging results in pilfering and loss of produce and the compounding of manual weighing errors over the entire load. The single weighing at ITC in which the entire wagon is weighed eliminates these losses.

  Both of these preceding factors contribute to lower transaction loss.

- **Professionalism and dignity**—The ITC procurement center is a well-maintained, professionally run operation where the farmer is treated with respect and actually serviced as a customer. The farmers we spoke with evinced great emotion for the dignity accorded to them by a professional process. Farmers mentioned simple touches such as a shaded area with chairs to await their paperwork as indicators of ITC's respect for them and their produce.

Even though intangible in the short term, the self-confidence created by the professional treatment is changing the way farmers conduct themselves. Sanchalaks, and even a commission agent, noted this change in farmer attitudes.

ITC's gains from the e-Choupal approach include the following:

- **Disintermediation savings**—The commissions paid to the agents were not excessive, but the true cost of intermediation, including the rent seeking, was between two and a half percent and three percent of procurement costs. A half percent commission to the sanchalak has replaced this.
- **Freight costs**—Direct reimbursement of transport costs to the farmer is estimated to be half of what ITC used to pay the commission agents for transport to their factory.
- **Quality control**—Removal of intermediary manipulation of quality and the capability to directly educate and reward quality in the customer base results in higher levels of quality in e-Choupal procurement. This results in higher post-processing yields.
- **Risk management**—The e-Choupal allows ITC to develop long-term supplier relationships with its farmers and attain some modicum of supply security over time. Risk is also managed in the e-Choupal world by a far stronger information infrastructure. Sanchalaks and samyojaks working on behalf of ITC provide excellent ground information on pricing, product quality, soil conditions, and expected yields. This information allows ITC to better plan future operations.

One of the most exciting aspects about the e-Choupal model is that it profitably provides an inaccessible village with a window to the world.

One of the most exciting aspects about the e-Choupal model is that it profitably provides an inaccessible village with a window to the world. The e-Choupal is the first and only PC in most of these villages. This fact, coupled with the higher remuneration and appreciation of the professional transaction, is causing several shifts in the social fabric.

Overall, the change brought about by the e-Choupal is overwhelmingly positive. It is, however, important to note that some parties are adversely affected in the short term. Diversion of produce to e-Choupals has caused soya volumes to shrink by 50 percent at mandis. Most people who have lost are closely connected to the mandi, as follows:

- **Commission agents**—Despite ITC's best efforts to maintain the mandi volumes and compensate the commission agents for lost income, there is little doubt that on the whole they have lower incomes after the e-Choupal than before.
- **Mandi laborers**—The workers in the mandi who weighed and bagged the produce have been severely impacted by the drop in volume. ITC's long-term vision is to employ many of these people in the hubs in much the same functions as they perform in the mandi. The Sonkach mandi has 28 tulavatis (weighers) and 300 laborers.
- **Bazaars near the mandi**—When farmers sold produce in the mandi, they would also purchase a variety of commodities at the local bazaars. This revenue has now been diverted to shops near the ITC hubs, which is actually more a diversion of revenue than its elimination.
- **Some mandi operations**—ITC still pays the mandi tax for all the grain procured through e-Choupals, but it now pays the tax to the mandi nearest to the procurement center. As a result, tax is being diverted from several mandis to the few mandis near procurement hubs. The result of this is that regional mandis have lost taxes that contribute to maintaining their infrastructure.
- **Competing processors**—Even before the advent of the e-Choupal, the soya-crushing industry suffered from severe overcapacity; half of all capacity was excess. The efficiency pressures imposed by the e-Choupal have spurred industry consolidation.

There are other challenges to the e-Choupal system of which ITC is aware. The computer in the village is revolutionary, but there is also no doubt that the villages are socially stratified to the point where not everybody can walk up to the sanchalak and ask to be shown the computer. There are clearly income levels and the entire adult female population who do not have access to the computer. The innate power of the computer to drive social change will not transcend this barrier unaided. This fact is by no means a reflection on ITC; it is a reflection on the nature of the underlying society in rural Madhya Pradesh. The solution might lie in observing where the system has driven social change. Village farmers belong to many social and economic strata. Yet, the sanchalaks are servicing all of them equally. In this case, the potential for commerce has broken a barrier that society has built. Similarly, engagement with the isolated demographics, especially women, might be possible through the active procurement and distribution through the e-Choupal of products tailored specifically to them.

ITC recognizes the limitations of today's e-Choupals in their manifestation as vehicles of procurement efficiency. Not every crop lends itself to such an intervention. In crops such as soya, where value is to be had, followers will soon imitate ITC and eliminate the competitive advantage. ITC's vision for the e-Choupals extends many generations as the e-Choupal evolves into a full-fledged orchestrator of a two-way exchange of goods and services between rural India and the world. At the very least, though, ITC has connected many rural villages to the rest of the world and taken real steps that while making a profit improve the condition and the situation of the rural poor.[1]

Endnotes

1. In April, 2005, P.M. Sinha, chairman of the Agriculture & Rural Development Committee of the Federation of Indian Chambers of Commerce and Industry, made a presentation at the Agricultural Summit in New Delhi, an excerpt of which follows:

   "At present, though agricultural production is largely free from controls, the same is not true of marketing and processing of agricultural commodities. The present agricultural marketing system is highly restrictive and regulated, owing to a large number of laws enforced by the states and the center. Monopolistic practices and procedures have prevented development of free and competitive trade in agri-products. The state governments alone are empowered to set up markets for agricultural commodities, in notified areas. Processing industries cannot buy directly from the farmers, except through the notified markets, where intermediaries take away a sizable share from the price of the produce. Currently, a study shows that the farmer receives only 30 to 35 percent of the end-consumer price, the intermediaries take up the balance. Hence we suggest:

   - Amend the Agricultural Produce and Marketing Act (APMC) to encourage direct marketing, to free the farmers to sell to whoever they want, enable them to get the best price for their produce, and create partnerships with banks, finance, and logistics companies, for lowest-cost financing and marketing. We feel states should be incentivized through budget allocation for speedy implementation of the amendments.

- Treat organization of markets as a service industry, and allow markets to be set up by the private sector and farmers' cooperatives. This will attract private investment in creation of much needed marketing infrastructure, create competition, and ensure better service to the farmers.
- Abolish the mandi tax system."

This case study was written by Kuttayan Annamalai and Sachin Rao under the supervision of Professor C.K. Prahalad. This case study is intended to be a catalyst for discussion and is not intended to illustrate effective or ineffective strategies.

Update: ITC e-Choupal

By S. Sivakumar, CEO, International Business Division, ITC Ltd.

1. The Ideas Behind e-Choupal

a. *Value creation:* As a physics student, I was deeply fascinated by Einstein's famous insight $e=mc^2$. Until he figured out the implication of the speed of light, energy and mass were two independent and unrelated fields. With one stroke of genius, he converged the two, and the world was never the same again. In a similar manner, capitalist markets, with the self-interest of the entrepreneur as the foundation, were never thought of as a means to achieve social equity. Interest of the disadvantaged communities, on the other hand, was always considered as the exclusive domain of government or community-based organizations or not-for-profits. Much later, when our experience at ITC had demonstrated that markets do deliver social equity when you co-create them together with empowered communities, I felt the same excitement as I did when I understood Einstein's equation. In other words, co-creation concept has converged the two independent domains of equity and markets. A new meaning to $e=mc^2$! And the core idea behind the value creation process in e-Choupal.
b. *Value delivery:* Another metaphor from physics, lever, helps in easily understanding the idea behind the value delivery process in the e-Choupal system. People at the BOP access markets under constrained conditions because of the voids in physical or institutional infrastructure, besides limitations in some of their own

capacities. Filling in these gaps in infrastructure can act as a multiplier (lever) and enable market access for the BOP consumers and producers. Investment in information and communication technologies was the key lever that made all the difference in the case of e-Choupal, through the process of price discovery in the village.

c. *Value capture:* Yet another physics principle, chaos theory, explains the most important idea in the e-Choupal model, namely the value capture mechanism. In the world of chaos, an attractor ensures stability and predictability. Much the same way, the orchestrator of the e-Choupal ecosystem—ITC—puts the network together and innovates the value capture mechanisms that do not strain the small wallets of the BOP customers. Win-win outcomes for all stakeholders can be achieved through logistics reorganization. Producers and buyers can get value through the ability to identify the source of the crops. This is an example of value creation.

2. *Evolution of e-Choupal*

a. *Scale:* The original report talks about 2,000 e-Choupals covering 11,000 villages servicing a million farmers. Today the network has scaled to 6,500 e-Choupals, 40,000 villages and 4 million farmers. The Hubs morphed into integrated Farmer Facility Centers, christened Choupal Saagars. There are 24 Choupal Saagars already operational. The business too has multiplied five-fold, demonstrating the scalability and replicability of the design that worked across product-service-geographic markets. While the basic character of agriculture is the same across India, value chains of different crops have their own intricate dynamics. So do the socio-economic characteristics of different regions. These complexities were factored in while operationalizing e-Choupal. The variations do nuance the supply chain designs, business processes, and revenue models across crops and geographies.

b. *Scope:* Underscoring the broader scope of evolution since the six waves were articulated in the original report, the multiple versions of e-Choupal are renumbered as 1.x and 2.x series. The original four waves are now called 1.1 to 1.4, describing the different models of agri-business. The rural marketing and distribution ideas described as wave 5 have been rolled out since then. They are renumbered as 2.1 to 2.6, covering agri-inputs (information, knowledge, risk management solutions, credit, seeds, nutrients, etc), consumer goods, financial services, retail hypermarkets at Choupal Saagars, health, and education respectively. The first four are full-fledged businesses, while the last two are in pilot scale. The different components under the 3.x series are being prototyped at this time. These cover new anchor businesses (much like the 1.x series in agriculture) and deeper personalization of the solution through the integration of mobile devices and analytics. These are likely to be scaled during 2009. The earlier wave 6 is now 4.x series, and work remains on the drawing board until the broadband reaches rural India at a substantially better price performance equation.

c. *Social impact:* Farmers benefited through better prices for crops as they are now able to make informed choices, through higher crop yields and improved quality enabled by better practices and quality inputs. Real-time information led to better alignment of production with markets, more valuable in perishable crops and organic produce. Research has concluded that information asymmetry between large mandies and small reduced in e-Choupal catchments. Competition from e-Choupal improved systems and efficiencies of the traditional mandi system. The success of e-Choupal inspired many other corporations to look at businesses in rural India more seriously, while the government has been comfortable reforming the various laws that constrained the entrepreneurial energies along the agriculture value chain. Above all, the optimism and confidence of a farmer arising from the freedom of choices is very visible. This is in great contrast to a mood of resignation.

3. *Principles in Operationalizing e-Choupal*

a. *Quality, cost, and experience—no trade-offs:* Trade-offs imply compromises and that some value needs to be given up to acquire some other value. It is envisaged from the beginning that the e-Choupal platform will offer full freedom of choice to the participants without any trade-off dilemmas. Better quality produce is acknowledged and rewarded with differentiated premium. Costs of participation are made near-zero to encourage rapid network build-up. Farmers participating on the platform were treated with dignity and respect that is not experienced by them in the alternate channels. Hypermarkets at Choupal Saagars not only offer quality screened products and services to the rural consumers at competitive prices but provide an in-store experience normally extended in high-end luxury store formats in cities.

b. *Multi-tiered innovation structures:* Institutional structures and the capacities to use them always existed in urban centers; the voids are acutely visible in rural hinterlands. Because of the institutional abilities, the enterprise activity in urban centers is vibrant and dynamic. In a sense, ITC e-Choupal catalyzed the diffusion of innovations to rural hinterlands and vice versa through a three-tier structure (i) village level, (ii) cluster level, and (iii) network orchestrator. This multi-tiered e-Choupal architecture is supplemented with the co-option of social capital in the form of Sanchalaks and Samyojaks, as well as ITC's field force recruited from villages and small towns. This combination led to a change in the interpersonal communication dynamics, leading to deeper engagement with farmers through culturally sensitive dialogue that generates ideas from the routine daily interactions. At the other end, collaborative effort across firms in the ecosystem versus the traditional competitive approach enabled opportunities for extraordinary value creation.

   In the case of wheat, for example, the transformation in the industry is led by e-Choupal's ability, through its processes and infrastructure, to bridge the disconnect between the way wheat is bought (physical properties), is processed (chemical properties), and the way the final product is bought by the consumer (rheological properties and organoleptic tests), which ensures the quality consistency in differentiated forms of Atta (Indian flour). This was just not possible—or too expensive—in the pre–e-Choupal days.

c. *Open yet self-regulating governance mechanisms:* When the ITC e-Choupal was first rolled out, mega successes of open source–based models such as Wikipedia or community-centric commerce platforms such as eBay were yet to happen. From day one, the e-Choupal model established a code of conduct quite unique to the business world with counterparty contracts based on moral contract rather than a written legal deed. Individual responsibilities and community ownership is emphasized and accentuated through processes and events. It is not in the interest of an individual to default on obligations because the peer-group enforces compliance. For example, if a farmer defaults on the quality of produce while delivering at the designated location, it gets identified and published. Once it gets known within the local community, the community actively discourages such behavior as it will impact the efficiency of the system.

Once every six months, large-scale face-to-face assemblies are arranged for all the participants, namely farmers, rural consumers, manufacturers, service providers. These assemblies serve to foster close-knit communities, reward innovators, and encourage behaviors that facilitate the realization of e-Choupal objectives.

4. Vision of e-Choupal

Another physics metaphor! *Black Holes for a Green World.* Curious? The next edition of the book will have the details.

Voxiva: Health Alerts for All

"We were able to get started because we raised money from people who thought what we were doing was important to the world and also thought there was a business."

—Paul Meyer

Over the past two decades, the spread of new diseases such as HIV/AIDS, severe acute respiratory syndrome (SARS), hepatitis C, and dengue haemorrhagic fever, and outbreaks of traditional diseases such as typhus and diphtheria, have generated a renewed awareness of the *global* threats posed by infectious diseases. Indeed, infectious diseases, such as cholera, meningococcal disease, and measles, cause 63 percent of all childhood deaths and 48 percent of premature deaths. Approximately 300 million people have acute cases of malaria, 90 percent of them in Sub-Saharan Africa.[1] Infections also cause cancers, cardiovascular, and respiratory/digestive deaths. The overall toll of infectious diseases is significant around the world.

The threat of rapid national, regional, and global spread of infectious diseases poses a new challenge: early detection and coordinated and rapid reaction by public-health authorities locally and globally. *A basic surveillance system built on a low-cost communications infrastructure is critical.* The innovation from Voxiva, Inc., in tackling such a challenge in Peru is proving to be

The threat of rapid national, regional, and global spread of infectious diseases poses a new challenge: early detection and coordinated and rapid reaction by public-health authorities locally and globally.

robust, with applications in developed countries such as the United States and developing countries such as Afghanistan, Iraq, China, and India.

Continuing threats of emergent diseases, such as SARS, threaten state and regional economies. According to the Asian Development Bank (ADB), the SARS outbreak will have a significant economic cost (in addition to the loss of life it will cause). ADB estimates that SARS will cost Asia approximately $7 billion in lost economic output, and the region as a whole could lose up to $28 billion.[2] However, early disease detection, clear and rapid communication, and coordinated action by health authorities can inhibit the spread of infectious diseases. According to the World Health Organization, "Reporting systems are the intelligence network that underpins disease control and prevention. Without this framework in place, it is impossible to track where disease is occurring, measure progress in disease control targets, monitor antimicrobial drug resistance, or provide an early-warning system for outbreaks and the emergence of new diseases." Surveillance data also is needed to assess where resources should go for maximum cost-effectiveness. Research in public health, around the world, has resulted in four simple conclusions to minimize the spread of disease:

1. We need widespread recognition that infectious diseases present a significant threat to global health, both in human and economic terms.
2. Active surveillance is critical for early detection. Often, the difficulty is the surveillance in remote regions of the developing world with poor communications and health infrastructure.
3. Early detection and subsequent relevant action reduce the probability of the spread of a communicable disease.
4. The ability to communicate between groups affected and public health authorities who can trigger the appropriate actions is critical.

Voxiva, Inc., considered these four factors when tackling a challenge with their technological solution. Though Voxiva first designed their platform around an epidemiological application, these criteria have applied to other types of cases found the world over, such as reporting crime, supplying blood to hospitals, and testing new vaccines. Though these solutions might seem obvious for people who never leave home without a mobile phone, Voxiva looked beyond the U.S. borders to rural areas where 70 percent of the world's poor live with limited access to telecommunications.[3]

Voxiva exists to bridge a communications gap, at the same time targeting a market that makes less than $2 a day. Its value added is socially admirable, and at the same time it seeks to be profitable. Its basic assumption is that there are a lot more telephones in the world than computers, and that telephones are a much more accessible and practical tool for conveying urgent data and information. Voxiva challenges an implicit assumption held by many: Computer usage must proliferate in rural communities to connect the poor. In bypassing this assumption, Voxiva provides a solution divorced from hardware configuration. Instead, it adds value by streamlining the flow of critical information through the existing telecommunications infrastructure.

Voxiva exists to bridge a communications gap, at the same time targeting a market that makes less than $2 a day. Its value added is socially admirable, and at the same time it seeks to be profitable.

Voxiva was co-founded by Paul Meyer and Dr. Pamela Johnson, who both have extensive experience in linking humanitarian projects with business enterprises. Meyer was founder and chairman of IPKO, the first and largest Internet service provider in Kosovo; Johnson was previously the coordinator for child survival at the U.S. Agency for International Development overseeing public health programs in fifty countries. Voxiva leverages the convergence between the public and private sector, creating a social venture with the goal of creating a better world by promoting public health in developing economies. These ventures are driven by *profits, scalability, and ROI* as much as by the social good they can do.

The health-care industry relies heavily on the management of critical information, and technological solutions hold great promise for providing support for challenging and complex interdependent managerial decisions and interventions that characterize health practice. The health-care sector is second only to the business sector as a major user and promoter of tools and methodologies to harvest knowledge through intensive use of ICT.[4] As a social venture, Voxiva (with its credibility and track record) has positioned itself not only as an expert in public health, but also as a business truly interested in solving public-health problems. As a result, Voxiva attracts a unique type of worker: The ideal Voxiva employee is part McKinsey consultant, part Microsoft technician, and part Peace Corps volunteer.

WHY PERU?

The Gates Foundation and the World Health Organization suggested Peru as a testing ground because it provided an environment in which Voxiva's unique data collection system could be more or less isolated and tested. Peru has a history of utilizing data to fight infectious diseases, a strong public-health orientation, and a demonstrable commitment to rural connectivity.

However, the missing link in Peru's existing disease surveillance was effective communication between central decision makers in Lima and the front-line health workers in rural areas. The two key elements that made Peru a fertile testing ground were its disperse rural populations and Voxiva's capability to identify and create two solid partnerships: with Telefónica, Peru's largest telephone company; and with a "superuser" at the operational level within the health-care system who took ownership of the pilot.

Finally, the importance of an active and involved user cannot be underestimated for the success of the pilot. Also known as a superuser, the role of Peru's Department of Epidemiology (OGE) was to actively help design the system, participate in its rollout, integrate it with its own training programs, and test it thoroughly to find the glitches and limitations. As Dr. Johnson emphasized, "The head of the OGE not only understood the role of information technology, but could see the power behind it. We worked with people who are really hungry for information so they can use it."

Voxiva's pilot launch application, Alerta, gave voice to marginalized communities in rural Peru that were only part of a health-care system according to a zone map, but not in practice. Voxiva's Alerta brought these remote and disaggregated groups into the fold years before their governments thought it was possible. Voxiva's primary challenge was to deconstruct a complex information reporting system into the "lowest common denominator" necessary to achieve the defined goals. This included not only the reporting structure, but also developing a user-friendly audio interface and assisting organizations accustomed to "snail mail" to leverage real-time information.

Voxiva piloted a system that connected approximately 204,000 individuals in two sparsely populated districts south of Lima to the national health surveillance system. The population density of Chilca-Mala was 15 residents and of Cañete 24 residents per square kilometer, respectively. The system incorporated 76 health clinics, health centers, and district centers (SBS) that are part of the four levels of the Ministry of Health. In total, Peru has 135 health posts (operations), 53 district-level health centers (or SBSs), and 34 state-level health centers (or DISAs that play a vital role in disaster-outbreaks management), along with the Department of Epidemiology (or the OGE), and the Ministry of Health (or the MINSA) located in the capital, Lima.

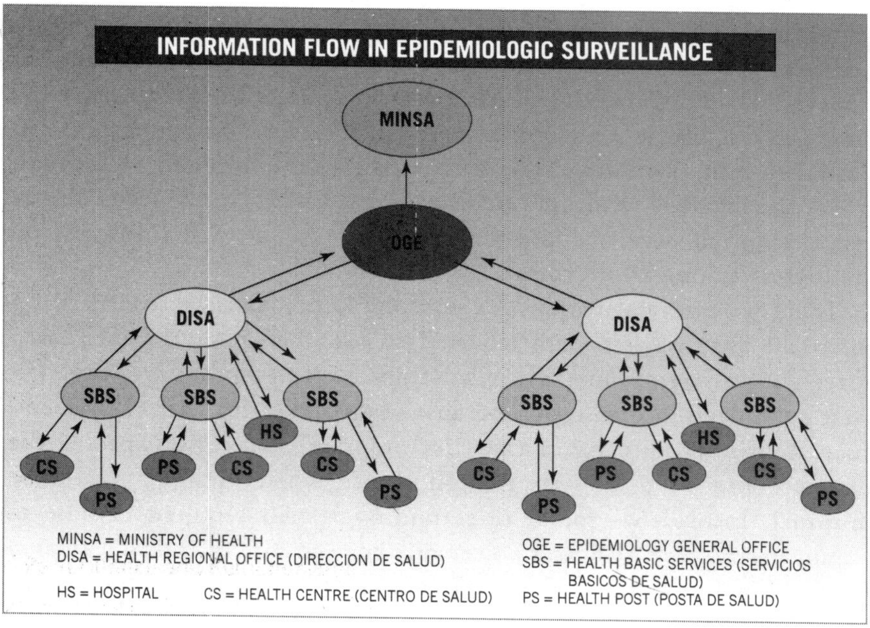

Figure 1 National public-health surveillance, Peru.

To improve communication, Voxiva's reports are available 24 hours a day, 365 days a year, in near real time, through text messaging to cell phones or e-mail.

The pilot ran from March 2002 through early September 2002. Preliminary results showed that prior to Alerta's installation, 28 health posts reported on a weekly basis, whereas 22 reported on a monthly basis to the Chilca-Mala SBS. The MINSA required that health posts and centers report on a weekly basis, but because of the cumbersome process of transporting the reports, many only reported monthly. After Alerta's deployment, 12 of the 22, which had previously reported on a monthly basis, began reporting on a weekly basis because of access to a telephone in their village. During the pilot, 26,264 cases were reported over 4,167 calls. Two hundred and four users, including front-line health workers and management, utilized the program.

A survey conducted in August, as the pilot neared its end, revealed that 90 percent of the respondents who used the system believed the faster responses from supervisors were the primary benefit of the system, and 70 percent of the users cited the increased communication with their colleagues and supervisors as a primary benefit of the system. In addition, 50 percent believed that reporting was easier, 40 percent believed more cases were reported, and 40 percent believed they saved time over the previous paper-based system. The time used to make a call has fallen from 3 minutes and 32 seconds to 2 minutes and 21 seconds, where the time has seemingly stabilized. Anecdotally, there seemed to be early adoption with younger medics and an increased interest in computers among all doctors.

There were several reasons for noncompliance. Because Alerta was a pilot, all health posts were required to use the previous paper-based surveillance system; some officials did not want to report twice. Reports were submitted inconsistently because of unfamiliarity with the system. Juan Rodriguez, director of the pilot program, said, "We expected the phone would be a familiar enough device where training would be minimal. Instead, we found that training is still required because of unfamiliarity with IVR and voicemail. For instance, a training session was held in July 2002 in Chilca-Mala to provide additional training for voicemail use."

The lessons learned from the Alerta pilot launch included the following:

- The environment and deployable resources will dictate the type of communication device used. For instance, the need to collect data from widely distributed communities entails the ability to accept data from a variety of input devices such as a computer, cell phone, or a land-line phone.

- Decreasing the cycle time in the data input and aggregation process to provide a near real-time assessment of the situation in the field will likely help prevent or decrease the duration of outbreaks. Responding quickly to events by incorporating near real-time data assessment into policy and public health decisions and communicating immediately with dispersed individuals via a suite of messaging and notification services will stem the rise of diseases.
- The system increases the quality and quantity of data available to facilitate decision making.
- The system must be cost-effective. The deployment of the Alerta system is inexpensive relative to other IT rollouts because it leverages the existing telecommunications infrastructure.
- The technology must be intuitive to facilitate adoption and use. Because a technology is only as good as the people using it, continuous training is critical, not only to familiarize the technicians with the hardware, but also to alter the culture.
- The technicians and doctors were receptive to the technology and liked connecting with the authorities on a regular basis.
- Only 21 percent of respondents used voicemail two times or more during July and August 2002 compared with 64 percent who used the system "never" or "occasionally." This usage pattern might be attributable to several factors, including unfamiliarity with use or the technology, no cases that would prompt voicemail usage, or that the telephone was in a public place the respondent thought was not conducive to sending a voicemail.
- Collaboration among customers, partners, and users drives problem solving.
- Remote locations with no access to the phone used the radio to contact a health post with a phone to report to the closest health post or clinic with a telephone.
- Health-care workers in remote locations used the voicemail system to communicate with their relatives.
- Group lists were created and used by directors or program coordinators to call for emergency meetings, workshops, courses, or staff meetings—something never done before on a regular basis.

- Industry-wide standard best practices must be adhered to, including those associated with security, flexibility to interoperate with other systems, and versatility of input devices and exportability.

The pace of business within international development is much slower than that of Wall Street. The benchmarks are different, and one significant indicator is the value of time. In the public sector, time is seen as a commodity; whereas with corporations, time translates into actual liquidity and must be accounted for in every respect. This clash of cultures is one tension Voxiva faces on several levels. Time spent on relationship building in the Peru office might or might not result in a funded proposal or pilot now but is crucial as a door opener for future possibilities.

In many ways, Voxiva's original intent to target the developing countries' health markets has paid off in the United States, where Voxiva seems to be a novelty based on its rare social mission as a start-up company with operations in Peru. In Peru, on the other hand, multi- and bilateral development aid in South America is big business. Many businesses position themselves as having a social mission or just convert to NGOs to gain more access to development funds. The idea of social responsibility for companies is an unfamiliar concept and as such misunderstood and distrusted. In the United States, however, any organizations associated with public funds, especially civil society, are seen as a threat to business sectors' status quo and regarded as inefficient and bureaucratic; moreover, NGOs from developing countries are suspected of being corrupt.

In short, Peru's development aid market is saturated; many groups are all vying for a piece of the pie. Voxiva-Peru's challenge is to become a viable business seeking public-sector funds. With pressure to realize new contracts quickly, the Lima office is applying two short-term tactics: networking within the circles of friends, former colleagues, family, and public offices with healthy budgets. In Peru, this translates into pitching to the mayors of wealthy districts of Lima and their corresponding municipalities. Alternatively, Voxiva Peru has a choice to cultivate inroads into the private sector, which has a greater ability traditionally to make faster decisions. This effort, however, is also filled with its own menu of complications. First, there is the risk that if they do find a market, as small as it might be, there will be competition within the IT market. Many large IT corporations who have deep pockets to court the donor community might be disposed to do so with the additional benefit of satisfying their role as a socially conscious business. Second, because Voxiva has no propriety ownership, a low profile might be in order. In addition to these factors, its positioning as an IT company within health has its complications, especially with operations in the developing world. The biggest worry with investors is recouping investment in a sector so heavily managed by the public sector in Latin America. It is harder to see the who, when, and how the payback will occur without the help of large international donors stepping in to fund the infrastructure of public services.

Two years after the successful launch of Voxiva and close to break even, Meyer still relentlessly challenged his employees to create innovative applications that deliver on two bottom lines: social and business. His track record and the story behind Voxiva were compelling to many investors. Trust, credibility, and social zeal helped him to raise another $3 million during the second quarter of 2003. Meyer is focusing on pulling in the right people who are smart and driven with initiative to innovate new solutions applying the formula of success: the power of the Internet, the reach of the phone. He constantly finds himself weighing the business opportunities versus the social benefits, short-term results over long-term impact, and fighting the inclination to grow all at once into different social sectors.

His successful run so far as a social entrepreneur is paying off. Over the summer of 2003, Voxiva-Peru launched its second application: Citizen's Alert, in Lima, Peru. This time the social good was safety. The pilot was funded by the mayor of Miraflores, a popular neighborhood of Lima with upscale restaurants and shops that cater to tourists. When the elite of Lima caught wind of this public service, they also demanded it be applied in their neighborhoods. The outcome favored all citizens of Lima because the four mayors consolidated their resources and scaled up the program to apply to the greater Lima area, population seven million. (The price structure is on a per-user basis.) Following on the heels of this launch were requests from their client base in the United States—proving again that challenges found in developing countries do not differ greatly from those in our backyard.

Endnotes

1. WHO Report on Global Surveillance of Epidemic-prone Infectious Diseases. WHO/CDS/CSR/ISR/2000.1, www.who/int/emc-documents/surveillance/docs/whocd-scsrisr2001.pdf/Introduction.pdf, May 2002.

2. "Economic Impact of SARS," Asian Development Bank, May 9, 2003, www.abd.org/Documents/News/2003/nr2003065.pdf.

3. The World Bank's Agriculture and Development home page, lnweb18.worldbank.org/ESSD/ardext.nsf/11ByDocName/AgricultureRuralDevelopment, October 2, 2003.

4. "Development and international cooperation in the 21st century: The role of IT in the context of a knowledge-based global economy," UN's Economic and Social Council, E/2000/52, August 2000.

This case study was written by Cynthia Casas and William C. Lajoie under the supervision of Professor C.K. Prahalad. This case study is intended to be a catalyst for discussion and is not intended to illustrate effective or ineffective strategies.

Update: Voxiva

By Paul Meyer, Chairman and President of Voxiva, Inc.

Eight years after starting, Voxiva is going strong—operating in 13 countries across Africa, Asia, and North and South America and employing more than 150 people. Although Voxiva is still focused on meeting the enormous need for innovative information services at the Bottom of the Pyramid, it is also taking what it learned there and applying those lessons in the U.S. health-care market.

When Voxiva started in 2001, there were only 750 million cell phones in the world. Many of the people approached with the idea for Voxiva thought it crazy to think that mobile phones could be leveraged to improve the delivery of health services to poor people in poor countries. Not only were there many fewer cell phones, but also technologies like Short Message Service were only just emerging and the mobile Internet was still a long way off.

Fast forward to 2009, and there are more than four billion cell phones in the world. For the first time in human history, it is possible to communicate, interact, and transact individually and in real-time with the majority of the people on the planet. For most people in the world, the cell phone is their first electronic connection to the outside world—not a landline phone, not e-mail, not the Internet. As a result, they use their phones for much more than making calls and texting their friends. They use their phones to access information, buy things, sell things, to send money, and much more—many of the things the Internet is used for in developed countries. Not only have developing countries leap-frogged the old telephone wire infrastructure and adopted wireless communications at a stunning rate, they have leap-frogged the old-fashioned PC-based Internet and adopted mobile information services at a much faster pace than their counterparts in developed countries. In health care, because developing countries are not burdened by the nightmarish jumble of legacy IT systems that plague developed countries, they are leap-frogging from paper straight to interactive mobile health services.

For Voxiva, the explosion in cell phone adoption in the last few years has meant that the company could extend the reach of its mobile health applications all the way to patients and consumers. In the early years, most of its end users were rural doctors or community health workers using the systems to report disease outbreaks or manage the supply of drugs. Now, in addition to providing applications that support health workers and health delivery systems, Voxiva provides a broad range of mobile health applications to help individuals manage their health. Although cell phones can't make diagnoses or dispense drugs, they can collect information, monitor patients, provide reminders, and give people timely information they can use to keep themselves healthy.

For example, in Mexico, Voxiva launched a series of mobile health services in partnership with Telcel, the leading mobile operator, the CARSO Health Foundation and Medical Clinica, the leading network of private health clinics serving lower-income populations. The Vidanet service allows HIV/AIDS patients to get medication and appointment reminders, access information and tips on living with HIV/AIDS, and track their treatment progress all via their mobile phones. The Diabediario lets diabetics track their glucose levels and other key metrics with their phone.

Given the chronic lack of trained health professionals in most of the developing world, these kinds of direct patient support services can result in significant improvements in health outcomes while reducing the burden on overtaxed health systems.

Voxiva's experience in the developing world and the credibility that stems from it have been invaluable as the company entered the U.S. health market. Unlike the developing world, Voxiva feels the U.S. health industry is just waking up to the potential of mobile health—the idea that the phones people carry around all day might be a better technology tool to help us live healthy lives than computers.

Part IV
Case Studies and CEO Comments

E+Co: Energy for Everyone

It is possible to combine clean and distributed energy development (a significant component of sustainable development) and provide access to electricity for the poor. The success of E+Co's investments in Tecnosol, in Nicaragua, with the local entrepreneur as the driving force in the market, demonstrates that locally based nongrid energy systems can work.

Globally, approximately 1.8 billion people lack access to electricity, and 2.4 billion people use wood fuels for cooking. The poor spend roughly $20 billion per year for ad-hoc solutions, such as kerosene lamps, candles, charcoal, firewood, dung fires, and batteries, just to meet basic energy needs.[1] Lack of modern forms of energy, particularly electricity, keeps people from escaping poverty and becoming more productive, and these substandard substitutes are often more expensive and more damaging than modern alternatives. For these reasons, electricity access has been a top priority for world governments, multilateral development organizations, and nongovernmental organizations for more than 50 years. However, the number of people without access to modern forms of energy has remained approximately the same despite these efforts.

Focusing on local entrepreneurs, E+Co combines the traditional training and support services of a nongovernmental organization with the capital investment strategies of private equity and banking firms.

In 1994, E+Co, a rural energy finance company, was formed to pioneer a different approach to the global energy problem. Focusing on local entrepreneurs, E+Co combines the traditional training and support services of a nongovernmental organization with the capital investment strategies of private equity and banking firms. The result could lead to a dramatic rethinking about how to reach and provide access to energy to the world's poor.

E+Co

E+Co had its genesis through pilot activities chartered by the Rockefeller Foundation, and led by Phil LaRocco, to develop new concepts for public-private partnerships in the area of rural energy. They saw an opportunity to install a fundamental building block that would support and reinforce every other important social need in rural societies, including increased economic output (and reduced waste); greater access to information and education; and improved health, especially from the reduction of pollution from wood, kerosene, and other fuels. The foundation recognized, however, that rural energy did not have a one-size-fits-all solution that could be developed in a lab, easily replicated, and scaled worldwide.

The organization quickly evolved and by 2002 had grown to include regional offices in South Africa, Nepal, and Costa Rica with an affiliate office in Bolivia and a global (main) office in Bloomfield, New Jersey. All together, these offices managed a $9 million loan and equity portfolio encompassing 62 active investments in more than 20 countries. In addition, a new office was in the process of being launched in northeastern Brazil. Each regional office, led by an E+Co manager, is responsible for sourcing deal flow, managing existing investments, and preparing investment recommendations for opportunities throughout their region.

Over 10 years, E+Co invested in 90 energy enterprises, reaching more than 200,000 people with modern energy across a variety of technologies and geographical contexts. The firm intentionally cast a broad net by working in more than 20 countries on multiple continents as it has sought to experiment, replicate, and prove its model. This phase of experimentation revealed four main conclusions:

1. There is a willingness and capacity to pay for modern forms of energy at the Bottom of the Pyramid.
2. Renewable energy technologies are an appropriate and increasingly reliable solution.
3. Private enterprises serving local markets are a necessary component for the provision of clean energy.
4. Local entrepreneurial talent with rural reach is a crucially valuable and widely available resource in communities around the world.

The demand for electricity in rural unelectrified areas is largely driven by the need for basic lighting and productive uses such as irrigating fields or operating machinery. One light bulb can keep a store open through the night or provide light for reading, household chores, and even basic security. An electric water pump can save hours of time fetching water. In addition, as globalization continues, there is increasing demand for telephone and even the Internet. When 60,000 poor people were asked to name the number one thing they wanted, they said technology and information, not food and charity. Poor people know that what keeps them poor is lack of competitiveness and knowledge.[2] Without electricity, there is little or no possibility these aspirations would come true.

When 60,000 poor people were asked to name the number one thing they wanted, they said technology and information, not food and charity.

Poorer countries tend to have the lowest levels of electrification because per-capita income and the percentage of a country that has electricity are unequivocally correlated. This is further supported by the observation that when a country's per-capita income is less than $300, typically 90 percent or more of the population uses firewood and dung for cooking. However, when incomes have exceeded

$1,000 per capita, most people switch to modern fuels, which further perpetuates their ability to earn greater income.[3]

Families in rural areas of developing countries spend approximately $10 per month on energy, which can represent between 10 percent and 40 percent of a family's income.[4] A billion people in rural markets have the ability to pay for energy, with many of these billion people spending $5 to $10 a month exclusively for lights.[5] Rural customers around the world are estimated to spend between $8 and $12 per month for lighting services, including candles, kerosene, dry cells, or battery charging.[6] These sources of energy are dirty and inefficient, and on a per-kilowatt basis, they cost anywhere from 5 to 100 times more than modern fuels and electricity. The paradox is that the poor are spending a disproportionate share of their income on a product that richer people can get cheaper and of higher quality.

Although the cost of energy would appear to be the main driving concern of rural households, experience indicates that high quality and reliability are the most valued attributes of an energy system. Willingness to pay for electricity that is reliable, safe, and of high quality is often higher than what is currently spent on energy services.

Modern distributed energy in developing nations might take many forms, but among the most exciting is the potential for widescale adoption of renewable energy technologies. Renewable energy is characterized as an energy resource that is inexhaustible in a reasonable period of time. The global renewable resource base is considered large but is currently being utilized far below its potential. The most advanced renewable energy technologies include solar photovoltaics, wind power, biomass, geothermal, and hydropower. A main advantage of renewable energy technologies is that the majority of the cost is up front, while the "fuel" costs are for the most part free.

Table 1 Renewable Energy Electricity-Generation Technologies

Technology	Description
Solar photovoltaics (PV)	Conversion of sunlight into electricity by means of a solar panel. A panel consists of multiple solar cells connected to each other and mounted on a support structure. The electrical output depends on the level of sunlight that falls on the panel.
Wind energy	Wind is used to drive a rotor (blades) connected through a power shaft to an electric generator. The amount of energy depends on the wind speed and the diameter of the rotor.

Technology	Description
Biomass energy	Plant or animal matter is used directly as a fuel or converted into gaseous or liquid fuels. Biomass typically refers to agricultural or municipal organic waste, forestry byproducts, wood or process waste, or special-purpose energy crops.
Geothermal energy	In geological zones that have been volcanically active, steam and/or hot water can be extracted through deep wells to provide a direct or indirect heat source for electric power generation or other uses.
Hydroelectricity	Moving water is used to drive a turbine that powers an electric generator. Large hydroelectric plants operate through the damming of rivers, and microhydroelectric plants can use the natural flow of a river to spin turbines.

Cost reductions in renewable energy technologies have driven renewed interest in the potential of alternative means to generate electricity. Technological advancements and economies of production supported by increased demand have led to this cost decline, which is predicted to continue as markets for renewable energy further develop. Wind power and solar photovoltaics in particular have been growing at more than 20 percent per year, while conventional sources of energy are barely growing or declining. The learning curve[7] for photovoltaics has been over 20 percent, resulting in an 80 percent cost reduction since 1980.[8] Wind power, currently the world's fastest-growing energy source, has grown at a rate of nearly 40 percent between 1997 and 2000; in locations with good wind resources, it is considered to be the lowest-cost energy option.[9]

Given that grid extensions can cost up to $10,000 per kilometer, renewable energy technologies are often a more cost-effective and appropriate solution to meeting the energy needs of rural noncontiguous areas in developing countries. Adoption of renewable energy technologies to meet energy needs in rural areas offers an opportunity to "leapfrog" the traditional development paradigm characterized by centralized electricity generation by fossil fuel power plants. Renewables also are a good solution in many developing markets because the amount of power they provide comes in scales that are quite appropriate to the demands of the market. Depending on the size, a photovoltaic array on the roof of an individual household can provide enough electricity to power a few lights, a radio, and television.

At the heart of a revolution in distributed energy is a series of success stories developed over the past decade. E+Co is transforming how the Bottom of the Pyramid obtains and uses energy by emphasizing "energy through enterprise," the delivery of clean energy through local entrepreneurs. In general, the prevailing view was one of generally large-scale, project-oriented investing implemented through government programs or grants to in-country nongovernmental organizations. Many of these projects and programs took the form of aid financing programs sponsored by multilateral institutions such as the World Bank Group for electricity grid extension or for subsidized "giveaway" programs to the rural poor. The expectation was that access to modern energy would generate a host of additional benefits, including greater economic prosperity. This prosperity would allow the government to repay the aid financing and would support further organic growth of the energy infrastructure. The fundamental flaw in many of these programs was how they distorted or ignored fundamental market forces and issues when targeting underdeveloped areas.

At the heart of a revolution in distributed energy is a series of success stories developed over the past decade. E+Co is transforming how the Bottom of the Pyramid obtains and uses energy by emphasizing "energy through enterprise," the delivery of clean energy through local entrepreneurs.

Often, with grid extension projects in areas where people were subsistence farming, the government or a nongovernmental organization would install power lines and lights, and then expect to charge a monthly bill at the same rates as for people in the city. Of course, the farmers had no significant disposable income, so the project would eventually fail.[10] In other cases, nongovernmental organizations would get a grant to install a certain number of solar panels at no cost in a region. This would be fine until the panels stopped working because of faulty installations, worn-out batteries, or other problems. Before then, the nongovernmental organization would have filed a final report with details on how many installations had been accomplished, how many households had been served, and so forth, and would have moved on to the next grant proposal. Many of these programs just were not sustainable in any kind of business sense.

In contrast to the top-down structured plans of the multilateral institutions and aid agencies, E+Co proposed to seek out and invest in entrepreneurs in developing markets who would develop new products and services to meet the energy needs in their communities. Because many of these entrepreneurs would not have significant business or even energy experience, the investment would be coupled with significant support services provided on a nonprofit basis.

In contrast to the top-down structured plans of the multilateral institutions and aid agencies, E+Co proposed to seek out and invest in entrepreneurs in developing markets who would develop new products and services to meet the energy needs in their communities. Because many of these entrepreneurs would not have significant business or even energy experience, the investment would be coupled with significant support services provided on a nonprofit basis.

Rather than focusing broadly on growth finance across multiple industries, E+Co was designed from the outset to accomplish a specific mission: the provision of clean, modern energy to the world's poor via locally developed, market-based solutions. By focusing on energy, E+Co expects to have substantial social, environmental, and economic benefits that will reinforce continued growth in each community in which it invests. Well beyond accomplishing a major feat of economic and social development, this strategy has important implications for the growth of E+Co and its investment portfolio. If successful, E+Co and its investors will realize a real return on their seed capital and create substantial opportunities for follow-on investments by commercial institutions.

By targeting the entrepreneur, E+Co shifts the focus away from technology, demonstrations, and donor programs to enterprise, markets, and competitive growth. A key metric of success is the capability of the businesses to grow to a point at which they are self-sustaining or can access larger, commercial sources of investment. E+Co's approach identifies market opportunities and business models through direct interaction with entrepreneurs and then provides them with the tools, training, and capital to mature their concept into successful, commercially viable businesses.

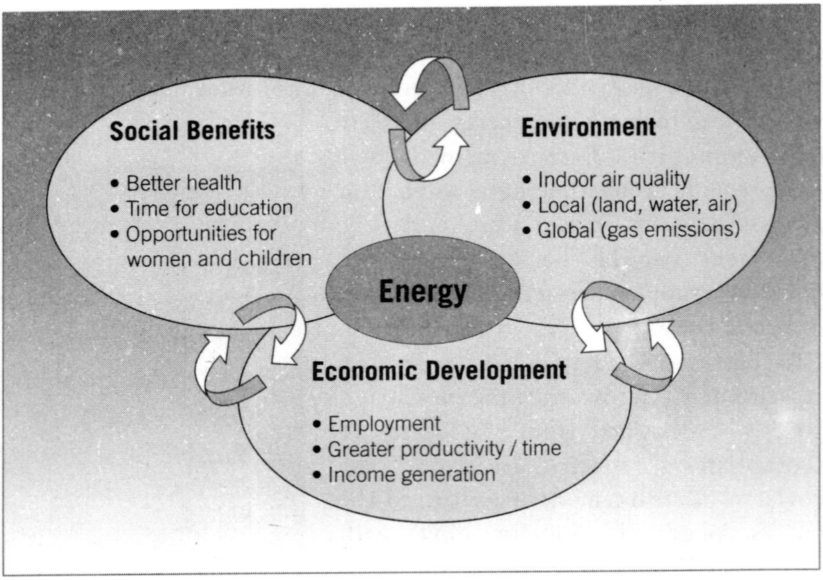

Figure 1 Modern energy is the key link to eliminating poverty, by stimulating social benefits and economic development in an environmentally sustainable manner.[11]

The initial relationship between the entrepreneur and E+Co or its partners is an opportunity to evaluate each other's goals and expectations. Contact between an entrepreneur and an E+Co representative typically begins with a training session in a given region publicized through local partners. During this "market opening," E+Co staff and local partners present success stories, describe the E+Co investment process, and provide general comments about opportunities that could qualify for potential investment. Basic business planning resources are distributed. During this and subsequent events, serious entrepreneurs are identified and engaged in more detailed discussions with investment officers who eventually select a limited number to participate in a more formal and detailed program of Enterprise Development Services. Roughly one in five entrepreneurs whom E+Co has any substantial contact with are selected to receive significant support; one in 20 might actually receive an investment.

The scope of E+Co's investments, although sometimes beginning at only a few thousand dollars, should not be confused with micro financing, which is generally designed for incremental economic activity such as short-term working capital for the purchase of individual livestock. Although the average E+Co investment is just more than $110,000, it varies widely by region with the mean investment in Africa being less than half that amount. E+Co also provides substantial support in attracting and negotiating follow-on investments for portfolio companies and in assisting them in raising their stature in their community. In many cases, the investment triggers increased access to commercial capital, better vendor financing terms, and increased positive attention from government policy officials.

Operating in an area between traditional development programs and commercial capital, E+Co's strategy incorporates elements of both approaches to investing. In combining these styles, the firm has pioneered several innovative strategies to meet its needs for investment capital, operational funding, and increased organizational impact in providing access to modern energy. As a provider of quasi-commercial capital, E+Co cannot earn true market rates of return on its early-stage investments. Therefore, to create a pool of investment capital, E+Co has targeted the philanthropic community to generate low-interest loans or outright grants from foundations, socially oriented investors, and corporations seeking a triple bottom-line return.[12]

E+Co's ideal investments are companies that have successfully penetrated the market with unique, defendable strategies and are now in a position to expand their business through next-stage growth capital. One such example is Tecnosol in Nicaragua. Tecnosol sells and installs distributed solar PV, wind, and hydroelectric power systems to mostly rural unelectrified populations throughout the country. Despite generally unfavorable economic conditions and a chronic shortage of working capital, the company has doubled its sales each year.

E+Co's ideal investments are companies that have successfully penetrated the market with unique, defendable strategies and are now in a position to expand their business through next-stage growth capital. One such example is Tecnosol in Nicaragua.

Tecnosol succeeded primarily on the strength of a market strategy that allows it to reach deep into rural markets with a clearly differentiated and well-publicized offering. Tecnosol also leveraged universal and regional knowledge in the field of rural and especially solar-based power business through close consultation with E+Co and its partners' broad experience base. This has allowed Tecnosol to significantly advance the sophistication of its business plan and has opened opportunities for new sources of capital (in particular, a major loan from E+Co). The combination of a superior market strategy and access to both dedicated business advisory support and growth capital is allowing Tecnosol to find new avenues for growth to better serve the large market for electricity in rural areas of Nicaragua. The company has installed more than 3,500 PV systems, 20 wind systems, and a few small hydroelectric systems. Growth has been highly organic and has benefited from a reputation for good quality and service. As the firm's reputation has spread, so has its growth.

TECNOSOL'S RELATIONSHIP WITH E+Co

Tecnosol was introduced to E+Co in 2001 as a potential candidate for Enterprise Development Services and follow-on investment, a phase that lasted nearly two years and included a detailed market study to confirm Tecnosol's claims about the market structure and opportunity. The market study confirmed Tecnosol's business model, indicating 91.4 percent of the population in four target regions in Nicaragua did not have access to electricity, and 60 percent of the population in those target regions had a strong interest in the company's products and could afford them. It also was determined this population could pay between $10 and $50 on a monthly basis for energy, and the richest farmers could spend between $50 and $200 per month. This was backed up by results; better targeting and the growing effects from positive word-of-mouth advertising had caused sales to jump to close to 700 systems per year, from around only 400 in the prior year.

E+Co's investment in the company, completed in early 2003, was designed to increase Tecnosol's working capital and expand the company's creditworthiness. Taking the form of a two-year, $100,000 loan at 11 percent interest, the investment has allowed Tecnosol to purchase additional inventory in one large-volume order, dramatically saving on shipping costs. The increase in inventory also allowed the company to extend a greater line of credit to its dealers so that they can increase their sales volume and carry a larger selection of products.

Tecnosol's business model is to sell renewable energy systems to customers primarily on a cash basis. In addition to complete packages for solar, wind, and hydroelectric systems, the company also sells accessories, including lighting systems, electric fencing, refrigerators, fans, water pumps, and water purification devices. If requested by the customer, the company will also place custom orders for various other electrical devices. Although margins on these additional requests are sometimes quite low, they are part of a strategy of providing complete service to meet the needs of the customer.

Tecnosol's business model is to sell renewable energy systems to customers primarily on a cash basis. In addition to complete packages for solar, wind, and hydroelectric systems, the company also sells accessories, including lighting systems, electric fencing, refrigerators, fans, water pumps, and water purification devices.

Tecnosol focuses primarily on customers who can more easily afford renewable energy systems, which mainly includes farmers and landowners. As pointed out by an E+Co investment officer, "Tecnosol taught us a lesson. It is not always necessary to go after the poorest people first—there are often many customers who are willing to pay higher amounts even in what would be considered underdeveloped areas."

A common means of accessing the capital needed to buy a system in such areas is through the sale of livestock. One interviewed customer, who was quite pleased with his purchases, described how he sold 6 cows for an illumination system and 10 cows for a water-pumping system. Even then, the addition of electricity to his property resulted in real monetary savings (about $40 per month in labor for carrying water and about $8 per month in the cost of kerosene candles[13]) and an overall increase in property value. To meet the needs of a range of potential customers, Tecnosol offers prepackaged systems for a variety of levels of affordability, including a small 14-watt PV system for the poorer people.

Tecnosol provides a full-service installation on all energy systems and gives verbal and written instruction to the customer on proper system maintenance. Two other smaller companies sell renewable energy systems in Nicaragua, but Tecnosol distinguishes itself by focusing on quality and customer service. Technicians travel any length to reach a customer (on horse if necessary), and if any problem is reported, a technician is always available to solve the problem. One lesson of previous rural electrification companies around the world is that quality is a key value driver in many rural markets because many people are skeptical the new technology will function as advertised, especially when compared to traditional solutions such as buckets (for carrying water), candles, and wood. Because word of mouth through existing customers is a primary driver of new buyers, quality and service satisfaction takes on an added importance. To support this spread of information, the company also uses a variety of media, including radio, newspaper, and market fairs, to advertise its products throughout the country. Tecnosol offers eight main packages for its customers, anywhere from a basic lighting system to a complex system for water pumping or refrigeration.

In what is an increasingly common revision of policy in many developing nations, the government of Nicaragua acknowledges it does not have the capacity to meet the energy needs of most people in the 50 percent unelectrified population in the country. As stated by Gioconda Guevara, the director of energy policy for the National Commission of Energy:

> Investment in the energy sector must be from private sources because the government does not have the capacity to make that necessary investment. Thus, Tecnosol or any other company that develops technology for energy projects will be looked upon highly. There are not many companies yet, but it is the government's intention to support private developers in the energy sector to augment the government's capacity.

As a response to the success of the private sector in serving the energy needs of rural communities, governments and multilateral institutions have started to adopt policies and build programs that support further expansion of private businesses for delivering energy services.

Companies selling and installing solar photovoltaics, wind, microhydro, and biomass power systems to unelectrified regions of developing countries are proving to be a lower-cost, cleaner, and faster way to deliver energy compared to traditional approaches. The historical perception of the energy problem as a "development issue" has been altered by a new approach that emphasizes local entrepreneurship in meeting the energy needs of underdeveloped communities. E+Co has effectively demonstrated that business models, technologies, and willingness to pay are not the limitations in meeting this energy need.

The main challenge is bringing the necessary investment to scale up currently profitable enterprises and to build new businesses in unserved markets. This new paradigm emphasizes market forces, sustainable business, and replication over technology demonstration, donor gifts, and individual projects.

Addressing the energy problem at the Bottom of the Pyramid involves elements relevant to both developing and developed countries:

- Sustainable development
- Clean and distributed energy technologies
- Local knowledge and global reach
- Private enterprise with supporting policies
- Investment (public and private) to reach scale

A new energy future is being sculpted in both developing and industrialized countries reflecting these themes. This future entails energy being generated from renewable sources and delivered close to the site where it will be consumed. Although technologies that are allowing this transition to take place have been formulated largely in the north, developing countries are taking the lead in their dissemination. The results from this phenomenon could significantly impact the way the energy sector evolves. Through both economies of scale in manufacturing and an approach that emphasizes locally managed and controlled energy delivery, the success of energy enterprises using renewable energy technologies at the Bottom of the Pyramid might prove to be the most important innovation in the energy sector for years to come.

Endnotes

1. World Development Report 1998/99.
2. "Voices of the Poor" study conducted by the World Bank, 2000.
3. Barnes, Douglas F. & Willem Floor, "Biomass Energy and the Poor in Developing Countries," *Journal of International Affairs*, 1996.
4. The Solar Electric Light Fund.
5. According to Dan Kammen at the University of California Berkeley, *The New York Times*, 2001.
6. Study by Michael Phillips and Brooks Browne.

7. The logarithmic relationship between price and cumulative sales.
8. Maycock, Paul D., *Photovoltaics Technology, Performance, Cost, and Market Forecast, Photovoltaics Energy Systems*, 2002.
9. *Wind Power Monthly*, 2002.
10. In one case, related by a government official in Latin America, a very poor area was given access to the electricity grid via a subsidized program organized by an out-of-country multilateral institution and was implemented through the country's utility. When the utility's rate collector began showing up, people in the area had no cash and so sold off their livestock (chickens and so forth) one by one to pay for the electricity. When the chickens were gone, many people chose to entirely abandon their electrified homes because they could not pay what the utility demanded for the ongoing cost of generation.
11. Adapted from 2002 E+Co business plan.
12. The triple bottom line: financial, social, and environmental performance, typically all measured in financial terms.
13. This customer also was aware the use of kerosene candles could have adverse long-term health effects and was pleased to not be using them any further.

This case study was written by Scott Baron and George Weinmann under the supervision of Professor C.K. Prahalad. The case study is intended to be a catalyst for discussion and is not intended to illustrate effective or ineffective strategies.

Update: E+Co/Tecnosol

By Mr. Phil LaRocco, CEO, E+Co

E+Co has grown from an experiment to a successful energy investment firm with a proven track record and 15 years of experience. E+Co has now invested in more than 250 energy businesses that, in turn, supply clean and modern energy to more than four and a half million people throughout Africa, Asia, and Latin America. In addition to increasing access to good-quality energy, E+Co's portfolio has reduced carbon dioxide emissions by more than three million tons, decreased deforestation, and improved indoor air quality. (And Tecnosol, the solar company highlighted in *Bottom of the Pyramid*, is now a ten-year-old, successful company, serving more than 100,000 households.)

To achieve these results, E+Co continues to rely on its enterprise-centered model of providing services and capital to entrepreneurs in developing countries. Over the years, E+Co has added innovations to this core model. In 2006, for instance, E+Co established E+Co Capital and the Central American Renewable Energy and Cleaner Production Facility (CAREC), a $20 million for-profit investment fund. This innovation allowed a concentration and focus that certain investors wanted. In 2007 and 2008, E+Co launched a carbon monetization program, including the creation of E+Carbon, a for-profit entity that bundles and monetizes the carbon dioxide offsets of E+Co's portfolio companies, and the entry of carbon sale arrangements with Goldman Sachs. Each of these innovations serves E+Co's core mission of increasing access to modern energy through the establishment of local energy businesses in developing countries. Other strategic partnerships with firms such as Accenture demonstrate the slow but steady recognition of the importance of small and growing businesses to the delivery of life expanding services to the poor.

In 2008, the *Financial Times*, the International Finance Corporation, named E+Co the *Sustainable Investor of the Year*. Based on such success, E+Co expects to grow to scale. By 2012, E+Co plans to serve more than 20 million people with access to clean energy—80 million by 2020.

Scaling up, however, is not without its challenges. Because of the additional costs of capacity building and asset management in emerging markets, there is a first-cost premium to investing in this space. Through the support of grant-makers, governments, specialized programs, social- and mission-related investors, and others, E+Co has funded this premium, to the point where the return on the all-in cost of creating successful enterprises, net of losses, produces a portfolio with a steady 3 percent rate of return. That is, if the world recognizes the social and environmental benefits of these companies and accepts a 3 percent regular return from this market, the scale that could be achieved in Bottom of Pyramid environments is enormous. There remains a wealth of entrepreneurs in developing countries who through appropriate training and access to capital can supply needed energy products and services to the Bottom of the Pyramid. There are reliable, affordable technologies to deliver modern energy. There are dozens of examples of success to emulate—these have names such as SELCO-India, Tecnosol (Nicaragua), SME-RE (Cambodia), Toyola (Ghana), Zara Solar (Tanzania), LaEsperanza (Honduras), and Red Ceramics (Bolivia). These are not rare exceptions. These examples are the product of a proven method of enterprise development and investment in emerging markets, a method underpinned by that most important and limitless resource: the power and desire of people to improve their quality of life.

E+Co has learned (in what could be called an accountant's argument) that a preliminary step to serving the Bottom of the Pyramid is to often serve the Middle of the Pyramid market segment. Entering with this market allows the establishment of basic business operations (and the coverage of fixed costs). Then it is more cost-effective (that is, with fixed costs covered) to expand into the lower market segments. In addition, it is also more strategic for the small business, in that it allows a deeper penetration into a market location and a greater diversity of product offerings without having to expand the business to new locations. Locally placed enterprises provide choices to unserved and underserved markets that represent development and business opportunities too often overlooked.

Biographies of the Researchers and Writers of the Success Case Studies from *The Fortune at the Bottom of the Pyramid*

Jennifer Anderson

Jennifer first developed her passion for economic development in emerging markets while working at an investment bank in New York City. Since then, she has traveled, volunteered, or consulted on projects in multiple countries across Asia, Latin America, the Middle East, and Africa. She is currently a management associate in a global leadership development program at Citigroup, where she also works with the Citi Micro finance group. Jennifer is actively involved in several other micro finance networks and is a proponent of poverty alleviation through entrepreneurship. In 2008, she received her MBA from the Stephen M Ross School of Business at the University of Michigan with a concentration in international business and entrepreneurship. Prior to that, she worked as a risk manager within the equities divisions of both Morgan Stanley and Banc of America Securities. Jennifer earned a BS in business from Wake Forest University, and in her spare time, she enjoys vetting new entrepreneurial endeavors and creative writing.

Kuttayan Annamalai

Kuttayan is from Tamil Nadu, India. He earned his bachelors degree in engineering from Birla Institute of Technology and Science, Pilani, India, in 1995. In 2004, Kuttayan earned his MBA from the University of Michigan Business School, with emphases in strategy and finance. Prior to his MBA, Kuttayan was a consultant at a technology services company, where he led initiatives to solve strategic technology issues for Fortune 500 clients. The Bottom of the Pyramid project was an eye-opener for him, as he explored innovative business models that not only catalyzed rural transformation but also redefined corporate social responsibility.

Scott Baron

Scott graduated in May 2004 from the University of Michigan and will earn his MS from the School of Natural Resources & Environment and his MBA from the Michigan Business School. Scott's focus is on renewable energy, particularly wind and hybrid power systems. Working with C.K. Prahalad for the past year, he was inspired to start his own business implementing renewable energy projects in Bottom-of-the-Pyramid markets. This venture won numerous distinctions at business plan competitions around the country, including Best Social Return on Investment at the Global Social Venture Competition. Prior to coming to Michigan, Scott worked in the field of climate change, where he helped start the Chicago Climate Exchange, a voluntary market for the trading of greenhouse gases. Scott is from Chicago and graduated from Northwestern University with a BS in economics and environmental policy.

Cynthia Casas

Cynthia, who cofounded the XMAP program with Praveen Suthrum, is a first-generation American of Mexican descent from El Paso, Texas. After obtaining her BS in international business from American University in 1994, she worked for GE Capital in London and then IBM in Singapore. In 1996, Cynthia embarked on a new career path, first at an environmental nonprofit organization in the United States and then at the World Bank, where she worked in the Corporate Strategy Group and External Affairs departments. In 2004, Cynthia earned her MBA from the University of Michigan Business School, where she brought together her backgrounds in business and economic development to bear on defining the role of the business sector in poverty alleviation. Through her work with C.K. Prahalad, she has had the chance to study profitable companies that seek to improve the economic viability of the regions and communities in which they operate. Copresident of the Emerging Markets Club and member of Net Impact while at Michigan, she is passionate about discovering and initiating business practices in developing countries that are both socially and environmentally sustainable.

Sami Foguel

Sami is from Salvador, Bahia, Brazil. He received his undergraduate degree in engineering from Universidade Estadual de Campinas in 1998 and worked for McKinsey and Company as a consultant mainly focused on financial institutions. In 2004, Sami earned his MBA from the University of Michigan Business School, where he concentrated in general management and finance. After graduation, Sami returned to McKinsey and Company in their São Paulo office. What impressed him most about his experience with Casas Bahia was the management's capability to understand and fulfill the untapped financing needs of the poor population in Brazil.

Nina Henning

Nina is motivated by her desire to improve economic conditions in emerging markets through innovative business ventures that respect the environment and indigenous cultures. She has experience in financing the commercialization and distribution of clean technologies, both internationally with the Acumen Fund and domestically with the University of Michigan's Frankel Commercialization Fund. In addition, Nina spent five years in Kathmandu, Nepal, as the managing director of Wild Earth Pvt. Ltd., a mission-driven herbal cosmetics company, where she led a turnaround from bankruptcy to profitability. Nina graduated from the University of Michigan in 2009, earning an MBA from the Ross School of Business and an MS from the School of Natural Resources & Environment. She earned her BA in history from Princeton University and is the coauthor of *Hybrid Organizations: New Business Models for Environmental Leadership* (Greenleaf Publishing, 2009).

Michael Hokenson

Michael is currently a second-year CEMP student, earning an MBA and an MS in environmental science from the University of Michigan. He was raised in New Jersey and received his undergraduate degree from St. John's College in Santa Fe, New Mexico, majoring in philosophy and mathematics. After traveling extensively in Asia in 1997, he founded MINLAM, Inc., a fair trade manufacturing firm designing handicraft products in Nepal in cooperation with the NGO Rugmark. Michael has worked in various entrepreneurial ventures, including the launch of Kinetix LLC in 2001, a consulting firm based in New York City whose mission is to assist businesses in the profitable alignment of financial goals with ethical and ecological principles. Michael believes the landscape of development currently taking place in emerging economies is transforming because of the need to balance development with environmental considerations. After graduation, Michael plans to focus on serving the capital and conservation management needs of small- and medium-sized enterprises in emerging economies.

William LaJoie

William is from Denver, Colorado, and his primary interests are the underlying factors that drive exponential growth. After obtaining his BA in English literature from the University of Notre Dame, he spent two years volunteering at the Working Boys' Center, a school for the working poor, in Quito, Ecuador, teaching in the elementary school, high school, and adult literacy program. After returning to the United States, William worked as a program manager for LinkShare Corporation, a provider of Internet-based affiliate solutions, where his clients included Dell and Ford. In 2004, William earned his MBA from the University of Michigan Business School, where he combined his interest in marketing, technology, and emerging economies. He is pursuing a career in market research and is looking forward to living happily ever after with his fiancée, Dana.

Scott Macke

Scott is from Marshalltown, Iowa, and graduated from Butler University in Indianapolis, Indiana, in 1996 with a degree in accounting. He worked in auditing and tax for an Indianapolis-based accounting firm for three years and then worked for two years conducting privately held business valuations for a regional CPA firm in Denver, Colorado. Scott is concentrating on finance and corporate strategy at the Michigan Business School and will work for Robert W. Baird in equity research after graduation.

Todd Markson

Todd is from Concord, Massachusetts. He graduated from Brown University in 1997 with a BA in political science and economics, having studied abroad for one semester at Yonsei University in Seoul, South Korea. After Brown, Todd entered the Peace Corps in Mali, West Africa, as a small enterprise development volunteer, working with native entrepreneurs in starting new ventures and attracting the flow of micro finance to underdeveloped communities. After returning to the United States, he was part of the founding team of two startups in the Bay Area of California, one a contact updating software company and the other an entrepreneurial incubator still in existence. Todd received his MBA with Distinction in April 2004 from the Michigan Business School with concentrations in corporate strategy, international business, and finance. Todd will be a senior associate at DiamondCluster, a strategy consulting firm, out of their London, England, office. The most intriguing aspect of this research is the realization that with business model modifications and innovative application of technology, vast new markets open up. Multinational companies can profitably expand their reach while providing individuals at the bottom of the economic pyramid with products and services that they need and desire.

Ruchi Misra

Ruchi is from Montville, New Jersey. After graduating from Barnard College, Columbia University, in 1997, she became a financial analyst for Salomon Smith Barney's Equity Capital Markets Group in both the New York and Hong Kong offices. Two years later, she was promoted to associate at Freeman & Co., a financial services management consulting firm in New York City. There she focused on mergers and acquisitions, strategy for asset management, and investment banking clientele. In 2004, Ruchi earned her MBA from the Michigan Business School and an MS in environmental science from the University of Michigan School of Natural Resources. At Michigan, Ruchi focused on corporate social responsibility and making the business case for sustainability.

Sharmilee Mohan

Sharmilee, a Class of 2003 MBA graduate, participated in the CEMEX project focusing on understanding Mexican society and CEMEX's (and competitors') strategy to provide housing for the poor profitably. She traveled to Guadalajara, Mexico, with no Spanish-speaking skills or a Spanish–English translator. She considered her one-week trip to Guadalajara an adventure and a huge success from an academic and cultural standpoint. She learned a lot about Mexican society, especially the poor, firsthand. As an Indian citizen, she is no stranger to a wide range of issues surrounding emerging economies today, such as poverty, gross domestic product growth, abundance of educated and semiskilled labor, corruption, globalization, exploding consumerism, outsourcing, and so on. Nevertheless, her experience in Guadalajara was an eye-opener when she approached the same issues and challenges that shroud emerging economies from a business perspective. Currently, she works for a management consulting firm in New York focusing on strategy and operations.

Mindy Murch

Mindy graduated from the Corporate Environmental Management Program, a dual masters program between the University of Michigan's School of Natural Resources & Environment and Business School in 2004. Prior to graduate school, Mindy worked for PricewaterhouseCoopers Management Consulting Service and the U.S. Department of Agriculture Forest Service in Washington, DC. Mindy holds a BA in Russian Language and Literature from Bowdoin College.

Marion Ntiru

A national of Uganda, Marion was born and raised in Nairobi, Kenya, before moving to New York City in 1992. After graduating from Mount Holyoke College in 2002 with a dual major in mathematics and economics, she worked as a consultant for Mercer HR Consulting (Retirement Practice) and PricewaterhouseCoopers, LLP (Risk and Compliance) in New York. In 2008, Marion earned her MBA in international business from the Stephen M. Ross School of Business at the University of Michigan. She is currently a management associate with Citi Cards in the New York office. Having lived in both developed and developing nations, she hopes one day to combine her background in business with economic development to alleviate poverty in Africa. Marion loves to travel and is on a quest to visit all seven continents of the world; she also enjoys dance and music.

Jeff Phillips

Jeff is from Olathe, Kansas. He graduated from the United States Air Force Academy in 1997 and served five years on active duty in the Air Force. At the Michigan Business School, he concentrated on corporate strategy and international business. After graduating in April 2004, Jeff began working for the management consultancy Booz Allen Hamilton in Cleveland, Ohio. What amazed him most about this experience was creating knowledge that will fundamentally alter the way companies view emerging economies. He hopes one day to own and operate a business incubator in a developing country.

Anuja Rajendra

Anuja grew up in Patiala, India, and Okemos, Michigan, a paradoxical combination that invoked her passion for global economic development. After earning a BS in industrial and operations engineering from the University of Michigan, Anuja worked in business development for American Power Conversion Corporation, where she was promoted three times in 18 months, becoming the regional sales support manager for the Northern United States. In 1997, the tragic death of her sister, Rachana, in an automobile accident motivated Anuja to start Moon-baked Creations Contemporary Art Lounge and Café in Okemos, Michigan. She later became the Director of Strategic Partnerships for a technology startup and then the Director of Development for a $1.5-million nonprofit organization. While a 2004 MBA candidate at the University of Michigan Business School, Anuja focused on global social entrepreneurship and hoped to start a business that served the Bottom of the Pyramid.

Sachin Rao

Sachin grew up in Mumbai, India, and holds an undergraduate degree in software engineering. He spent seven years executing, managing, and selling offshore software solutions for clients around the world before coming to the Michigan Business School to get his MBA. At Michigan, his focus has been on corporate strategy, international business, and watching his son, Dhruva, grow. Sachin's most enduring lesson from the experience is that at the BOP, social consciousness enables rather than compromises shareholder return.

Kate Reeder

Kate is from Providence, Rhode Island. She earned her MBA in April 2004 from the Michigan Business School, where she focused on marketing and corporate strategy. Prior to graduate school, Kate lived in San Francisco, California, and worked on a variety of projects as a creative services consultant for Sapient Corporation, a technology consultancy. She holds a BA in political science from Brown University.

Shara Senior

Shara is helping to start a U.S.-based BOP business incubator focused on creating businesses that improve health as a consultant to Ascension Health. Her career interests are in creating businesses that use holistic value chain approaches to providing critical goods and services by including the BOP as producers, consumers, and entrepreneurs. Shara graduated from the Stephen M. Ross School of Business at the University of Michigan with her MBA in 2008. Prior to Ross, Shara worked at Nissan North America as an engineer, and owned and operated a property management company. Shara is a native of Kingston, Jamaica, and holds a Bachelor of Science degree in mechanical engineering from the University of California, Los Angeles.

Tej Shah

Tej has a strong background in health care after spending three years at Deloitte Consulting. In 2004, Tej earned his MBA from the Michigan Business School, where he concentrated on marketing and corporate strategy. Tej became interested in emerging markets after developing grant applications for an HIV/AIDS nonprofit organization in Harare, Zimbabwe, in 2002. Working on this book allowed him to experience firsthand the power of an underserved community. Following graduation in 2004, Tej returned to Deloitte in its Chicago office as a senior consultant.

Ajay Sharma

Ajay is from Jaipur, India. After receiving a BTech degree in electrical engineering from the Institute of Technology in Varanasi, Ajay joined Infosys Technologies (India), where he provided IT solutions to Fortune 500 clients. He later worked in the Management Consulting Services group of PricewaterhouseCoopers (USA) as principal consultant. In 2004, he earned his MBA from the Michigan Business School, where he focused on Corporate Strategy and international business. From the Bottom of the Pyramid project, Ajay developed amazing insight into how developed economies can learn from innovations created in resource-constrained emerging economies.

Ajit Sharma

Ajit's native state, Bihar, is at the Bottom of the Pyramid in India, the poorest state in the nation. Paradoxically, it is the richest state in terms of natural resources. It has a glorious past, being the birthplace of two religions (Buddhism and Jainism), the place from where Ashoka ruled over India, the place where the first university (Nalanda) was established, and the place from where Gandhi started his fight for India's independence. Ajit believes that the BOP paradigm opens up new possibilities for the development of regions, like Bihar, caught in the downward spiral of poverty. For this reason, the concept is very close to his heart, and he hopes to use it someday for the development of his state. Ajit earned his BTech degree in manufacturing engineering from the National Institute of Foundry and Forge Technology (NIFFT), Ranchi; and his masters degree from NITIE, Mumbai. He completed his MBA from the University of Michigan in 2005. Ajit would like to express his gratitude to his parents, Shri Balram and Smt. Sushma, his brother Amit, and his wife Pratibha for their unconditional love and support.

Praveen Suthrum

Praveen, from Hyderabad, India, cofounded the XMAP program at the University of Michigan Business School. He obtained his BS in electrical engineering from the Mangalore University. Praveen then worked for six years with Satyam Computer Services, India's IT outsourcing leader, in various capacities, and more recently as a business manager serving Fortune 100 clients. In 2003, he adapted the eGovernance model, developed as part of the XMAP program, to aid reconstruction efforts in Iraq and presented the model to key dignitaries, including former Secretary of State Madeleine Albright and the Prime Minister of Iraqi Kurdistan, Dr. Barham Salih. Additionally, Praveen consulted with the U.S. Institute of Peace on the feasibility of eGovernance in Iraq. At the Michigan Business School, he has focused his studies on corporate strategy and emerging markets.

George Weinmann

George grew up in New Orleans, Louisiana. He graduated from the University of Virginia with a BS in aerospace engineering before working for the Boeing Company for five years, where he helped organize Boeing Ventures and led several new businesses in energy and telecommunications. At the Michigan Business School, George concentrated on entrepreneurship, strategy, and international business and was a student member of the Wolverine Venture Fund. After graduation in 2004, George pursued a career in international business. For George, this project impressed on him the power of entrepreneurship and investment to solve critical societal needs.

Andrew Wilson

Andrew received his undergraduate degree in business from Southern Methodist University and spent more than five years with Deloitte Consulting as an associate consultant focused on the energy sector. In 2004, Andrew earned his MBA from the University of Michigan Business School, where he concentrated in strategy and general management. What impressed him most about his experience with Casas Bahia was the management's hands-on role in changing the lives of customers. He is excited that the group's collective work is helping to shape global development.

PART V

Video Clips

- Jaipur Rugs
- Casas Bahia
- CEMEX
- Annapurna Salt
- Hindustan Lever Limited
- Jaipur Foot
- Aravind Eye Care
- ICICI Bank
- ITC e-Choupal
- EID Parry
- Voxiva
- E+Co/Tecnosol
- Andhra Pradesh

These videos are available on the book's CD and online at www.whartonsp.com/Prahalad. They include engaging success stories from the bottom of the pyramid, filmed on location in India, Peru, Mexico, Brazil, and Venezuela.

Index

A

B

D

E

F

G

H

I

J

K

L

M

Q–R

T

U

V

W

X–Z

Wharton School Publishing

In the face of accelerating turbulence and change, business leaders and polic makers need new ways of thinking to sustain performance and growth.

Wharton School Publishing offers a trusted source for stimulating ideas from thought leaders who provide new mental models to address changes in strategy, management, and finance. We seek out authors from diverse disciplines with a profound understanding of change and its implications. We offer books and tools that help executives respond to the challenge of change

Every book and management tool we publish meets quality standards set by The Wharton School of the University of Pennsylvania. Each title is reviewed by the Wharton School Publishing Editorial Board before being given Wharton's seal of approval. This ensures that Wharton publications are timely, relevant, important, conceptually sound or empirically based, and implementable.

To fit our readers' learning preferences, Wharton publications are available in multiple formats, including books, audio, and electronic.

To find out more about our books and management tools, visit us at whartonsp.com and Wharton's executive education site, exceed.wharton.upenn.edu.

Wharton
UNIVERSITY *of* PENNSYLVANIA

Pearson Education

watch
@ccess
more online
interact

Now see the book in action with its brand-new, interactive website

> **Interview with C.K. Prahalad**
Hear why he wrote *The Fortune at the Bottom of the Pyramid* and where the idea originated.

> **Supplemental videos**
See the featured case studies play out in videos.

> **Stories of real-world success**
Read letters from several CEOs who took the idea and successfully implemented it.

www.whartonsp.com/prahalad

Beyond the Best Practices

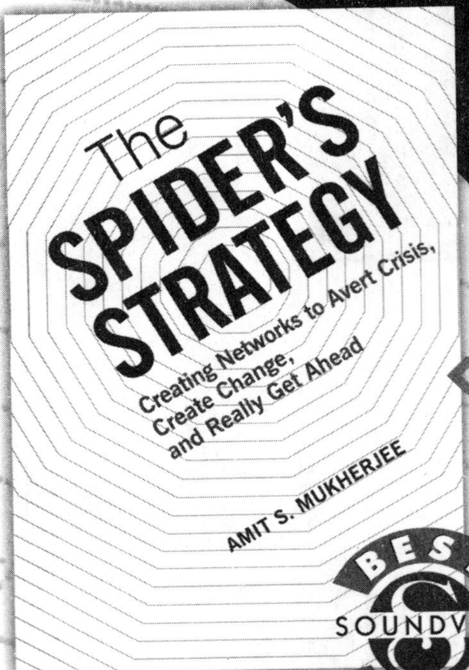

The Spider's Strategy
Amit S. Mukherjee
Price: 499.00
ISBN:9788131726204

BEST SOUNDVIEW BOOK

"One of the 30 Best Business Books of 2009"

In the 1980s, Lean transformed businesses, not because of JIT or SPC, but by fundamentally changing the philosophy of management and the roles of managers. Businesses that resisted change suffered; many went bankrupt. The Spider's Strategy takes you into the world of Adaptive businesses, which compete today as networks of companies. Through the experiences of leading edge companies like Nokia and Hewlett-Packard (which provided unprecedented research access) and Toyota, it illustrates how and why management must transform companies today.

"An 'adaptive organization' must count as the response in the increasingly connected world … A great read for the 'concerned' before they reach the stage of being 'tormented.'"

R. Gopalakrishnan, Executive Director, TATA Sons

"Beyond the obvious, this is a great and pragmatic book, demonstrating the incredible power of collaboration in action."

Jean-Francois Baril, SVP Nokia

"Once in a while … a book … makes me think "Why did I not write this?" … It takes a very experienced reflective practitioner, who in his heart is still an academic, to write such a wonderful book."

Luk Van Wassenhove, Professor, INSEAD

PEARSON

www.pearsoned.co.in